HANDBOOK OF RESEARCH METHODS ON HUMAN RESOURCE DEVELOPMENT

HANDBOOKS OF RESEARCH METHODS IN MANAGEMENT

Series Editor: Mark N.K. Saunders, *University of Surrey, UK*

This major series will provide the starting point for new PhD students in business and management and related social science disciplines. Each *Handbook* will give definitive overviews of research methods appropriate for particular subjects within management. The series aims to produce prestigious high-quality works of lasting significance, shedding light on quantitative, qualitative and mixed research methods. Each *Handbook* consists of original contributions by leading authorities, selected by an editor who is a recognized international leader in the field. International in scope, these *Handbooks* will be an invaluable guide to students embarking on a research degree and to researchers moving into a new subject area.

Titles in the series include:

Handbook of Research Methods on Intuition
Edited by Marta Sinclair

Handbook of Research Methods on Human Resource Development
Edited by Mark N.K. Saunders and Paul Tosey

Handbook of Research Methods on Human Resource Development

Edited by

Mark N.K. Saunders

Professor of Business Research Methods, Birmingham Business School, University of Birmingham, UK

Paul Tosey

Senior Lecturer in Management, Surrey Business School, University of Surrey, UK

HANDBOOKS OF RESEARCH METHODS IN MANAGEMENT

 Edward Elgar
PUBLISHING

Cheltenham, UK • Northampton, MA, USA

Published by
Edward Elgar Publishing Limited
The Lypiatts
15 Lansdown Road
Cheltenham
Glos GL50 2JA
UK

Edward Elgar Publishing, Inc.
William Pratt House
9 Dewey Court
Northampton
Massachusetts 01060
USA

A catalogue record for this book
is available from the British Library

Library of Congress Control Number: 2015933445

This book is available electronically in the **Elgar**online
Business subject collection
DOI 10.4337/9781781009246

ISBN 978 1 78100 923 9 (cased)
ISBN 978 1 78100 924 6 (eBook)

Typeset by Servis Filmsetting Ltd, Stockport, Cheshire
Printed and bound in Great Britain by T.J. International Ltd, Padstow

Contents

About the editors

Mark N.K. Saunders is Professor of Business Research Methods in the Birmingham Business School, University of Birmingham, UK. His research interests include human resource aspects of the management of change, in particular trust within and between organizations and learning; research methods, in particular methods for understanding organizational relationships and online methods; and small and medium sized enterprises. He holds visiting professorships at the School of Management and Accountancy, University of Malta, and Worcester Business School, University of Worcester, and is a Fellow of the British Academy of Management and a member of the Fellows' College. Mark has co-authored and edited a range of books including *Research Methods for Business Students* (currently in its seventh edition), *Organizational Trust: A Cultural Perspective*, *Handbook of Research Methods on Trust* and *Doing Research in Business and Management*. He is joint editor for Sage's *Understanding Research Methods for Business and Management Students* book series and editor for Edward Elgar's *Handbooks of Research Methods in Management* series. Mark's research has been published widely in journals including *Field Methods*, *Human Relations*, *Journal of Personnel Psychology*, *Journal of Small Business Management*, *Management Learning* and *Social Science and Medicine*.

Paul Tosey is a Senior Lecturer and Head of PhD Programmes in the Surrey Business School. His research interests include organizational learning, 'Clean Language', enquiry-based learning and leadership development. His work has been published widely in journals such as the *British Journal of Management*, *Management Learning*, *Innovations in Education and Teaching International* and *Human Resource Development Review*. Paul was awarded a National Teaching Fellowship by the Higher Education Academy in 2007; his career experience over 30 years also includes consultancy, coaching and line management. Paul is an active member of the University Forum for HRD, he was awarded the Alan Moon prize for best paper at the 2011 International HRD Conference and he chairs the UFHRD Programme and Qualification Activities Committee.

Contributors

Cinla Akinci is a Lecturer in Management at the School of Management, University of St Andrews, UK. Her research is focused on the role of intuition in decision making and organizational learning, particularly in the senior management context. She received her PhD from the University of Surrey's Business School in 2011, where she subsequently worked as Lecturer in Organizational Behaviour. Her research on intuition in decision making has received several awards, most notably the Best Paper Award twice from the British Academy of Management, and has been published in scholarly management journals and book chapters.

Nick Beech is Director of Executive Learning at Leeds Business School, Leeds Beckett University, UK and a National Teaching Fellow. His interests lie in executive talk and how language is used to shape meaning within boardrooms. He currently works with other co-researchers on key issues such as corporate governance, decision making and leadership. He has completed a DBA on the talk of boards of directors.

Kate Black is a Senior Lecturer at Newcastle Business School, Northumbria University, UK where she teaches, researches and supervises in the areas of manager development and professional learning. She is also the Programme Leader for the undergraduate HRM programme. Previously, Kate has worked in a teaching-led business school and as an HRD practitioner with a large UK retailer. Kate's research interests span a range of academic-practice areas examining such facets as the importance of informal learning for professionals in the contemporary knowledge economy, later-career learning, and student attendance and engagement. She has also worked to examine the relevance of the research methods and dissertation elements of management education in the light of the changing demographic of management students in UK universities. Kate's research adopts a largely qualitative approach to data generation, with particular emphasis upon visual methods such as photo-elicitation and the use of participant-generated pictures.

Jamie L. Callahan is Professor of Human Resource Development at Drexel University in Philadelphia, PA, USA and recently ended her term as Editor of *Human Resource Development Review*. Her research interests encompass leadership, the sociology of emotion, and contextual issues, such as organizational learning, organizational culture and communities of practice. She applies a critical theory perspective to the exploration of these issues.

Julia Calver is Senior Lecturer at The UK Centre for Events Management at Leeds Beckett University and Coordinator of the Yorkshire Events Network comprising 700 business members. Her particular research interests include micro industries within the creative sector, organizational learning and enterprise skills development applying action research principles.

David Coghlan is a Fellow Emeritus of Trinity College Dublin, Ireland. He specializes in organization development and action research and is active in both communities internationally. He is author of the internationally popular *Doing Action Research in Your Own Organization* (4th ed. 2014, Sage) and co-editor of *The SAGE Encyclopedia of Action Research* (2014).

Gary Connor is a Senior Lecturer at Coventry University, UK, and is responsible for the Human Resource Department's postgraduate dissertation programmes. He worked in the steel industry for over 20 years before starting his career in higher education at Coventry University. His main area of research is the assessment of students with regard to employability, fairness and equity.

Carole Elliott is Senior Lecturer in Management at Durham University Business School, UK. Her research interests include critical approaches to management and leadership learning; critical human resource development; and qualitative research methods, particularly the development of critical hermeneutic and visual methods in management and organization research. She is associate editor of *Human Resource Development International*.

Peter Evans is a Senior Teaching Fellow at the University of Edinburgh, UK, where he teaches on the MSc in Digital Education and the MSc in Education. His research interests are in digital environments for workplace and professional learning, organizational learning and knowledge management. Before starting his career in higher education, Peter worked in various roles in people and organizational development in the public, private and not-for-profit sectors.

Thomas Garavan is Research Professor, Leadership, at Edinburgh Napier University, UK. He specializes in leadership development, HRD and leadership, CSR and leadership and cross-cultural leadership. Thomas is a member of the Editorial Board of *Human Resource Management Journal, Human Resource Development Quarterly, Human Resource Development Review, Advances in Developing Human Resources* and

Human Resource Development International. He is the recipient of the Academy of Human Resource Development, Outstanding HRD Scholar Award 2013. His research interests include CSR and transformational leadership, cross-cultural dimensions of diversity training, tacit knowledge in manufacturing, international human resource management standards and human resource management in MNCs.

Jeff Gold is Professor of Organisation Learning at Leeds Business School, Leeds Beckett University and Visiting Professor at Leeds, Portsmouth and York St John universities, UK. His interests lie in the use of action modes of research to work collaboratively with others as co-researchers on key issues such as poverty, innovation and leadership that is distributed.

David E. Gray is Professor of Leadership and Organizational Behaviour at the University of Greenwich, UK. His research interests, and publication record, include research methods, management learning (particularly coaching and mentoring), action learning, reflective learning, learning in SMEs and the triggers for SME success. He has published books and articles on research methods, work-based learning, and coaching and mentoring. David has led a number of coaching research programmes for managers of SMEs, for unemployed managers who seek new employment opportunities and for unemployed managers who aim to start their own business.

Bob Hamlin is Emeritus Professor and Chair of Human Resource Development at the University of Wolverhampton, UK. His main research interest is exploring effective and ineffective managerial behaviour as perceived by managers and employees within public, private and third sector organizations. With various indigenous co-researchers he has replicated and continues to replicate his UK studies of perceived managerial and leadership effectiveness within a culturally diverse range of countries around the globe. His current aim is to use the results of these studies as empirical source data for conducting multiple-case, cross-sector, cross-nation comparative analytic studies based on replication logic in search of empirical generalizations that might lead to new HRD related theory development.

Victoria Harte is a PhD candidate at the University of Sheffield, UK, based in the Sheffield University Management School, as well as holding an Associate Lecturer position at Leeds Business School. Her PhD research is focused on the personal epistemologies of postgraduate management students and how these translate into the organization. Along with her PhD research, her other research interests are research-informed teaching and the impact of this on students and their learning experiences, teaching research methods and research philosophy.

Rosalie Holian is Associate Professor in the College of Business, School of Management, RMIT University, Melbourne, Australia. She is an Organizational Psychologist with a special interest in action research.

Claire Jones is the Managing Director of Inspiria Consulting Ltd. Her business is focused on helping organizations create and maintain alignment between strategic direction and individual objectives using coaching, facilitating and process consulting methods. She specializes in working with business alliances and is particularly interested in learning, trust and collaboration between organizations.

Christoph König is Researcher at the Institute of Educational Science at the University of Regensburg, Germany. His research focuses on teacher education systems, teacher allocation, learning in organizations and professional learning.

Dawn Langley is an independent researcher and organizational development consultant. Her research interests include organizational learning, curiosity and failure in organizations.

Almuth McDowall is course director for the MSc Human Resource Development and Consultancy at Birkbeck University of London, UK, and is currently working on a number of funded research projects. Her focus is on the application of psychological theory to personnel and HR issues on topics such as work–life balance, coaching, work performance and ethical behaviours.

Clíodhna MacKenzie is a lecturer in the School of Management and Marketing at University College Cork, Ireland. Her academic research focuses on 'dark side' organizational behaviour such as organizational narcissism, leadership derailment, counterproductive work behaviour, excessive risk-taking, unethical behaviour and corporate social irresponsibility. Her research interests include risk-taking behaviour, organizational strategy development and execution, corporate and organizational governance, ethics, corporate social responsibility and sustainability, human resource management/development, and leadership and organization development.

Sven De Maeyer is Associate Professor of Education at the Institute of Information and Education Sciences at the University of Antwerp, Belgium. His research focuses on educational measurement and the application of advanced statistics such as multilevel analysis, structural equation modelling and item response theory.

Diane Marks is a self-employed Executive Coach. She gained a Masters in Executive and Business Coaching at Leeds Business School, UK. She lives on the south coast.

Sharon Mavin is Chair of the University Forum for HRD, Professor of Organization and HRM and Director of Roehampton Business School, Roehampton University, UK. Sharon's research interests are doing gender well and differently; women's intra-gender relations; executive women and careers; and leadership, identity and emotion work in organizations. Sharon is Associate Editor of *International Journal of Management Reviews* and Co-editor of *Gender in Management: An International Journal* and has recent publications in *Gender Work and Organization, Organization, Human Resource Development Review, International Journal of Management Reviews, Gender in Management: An International Journal,* and the *British Journal of Management.*

Gerhard Messmann is Assistant Professor at the Institute of Educational Science at the University of Regensburg, Germany. His research interests include innovative work behaviour, informal learning at work and instructional design.

Regina H. Mulder is Full Professor of Pedagogy/Educational Science at the Institute of Educational Science at the University of Regensburg, Germany. Her research interests include a variety of topics in vocational education and training (VET) and on learning in organizations, such as evaluation of training, innovative work behaviour, informal learning at work, feedback and team learning.

Adrian Ogun is Executive Director of the Actionable Knowledge Research Centre, based in Nigeria, and a doctoral candidate at Leeds Business School, Leeds Beckett University, UK. His research interests include corporate governance and the study of how action modalities attempt to reconcile Western management theory with emerging market practice.

Rob F. Poell is Professor of Human Resource Development in the Department of HR Studies at Tilburg University, the Netherlands. His core field of expertise within HRD is workplace learning, especially viewed from the employees' perspective. His work has appeared in the *Journal of Vocational Behavior, Group & Organization Management, Management Learning, Small Group Research, International Journal of Nursing Studies, International Journal of Project Management, International Journal of Human Resource Management, Personnel Review,* and *Human Resource Development Quarterly.* He recently co-edited the *Routledge Companion to Human Resource Development,* which won the Forward Publishing Award of the Academy of Human Resource Development.

Clare Rigg works at the Institute of Technology Tralee, Ireland. Following an early career in economic development and urban regeneration, she developed an interest in collaborative working that was further fostered through encountering action learning as an approach to management development in 1990. For many years, based at the universities of Birmingham and Birmingham City, she worked with practitioners from across diverse sectors, integrating action research and action learning into development of public service networks, management learning and leadership development, continuing this work with a move to Ireland in 2005. She is particularly interested in the inter-relationships between multiple levels of learning and change and is co-editor of the *Journal of Action Learning: Research and Practice.*

Céline Rojon is a Lecturer in Human Resource Management at the University of Edinburgh Business School, UK. Her research interests include work performance, assessment, selection and development, research methods and cross-cultural studies.

Eugene Sadler-Smith is Professor of Organizational Behaviour in the Surrey Business School, University of Surrey, UK. His research interests at the moment are focused on the role of intuition in management and organization. His work has been published widely in peer-reviewed journals such as the *Academy of Management Executive, Academy of Management Learning and Education, British Journal of Psychology, Business Ethics Quarterly, Human Resource Development International, Journal of Occupational and Organizational Psychology, Journal of Organizational Behavior, Management Learning* and *Organization Studies.* He is the author of *Learning and Development for Managers: Perspectives from Research and Practice* (Blackwell, 2006), *Learning in Organizations* (with Peter J. Smith, Routledge, 2006), *Inside Intuition* (Routledge, 2008) and *The Intuitive Mind* (John Wiley and Sons, 2010).

Sally Sambrook is Professor of Human Resource Development, Director of the Centre for Business Research and former Deputy Head of School and Director of Postgraduate Studies at Bangor Business School, UK. Sally is a founding member of the University Forum for HRD and served as a Board member of the American Academy of HRD. Sally employs a critical and autoethnographic approach to HRD research, particularly management learning and doctoral supervision. She has published widely and holds various editorial roles on leading HRD, management education and ethnography journals.

Maura Sheehan is Professor of International Management at NUI Galway and Programme Director, MSc International Management. She is an Associate Editor of *Human Resource Development Quarterly* and the *Journal of Organizational Effectiveness: People and Performance*. She has published widely on HRM and performance, international HRM and labour markets. She was an EU Marie Skłodowska Curie Fellow, 2009–2012, and is currently heading an EU work package on self-employment under the EU-funded Strategic Transitions for Youth Labour in Europe (STYLE) project.

Tim Spackman is the Head of Organization Development at Skipton Building Society. He holds a Masters in HRM and is completing a Doctorate in Business Administration at Leeds Business School, UK in the practice of coaching as part of everyday life at work.

Valerie Stead is Lecturer in Management Learning and Leadership at Lancaster University Management School, UK. Her research interests include critical approaches to leadership and the learning of leadership, and the development and use of critical methodologies in qualitative research, with a particular focus on issues of power and gender in women's leadership

Jim Stewart is Professor of HRD at Coventry Business School and has previously held similar positions at Leeds and Nottingham Business Schools. His research interests span all aspects of HRD with recent emphasis being on higher education as a site of HRD practice, especially in relation to doctoral level education; the development of ideas on Critical HRD; and international comparisons of HRD professional practice. Jim is a former Chair of the University Forum for HRD and is currently its Executive Secretary. He also holds a number of appointed positions with the Chartered Institute of Personnel and Development, including being Chief Examiner for Learning and Talent Development.

Steven Tam is Assistant Professor of Management in the Department of Management and Marketing at Fort Hays State University. He received his PhD in Management from Surrey Business School, UK. His research interests include workplace learning, organizational behaviour, SME development, international business, strategic management and creativity.

Kiran Trehan is Professor of Leadership and Enterprise Development at Birmingham University, UK. Kiran is a key contributor to debates on diversity, leadership, and enterprise development and how it can be applied in a variety of business and policy domains. She has led a number of peer mentoring initiatives and extensively published journal articles, policy reports, books and book chapters in the field. Her publications are testimony both to the growing importance of this mode of research to small and medium size businesses, and to her success in advancing innovative approaches to enterprise development and mentoring in small and medium size businesses and policy-making circles. Kiran's work has been supported by grants from a full range of research funding bodies, including research councils, government departments, regional and local agencies and the private sector. Kiran also holds the positions of Visiting Professor at the universities of Lancaster and Chester. She is Editor of *Action Learning: Research and Practice*, the first international journal dedicated to the advancement of knowledge and practice through action learning.

Catherine L. Wang is Professor of Strategy and Entrepreneurship at the School of Management, Royal Holloway University of London, UK. Her research interests are in the areas of entrepreneurship and innovation from a strategic perspective, using quantitative (including structural equation modelling) and mixed methods. In particular, she focuses on how firms can effectively turn strategic and entrepreneurial resources into successful new products/services and bottom-line performance, primarily through the theoretical lens of the resource-based view of the firm, dynamic capabilities and organizational learning. Catherine's work has been published in journals such as *Entrepreneurship Theory and Practice, British Journal of Management, Journal of Business Research, International Small Business Journal, Journal of Small Business Management, European Journal of Information Systems* and *International Journal of Management Reviews*.

Russell Warhurst is Reader in HRM at Newcastle Business School, University of Northumbria, UK, and Adjunct Professor at Aalto University School of Business, Finland. Russell teaches research methods to master's and doctoral students and has coordinated a major Masters in Management Research programme. Russell's research interests include management and leadership learning, workplace learning, identity formation and learning in later careers. Russell is committed to methodological diversity in qualitative inquiry to ensure that multiple stories are heard as a basis for robust individual and collective action in organizations.

Helen Whitrod-Brown is the Associate Dean in the Carnegie Faculty, Leeds Beckett University, UK, responsible for the strategic leadership of Enterprise and Employability. She sits on the Sport Leeds Board and is a Trustee of the Leeds Rugby Foundation. She is holds a DBA on the use of sports coaching in business, and her interests lie in the transfer of training and the use of sport as a learning and development tool for sustainable performance improvement. She has developed a transfer model – the Transcoach – which uses sports coaching to embed business coaching skills, which contributes to the debate on the transfer problematic.

Christine S. Williams was formally Head of the Department of Marketing at Gloucestershire Business School, University of Gloucestershire, UK.

Jannine Williams is Lecturer in Human Resource Management and Organizational Behaviour at Bradford University, UK. Her research interests encompass processes of organizing; categories of social relations and constructions of difference, particularly disability and gender; women's intra-gender relations and friendship at work; and career studies with a focus upon boundaryless careers. Jannine is a member of the Chartered Institute of Personnel and Development and has presented at the Chartered Institute of Personnel and Development Professional Standards conference as well as University Forum for HRD conferences. Jannine co-edited the book *Deaf Students in Higher Education: Current Research and Practice* and has published in *Studies in Higher Education*, *International Journal of Management Reviews* and *British Journal of Management*.

Acknowledgements

In compiling the *Handbook of Research Methods on Human Resource Development,* we have been fortunate to work with a large number of friends and colleagues in the Human Resource Development (HRD) research field. Many of these people contributed chapters and even more commented on earlier drafts of these chapters. We are grateful to all of you for your help.

A number of the chapters in this book represent insights into methods that were, in an earlier form, presented at an annual conference of the University Forum for Human Resource Development (UFHRD). We thank the UFHRD organizers of their conferences over the years for supporting such a vibrant community of HRD scholars. We are also thankful for the assistance of Des Williamson of Surrey University Business School in the early stages of the project.

Invariably the genesis of this book owes a great deal to colleagues at Edward Elgar Publishing, in particular our commissioning editor Francine O'Sullivan. Francine and her colleagues Aisha Bushby and Benedict Hill have offered great support to this project and shown considerable patience as we brought it to fruition.

Mark N.K. Saunders
Paul Tosey

1. Introduction: the variety of methods for researching HRD

Mark N.K. Saunders and Paul Tosey

RESEARCHING HRD

Any scholar delving into the Human Resource Development (HRD) journals or textbooks for the first time would immediately be made aware of its multifaceted nature and the importance of HRD for both organizations and the people who work for and within them. They would also quickly become knowledgeable of a wide variety of issues associated with the development of people, the need to understand these fully and the importance of good quality research for doing this. However, what would not be so immediately apparent is the variety of research methods used by HRD scholars. Yet, as the chapters in this Handbook reveal, there are a wide range of methods available to, and used by, those researching HRD.

The last two decades have seen a plethora of research methods textbooks published. Some of these texts have taken broad disciplinary foci such as business and management (for example: Cameron and Price, 2009; Saunders et al., 2012), considering both quantitative and qualitative paradigms. Others have chosen to focus upon a particular grouping of methods within organizational research, such as quantitative or qualitative methods (for example: Symon and Cassell, 2012), or to concentrate on one specific method such as interviews (for example: Cassell, 2015) or questionnaires (for example: Ekinci, 2015). Whilst such books are both informative and insightful, their nature invariably means that the particular methodological challenges presented by HRD within a particular paradigm or for a particular method cannot be addressed fully.

As HRD research has developed, a growing variety of data collection methodologies and analysis techniques have been adopted, with research designs incorporating mono, multiple and mixed methods approaches. The knowledge and insights gained from the use of particular data collection and analysis techniques has been dissipated across a wide range of journals. These have included specialist HRD journals such as *Human Resource Development International* and the *European Journal of Training and Development*; Human Resource Management (HRM) journals such as *Human Resource Management* and *Personnel Review*; as well as more generalist business and management and organizational psychology journals. Whilst these journals and the associated articles highlight the methodological openness of the HRD field, they are rarely able to offer a comprehensive picture of the use of particular methods within HRD research. Rather their reading reveals the necessity for an up-to-date overview of the methods that are being used to help support HRD researchers in their use.

The aim of this book, therefore, is to draw the wealth of research methods experience gained by researchers working within HRD into one volume. Reflecting the methodological plurality revealed in the journals, the editors and contributors to this volume have explored and researched HRD from a variety of directions. The book therefore reflects and utilizes the research experiences of leading HRD scholars to provide a range of insights on methods for those researching HRD.

The development of HRD research has given rise to definitional debates, which are well addressed in the literature (Kuchinke, 2000; Lee, 1997, 2001; McLean and McLean, 2001; Wang and McLean, 2007). Drawing from the evolving nature of HRD from 'training' to 'training and development' to 'development' and its relationship with HRM, these debates focus on defining development through its purpose and end point (Lee, 1997). They consider what should be included or excluded within the definition; the functions and purpose of HRD, such as learning (Watkins 1991) and performance (Swanson, 1995); whether a unifying definition is appropriate given the different (national) contexts within which HRD operates (Wang and McLean, 2007); and if development should be considered a 'thing of being' or a 'process' (Lee, 2001). Another facet of these issues is that HRD is not confined to work organizations; Sambrook and Stewart (2010), for example, argue that higher education is itself a site of HRD practice. We have therefore taken a broad conceptualization of HRD in offering advice to our contributors, being guided by Lee's (1997) four overlapping forms of development:

- maturation, in which people progress through inevitable stages;
- shaping, in which people are moulded to fit the organization through named steps;
- a voyage, in which individuals are involved in a transformational shift through internal discovery;
- emergent, in which individuals develop through interaction with others.

In this volume we therefore both recognize and embrace the diversity of conceptualizations of HRD found in the literature, and this is reflected in variations between the chapters.

Invariably a volume such as this cannot be a research methods textbook, covering all areas of method as they apply to HRD. As editors we have sought to identify and draw together in one volume those areas that we, and our contributors, believe require particular attention when researching HRD. The task we set our contributors was to examine pertinent methodological issues and methods, emphasizing those practical concerns of particular relevance to both new and more experienced HRD researchers. In particular we wanted HRD researchers to share their experiences of these issues; of what works and what does not work, and of the challenges and innovations.

Each substantive chapter adopts a similar structure commencing with a short summary and an introduction. This is followed by a discussion of the method or issue and its application to HRD research. As pluralists we believe that no one method or methodology, be it quantitative, qualitative, used on its own or in combination, is superior to another. Rather we believe the choice of method is dependent upon the context, the research question and the researcher. We therefore asked our contributors to discuss their own experiences of the method or methodological issue when undertaking HRD research and to reflect upon these within their chapters. In doing so we wanted our contributors' chapters to inspire and inform their readers, rather than provide a full review of all the relevant literature. Consequently, following the discussion and list of references, each chapter also offers further annotated reading.

The book's 24 substantive chapters are organized into four parts: Conceptual Issues, Qualitative Research, Quantitative Research and, finally, Methodological Challenges.

PART I: CONCEPTUAL ISSUES

Part I considers a range of conceptual issues in HRD research. These include the philosophical and paradigmatic assumptions that underpin research, the purpose of research and the need for practitioner relevance, and systematic reviewing of existing literature.

The opening chapter (Chapter 2) is concerned with an issue of importance to all HRD researchers: how to locate and take ownership of both the paradigmatic and philosophical underpinnings of your research. Here Bob Hamlin outlines and offers insights from his personal experiences over a quarter of a century of HRD research. Within the chapter he outlines differing purposes of mono, multiple and mixed methods research designs and offers a simplified framework to support researchers in their own philosophical deliberations. In so doing his chapter also provides an overview of the epistemological and ontological debates that underpin the research strategies and methods discussed in subsequent parts of the book.

Chapters 3 and 4 are both concerned with the science of HRD research, addressing issues regarding the purpose of systematic enquiry and the need for practitioner relevance and usefulness. In Chapter 3 Eugene Sadler-Smith explores debates surrounding management as a design or explanatory science and the implications of these debates for HRD research. Within the chapter he contrasts the mission of design science to developing actionable knowledge with that of explanatory science, namely to describe, explain and predict. Posing the question as to whether HRD research might better be placed as the former, Eugene emphasizes how design science principles might help in the development of valid knowledge to support intellectually curious practitioners and assist in solving organizational field problems. The themes of relevance and usefulness are developed further in Chapter 4 by Jeff Gold and colleagues. They focus on the importance of scholarly practice within HRD research and its utility for tackling complex workplace issues. Acknowledging a relevance gap between academic research and practice, they explore and critique roles, strategies and behaviours for HRD scholar-practitioners, introducing Flyvbjerg's (2001) argument for making social science more relevant by moving in the direction of phronetic social science. Using six scholar-practitioners' voices, Jeff and colleagues consider how, when faced with competing or a plurality of values, phronetic social science's emphasis on practical wisdom and prudent judgements is articulated in HRD research.

The last chapter in Part I (Chapter 5) considers the use of systematic review to examine the extant HRD literature. Acknowledging that the need to review the literature is widely accepted by researchers, in this chapter Céline Rojon and Almuth McDowall outline how such an evidence-based approach can offer advantages in areas such as HRD where the literature is wide and fragmented. Drawing on their own experiences of conducting a systematic review, as well as that of other existing systematic reviewers, they outline the key features of the methodology. This is subsequently benchmarked against both traditional narrative reviews and the use of meta-analysis to consider the advantages and potential disadvantages of systematic review, alongside practicalities and challenges being discussed. In offering their insights, Céline and Almuth note that, although systematic review is time-consuming, taking skill, effort and determination, it supports a move towards evidence-based management within HRD.

PART II: QUALITATIVE RESEARCH

Part II focuses upon qualitative research, that is, research using non-numeric data, or data that have not been quantified. As such it includes chapters concerned with the use of specific strategies for qualitative research within HRD, such as action research and ethnography, as well as chapters focusing upon specific data sources and techniques such as social media and photo elicitation and systematic content analysis.

The first two chapters in this section are concerned with ethnography and the role of the researcher within this. In Chapter 6 Dawn Langley explores the distinct contribution of ethnographic research to understanding HRD practices, arguing that it enables the HRD researcher to gain a deeper understanding of the ways in which people make sense of their organizations. Within this she emphasizes the importance of building rapport between the researcher and participants, both outlining associated challenges and drawing on her own experiences to suggest ways these might be overcome. Dawn also highlights the impact for researchers of exposing the lives of others and themselves in their research and writing, noting the difference between talking about lived experiences and seeing these reported and recorded in print. The importance of self and the role of researcher are developed further in Chapter 7 by Sally Sambrook in her exploration of the use of autoethnography. Using the context of higher education, she illustrates the value of this method by outlining how the autoethnographic researcher can bring personal insight and understanding to wider sociological and cultural issues within sites of HRD practice. Sally offers three exemplars of using autoethnography within the higher education context, which might be adapted to other HRD contexts. She also exposes some of the challenges of adopting autoethnography, emphasizing the importance of self-awareness and the need to draw upon self as a source of data.

Chapters 8 and 9 are concerned with the use of visual methods. In Chapter 8 Kate Black and Russell Warhurst provide an overview of the contents of the visual methods toolbox from which HRD researchers might select. Following an exploration of the different traditions of visual methods and alternative research designs, they outline 17 different visual methods, providing more details for four of the five methods they consider to have notable potential for HRD research. Chapter 9, by Russell Warhurst and Kate Black, focuses on the fifth such method, photo-elicitation interviewing. Arguing that this method is, as yet, underutilized, Russell and Kate examine its development as a method and its value to HRD research. Using an illustrative example of non-formal workplace learning of professionals they note that the method can offer new and novel insights supporting inductively based theorizing. However, they also highlight shortcomings and potential pitfalls, not least the particular ethical concerns associated with using photographs.

Although action research can use both quantitative and qualitative data either separately or in combination, the inclusion of an illustrative example using qualitative data led us to locate Rosalie Holian and David Coghlan's chapter in this section on qualitative research. In this chapter (Chapter 10) Rosalie and David explore the theory and practice of action research, highlighting how it is an evolving process undertaken in a spirit of collaborative enquiry. They illustrate how, within an HRD context, it can be used both to bring about change in organizations and, through focusing on real organizational problems or issues, generate actionable knowledge of use to the world of organizations. In Chapter 11 Kiran Trehan and Clare Rigg focus on the use of critical action learning research, a development of the action learning approach in HRD research. Critical action learning emphasizes learning and development through critical engagement in both action and reflection. However, as in action research (discussed in Chapter 10), the research component incorporates the expectation that knowledge is created for the wider world.

The themes of undertaking HRD research that is useful to the world of organizations and of involving practitioners in that research are continued in Chapter 12. Here Mark Saunders and colleagues explore the application of the Service Template Extended Process (STEP) to HRD research to support applied HRD research in collaboration with practitioners. Adopting Schein's (1999) process consultation framework they outline how STEP can be used to surface values and underlying assumptions, acting as catalyst for both single- and double-loop learning.

Chapter 13 focuses upon the use of actor network theory and discourse analysis. Using the context of an online environment, Peter Evans describes how the theory and analysis can be used to investigate the social practices and community-forming activities associated with professional development. Within this Peter examines the usefulness and challenges of this research approach, highlighting its suitability for researching social media environments.

The last chapter in Part II (Chapter 14) offers new insights into the most frequently used qualitative method in HRD research, the interview. In this chapter Paul Tosey highlights the importance of designing and asking clear, unbiased questions in order to elicit data of good quality. Drawing on a project that investigated managers' metaphors of work–life balance that was informed by the practice called 'Clean Language', Paul shows how questions can be designed to minimize the risk of inadvertently introducing the interviewer's constructs, whether via their questions or their interpretation. In doing this he highlights a range of issues of relevance to all those using interviews. These include the difference between content-focused and epistemic conceptions of questioning, and the importance of precision in designing and using interview questions.

PART III: QUANTITATIVE RESEARCH

Part III commences with three chapters that look at different facets of the most prevalent method for collecting quantitative data, the survey. This is followed by a chapter exploring two data collection techniques less widely used in HRD research, namely the Critical Incident Technique and the Vignette Technique. The final two chapters in this part respectively offer overviews of the use of two quantitative analysis techniques: structural equation modelling and systematic content analysis.

In the first chapter (Chapter 15) on the use of surveys, Cinla Akinci and Mark Saunders provide an overview of the use of questionnaires in organizational HRD research, focusing on commonly occurring methodological issues and associated concerns. They illustrate this from their personal experience of four applied research projects within a large organization, emphasizing the importance of considering the entire process of questionnaire design, delivery and collection and data input and analysis as a whole rather than just its separate components.

This theme is developed with a particular focus on online and telephone surveys in Chapters 16 and 17. In Chapter 16, Jim Stewart and Victoria Harte focus on the issue of online survey non-response, arguing that reasons for this fall into three categories: design of the questionnaire, personal motivation of the respondents and the method used to distribute the questionnaire. Within this they note that the method of distribution is particularly significant in relation to the assumed online preferences of generation X (those born from the mid-1960s to early 1980s) and generation Y (those born from 1982 onwards and believed to engage automatically in web technologies). In Chapter 17, Maura Sheehan and colleagues consider issues of maximizing telephone survey response. Highlighting the continued utility of the telephone survey, Maura and colleagues focus upon ways of tailoring survey design and administration to leverage potential respondents' participation. They illustrate this with examples drawn from their international HRD research.

Chapter 18 explores how Critical Incident Technique (CIT) and the Vignette Technique (VT) can support HRD research. Using examples drawn from her research on informal learning and behaviour at work, Regina Mulder illustrates the relative advantages and disadvantages of both techniques in addressing challenges caused by the nature and the complexity of workplace HRD research settings. Within this she highlights how these techniques can be used to collect both quantitative and qualitative data, and addresses associated methodological issues, in particular the need to ensure context-boundedness and authenticity.

The final two chapters in this section discuss less widely used quantitative analytical techniques, which offer considerable potential for HRD researchers. In Chapter 19 Christoph König and colleagues discuss the use of structural equation modelling (SEM) in HRD research. They explain how SEM can offer a flexible quantitative data analysis tool to investigate complex problems generated by the hierarchical interdependencies between organizations, teams and individual employees and how these alter over time. Following a description of the method, Christoph and colleagues use the example of a study of the development of innovative work behaviours to illustrate its utility. Drawing on this they note the statistical rigour of SEM and the opportunities it can offer as a basis for improving organizational practice and policy. Finally in this part of the book, in Chapter 20 Rob Poell provides an overview of systematic content analysis, an approach to quantitatively analysing qualitative data. Rob's chapter looks briefly at its history and its main characteristics, advantages and disadvantages within HRD research. He illustrates these issues with an empirical example in which he shows how large amounts of qualitative data can be usefully summarized numerically, the resultant tables allowing scientific and practically relevant conclusions to be drawn.

PART IV: METHODOLOGICAL CHALLENGES

Methodological issues of researching HRD are highlighted throughout this volume as contributors discuss and reflect upon their own research. In Part IV our contributors devote entire chapters to common challenges of particular importance to HRD researchers. These are the adoption of a critical perspective, the use of mixed methods, gendered constructions, the need for reflexivity and alternative ways of researching extra-sensitive topics.

In Chapter 21 Jamie Callahan and Gary Connor return to the use of quantitative and qualitative paradigms first highlighted by Bob Hamlin in Chapter 2. In particular they challenge the hegemonic notion that critical paradigms, and in particular critical HRD research, necessitate qualitative research. Jamie and Gary argue that a focus on the qualitative epistemological underpinnings of critical theory is counterproductive to achieving critical social transformation, illustrating this with a mixed methods example. The practice of mixed methods in HRD research is explored further in Chapter 22 by Steven Tam and David Gray. They outline and illustrate how mixed methods research designs can allow critical insights to HRD research. Using an example drawn from an empirical study of learning practices in small and medium sized enterprises (SMEs), Steven and David highlight how qualitative and quantitative methods can be combined in a variety of ways and how one method can be used to provide focus for another. Like others in this volume, they also emphasize the importance of the research question.

Key issues for gender research in HRD are highlighted by Sharon Mavin and Jannine Williams in Chapter 23. Noting that gender research can be a highly political process, with significant negative or positive impact for both researchers and participants, they examine the importance of gender aware HRD and a range of issues in gender research. Sharon and Jannine present and illustrate these issues using research that operationalizes a Multi-Stakeholder Framework for analysing gendered media constructions of women leaders.

Returning to issues associated with research in action (introduced in Chapters 10 and 11), Carole Elliott and Valerie Stead explore in Chapter 24 how opportunities for research in action can be created through adopting a post-structuralist sensitivity to leadership development within the classroom. Using examples from their own experience, they illustrate how leadership development methods can also act simultaneously as methods of enquiry, constituting a research–teaching cycle. Building on those experiences, Carole and Valerie argue that reflexive enquiry requires a framework that exposes developmental activities to critique and informs the development of theory and continuing educational practice.

Our final chapter (Chapter 25), by Thomas Garavan and Clíodhna MacKenzie, considers the methodological challenges of researching HRD topics that are extra sensitive due to their potential for negative outcomes. In this they outline alternative innovative approaches to sourcing both primary and secondary data unobtrusively. Thomas and Clíodhna outline the advantages and associated issues of using data collection methods in comparison to more traditional methods and illustrate how the use of content analysis frameworks and Computer Aided Qualitative Data Analysis Software (CAQDAS) can augment such non-obtrusive collection methods.

MOVING FORWARD

As we intimated at the start of this introduction, this volume represents a sharing by HRD researchers of their thoughts, experiences and ideas about researching HRD. Whilst it is not a textbook, we believe it offers insights into a wide range of research methods, both mainstream and less frequently used, that HRD researchers will find both invaluable and useful. As editors we trust that this handbook will both inspire and inform HRD research and contribute to existing and future debates about researching HRD.

REFERENCES

Cameron, S. and Price, S. (2009) *Business Research Methods: A Practical Approach*. London: Chartered Institute of Personnel and Development.

Cassell, C. (2015) *Conducting Research Interviews for Business and Management Students*. London: Sage.

Ekinci, Y. (2015) *Designing Research Questionnaires for Business and Management Students*. London: Sage.

Flyvbjerg, B. (2001) *Making Social Science Matter*. Cambridge: Cambridge University Press.

Kuchinke, K.P. (2000) Debates over the nature of HRD: An institutional theory perspective. *Human Resource Development International*, 3 (3), pp. 279–283.

Lee, M. (1997) The developmental approach: A critical reconsideration, in J. Burgoyne and M. Reynolds (Eds.) *Management Learning* (pp. 199–214). London: Sage.

Lee, M. (2001) A refusal to define HRD. *Human Resource Development International*, 4 (3), pp. 327–341.

McLean, G.N. and McLean, L. (2001) If we can't define HRD in one country, how can we define it in an international context? *Human Resource Development International*, 4 (3), pp. 313–326.

Sambrook, S. and Stewart, J. (2010) Teaching, learning and assessing HRD: Findings from a BMAF/UFHRD research project. *Journal of European Industrial Training*, Special Issue, 34 (8/9), pp. 710–734.

Saunders, M., Lewis, P. and Thornhill, A. (2012) *Research Methods for Business Students* (6th edn). Harlow: Pearson.

Schein, E.H. (1999) *Process Consultation Revisited: Building the Helping Relationship*. Reading, MA: Addison-Wesley Longman.

Swanson, R.A. (1995) Performance is the key. *Human Resource Development Quarterly*, 6 (2), pp. 207–220.

Symon, G. and Cassell, C. (2012) *Qualitative Organizational Research*. London: Sage.

Wang, X. and McLean, G. (2007) The dilemma of defining international human resource development. *Human Resource Development Review*, 6 (1), pp. 96–108.

Watkins, K.E. (1991) Many voices: Defining human resource development from different disciplines. *Adult Education Quarterly*, 41 (4), pp. 241–255.

PART I

CONCEPTUAL ISSUES

2. Paradigms, philosophical prisms and pragmatism in HRD research
Bob Hamlin

SUMMARY

Following increasing numbers of calls for researchers to state their guiding paradigm when publishing their research, this chapter outlines personal experiences of striving to do this. It offers a simplified philosophical framework to aid researchers in locating and taking ownership of their philosophical perspective.

INTRODUCTION

Most research in business and management and other related fields including Human Resource Development (HRD) has been based on the 'scientific method', and there has been little expectation for researchers to declare their philosophical assumptions. However, with the ever increasing recognition and acceptability of qualitative research in the organizational, social and behavioural sciences, there has been in recent years an increasing number of calls for researchers to state their guiding paradigm when publishing their research. This chapter outlines my personal experience of striving to do just that, the difficulties encountered, the paradigmatic confusion that I found in the research methods literature, the resulting conundrum that confronted me, how this was resolved, and the development of a new 'simplified philosophical framework' to aid researchers in locating and taking ownership of their philosophical perspectives.

I have been engaged in academic research for over 25 years and have found it relatively straightforward and problem free in execution. In stark contrast my experience of getting the findings published has at times been frustrating and discouraging. I have struggled to classify much of my research paradigmatically because I have been unable to see it clearly located within either the 'positivist' or 'constructionist' paradigm. In the early 2000s, when I first declared the philosophical assumptions guiding my research, several journal reviewers were highly critical. It appeared they did not recognize my work as consistent with their understanding of the type of research they associated with my declared paradigmatic orientation. For example, one reviewer incorrectly inferred from my use of the term 'grounded theory mind-set' that I had actually engaged in conventional grounded theory research, which was not the case. Another was confused by the notion of 'multi-paradigm research' and my claim that the epistemology fell between post positivism and constructivism. Other reviewers were dismissive of my having located a study within the post positivist/critical realist paradigm because they could see no relationship between my work and their understanding of 'critical realist thinking', even though I had explained that from an ontological perspective I had been searching for variform universals, and that the study had adopted Fleetwood's (2005) notion of the 'ideally real' mode of critical realism.

Reviewers' rejections caused me to explore in some depth the 'philosophy of science'. This raised my awareness of (i) the 'science' and 'paradigm' wars of the 1980s and 1990s when 'purist' quantitative researchers were arguing vehemently about the superiority of 'hard generalizable' data, and similarly 'purist' qualitative researchers were arguing the superiority of 'deep, rich, thick' descriptive data; (ii) the dominance of paradigmatic privileging of what can be studied and how it can be studied; (iii) the emergence of the 'post positivist' and 'critical theory' paradigms; and (iv) the more recent emergence of 'pragmatism' and 'mixed-methods research' in the organizational, social and behavioural sciences. As a result I am now better placed to locate and articulate more accurately the paradigmatic orientation of my past and current research, as I will illustrate later.

In this chapter I provide an account of the difficulties I experienced in taking ownership of my orientation and how these were overcome. I discuss first my early research journey, during which I learned about the complexities and contradictions regarding the relationship between paradigms and philosophies and the considerable confusion existing across the research methods literature. This is followed by a discussion of specific insights gained from articles found in the counselling psychology, education and international relations literatures on multiple-paradigm research, mixed-methods research and pragmatism which helped me resolve my philosophical and paradigmatic conundrum. With the benefit of hindsight I close the chapter with a discussion of how my past studies should probably have been classified paradigmatically and present a derived 'simplified philosophical framework' which has helped me dispel personally much of the paradigmatic confusion found in the literature. I offer this framework in the hope that it will also be of help to other HRD researchers when they come to (i) select an appropriate paradigmatic orientation, ontology, epistemology, methodology and axiology for their next research inquiry, and (ii) articulate the philosophical prism through which their research should be perceived, evaluated and judged. Throughout the chapter the word 'philosophy' refers to the assumed ontology and epistemology that guide a researcher's study; and drawing on Guba (1990, p. 17) the word 'paradigm' refers to 'the net that contains the researcher's epistemological, ontological and methodological premises'. However, another definition that has resonance for this chapter is that offered by Bryman (1988, p. 4), who asserts that a paradigm is 'a cluster of beliefs and dictates which for scientists in a particular discipline influences what should be studied, how research should be done, [and] how results should be interpreted'. Although much is held in common between the definitional understandings of these two authors, there are some important differences that I will demonstrate and discuss later in the chapter.

MY EARLY RESEARCH JOURNEY AND PHILOSOPHICAL CONFUSION

I first engaged with HRD research in 1984 when I joined in mid career the Management Studies Department of 'The Polytechnic, Wolverhampton' (UK), which in 1992 became the University of Wolverhampton. To pursue a long term career in Higher Education I decided I needed a research qualification, and within three years of part time study I had gained an MPhil degree on the 'criteria of managerial effectiveness' in UK secondary schools. When I embarked on the study no guidance was given regarding the 'philosophy of science'; nor was I given any formal training on research methodology and methods. My personal development as an academic researcher came about through experiential learning and informal mentoring from my director of studies. Nevertheless, the research was rated highly by two external examiners, and one of them arranged for my MPhil thesis to be published in an academic journal (Hamlin, 1988).

By 1989 I had become a divisional manager at the polytechnic, and it was not until eight years later that I had the time and opportunity to engage actively once more with academic research. I was commissioned by the Executive Head of the Anglia Region of HM Customs and Excise – a major department of the British Civil Service – to conduct in conjunction with his internal researcher an organization-wide study of 'managerial and leadership effectiveness' using the same qualitative critical incident technique (CIT) and quantitative factor analytic methods adopted for my MPhil study. As before the research was published without any reference to any philosophical or paradigmatic issues (see Hamlin et al., 1998). However, by the time of my next CIT/factor analytic replication study carried out in a UK public sector hospital, I had become aware of the desirability to declare at least my assumed methodological stance. Consequently, I stated that I had adopted an 'inductive approach' within a 'grounded theory mind-set' – thus indicating that I had not engaged in conventional ('pure') quantitative ('positivist') research or qualitative ('interpretivist–constructivist') research (see Hamlin, 2002). Similarly, when reporting the results of a subsequent cross-case comparative analysis of findings obtained from my MPhil study and the two aforementioned replication studies (see Hamlin, 2004), I stated that I had adopted an 'inductive' and a 'deductive approach' within a 'grounded theory mind-set'. However, knowing that I had not used the conventional grounded theory 'constant comparative method', I decided I needed to increase my understanding of the 'philosophy of science' so that I could locate more accurately and state with more confidence my paradigmatic orientation and philosophical assumptions, and thereby articulate the philosophical prism though which my research should be viewed.

This decision chimed with various contemporary and subsequent calls in psychology and organizational science for researchers to (i) take ownership of their perspective when publishing qualitative research by understanding and stating their guiding paradigm, methodology and personal orientation (Elliott et al., 1999; Morrow, 2007); (ii) locate their research studies within a specific research paradigm (Ponterotto, 2005); and (iii) articulate more openly the basis and appropriateness of their research methods (Buchanan and Bryman, 2007). Inferring that these calls were relevant to HRD related researchers, and in the absence of any HRD research methods book that specifically discussed the issue of research philosophy, I turned first to the work of Guba and Lincoln (1994). These 'experts' had identified four competing basic belief systems (paradigms) for guiding qualitative research in the 'social science' disciplines. They labelled them as 'positivism', 'postpositivism', 'constructivism' and 'critical theory and related ideological positions'; and they also described the associated ontological, epistemological and methodological assumptions.

According to Guba and Lincoln, positivism is based on (i) a 'realist' ontology (commonly called 'naïve realism') which assumes the existence of an apprehendable reality and (ii) a 'dualist/objectivist' epistemology where the researcher and the investigated object are assumed to be independent entities and the researcher studies the object without influencing it or being influenced by it. Post positivism is based on (i) a 'critical realist' ontology which assumes the existence of an imperfectly apprehendable reality because of basic flaws in human intellectual activity and the intractable nature of life's phenomena which prevents the capture of a 'true' reality and (ii) a modified 'dualist/objectivist' epistemology where researchers acknowledge they may have some influence on that being researched but strive for objectivity and researcher–object/subject independence. Constructivism is based on (i) a 'relativist' ontology which assumes realities are apprehendable in the form of multiple, intangible, mental constructions that are socially and experientially based, local, and specific in nature, and dependent for their form and content on the individual persons or groups holding the constructions, and consequently are alterable, and (ii) a 'transactional/subjectivist' epistemology where the researcher and the investigated object are assumed to be interactively linked so that the findings are literally created as the research proceeds. Critical theory and related ideological positions are based on (i) an 'historical realist' ontology which assumes the existence of an apprehendable reality that has been shaped over time by social, political, cultural, economic and other such factors, and then crystallized into structures that are taken as natural and immutable, and (ii) a 'transactional/subjectivist' epistemology where the researcher and the investigated object are interactively linked, with the values of the researcher (and of situated other people) inevitably influencing the inquiry such that the findings are value mediated.

I then contrasted Guba and Lincoln's US derived perspectives on competing paradigms against Bryman and Bell's (2003) UK derived perspectives in the field of business research.[1] These writers identified three epistemological positions (positivism–realism–interpretivism) and two ontological positions (objectivism–constructionism). They argued that positivism is concerned with applying methods of the natural sciences to the study of social reality and beyond and is aimed at testing theories and providing evidence for the development of laws. Regarding realism they argued it has two major forms which share two features with positivism, namely a belief that the natural and social sciences should apply the same kinds of approach to data collection and explanation and that there is an external reality separate from descriptions of it. The first form is empirical realism, which simply asserts that through the use of appropriate methods reality can be understood and that it is this meaning to which writers refer when they employ the term 'realism' in a general way. According to Saunders et al. (2012), this form of realism, which they refer to as direct realism, asserts that what people experience through their senses portrays the world accurately. In contrast, critical realism is conceptualized as a specific form of realism which seeks to identify the structures at work that generate events and discourses in the natural order of the social world, with the aim of understanding and so changing them. Bryman and Bell (2003) define objectivism as an ontological position which asserts that social phenomena and their meanings have an existence independent of social actors, and constructionism is an ontological position which asserts that social phenomena and their meanings are continually being accomplished by social actors. Additionally, they draw upon Burrell and Morgan's (1979) four possible paradigms/paradigmatic positions that researchers can adopt for the study of organizations, namely functionalist, the dominant framework which is based on problem-solving that leads to rational explanations; radical structuralist, in which researchers view organizations as products of structural power relationships that result in conflict; interpretative, which questions whether organizations exist in any real sense beyond the conceptions of social actors, which means that understanding must be based on the experience of those who work within them; and radical humanist, in which researchers see organizations as social arrangements from which individuals need to be emancipated as guided by the need for change identified by their research.

More recently, Swanson (2005) asserted that there are three alternative paradigms and methods considered relevant to scholars across multiple disciplines including HRD: positivism, interpretivism and critical science. Positivism assumes the world is objective and that researchers generally explore relationships among variables and focus on quantitative methods to test and verify hypotheses. Interpretivism is concerned with subjective meaning and seeks to reveal how organizational members apprehend, understand and make sense of events and situations; thus there is no objective knowledge apart from individual interpretations by reasoning humans. A variant of interpretivism is 'social constructionism', which seeks to investigate how the objective features in the social world of organizations emerge from, depend upon and are constituted by subjective meanings of individuals and intersubjective processes such as discourses or discussions in groups. Critical science is a combination of critical theory and postmodernism, whereby researchers either seek to challenge the 'domination, injustice and subjugation' within organizations that they believe capitalism produces, or endeavour to provide historical understandings of important events and to surface unacknowledged forms of exploitation and domination. However, Swanson provides no cited evidence in support of this latter paradigmatic conceptualization, which could be contested by other research methods experts. Furthermore, he omits to discuss specifically the ontological and epistemological assumptions upon which his three asserted paradigms are based.

Despite the various similarities and overlaps across the offered sets of paradigmatic insights, what particularly confused me were the conflicting and contradictory terms used by Guba and Lincoln (1994) and by Bryman and Bell (2003) in labelling their respective near equivalent paradigmatic definitions. As can be seen in Table 2.1, they use quite different labels to describe paradigms that appear substantively the same, and in

Table 2.1 *Conflicting and confusing labelling*

	Authors	Labelling			
Paradigm	Guba and Lincoln (1994)	Positivism	Post-positivism	Critical theory and related ideological positions	Constructivism
	Bryman and Bell (2003), Burrell and Morgan (1979)	Functionalist	Radical structuralist	Radical humanist	Interpretive
	Ponterotto (2005)	Positivism	Post-positivist	Critical–ideological	Constructivism–interpretivism
	Swanson (2005)	Positivism		Critical science	Interpretivism
Ontological characteristics	Guba and Lincoln (1994)	Realism (*Naïve realism*)	Critical realism	Historical realism	Relativism
	Bryman and Bell (2003)	Objectivism	Objectivism	Constructionism (*Constructivism*)	Constructionism (*Constructivism*)
	Ponterotto (2005)	Naïve realism	Critical realism		Relativism
Epistemological position	Guba and Lincoln (1994)	Dualist/objectivist	Modified dualist/objectivist	Transactional/subjectivist	Transactional/subjectivist
	Bryman and Bell (2003)	Positivism	Empirical realism and critical realism		Interpretivism
	Ponterotto (2005)	Dualism/objectivism	Modified dualism/objectivism	Transactional/subjectivist	Transactional/subjectivist

some cases the same label has been used to describe different ontological or epistemological characteristics of a paradigm. For example, Bryman and Bell (2003) deploy the term 'constructionism' (or alternatively constructivism) to describe the ontology that they associate with Burrell and Morgan's (1979) subjectivist radical humanist and interpretive paradigms, whereas Guba and Lincoln (1994) use the same term for a paradigm label. Similarly, Bryman and Bell deploy the term 'positivism' to describe an epistemological position, whereas Guba and Lincoln use it as a paradigm label. Additionally, the term 'critical realism' is used by Guba and Lincoln to describe the ontology associated with their post positivist paradigm, whereas Bryman and Bell deploy it to describe one form of the epistemology they associate with Burrell and Morgan's (1979) objectivist radical structuralist paradigm. Related to these two equivalent paradigms, it will be noted that whereas the term 'objectivist' is part of Guba and Lincoln's epistemological description, Bryman and Bell use the related term 'objectivism' as an ontological description. As Walton (2008) observed, compared to 'positivism', which is relatively straightforward, when one starts to explore the philosophical concepts of 'critical realism', 'post positivism', 'constructivism' and their variants it becomes very complex and often contradictory.

These conflicting and confusing descriptors of the different worldview characteristics of competing paradigms posed for me a considerable philosophical/paradigmatic conundrum, particularly as I could not locate my replication and cross-case comparative studies within a single paradigm. Consequently, I continued to be deterred from taking ownership of and declaring my paradigmatic orientation.

RESOLVING MY PHILOSOPHICAL AND PARADIGMATIC CONUNDRUM

Resolution of my philosophical and paradigmatic conundrum came about through insights gained from reading relevant articles found in the counselling psychology, education and international relations literatures on the issues of multiple-paradigm research, mixed-methods research and pragmatism respectively.

Multiple-Paradigm Research

Ponterotto (2005) describes four research paradigms applying within counselling psychology, which are similar to the conceptualizations offered by Guba and Lincoln (1994) and Lincoln and Guba (2000). Of particular interest to me was Ponterotto's (2005) discussion of the 'universe of qualitative approaches and locating them within research paradigms', and his illustration of the process as applied to an example of consensual qualitative research (CQR) in counselling psychology. He argues that what can be studied and how it can be studied does not have to be privileged and governed by one specific paradigm, but instead can be influenced by the ontology and/or epistemology of other paradigms. For example, CQR relies on 'research team member and external auditor consensus' in arriving at domains and core ideas, and it assumes there is one true 'approximal reality' rather than multiple equally valid realities (ibid., p. 133). Consequently, Ponterotto claims that the ontology of CQR can be characterized as post positivist. However, with reference to epistemology he notes that CQR researchers often conduct semi-structured interviews (30–60 minutes) which are unlikely to lead to intense researcher–participant interaction or extensive discovery; and that they follow an overall interview protocol, which does not change from interview to interview as in the constructivist paradigm. Hence, he classifies the epistemology of CQR as falling somewhere between post positivism and constructivism but leaning towards post positivism.

With this greater awareness of the possibility of locating social and behavioural science related research within multiple paradigms, I became more confident in classifying and reporting the assumed ontology and epistemology of my then recently completed and on-going qualitative replication studies. Because I had in mind to use in due course the findings of these single and multiple organization studies as source data for a subsequent derived etic[2] multiple cross-case comparative study that sought to identify generalizations across organizations and organizational sectors in the UK and ultimately across nations, and if possible to deduce generic and ultimately universalistic behavioural criteria of perceived managerial and leadership effectiveness, I concluded I could claim I was adopting ontological assumptions associated with the post positivist paradigm. Furthermore, because the CIT component of the emic source studies had deployed semi-structured interviews to elicit critical incidents through 'social discourse', which involved 'probing', 'follow-up' and 'explicatory' questions, I thought my assumed epistemology could be classified as constructivist–interpretivist (see Hamlin and Serventi, 2008). However, after re-reading Ponterotto's (2005) primer on research paradigms, and reflecting further on the fact that the typical CIT interview duration had been 75 minutes or less and that the respective researchers had had limited interpersonal interaction with their informants, I concluded the epistemology would be better classified as falling between post positivism and constructivism–interpretivism (see Hamlin et al., 2010).

Pragmatism and Mixed-Methods Research

In the field of educational research, Burke Johnson and Onwuegbuzie (2004) and Onwuegbuzie and Leech (2005) highlight the long-standing divide between positivists and interpretivists, particularly within the social and behavioural sciences where quantitative and qualitative researchers have engaged in ardent dispute and vehement debate. They refer to the two resulting dominant paradigms, with one research sub-culture (quantitative 'purist') professing the superiority of 'hard generalizable' survey data and the other sub-culture (qualitative 'purist') professing the virtues of 'deep, rich, thick' interview data. However, as these writers also observe, there are many similarities between quantitative and qualitative research, with both types of researcher using empirical observations to address research questions, often triangulating their data, applying techniques to verify their data and deploying analytic methods to reduce their data. Furthermore, in both paradigms the role of theory is central, with quantitative research being concerned with theory testing and theory modification and qualitative research being concerned with theory initiation and theory building. However, they claim that neither approach can encompass all that which needs to be researched in order to understand a phenomenon fully and that both approaches need to gain a more complete understanding. Hence, these writers argue the case for epistemological ecumenism (unity) and methodological pluralism and advocate the advantages of becoming a pragmatic and often a mixed-methods researcher. Echoing Cresswell's (2003) definition of mixed-methods research, Burke Johnson and Onwuegbuzie (2004, p. 17) define it as 'the class of research where the researcher mixes or combines quantitative and qualitative research techniques, methods, approaches, concepts or language into a single study', with researchers mindfully creating designs that effectively answer their research questions in order to better understand the research problems being explored. Additionally, they argue that mixed-methods research is the natural complement to traditional quantitative and qualitative research and that pragmatism is its philosophical partner. However, it should be noted that the mixing of methods does not necessarily have to be undertaken from a pragmatist perspective. For example, the type of data collected and methods deployed by post positivist researchers can be privileged as either quantitative or qualitative, or as a combination of both types. Furthermore, mixed-methods research should not be confused with the notion of multiple-methods research, which refers to qualitative studies that consist of two or more components using qualitative methods or quantitative studies that consist of two or more quantitative components using quantitative methods (Saunders et al., 2012).

In the field of social science and educational research, Maxcy (2002) argues that what is healthy about mixed-methods research within a pragmatist philosophy is that (i) a number of projects are allowed to be undertaken without the need to identify invariant prior knowledge, laws or rules governing what is recognized as 'true' or 'valid'; (ii) only results count; and (iii) researchers do not require a single foundational discourse of research methodology to warrant their activities. This view is supported by Bryman (2006), who argues that in place of the primacy of philosophical principles associated with positivism and constructionism, pragmatism prioritizes the research question, relegates ontological and epistemological debates to the sidelines and clears the path for inquiries that combine qualitative and quantitative research methods. Maxcy's view is also supported by Morgan (2007), who argues that rather than the choices researchers make about what questions are most important to study and which methods are most appropriate for conducting those studies being governed/privileged by the ontological–epistemological stance of a particular paradigm, these choices can instead be pragmatically determined by the system of beliefs and practices shared among their own community of scholars, and/or by their individual personal history, social background and cultural assumptions. However, irrespective of these influences, the nature of the research question or questions can be the predominant determinant as to whether a 'mixed-method', 'multiple-method' or 'mono-method' research design should be adopted (Saunders et al., 2012). Morgan (2007) suggests that the 'pragmatic approach', which he prefers not to regard as another paradigm, has three distinctive features: abduction–intersubjectivity–transferability. In the pragmatic mode of research, connection of theory and data relies on 'abductive' reasoning which moves back and forth between induction and deduction. Thus, for example, the results from a qualitative approach can serve as inputs to the deductive goals of a quantitative approach, and vice versa. The relationship between the researcher and the research process in the 'pragmatic approach' does not require the usual forced dichotomy between subjectivity and objectivity, but instead recognizes that many practising researchers typically have to work back and forth between various frames of reference. This duality is captured by the pragmatic 'intersubjectivity' approach. Intersubjectivity also means that there is no problem with a researcher asserting in a single study that there is a single 'real truth'; also that all individuals have their own unique interpretations of the world. Another significant insight offered by Morgan is the widely accepted option in pragmatic research of either separating the metaphysical aspects of ontology from epistemological and methodological issues, or treating them as 'loosely coupled'.

Taking a pragmatic and pluralist philosophical position, Burke Johnson and Onwuegbuzie (2004) have offered a typology of nine mixed-methods research designs based on whether the respective qualitative and quantitative methods have either 'equal' or 'dominant' status and are deployed either 'concurrently' or 'sequentially'. Similarly, in the field of public health research, Curry et al. (2006) have identified eight variations of 'mixed-methods research', whilst in the field of counselling psychology, Hanson et al. (2005) have conceptualized a taxonomy comprising six designs. An integration and summary of the conceptualized pragmatic mixed-methods research designs that are held in common across these widely different fields of study is presented in Table 2.2. The table also includes conceptualizations of 'multiple-method' and 'mono-method' designs in HRD research.

RELOCATING MY RESEARCH WITHIN A SPECIFIC PARADIGMATIC ORIENTATION

As a result of my exploration of the philosophy of science I concluded, with the benefit of hindsight, that in the main I had unconsciously adopted a pragmatic approach and had engaged in mixed-methods research. For example, with reference to Table 2.2, my three early single organization 'emic' CIT/factor analytic studies could be classified as 'QUAL→quan' mixed-methods research where the *sequential* quantitative component was used to identify patterns, themes and concepts within the collected qualitative data. In each study the behavioural statements derived from the collected qualitative CIT data were used to create a survey instrument, namely a behavioural item questionnaire (BIQ) with a Likert scale attached. The BIQ was subsequently administered widely within the particular collaborating organization and the quantitative survey data then subjected to factor analysis in order to reduce and classify the behavioural items and ultimately identify an organization-specific 'lay model' of perceived managerial and leadership effectiveness. This research process fits closely with Hanson et al.'s (2005) notion of 'sequential exploratory designs' for studying phenomena where the study variables are not known; for developing new assessment criteria and instruments based on the initial qualitative analysis; and for generalizing qualitative findings to a specific population. Most of my subsequent 'emic' single organization and multiple organization replication studies, carried out in the UK and other countries with various co-researchers, could also be classified as pragmatic 'QUAL→quan' mixed-methods research but using a concurrent nested design. In each of these studies the core inductive qualitative CIT component had dominant status, the primary aim being to identify

Table 2.2   Mono-, multiple- and mixed-methods research designs

Design	Method	Purpose
Mono-method		
QUAL	Single qualitative component	Exploratory
QUANT	Single quantitative component	Explanatory
Multiple-method		
QUAL→QUAL	Two or more qualitative components (no quantitative component)	Exploratory or triangulation
QUANT→QUANT	Two or more quantitative components (no qualitative component)	Explanatory or triangulation
Mixed-methods sequential and dominant status		
QUAL→quan	Qualitative core component (inductive) which inputs a sequential quantitative component	Exploratory
	Qualitative core component (inductive) which inputs a sequential quantitative component using an explicit advocacy lens (e.g., feminist perspectives, critical theory)	Transformative
QUAN→qual	Quantitative core component (deductive) with a sequential qualitative supplementary component	Explanatory
	Quantitative core component (deductive) with a sequential qualitative supplementary component using an explicit advocacy lens (e.g., feminist perspectives, critical theory)	Transformative
Mixed-methods concurrent and equal status		
QUAL+QUAN	Core qualitative (inductive) component and core quantitative (deductive) conducted simultaneously	Triangulation
	Core qualitative (inductive) component and core quantitative (deductive) conducted simultaneously using an explicit advocacy lens (e.g., feminist perspectives, critical theory)	Transformative
Mixed-methods concurrent and unequal status		
QUAL+quan	Qualitative core component (inductive) with a simultaneous but lower priority quantitative supplementary component to help answer altogether different research questions	Nested
QUAN+qual	Quantitative core component (deductive) with a simultaneous but lower priority qualitative supplementary component to help answer altogether different research questions	Nested

how managers and employees of the collaborating organization defined managerial and leadership effectiveness. The subsequent qualitative comparative analysis that compared the core component findings against an equivalent replication study in search of similarities and differences across different organizations, and in some cases across organizational sectors and/or national settings, contained a small embedded ('nested') quantitative component. Its purpose was to quantify the extent of the identified convergence and divergence through the use of simple descriptive statistics. My two 'derived etic' multiple cross-case comparative studies in search of generic/universalistic behavioural criteria of perceived managerial and leadership effectiveness (Hamlin, 2004; Hamlin and Hatton, 2013), which used as empirical source data the results of various aforementioned 'emic' replication studies (cases), could be classified as examples of abductive 'pragmatic approach' research.

DISCUSSION

As previously mentioned, over the past ten years or so some peer reviewers have questioned and criticized the respective paradigmatic orientations that I have reported in the articles submitted to their particular journals. This experience has led me to conclude that (i) the way in which 'post positivist/ critical realist' and 'constructivist/constructionist' paradigms are understood and applied by some researchers in 'business and management' can be quite different to the way they are understood and applied by researchers in counselling psychology and in other parts of the organizational, social and behavioural sciences, (ii) qualitative research that is claimed to emanate from a 'multiple paradigm' epistemology can be confusing and unacceptable to some researchers and (iii) striving to take ownership of your paradigmatic stance or position by stating your 'guiding paradigm, methodology, and personal orientation' as advocated by Elliott et al. (1999) and other experts can be complicated and problematic, particularly when your research approach does not clearly fall within, or has not been ontologically privileged/governed by one of the four dominant paradigms.

To help reduce some of the paradigmatic confusion outlined earlier in this chapter, and to aid other researchers when making choices about the most appropriate paradigmatic orientation to adopt for a particular study, I have developed a 'simplified philosophical framework' by integrating and summarizing my interpretation and understanding of the various conceptualizations of (i) the four main paradigms, (ii) pragmatism and (iii) mono-, multiple- and mixed-methods research designs (see Figure 2.1). The structure and content of this framework have been

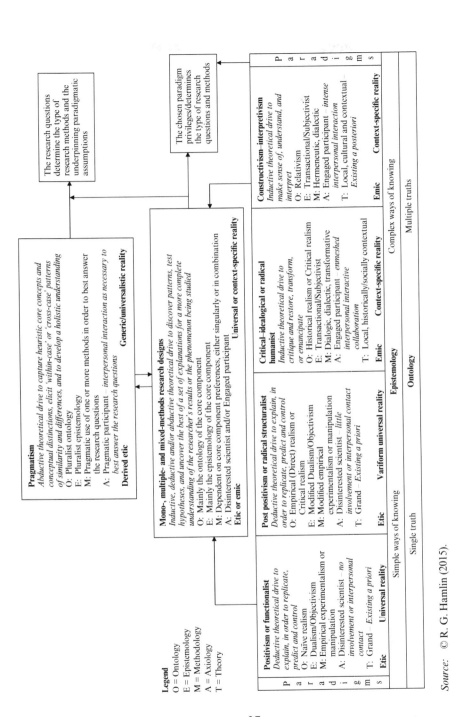

Legend
O = Ontology
E = Epistemology
M = Methodology
A = Axiology
T = Theory

Positivism or functionalist
Deductive theoretical drive to explain, in order to replicate, predict and control
- O: Naïve realism
- E: Dualism/Objectivism
- M: Empirical experimentalism or manipulation
- A: Disinterested scientist – no involvement or interpersonal contact
- T: Grand – *Existing a priori*

Etic   **Universal reality**

Post positivism or radical structuralist
Deductive theoretical drive to explain, in order to replicate, predict and control
- O: Empirical (Direct) realism or Critical realism
- E: Modified Dualism/Objectivism
- M: Modified empirical experimentalism or manipulation
- A: Disinterested scientist – little involvement or interpersonal contact
- T: Grand – *Existing a priori*

Etic or emic   **Variform universal reality**

Mono-, multiple- and mixed-methods research designs
Inductive, deductive and/or abductive theoretical drive to discover patterns, test hypotheses, and uncover the best of a set of explanations for a more complete understanding of the researcher's results or the phenomenon being studied
- O: Mainly the ontology of the core component
- E: Mainly the epistemology of the core component
- M: Dependent on core component preferences, either singularly or in combination
- A: Disinterested scientist and/or Engaged participant

Etic or emic   **Universal or context-specific reality**

Pragmatism
Abductive theoretical drive to capture heuristic core concepts and conceptual distinctions, elicit 'within-case' or 'cross-case' patterns of similarity and differences, and to develop a holistic understanding
- O: Pluralist ontology
- E: Pluralist epistemology
- M: Pragmatic use of one or more methods in order to best answer the research questions
- A: Pragmatic participant – *interpersonal interaction as necessary to best answer the research questions*

Derived etic   **Generic/universalistic reality**

The research questions determine the type of research methods and the underpinning paradigmatic assumptions

The chosen paradigm privileges/determines the type of research questions and methods

Critical-ideological or radical humanist
Inductive theoretical drive to critique and restore, transform, or emancipate
- O: Historical realism or Critical realism
- E: Transactional/Subjectivist
- M: Dialogic, dialectic, transformative
- A: Engaged participant – *enmeshed interpersonal interactive collaboration*
- T: Local, historically/socially contextual

Emic   **Context-specific reality**

Constructivism–interpretivism
Inductive theoretical drive to make sense of, understand, and interpret
- O: Relativism
- E: Transactional/Subjectivist
- M: Hermeneutic, dialectic
- A: Engaged participant – *intense interpersonal interaction*
- T: Local, cultural and contextual – *Existing a posteriori*

Emic   **Context-specific reality**

Simple ways of knowing	Complex ways of knowing
Single truth	Multiple truths
Epistemology	
Ontology	

Source: © R. G. Hamlin (2015).

Figure 2.1   A simplified philosophical framework of research in HRD and other applied fields

27

informed partly by Worrall's (2005) 'four quadrant' ontological–epistemological framework and by Lincoln and Lynham's (2011) recent explication of the 'three major paradigms of inquiry' used in applied fields,
which they define as conventional (positivism and post positivism), critical
(emancipatory) and interpretive. My deduced framework has helped me to
see more clearly and locate more accurately the philosophical assumptions
that have guided my past and on-going research. As already mentioned,
despite the personal paradigmatic twists and turns outlined in this chapter,
it is my strong belief that all HRD researchers should endeavour to take
ownership of their adopted paradigmatic orientation and to explain fully
their choice of methodology/methodologies and method(s) for the following reasons. First, to ensure that readers can see that there is no mismatch
between the research question(s) and the research design, and that the
study is capable of answering the question(s). Second, to ensure sufficient
information is provided so that someone can either (i) replicate the study
and get the same results if they use exactly the same procedure and data
or (ii) conduct multiple replication studies in different organizational
contexts and cultural settings – following as closely as possible the same
design and procedure – with the aim of searching for commonalities and
generalizations across cases which might then lead to theory development.
Third, to ensure that readers clearly know the paradigmatic orientation that informed the research design and also the philosophical prism
through which the research should be perceived, evaluated, and judged.

I suggest the first step would be for HRD researchers to update their
understanding of the latest expert thinking and practice on what is
accepted as 'legitimate' research by all 'researcher communities' within
their own field or fields of study. Whereas Lincoln and Lynham (2011)
have made explicit the relevance and utility of 'positivist', 'post positivist', 'critical (emancipatory)' and 'interpretive (social constructivist)'
paradigms of inquiry in the HRD domain, I would like to believe that
'pragmatism' and 'mixed-methods research' are (or will become) equally
recognized and valued in HRD. Assuming this is (or will become) the case,
I suggest that at the outset of an inquiry researchers should be careful and
rigorous in the way they choose the paradigmatic worldview characteristics and philosophical assumptions that guide their research. For example,
is the nature of the inquiry consciously influenced by the school of thought
which argues (i) that research designs must be privileged/governed by a
pre-selected paradigm; or (ii) that the posited research questions should
determine the researcher's ontological/epistemological assumptions and
methodology (i.e. founded on pragmatism); or (iii) that a more complete
understanding of research results and/or a more holistic explanation of
the phenomenon being studied can be gained by adopting an appropriate

'mixed-methods research' approach. Reference to Figure 2.1 might help clarify their thinking when making philosophical/paradigmatic choices at the research design stage.

When researchers come to reporting their findings I suggest careful thought needs to be given to how best to articulate their adopted paradigmatic/philosophical position. A single sentence should suffice when reporting the adoption of either the dominant 'positivist' or 'constructivist–interpretivist' paradigms. However, as previously discussed, I suggest a fuller explanation and justification is required when reporting the adoption of the other two paradigms; also of pragmatism and/ or of mixed-methods research designs. This would likely prevent readers, particularly journal editors and peer reviewers, from drawing wrong inferences or conclusions regarding the paradigmatic orientation and philosophical assumptions that had guided and underpinned their studies. Doing this should increase the probability of the research being viewed through the same philosophical prism as that used by the researchers and, consequently, it being perceived, evaluated and judged appropriately.

NOTES

1. Bryman and Bell's UK derived perspectives in the field of business research are also covered in the 2011 (3rd) edition of their book, which was first published in 2003.
2. The term 'derived etic' was coined by Berry (1989) in the field of cross-cultural psychology research. Using Pike's (1967) notions of emic research, which studies behaviour as from outside a particular system or culture, and etic research, which studies behaviour as from inside the system or culture, Berry argues that there are benefits for using a combined emic–etic approach to reach valid derived etic generalizations. In derived etic research the same phenomena is explored in more than one specific context/cultural setting, and in the same way. A cross-case comparative analysis of the emic findings is then carried out. If common features begin to emerge the comparison is possible. Without necessarily assuming universality, this combined emic–etic approach provides the possibility of drawing conclusions about derived etics across the compared cases and progressively across more and more specific contexts and cultural settings. This approach contrasts sharply with conventional imposed etic research in which the researcher is usually armed with an emic concept or instrument rooted in their own culture and assumes it is a valid basis for studying a phenomenon in another culture and then to compare the phenomenon in the two cultures.

REFERENCES

Berry, J. W. (1989) 'Imposed etics–emics-derived etics: The operationalization of a compelling idea', *International Journal of Psychology*, Vol. 24, pp. 721–35.
Bryman, A. (1988) *Quantity and Quality in Social Research*. London: Routledge.
Bryman, A. (2006) 'Paradigm peace and the implications for quality', *International Journal of Social Research Methodology*, Vol. 9, No. 2, pp. 111–26.

Bryman, A. and Bell, E. (2003) *Business Research Methods.* Oxford: Oxford University Press.
Buchanan, D. A. and Bryman, A. (2007) 'Contextualizing methods choice in organizational research', *Organizational Research Methods,* Vol. 10, No. 3, pp. 483–501.
Burke Johnson, R. and Onwuegbuzie, A. J. (2004) 'Mixed methods research: A research paradigm whose time has come', *Educational Researcher,* Vol. 33, No. 7, pp. 14–26.
Burrell, G. and Morgan, G. (1979) *Sociological Paradigms and Organisational Analysis.* Aldershot, UK: Gower.
Cresswell, J. W. (2003) *Research Design: Qualitative, Quantitative, and Mixed Methods Approaches* (2nd edn). Thousand Oaks, CA: Sage.
Curry, L., Shield, R. and Wetle, T. (2006) *Improving Aging and Public Health Research: Qualitative and Mixed Methods.* Washington, DC: American Public Health Association and the Gerontological Society of America.
Elliott, R., Fischer, C. T. and Rennie, D. L. (1999) 'Evolving guidelines for publication of qualitative research studies in psychology and related fields', *British Journal of Clinical Psychology,* Vol. 38, pp. 215–29.
Fleetwood, S. (2005) 'Ontology in organization and management studies: A critical realist perspective', *Organization,* Vol. 12, pp. 197–222.
Guba, E. G. (ed.) (1990) *The Paradigm Dialog.* Newbury Park, CA: Sage.
Guba, E. G. and Lincoln, Y. S. (1994) 'Competing paradigms in qualitative research', in N. K. Denzin and Y. S. Lincoln (eds.), *Handbook of Qualitative Research* (pp. 105–17). London: Sage.
Hamlin, R. G. (1988) 'The criteria of managerial effectiveness in secondary schools', Published MPhil thesis in *CORE: Collected and Original Resources in Education, International Journal of Educational Research in Microfiche,* Vol. 12, No. 1, pp. 1–221.
Hamlin, R. G. (2002) 'A study and comparative analysis of managerial and leadership effectiveness in the National Health Service: An empirical factor analytic study within an NHS Trust Hospital', *Health Services Management Research,* Vol. 15, pp. 1–20.
Hamlin, R. G. (2004) 'In support of universalistic models of managerial and leadership effectiveness', *Human Resource Development Quarterly,* Vol. 15, No. 2, pp. 189–215.
Hamlin, R. G. and Hatton, A. (2013) 'Towards a British taxonomy of perceived managerial and leadership effectiveness', *Human Resource Development Quarterly,* Vol. 24, No. 3, pp. 365–406.
Hamlin, R. G., Nassar, M. and Wahba, K. (2010) 'Behavioural criteria of managerial and leadership effectiveness within Egyptian and British public sector hospitals: An empirical study and multiple-case/cross-nation comparative analysis', *Human Resource Development International,* Vol. 13, No. 1, pp. 43–64.
Hamlin, R. G., Reidy, M. and Stewart, J. (1998) 'Bridging the HRD research–practice gap through professional partnership', *Human Resource Development International,* Vol. 1, No. 3, pp. 273–90.
Hamlin, R. G. and Serventi, S. (2008) 'Generic behavioural criteria of managerial effectiveness: An empirical and comparative study of UK local government', *Journal of European Industrial Training,* Vol. 32, No. 4, pp. 285–302.
Hanson, W. E., Creswell, J. W., Plano Clark, V. L., Petska, K. S. and Creswell, J. D. (2005) 'Mixed methods research designs in counseling psychology', *Journal of Counseling Psychology,* Vol. 52, No. 2, pp. 224–35.
Lincoln, Y. S. and Guba, Y. S. (2000) 'Paradigmatic controversies, contradictions, and emerging confluences', in N. K. Denzin and Y. S. Lincoln (eds.), *Handbook of Qualitative Research* (2nd edn, pp. 163–88). Thousand Oaks, CA: Sage.
Lincoln, Y. S. and Lynham, S. A. (2011) 'Criteria for assessing theory in human resource development from an interpretive perspective', *Human Resource Development International,* Vol. 14, No. 1, pp. 3–22.
Maxcy, S. (2002) 'Pragmatic threads in mixed methods research in the social sciences: The search for multiple modes of inquiry and the end of the philosophy of formalism', in A. Tashakkori and C. Teddlie (eds.), *Handbook of Mixed Methods* (pp. 51–89). London: Sage.

Morgan, B. L. (2007) 'Paradigms lost and pragmatism regained: Methodological implications of combining qualitative and quantitative methods', *Journal of Mixed Methods Research*, Vol. 1, pp. 48–76.
Morrow, S. L. (2007) 'Qualitative research in counselling psychology: Conceptual foundations', *The Counselling Psychologist*, Vol. 35, pp. 209–36.
Onwuegbuzie, A. J. and Leech, N. L. (2005) 'On becoming a pragmatic researcher: The importance of combining quantitative and qualitative research methodologies', *International Journal of Social Research Methodology*, Vol. 8, No. 5, pp. 375–87.
Pike, K. L. (1967) *Language in Relation to a Unified Theory of the Structure of Human Behaviour*. The Hague, the Netherlands: Mouton.
Ponterotto, J. G. (2005) 'Qualitative research in counseling psychology: A primer on research paradigms and philosophy of science', *Journal of Counseling Psychology*, Vol. 52, No. 2, pp. 126–36.
Saunders, M., Lewis, P. and Thornhill, A. (2012) *Research Methods for Business Students*. Harlow, UK: Pearson Education.
Swanson, R. A. (2005) 'The process of framing research in organizations', in R. A. Swanson and E. F. Holton III (eds.), *Research in Organizations: Foundations and Methods of Inquiry* (pp. 11–26). San Francisco: Berrett-Koehler.
Walton, J. S. (2008) 'Scanning beyond the horizon: Exploring the ontological and epistemological basis for scenario planning', *Advances in Developing Human Resources*, Vol. 10, No. 2, pp. 147–65.
Worrall, L. (2005) 'Fiat lux: A reflection on management research', *International Journal of Management Concepts and Philosophy*, Vol. 1, No. 3, pp. 248–60.

ANNOTATED FURTHER READING

Saunders, M., Lewis, P. and Thornhill, A. (2012) *Research Methods for Business Students*. Harlow, UK: Pearson Education. This contains excellent chapters (4 and 5) on understanding research philosophies and formulating research designs.
Swanson, R. A. and Holton, E. F. III (2005) *Research in Organizations: Foundations and Methods of Inquiry*. San Francisco: Berrett-Koehler. In Chapter 18, John Cresswell and David Cresswell provide an excellent introduction to mixed-methods research, the types of designs and the critical philosophical and methodological issues in conducting this form of inquiry.

3.   HRD research and design science
Eugene Sadler-Smith

SUMMARY

This chapter explores the debates surrounding management as a design science rather than as an explanatory science. Taking the mission of design science as being to develop actionable knowledge, the positioning of HRD research is considered and the question asked: can HRD research be considered a design science?

INTRODUCTION

Nobel Laureate Herbert A. Simon (1916–2001) in his book *The Sciences of the Artificial* (1969/1996) described management as a 'design science' with a principal role to develop 'valid knowledge to support thoughtful, designing practitioners' and enable 'organizational problem solving in the field' (Huff, Tranfield and van Aken, 2006, p.413). The 'classical' design sciences, such as medicine or engineering, have the mission to develop actionable knowledge that doctors and engineers can use to design solutions for their field problems, as distinct from 'pure' knowledge problems (van Aken, 2007, p.68). On the other hand the mission of explanatory sciences, which includes disciplines such as sociology or psychology (these are in addition to the natural sciences such as physics, chemistry and biology referred to by Simon), is to 'develop knowledge to describe, explain and predict' phenomena in the natural or social world (van Aken, 2005, p.20), see Figure 3.1.

The chapter begins by considering Simon's original conception of design science (Simon, 1969/1996); this is followed by a more detailed discussion of management as a design science and, in particular, the work of van Aken and his colleagues (e.g. van Aken, 2004, 2005, 2007; van Aken and Romme, 2009); the chapter concludes by considering the positioning of Human Resource Development (HRD) research vis-à-vis these debates and asks the question: can HRD research be considered a design science?

Explanatory
Sciences
Describe, explain
and predict phenomena
in natural/social world

Design
Sciences
Develop actionable
knowledge to solve field
problems

Figure 3.1   The missions of explanatory and design sciences

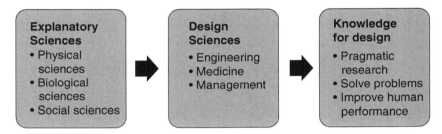

Figure 3.2a   Explanatory sciences and design sciences

DESIGN SCIENCES

The concern of the design sciences is for the *design* of artefacts and interventions which change situations from how they are now to how 'they ought to be in order to attain goals' (Simon, 1996, p.4). In speaking to an HRD audience I use the term 'intervention' (Korth, 1997; Sadler-Smith, 2014) in tandem with 'artefact' but the former is not a term that Simon himself used. However, design sciences do not merely consume or apply theory from the explanatory sciences (Figure 3.2a); they generate extensive and significant knowledge ('knowledge-for-design') of their own through research of a pragmatic nature which helps professionals to take decisions and solve problems in pursuit of improving human performance (van Aken, 2005). Design science offers solutions to field problems, enables a 'better reality' and contributes to improving the human condition (van Aken, 2007, p.68), see Figure 3.2b.

The product of design science is not action per se; rather, it is a particular type of scientific knowledge which may be used for the design of artefacts and interventions and to support their use by professionals (van Aken, 2004). In Simon's original conceptualization, artefacts represent a 'meeting point' or interface between an inner environment (i.e. the substance and

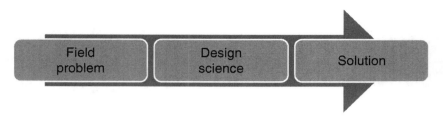

Figure 3.2b   The relationship between field problem and design science

organization of the artefact itself with its underlying natural laws which constrain but do not dictate the fabrication of the artefact) and an outer environment (i.e. the surroundings in which it operates). He offers the example of a ship's clock: if it is immune to buffeting it will serve its purpose well as a ship's chronometer; if it is not, it will not. The properties of the artefact 'lie on the thin interface between the natural laws within it and the natural laws without', and it is at this interface between the inner and outer environment which the artificial world is centred (1996, p.113). For example, an 'artefactual science' of entrepreneurship would study 'new organizations, new markets and new institutions *as artefacts* fabricated by human beings' (Sarasvathy, Dew, Read and Wiltbank, 2008, p.331, emphasis added).

The prescription-driven products of design science are holistic 'technological rules' derived ultimately from description-driven explanatory research. These technological rules (also referred to as design propositions) follow Bunge's (1967) 'logic of prescription': 'if you want to achieve outcome O in context C, then use intervention type I.' The desired outcome is produced in a given context as a result of the operation of particular generative mechanisms (M) and is testable on the basis of pragmatic validity (Denyer, Tranfield and van Aken, 2008). For these reasons this logic of prescription is sometimes referred to as CIMO-logic (i.e. 'what to do', 'where/when to do it', 'to what effect' and 'why it happens'); an example is offered by Denyer et al. (2008): 'If you have a project assignment for a geographically distributed team (class of contexts, C), use a face-to-face kick-off meeting (intervention type, I) to create an effective team (intended outcome, O) through the creation of collective task insight and commitment (generative mechanisms, M)' (p.396).

Organizations are highly complex, and it is unlikely that a single intervention will provide sufficient leverage on a given problem, hence it is more likely that an effective design proposition will consist of several interventions (I) combined together to mobilize contextually grounded 'generative mechanisms' (M), and their effects on outcomes (O) in a given

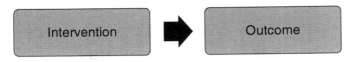

Figure 3.3a   IO-logic

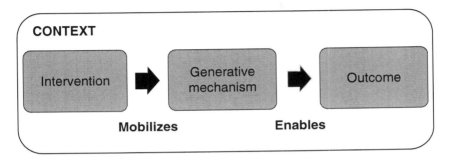

Figure 3.3b   CIMO design science logic

context (C) are 'proven' (or otherwise) by the methods of field testing and evaluation (Denyer et al., 2008), see Figure 3.3a and Figure 3.3b.

The method and products of design science research can be distinguished from the managerial anecdotes often found in the popular management literature which tend to rely more on an IO- than a CIMO-logic (see Figure 3.3a and Figure 3.3b and below) and are likely to be limited in their transferability to different contexts (Denyer et al., 2008; Hodgkinson and Healey, 2008; van Aken, 2004). An example of the requisite complexity is offered by Hodgkinson and Healey (2008), who drew on the principles of social identity theory, self/social categorization theory and the Five-Factor Model of human personality from the disciplines of personality and social psychology to offer propositions for the design of scenario planning interventions:

> To ensure effective coping with change and willingness to explore new avenues of inquiry, and to facilitate novel thinking, the exchange of diverse perspectives and ideas, meaningful consideration of challenging scenarios and the generation of high-quality strategic responses to scenarios, wherever possible select participants high in [the personality trait of] Openness to Experience. (p.445)

Hodgkinson and Healey (2008) also drew attention to the fact that it is entirely feasible, and indeed desirable, within the management and organization field to develop design propositions/technological rules that draw upon the existing and well-validated corpus of theory rather than embarking upon an ambitious and potentially exhausting, time-consuming and resource-hungry programme of basic empirical research to solve the field problem from scratch. Such propositions should be amenable to falsification and result in a design science which is high in both scientific rigour and practical relevance (Anderson, Herriot and Hodgkinson, 2001; Hodgkinson and Healey, 2008).

Effective problem solving using technological rules/design propositions is not only a mechanistic affair; it is also an 'art' or 'craft' and involves the skilled use of professional knowledge and expertise grounded in an intimate knowledge of what is likely to work in a given context (Denyer et al., 2008; Schön, 1983). As noted above, Denyer et al. (2008) contrast the CIMO-logic with a simpler IO-logic (i.e. 'If you want A then do B') in order to underline the point that in organizations it is rarely the case that propositions can be reduced to a simple and arguably impoverished IO algorithm, see Figure 3.3a. Moreover, the variables in real-world organizational systems may often be drowned in 'noise' such that researchers are forced to investigate short causal chains rather than ultimate variables such as overall organizational performance (van Aken, 2004).

IS MANAGEMENT A DESIGN SCIENCE?

Van Aken makes a number of salient points regarding design science in general: firstly, that most people who study design sciences are not trained as researchers, rather they are trained as professionals (e.g. as engineers or doctors in engineering and medical schools rather than as physical or medical scientists); secondly, the schools in which design sciences are located, such as medical schools and engineering schools, are professional schools. Many people see business schools as professional schools; however, there is a potential tension between management and organization research as practised in business schools and the concept of design science as articulated by Simon (1996) and van Aken (2004). Researchers in business schools tend not to be trained as practitioners (although some are, whilst others may have a professional background or ongoing connections with practice through activities such as consulting). The research that is carried out in business schools has become 'by and large [to be] based on the paradigm of the explanatory sciences rather than on the paradigm of the design sciences' (van Aken in Huff et al., 2006, p.414). Van Aken remarks that business and management appears to have strayed away from its origins as a design science (Simon, 1969/1996; Thompson, 1956) and towards attempting to define itself as a 'pure' (explanatory) social science. Moreover, this distinction and trend is important since it drives the type of research questions asked and the knowledge products which the research yields (e.g. descriptive knowledge versus prescriptive knowledge) (Huff et al., 2006).

In evaluating the status of management as a design science, van Aken (2005, p.33) commented that: (1) many in the management and organization studies research community in business schools see their missions as being to conduct explanatory research but overlook the potential of the design sciences to 'produce respectable academic research products'; (2) the 'highway to academic reputation', respectability and reward in business schools is seen to be via the explanatory route; and (3) as noted earlier, it is not automatically the case that management and organization researchers were trained as professionals prior to becoming academics. Van Aken (2005) concludes that management is not yet a design science because it is a young field, but that it can become one and to do so is desirable, valuable and potentially rewarding.

Whether or not management is or should be considered a design science continues to be debated (Pandza and Thorpe, 2010). As noted by van Aken and Romme (2009), in any given discipline (or field) it is perfectly possible for design science research to be a minor research stream, whereas 'if it is mainstream research, as in medicine and engineering, that discipline [or field] can be called a design science' (p.7). Van Aken (2004) also noted that the situation in fields such as Human Resource Management (HRM) (and arguably HRD as well) is different from that in the mainstream of management and organization studies. Professional associations, with their various conferences and publications (such as the Chartered Institute of Personnel and Development (CIPD) in the UK with its annual HRD Conference and widely circulated publication *People Management*), bring together practitioners and academic researchers. Moreover, in the field of HRD, the latter tend to have mixed academic/professional backgrounds and therefore are more likely to have an interest in the utility of the community's research products than are researchers who have followed a purely academic route (van Aken, 2007).

Having outlined some general principles regarding design science in general, and the design science of management in particular, attention will now be focused on defining and conceptualizing HRD research in relation to design science.

DEFINING AND CONCEPTUALIZING HRD

HRD, like management, is a young field and is seeking to establish an identity. Tranfield argues that such emergent fields need to attend to issues of identity by establishing their boundaries and providing a credible answer to the question 'what is the nature of the beast?' (Huff et al., 2006, p.415). Likewise, HRD research, with its acknowledged overlaps and commonalities with other sub-fields of management such as HRM, needs to attend to issues of its identity and boundaries. HRD has been defined in various ways, though some have refused to define it on theoretical, professional and practical grounds (Lee, 2004). Davis and Mink (1992) defined HRD as a 'wide range of interacting, integrating processes aimed at developing greater purpose and meaning, higher levels of performance and achievement and greater capacity for responding to an ever-changing environment leading to more effective individuals, teams and organizations' (p.201). The definition of HRD offered by McLean and McLean (2001) is apposite for present purposes: 'Any process or activity that, either initially or over the long term, has the potential to develop adults' work based knowledge, expertise productivity and satisfaction, whether for personal or group/team gain or for the benefit of an organization, community, nation or *ultimately the whole of humanity*' (p.314, emphasis added).

HRD is differentiated from related fields such as HRM (also concerned with performance improvement) in that the interacting and integrating processes and activities relate specifically to leveraging learning and development. Moreover, inherent in Davis and Mink's definition is *prescription*, that is processes (often in the form of learning-related 'interventions', see Korth, 1997; Sadler-Smith, 2014) which enable individuals, teams and organizations to respond to problems through learning and development and achieve desired outcomes.

Given the fact that HRD still is a young field, it is unsurprising that scholars have debated its nature, identity and scope. For example, Swanson (2001) contended that HRD is an emerging discipline based on a 'logical set of foundational theories' from economic theory, system theory and psychological theory and that these make up the 'foundational theory of HRD' (p.307). An alternative view is that these various theories, which do not present an exhaustive list, are better seen as 'base disciplines' or 'source disciplines' of HRD which are themselves explanatory sciences, for example psychology, sociology, economics and philosophy (Sadler-Smith, 2006, p.99). Swanson (2001) further argued that HRD, at the time of writing, was 'full of atheoretical models (not theories) and espoused theories that are unsubstantiated', and the challenge as Swanson saw it was to develop more HRD theories rather than continuing to 'wallow in atheoretical explanations' (Swanson, 2001, p.309). It is undeniable that the practice of HRD, often for the best of motives, sometimes seeks 'quick fixes to organizational problems' but as a result may expose itself to the vagaries of atheoretical fads and panaceas. In so far as the status of HRD as a discipline in its own right is concerned, Kuchinke (2001) drew a hierarchical distinction between the basic sciences, disciplines and fields and argued that HRD is decidedly not a discipline, describing it instead as an 'emerging professional field' (p.291).

Short, Bing and Kehrhahn (2003), whilst celebrating the vitality of the field, also raised a number of important concerns and questions about HRD, namely its inner-directedness, its preaching to the converted, the encroachment of other professionals into HRD's territory, the lack of meaningful evaluation of the impact of HRD interventions, the gaps between HRD research and real-time organizational problems, and it being prone to faddishness and 'false short-term training panaceas' (Short et al., 2003, p.239). Short and colleagues identified five challenges that HRD research must overcome in coming years to ensure its success. One of these was that HRD research should focus on providing solutions to 'real' problems. HRD researchers should not only concern themselves with those things that matter to HRD researchers themselves but also to those that matter to stakeholders in organizations; that is, to go beyond a 'silo mentality' and embrace the perspective that 'organizational problems are systemic and [therefore] require systemic solutions' (Short et al., 2003, p.242). This means that HRD researchers and practitioners must work in 'problem-focused, solution-driven, multidiscipline teams within organizations' (Short, et al., 2003, p.242). This view resonates strongly with a design science perspective.

As far as HRD research developing its own theories is concerned, Torraco (2004) was optimistic about the progress that had been made and for the field's prospects. He argued that there is an increasing number of theoretical and conceptual articles in HRD being published in that 'new and enhanced theories, concepts, theory-building research methods, conceptual articles, research on the foundations and philosophy of HRD, and integrative literature reviews for theoretical purposes' all appear regularly in the literature (Torraco, 2004, p.171). He cited theoretical work in areas such as theories of learning, models of managerial work, philosophies and foundations of HRD, major constructs, theory-building methodologies and new conceptual models. This stream of work is productive to the extent that there is now a forum, *Human Resource Development Review*, devoted to conceptual and theoretical work as well as integrative literature reviews.

In this chapter I do not propose to review or appraise the question of whether HRD is a discipline, its relationship to HRM, or if it has developed a substantive theoretical base of its own or 'needs more theory'. Instead I will examine the potential of a design science perspective as an under-explored avenue for making sense of HRD's current status and its potential contribution to solving field problems through learning and development interventions.

IS HRD RESEARCH A DESIGN SCIENCE?

HRD requires an understanding of phenomena that occur at the intersection of people, organizations and learning. The theories which are thus developed should not only enable description, explanation and prediction, they should also enable researchers and practitioners to design learning and development interventions and systems that 'improve organizational performance' (see March and Storey, 2008, p.725). This entails the design and development of actionable knowledge that practitioners in organizations can use in order to solve their pressing field problems, thereby 'changing existing situations into preferred ones' (Simon, 1996, p.111). Given the field's strong tradition of an applied focus, HRD researchers and practitioners have always sought through their interventions (e.g. models, methods, technologies and processes) to change existing situations into preferred ones. Artificial or 'designed' solutions are produced 'by art rather than by nature' (Simon, 1996, p.4) and accomplished by blending processes which on the one hand are natural, creative and intuitive (cf. Schön's (1983) notion of 'professional knowledge') but on the other must be knowledge intensive, drawing on 'valid procedural knowledge concerning how to design solutions for field problems in a professional way, and with valid substantive knowledge on alternative solutions for various types of field problems' (van Aken, 2007, p.69).

As noted above, design sciences are more concerned with generating their own particular type of knowledge rather than with action per se. Can HRD research generate its own knowledge-for-design and thereby enhance organizational and individual learning processes and outcomes and by doing so bring about beneficial changes within and beyond organizational boundaries (see Hamlin, 2007a, 2007b)? HRD research (as distinct from HRM research or HRD practice) is concerned with the development of actionable knowledge that members of the HRD, HR and management professions can use can use in order to design, develop and implement learning and development interventions which offer solutions to field problems (Sadler-Smith, 2014). Following a design science philosophy is likely to entail HRD research following the CIMO-logic of prescription in producing technological rules/design propositions of the form: 'if you want to achieve outcome O in context C, then use intervention type I.' For example, emerging evidence from neuroscience on social encoding which relies on the 'mentalizing network' (i.e. a set of brain regions that support thinking about the thoughts, feelings and goals of others) suggests that learning new material for the sake of teaching it to others rather than for being tested is likely to 'trump intentional memorization' in terms of memory performance (Lieberman, 2012, p.7). Hence a general design proposition applicable to a variety of specific field problems (e.g. newcomers' learning about an organization's mission) is: To ensure effective encoding of new information, new material should be learned for the purposes of teaching it to others rather than for the sake of being tested on it.

In using and evaluating such a proposition as the basis for interventions to solve the field problem of 'enhancing the effectiveness of learning' across a variety of settings (thereby enhancing its generalizing remit), HRD research would be drawing upon an extensive body of theory and research in social psychology and neuroscience (e.g. Mitchell, Macrae and Banaji, 2004). This problem-focused approach is to be preferred over embarking upon an ambitious and potentially redundant programme of basic empirical research outside of its zone of competence.

If more theoretical work is needed in HRD (Torraco, 2004), the question of what kind of theoretical research is needed comes to the fore, as do debates about the extent to which the purpose of HRD research interfaces with the motivations of individual researchers. The focus of attention is switched away from understanding fundamental mechanisms and microprocesses towards operationalizing the value that fundamental research can add to HRD practice. The situation in HRD possesses similarities with that of organization development as identified by van Aken (2007, p.72), in that it is significantly influenced by behavioural science giving it a 'tilt toward explanatory research' whilst simultaneously leaning towards design science research through an 'engagement with field problems, its interests in applying behavioural science to solve these problems, and a far greater interaction between researchers and practitioners than found in most other subfields of management' (van Aken, 2007, p.72). HRD research that has a design science orientation should involve stakeholders as co-designers rather than as 'passive recipients' or 'troublesome puppets' (ibid.). It should also practise foresight aimed at developing an intended solution, rather than piggybacking solutions with hindsight on explanatory research (as is often witnessed in the obligatory 'practical or managerial implications' section of traditional management papers), see van Aken (2007, p.81). Van Aken recommends the use of multiple case studies as an effective strategy for research design which aims to produce and test technological rules/design propositions. This would involve working with practitioners whereby 'each individual case is primarily oriented at solving the local problem in close collaboration with the local people'

(Van Aken, 2004, p.232). Such an approach may address the issue identified by Saunders (2011, p.246) for 'research at the interface' which aims to
satisfy the academic and practitioner foci of interest. Within the HRD-as-
design-science perspective the focus of the researcher's attention is a field
problem which by definition meets practitioners' needs and interests.

DISCUSSION

A general implication of this chapter is that HRD may not be positioned
as an academic discipline (Kuchinke, 2001), or as subordinate or super-
ordinate to HRM (see Stead and Lee, 1996). Instead, on the basis of
HRD defined as 'planned activities and processes *designed* to enhance
organizational and individual learning, develop human potential, maxi-
mize organizational effectiveness and performance, and help bring about
effective and beneficial change within and even beyond the boundaries
of the organization' (Hamlin, 2007a, p.43, emphasis added), the question
is posed: 'can HRD research be better positioned as a solution-oriented
"design science" rather than making unwarranted claims to be a discipline in its own right or by seeking merely to define itself in relation to
HRM?'

To the extent that the field of management and organization studies
(including HRD research) should be problem-led (Hodgkinson, 2013),
there is a multiplicity of ways in which HRD research might respond
to learning-related problems faced by organizations. By drawing upon
insights from its explanatory science source disciplines, HRD research
might contribute usefully to the 'general problem of *design*' for management and organization studies (Hodgkinson, 2013, p.149, emphasis
added), that is, creating systems of management that are better fit for
purpose than those which we currently have (Tranfield and Starkey,
1998). The danger is that failure to address these issues might result
in HRD research being sidelined, populated by a 'gradually shrinking
number of people who write for themselves' and 'reacting ineffectively to
demands long after they have been formulated' (Short et al., 2003, p.242).
Hodgkinson and Healey's (2008) exhortations for bringing a design
science perspective to bear on strategic management problems apply also
to HRD research: the principles of design science may help to elevate
HRD research to a high rigour/high relevance pragmatic science which
develops valid knowledge of its own to support intellectually curious artful
practitioners and assist them in solving their pressing organizational field
problems, thereby changing situations from how they are to how they
ought to be (see Sadler-Smith, 2014).

REFERENCES

Anderson, N., Herriot, P. and Hodgkinson, G.P. (2001), 'The practitioner–researcher divide in Industrial, Work and Organizational (IWO) psychology: Where are we now, and where do we go from here? *Journal of Occupational and Organizational Psychology*, Vol.74, No.4, pp.391–411.

Bunge, M. (1967), *Scientific Research II: The Search for Truth*. Berlin: Springer Verlag.

Davis, L.N. and Mink, O.G. (1992), 'Human resource development: An emerging profession – an emerging purpose', *Studies in Continuing Education*, Vol.14, No.2, pp.187–202.

Denyer, D., Tranfield, D. and van Aken, J.E. (2008), 'Developing design propositions through research synthesis', *Organization Studies*, Vol.29, No.3, pp.393–413.

Hamlin, R.G. (2007a), 'An evidence-based perspective on HRD', *Advances in Developing Human Resources*, Vol.9, No.1, pp.42–57.

Hamlin, R.G. (2007b), 'Generating HRD related general knowledge from mode 2 design science research: A cumulative study of manager and managerial leader effectiveness', *Online Submission*.

Hodgkinson, G.P. (2013), 'Organizational identity and organizational identification: A critical realist design science perspective', *Group and Organization Management*, Vol.38, No.1, pp.145–157.

Hodgkinson, G.P. and Healey, M.P. (2008), 'Toward a (pragmatic) science of strategic intervention: Design propositions for scenario planning', *Organization Studies*, Vol.29, No.3, pp.435–457.

Huff, A., Tranfield, D. and van Aken, J.E. (2006), 'Management as a design science mindful of art and surprise: A conversation between Anne Huff, David Tranfield, and Joan Ernst van Aken', *Journal of Management Inquiry*, Vol.15, No.4, pp.413–424.

Korth, S.J. (1997), 'Planning HRD interventions; what, why, and how', *Performance Improvement Quarterly*, Vol.10, No.4, pp.51–71.

Kuchinke, K.P. (2001), 'Why HRD is not an academic discipline', *Human Resource Development International*, Vol.4, No.3, pp.291–294.

Lee, M. (2004), 'A refusal to define HRD'. In J. Woodall, M. Lee and J. Stewart (eds.) *New Frontiers in Human Resource Development*. London: Routledge, pp.27–39.

Lieberman, M.D. (2012), 'Education and the social brain', *Trends in Neuroscience and Education*, Vol.1, pp.3–9.

March, S.T. and Storey, V.C. (2008), 'Design science in the information systems discipline: An introduction to the special issue on design science research', *MIS Quarterly*, Vol.32, No.4, pp.725–730.

McLean, G.N. and McLean, L. (2001), 'If we can't define HRD in one country, how can we define it in an international context?' *Human Resource Development International*, Vol.4, No.3, pp.313–326.

Mitchell, J.P., Macrae, C.N. and Banaji, M.R. (2004), 'Encoding-specific effects of social cognition on the neural correlates of subsequent memory', *Journal of Neuroscience*, Vol.24, No.21, pp.4912–4917.

Pandza, K. and Thorpe, R. (2010), 'Management as design, but what kind of design? An appraisal of the design science analogy for management', *British Journal of Management*, Vol.21, No.1, pp.171–186.

Sadler-Smith, E. (2006), *Learning and Development for Managers: Perspectives from Research and Practice*. Oxford: Blackwell.

Sadler-Smith, E. (2014), 'HRD research and design science: Recasting interventions as artefacts', *Human Resource Development International*, Vol.17, No.1, pp.1–16.

Sarasvathy, S.D., Dew, N., Read, S. and Wiltbank, R. (2008), 'Designing organizations that design environments: Lessons from entrepreneurial expertise', *Organization Studies*, Vol.29, No.3, pp.331–350.

Saunders, M.K. (2011), 'The management researcher as practitioner: Issues from the interface'. In C. Cassell and B. Lee (eds.) *Challenges and Controversies in Management Research*. Abingdon, UK: Routledge, pp.243–257.

Schön, D. (1983), *The Reflective Practitioner*. New York: Basic Books.
Short, D.C., Bing, J.W. and Kehrhahn, M.T. (2003), 'Editorial: Will human resource development survive?' *Human Resource Development Quarterly*, Vol.14, No.3, pp.239–243.
Simon, H.A. (1969/1996), *The Sciences of the Artificial*. Cambridge, MA: MIT Press.
Stead, V. and Lee, M. (1996), 'Intercultural perspectives on HRD'. In J. Stewart and J. McGoldrick (eds.) *Human Resource Development: Perspectives, Strategies and Practice*. London: Pitman, pp.47–70.
Swanson, R.A. (2001), 'Human resource development and its underlying theory', *Human Resource Development International*, Vol.4, No.3, pp.299–312.
Thompson, J.D. (1956), 'On building an administrative science', *Administrative Science Quarterly*, Vol.1, pp.102–111.
Torraco, R.J. (2004), 'Challenges and choices for theoretical research in human resource development', *Human Resource Development Quarterly*, Vol.15, No.2, pp.171–188.
Tranfield, D. and Starkey, K. (1998), 'The nature, social organization and promotion of management research: Towards policy', *British Journal of Management*, Vol.9, No.4, pp.341–353.
van Aken, J.E.V. (2004), 'Management research based on the paradigm of the design sciences: The quest for field-tested and grounded technological rules', *Journal of Management Studies*, Vol.41, No.2, pp.219–246.
van Aken, J.E. (2005), 'Management research as a design science: Articulating the research products of mode 2 knowledge production in management', *British Journal of Management*, Vol.16, No.1, pp.19–36.
van Aken, J.E. (2007), 'Design science and organization development interventions aligning business and humanistic values', *Journal of Applied Behavioral Science*, Vol.43, No.1, pp.67–88.
van Aken, J.E. and Romme, G. (2009), 'Reinventing the future: Adding design science to the repertoire of organization and management studies', *Organization Management Journal*, Vol.6, No.1, pp.5–12.

ANNOTATED FURTHER READING

The classic text on design science is Simon's 1969/1996 book *The Sciences of the Artificial*. Simon's book is an essential work for scholars of design science. The following articles build on Simon's foundational contribution and offer a more in-depth treatment of the topic in relation to management and organization research and HRD research respectively:

Denyer, D., Tranfield, D. and van Aken, J.E. (2008), 'Developing design propositions through research synthesis', *Organization Studies*, Vol.29, No.3, pp.393–413.
Sadler-Smith, E. (2014), 'HRD research and design science: Recasting interventions as artefacts', *Human Resource Development International*, Vol.17, No.1, pp.1–16.

4. Scholarly practice in HRD research

Jeff Gold, Tim Spackman, Diane Marks,
Nick Beech, Julia Calver, Adrian Ogun and
Helen Whitrod-Brown

SUMMARY

For the usability of research in HRD to progress, more attention needs to be given to scholarly practice. Roles, strategies and behaviours for HRD scholar-practitioners are explored and critiqued, before the key features of research as a 'phronetic social science' are presented. HRD scholar-practitioners' voices are considered and discussed.

INTRODUCTION

For several years there has been growing concern about the disconnection between Human Resource Development (HRD) scholarship, exemplified by research and theory development in academe, and those who practise HRD, exemplified by professionals within organisations and consultants (Short et al. 2009). This disconnection is related to broader concerns in management and the social sciences where rigour is prioritised at the expense of relevance in scholarship so that research outputs can meet the requirements of largely US-based journals. Perhaps as a consequence, doubts are expressed about the value of a business school education based on accepted but 'amoral' theories, which have the potential to promote 'bad' practices (Ghoshal 2005).

There have been various efforts to redress this problem by adopting approaches that frame research in relation to the context of application so that it becomes relevant to practice, often referred to as Mode 2 research (Gibbons et al. 1994), but progress still needs to be made (Hodgkinson and Starkey 2011). If anything, management research in academe has seen a reduction in the actionability of its outputs in recent years (Pearce and Huang 2012). By contrast, Van de Ven's (2007) engaged scholarship and the working of the design science analogy in a management context (Panza and Thorpe 2010) do go some way towards jumping the 'double hurdle' of rigour and relevance, but in both cases the power to research and theorise remains with the academic rather than the practitioner. Aram and Salipante (2003) argue for a 'bridging scholarship' which seeks to 'meld rigour and relevance' (p. 201). This has to begin and continue with the problems of those facing challenges in practice, and in recent years there has been some attempt in HRD to build bridges between academe and practitioners (Stewart and Gold 2011). In this chapter, we consider those who seek to tackle complex HRD issues at work in a more scholarly fashion through *scholarly practice*. We will proceed as follows. Firstly, we will briefly consider some of the key ideas and debates relating to the status of the HRD profession. Secondly, we will explore some key ideas relating to scholarly practice before hearing from those involved in such work. They will indicate how they do this and describe the impact on their lives. Lastly, we will provide some learning points for further development of scholarly practice in HRD.

HRD AS A PROFESSION AND SCHOLARLY PRACTICE

As a profession and field of practice, HRD has a contentious status and identity, and a controversial territory that requires a frequent re-positioning by practitioners in order for them to be proactive in their approach to change (Mankin 2001). Like all other professions, claims of expert knowledge need to persuade others – clients and customers who face uncertainty and difficulty – to be seen as legitimate (Gold et al. 2003). Further, to underpin such claims there needs to be an identifiable body of knowledge which can be applied to satisfy others, thus reinforcing the recognition of expertise. The existence of such a body of knowledge is cited as a key feature of any profession, underpinning its skills and claims for a special status (Friedson 2001). Such knowledge is usually considered as theoretical or abstract knowledge which is available publicly and provides the propositions that can be generally considered for practice (Eraut 2000). For Abbott (1988), this knowledge is foundational and allows a profession to differentiate itself from others. New entrants to a profession are required to prove their understanding of such knowledge and how it can be applied in various situations they will face as professionals.

In HRD there have been quests to build a degree of unity in theory development, in order to secure underpinning principles for practice so that actions can be justified (Swanson 1999; McLean 1998). Further, in recent years, as we have already suggested, there has been a significant increase in the outputs of HRD academic journals which add to the development of the body of knowledge. Of course, the vagaries and shenanigans that accompany academic journal status and positions may well have distorted the development of theories and ideas, thereby adding to the gap between academe and practice. Even when theories find their way into professional programmes, such as Chartered Institute of Personnel and Development's (CIPD's) professional development scheme, there is no certainty that they will be utilised or valued once the world of practice is entered. Evidence suggests that, generally, Human Resource Management (HRM) practitioners suffer overload and ambiguity at work and are more likely to be required to serve the interests of line managers (Harrison 2011). Thus, like all professionals, HRD practitioners have to adapt to the contingencies and vicissitudes of life within their domain of practice. In this way, however well HRD practitioners command expertise based on foundational knowledge, they have to also to localise such expertise by developing a personal knowledge (Eraut 2000) which is 'grounded' in the various situations of professional work (Cheetham and Chivers 2000, p. 381). However, while it may enable an HRD professional to satisfy clients, such knowledge can also become more privileged in practice but also carry negative consequence for the position of HRD against other groups, such as line managers, finance managers and so on. It is easy to see why HRD might become a 'weakened profession' (Short et al. 2009, p. 421) through a requirement to play a subservient role with respect to other groups and because it may rely on knowledge which lacks robustness and proof of value-added in tackling key issues arising from its activities. Typical of such weakness might be an adherence to traditional and idealistic notions or models, such as the four stage systematic training model which has the advantage of simplicity and therefore becomes a normative sequence for planning and action (Buckley and Caple 2007). Similar staged models with the normative connotation of systematic can be found in evaluation, change management and learning models, even if the stages are re-presented as cycles. Crucially, the simplicity of such models falls foul of an acceptance of linearity that hides and camouflages the impact and presence of contextual inhibitors embedded in organisation cultures and histories (Chiaburu and Tekleab 2005). However, there remains an attraction in keeping the models simple even if this feeds the gullibility of HRD practitioners in the face of the plethora of 'new' products, services and fads available from an HRD provider industry (Short et al. 2003). Evidence for the tendency to prefer simplicity comes from recent surveys of HRD practitioners by CIPD (2012). For example, it was found that many practitioners adhered to familiar models of learning styles and team roles but were not aware of more complex ideas from research in areas such as neuroscience, social psychology, economics, computing and the natural sciences. The same survey suggested that recession had reduced HRD budgets, with particular concern in the public sector for the future of HRD.

TOWARDS SCHOLARLY PRACTICE IN HRD

Acknowledgement of the gap between academe and practice has been evidenced by a range of activities which have been designed to accommodate the interests of both parties. The Academy of HRD (AHRD), for example, includes keynote addresses from practitioners at its annual conference as well as pre-conference workshops that combine research and practice and a scholar-practitioner track (Short 2006a). Scholarly practice is also the focus of one of its 'Awards for Excellence', given for 'excellence in applying scholarly HRD theory and research to practice in a manner that brings measurable improvement to an organization and/or has the potential to advance the field of HRD' (see http://www.ahrd.org/displayemailforms.cfm?emailformnbr=183638).

In Europe, too, there is growing interest in bringing academe and practitioners together through the creation of a scholarly practice stream at the annual conference. However, on both sides of the Atlantic, it is recognised that such efforts remain limited, with many thousands of practitioners not yet tempted to engage. Nevertheless, it is argued that for HRD to make progress, and given that such progress has to be measured by the usability of research in the workplace, there needs to be more attention given to scholarly practice and the creation of a special kind of knowledge and expertise based on a connection or nexus between evidence, enquiry and evidence from intervention, underpinned by critical thinking (Keefer and Yap 2007).

The term scholarly, derived from the Latin *scolaris*, according to dictionary definitions immediately suggests learning and a deep knowledge of a subject. As an adjective, it qualifies the behaviour and approach of someone who engages in the practice of a particular area. Like many such terms which are combined, there is a degree of tension between apparently contradictory behaviours. However, such contradictions can also become a source of creativity, from which practical knowledge is produced, and, as a consequence, the actionability of such knowledge has the potential to advance understanding of HRD. Since scholar-practitioners must accept that their knowledge is insufficient, it becomes crucially important to provide approaches to research that are oriented towards knowledge which is actionable rather than made as a form of representation or truth that might be actionable; this requires some degree of involvement or collaboration with those taking action so that contextuality and use take precedence. However, the precedence given to contextuality, as a route to making research relevant, should not be an excuse for a lack of rigour. The hallmark of scholarly practice is how enquiry can become an exercise of *both* relevance *and* rigour. This presents the scholarly practitioner with something of a dilemma, necessarily inherent in the combination of terms as we have suggested above. A polarisation of the notion of being scholarly emphasises the rigour to produce research for general knowledge without the need for a practical purpose. By contrast, a polarisation of the notion of practice, where research only focuses on application, can tend towards ill-considered quick fixes with short-term benefits.

One way of avoiding the competing and conflicting tendencies is to seek reconciliation to a combined position which can bring such worlds together. Scholar-practitioners become the bridge between each world because they are intentionally and uniquely placed to cross the boundary from one to another, providing interpretations and translations of both research and practice (Moats and McLean 2009; Wasserman and Kram 2009). Simultaneously, as the process unfolds, they can improve their skills and ability to make conscious use of knowledge in practice.

Short (2006b) argues that HRD scholar-practitioners complete five roles. They:

1. Operate as a bridge between research and practice to improve understanding and the practice of HRD
2. Become champions for research and the use of theory at work and in professional associations
3. Use research and theory in their own practice
4. Complete and disseminate the findings from their research and practice
5. Work in partnership with academics and practitioners.

An interesting feature of these roles is how the metaphor of bridge moves from a physical image to an embodied image where scholar-practitioners become the bridge by enacting a particular way of working. Moats and McLean (2009) focus more on the way of working by positioning the scholar-practitioner as an interpreter, 'to help scholars and practitioners understand each other' (p. 515), and they provide four strategies to start the necessary relationships. These are:

1. Establish and broker meaningful relationships between scholars and practitioners
2. Broker opportunities for collaborative research
3. Broker opportunities for collaborative practice
4. Improve the dissemination of knowledge.

BOX 4.1   SCHOLAR PRACTITIONER COMPETENCIES

1. Dealing with ambiguity
2. Ethics and values
3. Integrity and trust
4. Problem solving
5. Business acumen
6. Written communication
7. Intellectual horsepower
8. Organizational agility
9. Listening
10. Creativity
11. Strategic agility
12. Interpersonal savvy
13. Political savvy
14. Decision quality
15. Presentation skills
16. Functional/technical skills

Source: Kormanik et al. (2009, p.496).

In undertaking such strategies, scholar-practitioners need to employ a range of skills and behaviours. Kormanik et al. (2009) therefore seek to elucidate HRD scholar-practitioner behaviours by developing a competency model. Based on findings from a sample of self-identified HRD scholars, scholar-practitioners and practitioners, the framework developed was composed of 16 competence headings, shown in Box 4.1.

Roles, strategies and behaviours as competences do articulate a degree of clarity for the work of scholarly practice, although there can also be a tendency for such frameworks and lists to become normative, providing the knowledge for how scholarly practice should proceed and obscuring the reality of practice with a representation of practice (see Bolden and Gosling 2006). Perhaps this is the inevitable result of the research interest in scholarly practice that has occurred in recent years. As well as carrying the possibility of normative force, these expressions can also represent scholarly practice in rather static terms rather than as processes of dynamic encounters and events. Therefore, in addition to the image of the bridge, or the broker between worlds, we would like to bring into consideration a more processual view of scholarly practice. Undoubtedly, the scholarly practitioner needs to move and indeed give preference to different aspects of scholarly and practical knowledge. Crucially, as the work proceeds, we argue that there is an ongoing tension that feeds a creative process of being both a scholar and a practitioner, and this can be grasped to reveal new possibilities. We see this as important, since like many other domains within the social sciences, HRD has to give attention to the randomness and volatility of human responses and the failure of prescriptive notions. It is no accident that the most prominent heading in Box 4.1 is 'dealing with ambiguity'. We would extend this to include equivocality too, that is, situations when several or many meanings can be present (see Weick 1979). To understand this further, we can employ Aristotle's term *phronesis* and its relationship to his other terms of *episteme* and *techne*.

Flyvbjerg (2001) has presented an argument for making the social sciences more relevant in the world by moving in the direction of what he calls a 'phronetic social science' (p. 62). Working with Aristotle's term *phronesis*, which can be understood as practical wisdom in the face of competing or a plurality of values, it is argued that in such situations a person with *phronesis* knows how to behave and act, based on grasping the values and a judgement of what is good or bad, where experience can play a part too. Such judgement is not the same as producing something or applying knowledge (*techne* – or *know-how*), but it might lead to such action; nor is it the same as the use of universal ideas and theory (*episteme* – or *know-what*), but it might draw from these. The crucial difference is the response to particular circumstances and the situation, where phronesis provides the point of intersection between know-what and know-how. In addition, as part of the formation of judgement, a person's past experience is bound to have an influence. Another term from Aristotle, *nous*, becomes relevant (Eikeland 2007), whereby according to the particulars of a situation, a judgement can be justified based on an 'infallable intuitive faculty' for the principles which are appropriate to the sense of the situation (Aydede 1998). Justifications based on *nous* can only occur phenomenologically on the basis of a pre-understanding, a tradition and a history.

METHOD

In order to explore the work of scholar-practitioners against our consideration of 'phronetic social science', we contacted six participants in doctorate and master's programmes at Leeds Beckett University. The programmes were:

1. MA in Executive and Business Coaching (MAEBC)
2. Doctorate in Business Administration (DBA)

Such programmes are characterised by the possible use of action modes of enquiry (Raelin 2009), if seen as appropriate. In all cases, however, the purpose is to make a contribution to practitioner knowledge as well as meet the standards of a rigorous academic qualification. The participants selected are all involved in HRD in some form or other, either as practitioners or academics with a practice interest. Each person was asked to supply a short response to aspects of their work, explaining how scholarly becomes part of their practice. Based on the responses, we will consider how phronetic research is articulated.

SCHOLAR-PRACTITIONER VOICES

BOX 4.2   TIM – ORGANISATION DEVELOPMENT MANAGER, SKIPTON BUILDING SOCIETY

Completing a DBA on Workplace Coaching and Employee Engagement

Working on a DBA in the areas of workplace coaching and employee engagement has enabled me to consider how I and others might develop coaching frameworks which better serve the individual and collective interests of those who work within organisations. I have shared some of the knowledge I have gained from my Literature Review directly with managers within the organisation with a view to helping them develop their understanding and practice. A critical approach to my research topics has enabled me to be more balanced in my advocacy of strategies relating to coaching and engagement. I ask myself seemingly big questions such as who I am as a practitioner, what I stand for, what can I meaningfully contribute and is it 'enough'? I aspire to develop a deep knowledge of the subjects for which I have some responsibility so that I can give of my best but recognise that this knowledge will always be incomplete, limited and insufficient. Most significantly perhaps I find myself critiquing pretty much everything (including the brief for this response where I found myself asking 'According to whom?'!).

BOX 4.3   DIANE – COACH AND FACILITATOR

Completed a MA in Executive and Business Coaching

The MA significantly enhanced my learning about my practice and about myself. The combination of academic rigour with the supported freedom to so fully explore a specific issue of interest has directly impacted my coaching practice ongoing as I have become more aware of who I can be as a coach. I have come to realise that my being scholarly continues without the formality and structure of a course. I continue to develop my 'living theory' about my work, 'researching' by means of reading, accessing coaching for myself and shortly to involve others through a workshop around my area of interest. Throughout this evolving 'living theory', my practice and being scholarly are intertwined.

BOX 4.4 NICK – ACADEMIC

Completed a DBA on Board Decision Making and Learning

The research focuses on discourse within the boardroom and explores the myths and micro linguistic tools that directors employ in their day-to-day talk to shape meaning and make sense of their world. Predominately I adopted ethnomethodology to observe and interpret events as they unfolded but further scrutinised the narrative and surrounding events and context with the employment of critical discourse analysis considering macro, meso and micro context. Of particular interest has been the ebb and flow of power and how the invisible hand of protocol, culture and belief orchestrates events. Further, how this helps those in possession of the appropriate linguistic resources and context awareness can shape events to their favour.

Scholarly practice has allowed me to gain greater insight, not only into how things are actually achieved, but to grasp the deeper narrative of why and the politically driven drivers that measure success. I have a greater understanding of humans and their interactions and how they use discourse, text and symbols to consciously or subconsciously drive their personal agenda. I see much more clearly now what is going on in the room and often marvel at the way linguistic practitioners can manage others' beliefs and move them to a virtually predetermined outcome without their subject even realising it. I understand what power in action really is and how to effectively deal with these forces so that they work in favour of my people.

BOX 4.5 JULIA – ACADEMIC AND FACILITATOR

Completing a DBA on Making Connections between the World of Business and University

It is the role of the 'intermediary' that provokes my academic curiosity. As an action researcher, I am interested in understanding the practice, the engagement processes and the relationship dynamics involved in establishing linkages between the cultural and creative sector and universities. As part of my doctoral studies I am investigating university and cultural and creative industries collaboration. My philosophical approach is informed by pragmatism, that is, managing and observing the bringing of people together to find out how connections work or do not work. I am looking to identify patterns both practically and conceptually.

Through a series of action learning cycles I am exploring the role of the intermediary in the process of network creation in order to impact on my approach. This is explored through abductive reasoning and involves three action learning cycles. The first cycle starts with my own approach in facilitating a network; the second cycle explores a chain of intermediaries in engaging businesses; and the third cycle draws on external examples. Through this approach it is anticipated that there will be shared understanding, both externally as well as with those colleagues with whom I work, of the role of an intermediary in the development of cultural and creative businesses and universities.

BOX 4.6   ADRIAN – DIRECTOR

Completing a DBA to Develop a Practice-based Model of Board Governance

My project aims to develop a practice-based model of board directorship that reflects the cultural, political and economic operating environment of an emerging market while satisfying Trans-National Institutional theoretical goals for corporate governance. The methodology employed is Reflexive Grounded Critical Action Learning Research and my approach acknowledges grounded theory's scholarly rigour and the scholarship of practitioner sense making inherent in action modalities, such as Action Learning, Action Research and Activity Theory's dialogic interventions. Critical Action Learning is the study's focus because it invites practitioners to question directly the programmed learning of international theories promoted by Trans-National Institutions (e.g. the World Bank and the International Monetary Fund (IMF)).

A scholarly distinction between a processual approach to board directorship and a quasi-experimental causal approach has focused my practice on trying to understand the process of board directorship in emerging markets. As a practising board director for emerging market companies, I seek to explain the process of applying international board principles in terms of the actions, goals, motives and world views of fellow board directors that inform decision making aimed at resolving corporate governance dilemmas. Furthermore, the scholarly distinctions between entitative, emergence and activity theory fuel my critical questioning of the compatibility of western individualism and liberalism (underpinning board directorship models promoted by Trans-National Institutions) with the communitarian culture and context of many emerging markets.

BOX 4.7   HELEN – ACADEMIC

Completed a DBA on the Transfer of Sports Coaching in a Business Context

Using sports coaching principles and practice in a business coaching context to inform my research direction of travel has provided me with the opportunity to develop an evidenced-based and contextualised coaching transfer model termed 'transcoach' for Retail Company X. I have sought to expose the reality and experiences of the participants on the Coaching for Performance Programme within Retail Company X to identify significance and meaning, particularly in relation to the sporting elements, to inform future practice adopting a constructivist grounded theory approach.

As a scholar-practitioner my understanding of the theory – practice link and academe–work relationships – has grown through my immersion in the organisation in which I am a participant researcher. Early on the misunderstandings, tensions and miscommunications between my organisation and Retail Company X led me to seek an explanation of this scholar-practitioner divide from others more experienced than myself. Translation theory (Latour 1987) and wicked problems (Rittel and Webber 1973) are some of the scholarly works which supported me on my early journey from academic and early researcher into a scholar-practitioner.

DISCUSSION

As with the findings from Wasserman and Kram (2009), a consideration of how scholar-practitioners work reveals complexity, variety, dilemmas and tensions. Working with the idea of phronesis, it becomes possible to discern the good intentions being pursued and the value judgements that underpin such intentions. Both the DBA and MAEBC are purposely developed for setting out a direction for action, and that requires change. Tim seeks to 'serve the individual and collective interests' (Box 4.2). Julia, in pursuit of university and cultural and creative industries collaboration, and having come to the academic world from a place in the creative sector world of practice, wants to bring 'people together to find out how connections work or do not work' (Box 4.5). Nick and Adrian are concerned with 'effective governance' and 'a practice-based model of board directorship' (Box 4.4 and Box 4.6), Helen, a sports academic and practitioner, pursues a model that uses 'sports coaching . . . in a business coaching context' (Box 4.7) and Diane, already a coach of considerable experience, moves beyond the structure of a qualification by continuing 'to develop my "living theory" about my work' (Box 4.3). Phronesis is concerned with judgements that are prudent, in pursuit of a purpose; it is a value judgement and therefore an aspect of a person's virtuous identity or character. Aristotle made a key point on the relationship between virtue, which makes a goal right, and phronesis as a judgement to move practically towards a goal. Intriguingly, the meaning of this point has been the subject of much discussion among philosophers and ethicists. Crucially, it is argued that virtue can be distinguished from a rational intellectual process to judge what is right to do, with phronesis providing the way to do it (Moss 2011). We might suggest that scholar-practitioners can be characterised in this way, rather than the judgements on what is right made by scholars, where the ends might be more prone to an intellectual process? As we argued earlier, in HRD scholarship and management more generally, there has been a tendency in recent years to decide what it is right to work on based on the need to publish in peer-reviewed journals. Judgements can be reduced to where to publish and how best to do it.

Phronetic research draws upon the prudence of the researcher, which is based on their experience. Even those who are starting as academics can draw on experience. Julia, for example, has a long history of working with cultural and creative organisations and continues to do so. Nick and Helen also work closely with organisations, and such closeness allows scholar-practitioners to focus more carefully on what is practical and what is particular in a specific case. Aristotle (1987) considered how prudence is a 'practical virtue' and has to 'do with particulars'. It can capture what is unknown, unpredictable and subject to variation, and in this way, phronesis can draw on or feed universal understanding. However, crucially, phronesis does not become universal as either theory or technique; a phronetic researcher retains value judgement.

Sherman (1999) points to how phronesis as particularism gives emphasis to 'an obligation to know the facts of the case, to see and understand what is morally relevant and to make decisions that are responsive to the exigencies of the case' (p. 38), which requires not just a knowledge of universal rules but a 'bottom-up' narrative of specific circumstances (p. 39). As the scholar-practitioner develops practical knowledge through phronesis, it leads to a deepening and questioning of the particulars, the potential for theorising through abductive reasoning (Gold et al. 2011) and a potential advance in universal knowledge (Dunne 1999). In all the cases reported by Tim, Diane, Adrian, Julia, Helen and Nick there are efforts to take contextualisation seriously and set the research within a particular location and case. This is not always easy or without tensions (Helen). There is also a need to consider the power-laden features of context and how history, culture and sociality is made manifest or works in the background (Searle 2011) (Nick and Adrian).

Setting their research in context, scholar-practitioners make their work relevant to practitioners by identifying the problems that are troubling and cause difficulty. There is involvement with groups and communities in the context of their practice. Nick and Adrian are concerned with boards of directors, Helen with the transfer of learning from coaching, Julia with her links with the cultural and creative sector, Tim with others who might develop a coaching framework and, intriguingly, Diane with an evolving 'living theory' (Whitehead 2009) about her practice. Whatever the context chosen, the research process produces data or text that is complementary, and this enhances the sense of the work and reduces the potential for the production of non-sense. Phronetic research matters, and such an achievement cannot be brought about without some attempt to focus on the values and getting close to practice (Flyvbjerg 2004). These are key feature of the methodology and methods that are selected by scholar-practitioners. There is a concern for participation and recognition that there are a variety of voices and viewpoints which must be accepted into the research. Adrian and Julie use the newly emerging methodology of action learning research (Coghlan and Coughlan 2010), Nick works with ethnography and participant observation, Helen is a participant researcher through immersion in her organisation, Diane intertwines scholarliness with her own practice and Tim works directly with managers helping them develop understanding and practice. These approaches allow scholar-practitioners to work closely with others that they both study and involve in any analysis completed. Data reflect the values and interests of the participants, and any movement beyond data as ideas, possible models and theories developed through the rigour of scholarship is likely to be relevant to participants, enabling them to reflect on their values and practice. It is an iterative process of learning that will improve the value of the research (Flyvbjerg 2004).

At a time when the practice of HRD in organisations is facing something of crisis in terms of influence and resources devoted to it, as well as the tendency for practitioners to adhere to outdated models to inform their practice (CIPD 2012), the gap between academe and practitioners is a continuing but unnecessary burden. It is becoming clearer that for the HRD profession to advance, there needs to be much better collaboration between researching and practising; we suggest that the scholar-practitioners need to be at the forefront of such advances.

To be fair, HRD academics in both the US and Europe have sought to find the space for practitioners to take steps to join them in their conferences and through their journals. As this chapter has shown, as part of this effort to bring the two worlds closer, there have been efforts to promote scholarly practice through awards and devoted streams at conferences. In addition, with the prospect that scholar-practitioners carry the potential to deal with the double hurdle of rigour and relevance, there has been an interest in helping this process by identifying roles, skills and competencies. Thus scholar-practitioners become bridges, brokers, translators and boundary spanners. In addition, they need to develop competences such as problem solving, intellectual horsepower and organisational agility. We have no problem with the work on this front; it is a part of the unfolding of understanding that is needed to help scholar-practitioners in HRD make their mark. However, we also felt that such tendencies needed to be countered with a more emergent framework that captures the dynamic nature of working as a scholar-practitioner, including the difficulties, tensions and grasping of values needed to make such work rigorous and relevant.

Our response was to answer the call of Bent Flyvbjerg (2001) to make social science matter by moving in the direction of 'phronetic social science'. We see how scholar-practitioners, by operating between academe and practice, need to show *phronesis* or prudence/practical wisdom and know how to behave by grasping the values they face so that judgements can be made to reflect the contextualised source of such values. Phronesis is shown in the midst of their practice, and in this chapter we sought to provide examples of this through the voices of six scholar-practitioners, all completing or having completed a master's or DBA at Leeds Beckett

University. In all the cases, the work presented shows how the focus on values leads their efforts to bring about change to practice for individuals, groups, organisations and, in one case, a whole country. Importantly, such a focus leads the scholar-practitioner into contexts, situations and relationships with others who become connected to the study and therefore are most likely to benefit in terms of change to practice. At the same time, the requirements for rigour ensure that scholar-practitioners are able to stand back from the demands and 'hurly burly' of everyday practice in which they are working.

In some ways, it does become possible to specify how phronetic research can proceed. Flyvbjerg (2004), for example, provides what he calls 'methodological guidelines for planning phronetic research' (p. 295), including calls for

1. Focusing on values
2. Placing power at the core of analysis
3. Getting close to reality
4. Emphasizing 'little things'
5. Looking at practice before discourse
6. Studying cases and contexts
7. Asking 'How?', do narrative
8. Moving beyond agency and structure
9. Doing dialogue with a polyphony of voices.

We would prefer to see this list not as a set of competences or skills, but as an approach and attitude to take into scholarly practice. We would, however, see much value in prompting the direction of scholarly practice through key questions for phronetic research, which Flyvbjerg (2001, p. 60) summarises as:

1. Where are we going?
2. Is this desirable?
3. What should be done?

Such questions might also serve as the guidance for the work of scholarly practice. In addition, Flyvbjerg provides a further question to reflect the importance of politics and power:

4. Who gains and who loses?

We also would include a question to allow the revelation and critique of prejudice:

5. How does tradition and history enable or constrain our understanding?

These questions provide a framework for scholar-practitioners in HRD, when completed as part of a formal programme, such as the DBA and masters reported here, but also for those in academe and practice who seek to make their work both rigorous and relevant.

REFERENCES

Abbott, A. (1988). *The System of Professions*. Chicago: University of Chicago Press.

Aram, J.D. and Salipante, P.F. (2003). Bridging scholarship in management: epistemological reflections. *British Journal of Management*, 14(3): 189–205.

Aristotle (1987). *The Nichomachean Ethics*, Translated by J.E.C. Welldon. New York, NY: Prometheus Books.

Aydede, M. (1998). Aristotle on episteme and nous: the posterior analytics. *Southern Journal of Philosophy*, 36(1): 15–46.

Bolden, R. and Gosling, J. (2006). Leadership competencies: time to change the tune? *Leadership*, 2(2): 147–163.

Buckley, R. and Caple, J. (2007). *The Theory and Practice of Training*. London: Kogan Page.

Cheetham, G. and Chivers, G. (2000). A new look at competent professional practice. *Journal of European Industrial Training*, 25(5): 374–383.

Chiaburu, D. and Tekleab, A. (2005). Individual and contextual influences on multiple dimensions of training effectiveness. *Journal of European Industrial Training*, 29(8): 604–626.

CIPD (2012). *Learning and Talent Development Survey*. London: Chartered Institute of Personnel and Development.

Coghlan, D. and Coughlan, P. (2010). Notes toward a philosophy of action learning research. *Action Learning: Research and Practice*, 7(2): 193–203.

Dunne, J. (1999). Virtue, phronesis and learning. In D. Carr and J. Steutel (Eds.), *Virtue Ethics and Moral Education* (pp. 49–64). London: Routledge.

Eikeland, O. (2007). *The Ways of Aristotle*. Bern: Peter Lang.

Eraut, M. (2000). Non-formal learning and tacit knowledge in professional work. *British Journal of Educational Psychology*, 70: 113–136.

Flyvbjerg, B. (2001). *Making Social Science Matter*. Cambridge: Cambridge University Press.

Flyvbjerg, B. (2004). Phronetic planning research: theoretical and methodological reflections. *Planning Theory and Practice*, 5(3): 283–306.

Freidson, E. (2001). *Professionalism*. Cambridge: Polity Press.

Ghoshal, S. (2005). Bad management theories are destroying good management practices. *Academy of Management Learning and Education*, 4: 75–91.

Gibbons, M., Limoges, C. and Nowotny, H. (1994). *The New Production of Knowledge/The Dynamics of Science and Research in Contemporary Society*. London: Sage.

Gold, J., Rodgers, H. and Smith, V. (2003). What is the future for the human resource development professional? A UK perspective. *Human Resource Development International*, 6(4): 437–456.

Gold, J., Walton, J., Cureton, P. and Anderson, L. (2011). Theorising and practitioners in HRD: the role of abductive reasoning. *Journal of European Industrial Training*, 35(3): 230–246.

Harrison, P. (2011). Learning culture, line manager and HR professional practice. *Journal of European Industrial Training*, 35(9): 914–928.

Hodgkinson, G. and Starkey, K. (2011). Not simply returning to the same answer over and over again: reframing relevance. *British Journal of Management*, 22: 355–369.

Keefer, J. and Yap, R. (2007). Is HRD research making a difference in practice? *Human Resource Development Quarterly*, 18(4): 449–455.

Kormanik, M., Lehner, R.D. and Winnick, T.A. (2009). General competencies for the HRD scholar-practitioner: perspectives from across the profession. *Advances in Developing Human Resources*, 11(4): 486–506.

Latour, B. (1987). *Science in Action: How to Follow Scientists and Engineers through Society*. Boston, MA: Harvard University Press.

Mankin, D.P. (2001). A model for human resource development. *Human Resource Development International*, 4(1): 65–85.

McLean, G.N. (1998). HRD: a three-legged stool, an octopus, or a centipede? *Human Resource Development International*, 1(4): 291–294.

Moats, J.B. and McLean, G.N. (2009). Speaking our language: the essential role of scholar-practitioners in HRD. *Advances in Developing Human Resources*, 11(4): 507–522.

Moss, J. (2011). Virtue makes the goal right: virtue and phronesis in Aristotle's ethics. *Phronesis: A Journal for Ancient Philosophy*, 56(3): 204–261.

Panza, C. and Thorpe, R. (2010). Management as design, but what kind of design? An appraisal of the design science analogy for management. *British Journal of Management*, 21: 171–186.

Pearce, J. and Huang, L. (2012). The decreasing value of our research to management education. *Academy of Management Learning and Education*, 11(2): 247–262.

Raelin, J. (2009). Seeking conceptual clarity in the action modalities. *Action Learning: Research and Practice*, 6(1): 17–24.

Rittel, H.W.J. and Webber, M.W. (1973). Dilemmas in a general theory of planning. *Policy Sciences*, 4: 155–169.

Searle, J. (2011). Wittgenstein and the background. *American Philosophical Quarterly*, 48(2): 120–128.

Sherman, N. (1999). Character development and Aristotelian virtue. In D. Carr and J. Steutel (Eds.), *Virtue Ethics and Moral Education* (pp. 35–48). London: Routledge.

Short, D.C. (2006a). Closing the gap between research and practice in HRD. *Human Resource Development Quarterly*, 17(3): 343–350.

Short, D.C. (2006b). HRD scholar-practitioners: a definition and description of core activities. *2006 AHRD Conference Proceedings* (pp. 258–264). Bowling Green, OH: AHRD.

Short, D.C., Bing, J.W. and Kehrhahn, M.T. (2003). Will human resource development survive? *Human Resource Development Quarterly*, 14(3): 239–243.

Short, D., Keefer, J. and Stone, S.J. (2009). The link between research and practice: experiences of HRD and other professions. *Advances in Developing Human Resources* 11(4): 420–437.

Stewart, J. and Gold, J. (2011). Theorising in HRD: building bridges to practice. *Journal of European Industrial Training*, 35(3): 199–299.

Swanson, R.A. (1999). HRD theory, real or imagined. *Human Resource Development International*, 2(1): 2–5.

Van de Ven, A. (2007). *Engaged Scholarship: A Guide for Organizational and Social Research*. Oxford: Oxford University Press.

Wasserman, I.C. and Kram, K. (2009). Enacting the scholar-practitioner role: an exploration of narratives. *Journal of Applied Behavioral Science*, 45(1): 12–38.

Weick, K. (1979). *Social Psychology of Organizing*. Reading, MA: Addison-Wesley.

Whitehead, J. (2009). Using a living theory methodology in improving practice and generating educational knowledge in living theories. *Educational Journal of Living Theories*, 1(1): 103–126.

ANNOTATED FURTHER READING

Flyvbjerg, B., Landman, T. and Schram, S. (2012). *Real Social Science: Applied Phronesis.* Cambridge: Cambridge University Press. An edited book of several studies completed through the lens of Aristotelian phronesis.

Scully-Russ, E., Lehner, R. and Shuck, B. (2013). A scholar-practitioner case approach. *Advances in Developing Human Resources*, 15(3): 243–251. A special edition of the journal devoted to scholar-practitioner research in HRD.

5. Using systematic review methodology to examine the extant literature

Céline Rojon and Almuth McDowall

SUMMARY

This chapter explicates systematic review methodology as an evidence-based approach for examining literature, drawing on the authors' experience of conducting a systematic review as well as on the discussion of other existing systematic reviews. Introducing key tenets, the methodology is benchmarked against alternative reviewing approaches, discussing advantages and potential disadvantages, alongside practicalities and challenges.

INTRODUCTION

Human resource development (HRD) is by nature a wide, fragmented field, encompassing plurality in topics, foci and methods. This can make it challenging to obtain a distinct and concise overview of current evidence, highlighting the need to synthesize and integrate what is 'out there' to guide best practice and future research. To this effect, Briner, Rousseau and fellow scholars (e.g. Briner and Rousseau, 2011; Rousseau and Barends, 2011; Briner, Denyer and Rousseau, 2009) call for an evidence-based rather than an intuitive approach to management, building sound practice based on the integration of findings which have not only been synthesized, but also checked for quality. We acknowledge here that others think differently. Cassell (2011) for instance openly raises the issue of what 'evidence' actually is and highlights its context-dependent nature. Be the discussion as it may, we assert that there will always be instances when there is a need to integrate an existing knowledge-base and 'take stock'. This is where systematic review methodology comes into its own, being particularly suitable when the aim is to establish current best evidence as well as gaps in the literature with regard to a (set of) specific review question(s).

CHAPTER STRUCTURE

This chapter will familiarize the reader with systematic review methodology, commencing with an introduction to its key tenets. We further benchmark systematic review methodology against other reviewing approaches, using a table to guide the reader. Within this comparison, we also critically reflect on caveats and potential disadvantages of the methodology, given that systematic reviews are time-consuming and laborious to conduct. Our discussion will provide the reader with guidance on whether this methodology is suitable and applicable for their research questions. Finally, we discuss the practicalities of carrying out a systematic review in an HRD context. We hereby draw upon our own experience of conducting a systematic review on the topic of individual workplace performance. Specifically, we explain the six stages that are usually followed when doing a systematic review and provide hints and tips for each based on our own experience with this methodology. We also discuss the various challenges that we came across when undertaking our systematic review (e.g. the very large number of references located) and identify potential solutions on how to deal with these.

AN OVERVIEW OF SYSTEMATIC REVIEW METHODOLOGY

In essence, systematic review methodology is a particular way of conducting literature reviews using clear and replicable protocols and criteria to draw conclusions from any evidence. More explicitly, according to Denyer and Tranfield (2009), systematic review can be understood as 'a specific methodology that locates existing studies, selects and evaluates contributions, analyses and synthesizes data, and reports the evidence in such a way that allows reasonably clear conclusions to be reached about what is and is not known' (p. 671). Drawing upon detailed guidelines/a research protocol determined in advance, the available literature is critically examined in regard to how each single publication will contribute to answering one or more specific question(s) formulated at an early stage of the systematic review. Information is then analysed, synthesized (qualitatively and/or quantitatively) and discussed. Comparing systematic review methodology to the more traditional forms of literature review including narrative approaches, the following key differences have been noted (Petticrew and Roberts, 2006). First, by attempting to identify, appraise and synthesize all studies that are relevant to the review question(s), systematic reviews aim to limit systematic error (bias) in following a set of scientific processes, as opposed to traditional reviews, which can be somewhat selective in the studies included. The second, interrelated difference is that these processes are defined a priori and reported in sufficient detail to enable replication for systematic reviews, which is not necessarily the case for other types of literature review.

Systematic review methodology, which originated in the Medical Sciences, gained acceptance also in other disciplines, such as the Social Sciences, over the past two decades (Harlen and Crick, 2004). More recently, its value for evidence-based research has further been acknowledged by researchers in the Management and Organization Sciences (MOS), who have adapted this reviewing approach to suit the particular needs of their field (e.g. Denyer and Tranfield, 2009). Considering the field of HRD more specifically, systematic review methodology has started to gain popularity here also. One of the earlier examples of a systematic review in HRD is Cho and Egan's (2009) examination of the action learning literature. This study resulted, amongst others, in the development of a conceptual framework illustrating key dimensions of action learning, grouped under the four headings of antecedents (initiation of action learning), process (action learning intervention deployment), proximal outcomes (action learning implementation) and distal outcomes (action learning evaluation). Recent examples of systematic reviews in HRD include studies by Greer and Egan (2012) as well as Olckers and Du Plessis (2012). In the first of these, the authors systematically reviewed the literature on role salience and its implications for employees and organizations (e.g. in relation to organizational policies, HRD practices or employee performance) as well as for HRD professionals. The second study by Olckers and Du Plessis is a systematic review of the literature on psychological ownership. Based on their findings, these scholars conclude that psychological ownership is a multidimensional construct that can be distinguished from other, similar constructs (e.g. work-related attitudes); further, they highlight the importance of psychological ownership in regard to the retention of skilled employees within organizations.

Systematic reviews are meant to adhere to four core principles in the MOS (Denyer and Tranfield, 2009). First, they aim to be transparent, in other words open and explicit about the process and methods employed as well as any underlying assumptions, such as prior knowledge held by the reviewer(s). Second, systematic reviews should be inclusive, meaning the reviewer needs to consider carefully whether or not a publication contributes to answering the review question(s) and adds something new to the understanding of the field (Pawson, 2006; cited in Denyer and Tranfield, 2009). When deciding whether or not to include a primary study in the review, a quality checklist is used to specify and justify inclusion/exclusion criteria (Wallace and Wray, 2006). The third principle is about the systematic review being explanatory; this relates to the synthesis of the included publications, which can be undertaken qualitatively (e.g. interpretive and explanatory syntheses) and/or quantitatively (e.g. meta-analysis). Finally, systematic reviews should strive to be heuristic, in that any conclusions made (e.g. heuristic conclusions, such as generic suggestions on how to progress both in academic and organizational settings) should refer back to the specific review question(s) asked.

These four principles can be applied by adhering to the six distinct stages of systematic reviewing as suggested by Denyer and Tranfield (2009; also Petticrew and Roberts, 2006; Wallace and Wray, 2006). The first stage is a pre-review scoping study, undertaken to determine (i) if a systematic review is required in the first place (or would rather be mere replication of existing reviews) and (ii) the basis of the literature search. This is followed by determining one or more questions used to guide the systematic review. At this stage of the process, to assist with specifying the review questions, a range of stakeholders (e.g. scholars in the subject area, practitioners and/or policy makers with a relevant background and experience, librarians with subject knowledge), functioning as an advisory panel, is usually involved. Upon having determined the questions, the reviewer carries out an exhaustive search of the literature, by way of attempting to examine all the evidence available that will contribute to addressing the questions; this should take account of a range of sources (e.g. databases, conference proceedings, personal requests to scholars in the field). Next, using pre-determined criteria for judging the relevance and quality of any references found in the literature search, it is necessary to select and evaluate them, to assert which ones will be useful for addressing the review questions. Having decided upon those publications to be employed for answering the review questions, this body of literature needs to be integrated in either a narrative way, in other words by describing, summarizing and relating the studies to one another, and/or statistically, by means of a meta-analysis. Last, once all the available evidence pertaining to the review questions has been analysed and synthesized, findings are summarized and discussed overall in terms of what we know, what we do not know yet and where future research should take up; some thought might also go into how the findings might inform future research and practice.

We provide further detail about these six stages in the section explaining our personal experience of applying systematic review methodology in the field of HRD.

ADVANTAGES AND POTENTIAL DISADVANTAGES OF SYSTEMATIC REVIEW METHODOLOGY

Undertaking a systematic review is often a time-consuming and laborious activity, reportedly taking a team of reviewers an average of seven months (Allen and Olkin, 1999). Yet, this disadvantage in terms of increased use of resources is seen to be offset by some distinct advantages (e.g. Rojon, McDowall and Saunders, 2011; Briner and Rousseau, 2011; Denyer and Tranfield, 2009; Petticrew and Roberts, 2006) the methodology offers over alternative reviewing and synthesis methods, such as meta-narrative approaches (e.g. Greenhalgh et al., 2005), critical appraisals (e.g. Hill and Spittlehouse, 2003) and realist reviews (e.g. Pawson et al., 2005). We outline these advantages in Table 5.1, which directly compares systematic review methodology to two of the most commonly used reviewing approaches, namely traditional narrative review (cf. Jesson, Matheson and Lacey, 2011) and (statistical) meta-analysis (cf. Hunter and Schmidt, 2004).

THE SCOPE OF SYSTEMATIC REVIEWS

Systematic reviews vary greatly in the scope (from narrow to wide) and nature of their research questions and the number of primary studies reviewed and included. Some systematic reviews can take years to complete, particularly where evidence is difficult to obtain or time-consuming to interpret. Review scope is concerned with the breadth of the research questions covered. Our own review, discussed below, can be considered to have a wide scope, as it cuts across two strands of research (MOS and also Industrial/Organizational (I/O) Psychology). Yet, a systematic review might also change from having a wide scope at the outset to a narrow scope once it has been completed. An example of the latter is Joyce and colleagues' review of interventions relevant to flexible working (Joyce et al., 2010) and their impact on health outcomes. The authors started off reviewing a large number of databases ($N = 12$), eliciting a huge number of potentially relevant 'hits'. Due to their stringent inclusion criteria (randomized controlled trials, interrupted time series or controlled before and after studies examining the effects of flexible working interventions on employee health and wellbeing), in the end the authors only reviewed ten primary studies by means of narrative synthesis, offering tentative conclusions, such as 'these findings seem to indicate that flexibility in working patterns which gives the worker more choice or control is likely to have positive effects on health and wellbeing' (Joyce et al., 2010, p. 2).

Table 5.1   Advantages of systematic reviewing in comparison to alternative approaches for reviewing literature

Systematic review methodology (e.g. Denyer and Tranfield, 2009; Petticrew and Roberts, 2006)	Traditional narrative review (e.g. Jesson et al., 2011)	Meta-analysis (e.g. Hunter and Schmidt, 2004)
Greater rigour, replicability, thoroughness and objectivity possible by adhering to a set of review principles and stages	• Less rigour, transparency and replicability, as usually no formal methodology • Yet: more flexibility possible in exploring researcher's own ideas	Processes of locating, evaluating, selecting and coding studies need to be documented in detail to enable replicability (e.g. for statistical meta-analysis)
• Especially useful when aware of main themes, but unsure of the actual evidence in relation to the review topic, since all potentially relevant sources of information are considered and reconciled • As such: comprehensive collation of all existing evidence across relevant studies and integration of different schools of thought and research findings	Possibility/danger that scholars concentrate on a personal, purposive selection of materials they believe to be important (e.g. 'preferred' journals), thus potentially introducing a one-sided (or even biased) argument	Potential danger of researcher bias: • Scholars can be very selective as to which studies to include in their meta-analysis • Not always evident why some studies have been included when others have not been
Where researchers are faced with a vast and heterogeneous body of literature, reviewing of a topic is facilitated by following an a priori developed protocol that specifies tasks and stages in the reviewing process	Scholars might have difficulty in identifying and reviewing a topic when faced with a vast and heterogeneous body of literature, since there is no set protocol to follow in most cases	Adherence to statistical and psychometric principles of meta-analysing data can allow for greater ease in dealing with a large number of studies – especially if findings are contradictory
Possibility to combine methods of analysis and synthesis (e.g. integration of qualitative and quantitative reviewing elements)	Review usually focuses on narrative component (qualitative synthesis) only	Review usually focuses on meta-analytical component (quantitative synthesis) only

Source: Adapted from Rojon, McDowall and Saunders (2011).

This example illustrates that whilst the field of flexible working is wide, as arguably is the range of potential health outcomes, resulting in a wide research question, a systematic review's scope will also be defined by its inclusion criteria.

PERSONAL EXPERIENCE OF APPLYING SYSTEMATIC REVIEW IN HRD

As part of a large research project aimed at closely examining how individual workplace performance can be defined, conceptualized and measured, a systematic review was conducted at the outset (in 2009/2010). This was to provide the basis for subsequent studies by way of determining what the current understanding is of individual workplace performance, what is not yet known and how future research can contribute to the existing body of evidence. A systematic review was considered a particularly useful approach in our context for examining the literature, because its structured, standardized and rigorous procedure was perceived to facilitate integration of the large and heterogeneous body of evidence across MOS, I/O Psychology and related areas.

As outlined above, there are usually six stages in the process of systematic reviewing. We will now explain how we conducted our systematic review on aspects of individual workplace performance along those stages, in so doing also outlining the various challenges we encountered and how these might be dealt with.

1) Pre-review Scoping Study

An exploratory scoping study, aimed at determining the scope and focus of the literature search, typically precedes the actual systematic review. This was undertaken by (i) assessing the types of studies carried out to date and where these had been published, (ii) identifying the focus of the investigation and (iii) considering whether, and if so how, the systematic review would contribute to the knowledge in the field. We had determined during this stage that our systematic review would be the first of its kind on the topic of workplace performance. Whilst there are a number of important meta-analytical studies (e.g. Viswesvaran, Schmidt and Ones, 2005) and traditional literature reviews (e.g. Arvey and Murphy, 1998) examining aspects of workplace performance, none of these can be characterized as a systematic review, suggesting a need for such an approach. In general, it is important to examine whether or not previously conducted systematic reviews have focused on your topic of interest to minimize the risk of duplication.

Results of the scoping study indicated that there are a variety of understandings of the construct of individual workplace performance, in particular concerning its definition and conceptualization and, as a consequence, its measurement. One fundamental question, for example, was whether performance is unidimensional (one general factor) or multidimensional (different elements) (e.g. Borman and Brush, 1993; Bartram, 2005). This general lack of a common consensus pointed to a need for further investigation. The matter of understanding and conceptualizing workplace performance, particularly concerning its potential underlying structure, was therefore chosen as the central point of investigation for the systematic review.

2) Determination of Review Question(s)

Clearly framed research (review) questions were formulated, being defined precisely to facilitate the decision as to whether or not a potentially relevant publication would contribute to answering them (Greenhalgh and Peacock, 2005). We involved a range of stakeholders as an advisory group to assist with specifying the review questions. Members of such a group are usually individuals with academic knowledge and practical expertise in the subject area (Denyer and Tranfield, 2009; Petticrew and Roberts, 2006; Tranfield, Denyer and Smart, 2003), where each subject matter expert should bring unique insights to the panel to represent a range of interests and perspectives. As such, we recruited a heterogeneous group of ten individuals: academics with a research interest in workplace performance, but each with a different focus of interest, as well as private and public sector practitioners (personnel/HR professionals). Broad semi-structured telephone interviews were conducted with each person, questions focusing on individuals' definition and understanding of individual workplace performance, how the literature (e.g. academic articles, trade magazines) links to this view, pertinent practical concerns research should address and any specific questions they would like to see addressed in a literature review. By adopting a flexible approach to interviewing, we aimed to ensure that any resulting review questions would be useful and practically relevant to a wider audience, whilst still being aligned with the focus of our review as deduced from the scoping study.

Qualitative content analysis of the interviews determined main themes, the degree of consensus between panel members and questions suggested for the review. One of the main themes centred on performance being a complex construct in a number of ways, for example in terms of different levels of performance (individual, team/group and organizational performance), relationships between individual input and organizational output or underlying performance components (e.g. task and contextual performance). Further, individuals indicated that not enough research had concerned itself with the underlying structure of performance and how to operationalize and measure it, this being similar to findings from the scoping study. When asked specifically about areas or questions research should address, panel members mentioned again that more research should look at how to measure performance (e.g. objectively versus subjectively) and that further exploration is required as to whether performance should be assessed in terms of overall job performance or in a more differentiated way. A related aspect is that of the validity of predictors of performance – how can different performance criteria be predicted best? In summary, experts were mostly interested in seeing questions concerning the conceptualization and measurement of performance being addressed. Overall, we note that it was not always easy to reconcile different stakeholder perspectives; this we tried to address by balancing academic and practitioner foci in the final review questions. As such, resulting from the scoping study and the findings from the expert interviews, we deduced the following specific research questions for the systematic review, which were fed back to the experts to obtain their approval (Dillman et al., 2009):

1. How is individual workplace performance defined and conceptualized?
2. How is individual workplace performance measured? What are the reasons for using certain methods of measurement and how solid are the arguments presented for different approaches?
3. What are the relationships, if any, between overall versus criterion-specific measures of individual workplace performance and established predictors (i.e. ability and personality measures)?

3) Search of the Literature

An exhaustive search of the literature was carried out to enable us to examine all the evidence available in relation to the three review questions. Upon having undertaken pilot database searches by way of assessing the utility of search strings and determining a start date, we decided to combine four search strings for databases searches. Each of these refers to a key concept addressed by the systematic review, the asterisk enabling searching on truncated word forms; synonymical words or similar concepts were included in each string to ensure that any relevant references would be found in the searches:

1. perform* OR efficien* OR productiv* OR effective* (key concept captured is performance)

2. work* OR job OR individual OR task OR occupation* OR human OR employ* OR vocation* OR personnel (key concept: workplace)
3. assess* OR apprais* OR evaluat* OR test OR rating OR review OR measure OR manage* (key concept: measurement)
4. criteri* OR objective OR theory OR framework OR model OR standard (key concept: criterion)

Several sources of evidence were considered in the searches to help ensure maximum saturation and inclusion of any potential key references, namely 12 databases (e.g. Business Source Complete, PsycInfo, Chartered Institute of Personnel and Development database), alongside proceedings and contributions from four conferences (e.g. Academy of Management Annual Meeting). Moreover, manual searches of three journals inaccessible through the databases (e.g. *The Industrial-Organizational Psychologist*) were conducted and requests for further publications (e.g. papers still in preparation) sent to scholars with relevant research interests (outside the advisory group).

The searches took approximately two weeks (full-time). All the results were exported into a program designed for the management of references. Upon removal of duplicate references, we retained 59,465 references.

4) Selection and Evaluation of References

All references retrieved by the literature search underwent an initial screening, first by title only and second by both title and abstract. The purpose of this was to exclude any papers that did not appear to address any or all of the specific review questions at least to some extent from any further investigation. It was crucial hereby to apply caution and not to discard any potentially relevant references prematurely.

This initial screening led to a radical reduction in reference numbers: screening by title alone, which involved an examination of all publications' titles with regard to their applicability to the review questions, reduced their number from 59,465 to 3,010. The vast majority of these irrelevant references pertained to areas completely unrelated to the topic of investigation, such as medicine (mostly concerned with various illnesses and conditions and their treatments), chemistry and physics, technology (e.g. automobile industry), marketing and so forth.

Screening further by title and abstract reduced the number to 315. This second screening was more challenging, as it was not always immediately obvious when a reference was potentially relevant or not. In order not to lose focus, it was therefore important at this stage to keep in mind the specific questions the systematic review set out to answer. Any research outputs for which the abstract indicated potential relevance for the review questions were kept at this stage. References that were sifted out pertained, amongst others, to the broader area of performance management, to organizational performance, to methods of administering appraisal feedback and so forth.

Next, upon having obtained full text copies of the remaining references, these were examined in more detail by way of deciding which publications to use in addressing the review questions. As such, we read the full text critically by applying 13 previously determined criteria for inclusion/exclusion (e.g. Is the paper well informed by existing theory? Are the methods chosen appropriate to the stated purpose? Are the conclusions well linked to the purpose and aims of the research?), which were derived and adjusted from guidelines/criteria for the evaluation of academic publications (Cassell, 2010; Briner, Denyer and Rousseau, 2009; Denyer, 2009; Cuevas, 2006). A total of 172 publications met the inclusion/exclusion criteria relating to both contribution to answering the review questions and satisfactory quality. To facilitate the synthesis of the evidence retrieved, we completed a data extraction form for each of these, summarizing key points.

We note at this point that the selection and evaluation of references was a time-consuming process, which took us approximately three months. To avoid digression, it was necessary at this stage to ensure a constant focus on the review questions and to only accept those publications for the final pool of references that met the inclusion/exclusion criteria.

5) Analysis and Synthesis of Findings

Descriptive statistics (i.e. document type, publication outlet, year of publication and quality) were obtained for the final pool of references. We found that the vast majority of references were peer-reviewed journal articles, having been published in a wide variety of journals ($N = 52$), but with half coming from six different journals only. Literature outputs had been published between the years of 1959 and 2010; yet more than 75 per cent were concerned with research conducted in the last 20 years.

The body of evidence from the data extraction forms was integrated in two ways, combining analytical methods. For review questions 1 and 2, findings were integrated in a narrative, qualitative manner by describing and summarizing the studies and further determining how they relate to each other (Rousseau, Manning and Denyer, 2008). For review question 3, findings were aggregated quantitatively by means of statistical meta-analysis (Hunter and Schmidt, 2004).

6) Discussion and Utilization of Findings

Upon having analysed and synthesized all the available evidence pertaining to the three review questions, we summarized and discussed findings in terms of what is known, what is not yet known, where future research should take us and potential implications for practice and policy.

At this point, we would like to draw the reader's attention to three challenges that we faced across the six stages of the review. The first of these pertains to time management: systematic reviewing is a time-consuming, laborious activity, and the reviewer (or indeed reviewing team) should be aware that many tasks will take longer than anticipated. Further, time should be factored in for the acquisition of potentially required knowledge, skills and abilities in relation to the systematic review process (e.g. how to use reference management software). The second overarching challenge is linked to the first and relates to a potential danger of decreasing motivation; we tried to avoid this by regularly discussing progress and next steps amongst ourselves as well as with other scholars involved in conducting systematic reviews. The third, and perhaps biggest challenge in our case, was handling the very large number of references our literature search had revealed. We believe this may have been a result of our review questions being relatively comprehensive and would therefore recommend that the reader consider his/her own review question(s) carefully, ensuring these are sufficiently focused.

DISCUSSION

We are advocates of systematic review methodology, given its power to assist researchers in synthesizing diverse and potentially variable original sources to evaluate current evidence. This power lies in the transparency, the replicability and the firmness of conclusions if the systematic review has been done well. Our own work illustrates that the process is laborious and not without motivational challenges, but offers worthy rewards in the end. The biggest challenge in our view is that systematic review methodology in itself can be considered simultaneously a strength and a weakness. The strength lies in the fact that protocols are so clearly stipulated in advance, detailed and easily replicable. Such a priori protocols necessitate clarity throughout the review process and render the researcher(s) very accountable for their work. As a result, we have become very sensitized to other, more narrative reviews, which claim to offer state-of-the-art evidence, but fail to justify which primary studies were included in the review and which ones were not. Yet, stipulating the process in advance also has disadvantages. For instance, when we conducted our own review, our search strategy elicited many more hits than we had originally anticipated, meaning that it became a rather fulsome task to do full justice to all three review questions. Researchers might at this point in time be tempted to change or abandon the process, but 'pure' systematic review methodology would caution against any post hoc changes. So the benefit of hindsight can be a wonderful thing, but does not always work to the advantage of conducting a systematic review! By offering this insight, we do not mean to deter other HRD researchers from carrying out systematic reviews, but would rather like to make explicit that such a review should not be undertaken lightly. The process takes time, skill, effort and considerable determination. But without systematic reviews, moving the HRD field towards evidence-based management will be difficult.

REFERENCES

Allen, E. and Olkin, I. (1999) 'Estimating time to conduct a meta-analysis from number of citations retrieved' *Journal of the American Medical Association*, Vol. 282(7), pp. 634–635.
Arvey, R. D. and Murphy, K. R. (1998) 'Performance evaluation in work settings' *Annual Review of Psychology*, Vol. 49, pp. 141–168.
Bartram, D. (2005) 'The Great Eight competencies: A criterion-centric approach to validation' *Journal of Applied Psychology*, Vol. 90(6), pp. 1185–1203.
Borman, W. C. and Brush, D. H. (1993) 'More progress towards a taxonomy of managerial performance requirements' *Human Performance*, Vol. 6(1), pp. 1–21.
Briner, R. B., Denyer, D. and Rousseau, D. M. (2009) 'Evidence-based management: Concept cleanup time?' *Academy of Management Perspectives*, Vol. 23(4), pp. 19–32.
Briner, R. B. and Rousseau, D. M. (2011) 'Evidence-based I-O Psychology: Not there yet' *Industrial and Organizational Psychology: Perspectives on Science and Practice*, Vol. 4(1), pp. 3–22.
Cassell, C. (2010) 'Criteria for evaluating papers using qualitative research methods' *Journal of Occupational and Organizational Psychology (JOOP)*. Retrieved 3 January 2010 from http://onlinelibrary.wiley.com/journal/10.1111/(ISSN)2044-8325/homepage/ qualitative_guidelines.htm.
Cassell, C. (2011) 'Evidence-based I-O Psychology: What do we lose on the way?' *Industrial and Organizational Psychology*, Vol. 4, pp. 23–26.
Cho, Y. and Egan, T. M. (2009) 'Action learning research: A systematic review and conceptual framework' *Human Resource Development Review*, Vol. 8(4), pp. 431–462.
Cuevas, J. M. (2006) 'Learning and knowledge processes in an academic-management consulting research programme. The case of the MC Centre' Unpublished doctoral dissertation. School of Management, Cranfield University, UK.
Denyer, D. (2009) 'Reviewing the literature systematically' Cranfield: Advanced Institute of Management Research (AIM), UK. Retrieved 26 October 2009 from http://aimexpertresearcher.org/.
Denyer, D. and Tranfield, D. (2009) 'Producing a systematic review'. In Buchanan, D. and Bryman, A. (eds.) *The SAGE handbook of organizational research methods*. London: Sage, pp. 671–689.
Dillman, D. A., Phelps, G., Tortora, R., Swift, K., Kohrell, J., Berck, J. and Messer, B. L. (2009) 'Response rate and measurement differences in mixed-mode surveys using mail,

telephone, interactive voice response (IVR) and the Internet' *Social Science Research*, Vol. 38(1), pp. 1–18.

Greenhalgh, T. and Peacock, R. (2005) 'Effectiveness and efficiency of search methods in systematic reviews of complex evidence: Audit of primary sources' *British Medical Journal*, Vol. 331(7524), pp. 1064–1065.

Greenhalgh, T., Robert, G., Macfarlane, F., Bate, P., Kyriakidou, O. and Peacock, R. (2005) 'Storylines of research in diffusion of innovation: A meta-narrative approach to systematic review' *Social Science and Medicine*, Vol. 61(2), pp. 417–430.

Greer, T. W. and Egan, T. M. (2012) 'Inspecting the hierarchy of life roles: A systematic review of role salience literature' *Human Resource Development Review*, Vol. 11(4), pp. 463–499.

Harlen, W. and Crick, R. D. (2004) 'Opportunities and challenges of using systematic reviews of research for evidence-based policy in education' *Evaluation and Research in Education*, Vol. 18(1–2), pp. 54–71.

Hill, A. and Spittlehouse, C. (2003) 'What is critical appraisal?' *Evidence Based Medicine*, Vol. 3(2), pp. 1–8. Retrieved 3 October 2010 from http://www.whatisseries.co.uk/ whatis/pdfs/What_is_crit_appr.pdf.

Hunter, J. E. and Schmidt, F. L. (2004) *Methods of meta-analysis: Correcting for error and bias in research findings* (2nd edn). Thousand Oaks: Sage.

Jesson, J. K., Matheson, L. and Lacey, F. M. (2011) *Doing your literature review: Traditional and systematic techniques*. London: Sage.

Joyce, K., Pabayo, R., Critchley, J. A. and Bambra, C. (2010) 'Flexible working conditions and their effects on employee health and wellbeing' *Cochrane Database of Systematic Reviews*, Issue 2. Art. No.: CD008009. DOI: 10.1002/14651858. CD008009.pub2.

Olckers, C. and Du Plessis, Y. (2012) 'The role of psychological ownership in retaining talent: A systematic literature review' *SA Journal of Human Resource Management/SA Tydskrif vir Menslikehulpbronbestuur*, Vol. 10(2), pp. 1–18.

Pawson, R., Greenhalgh, T., Harvey, G. and Walshe, K. (2005) 'Realist review – a new method of systematic review designed for complex policy interventions' *Journal of Health Services Research and Policy*, Vol. 10(1), pp. 21–34.

Petticrew, M. and Roberts, H. (2006) *Systematic reviews in the Social Sciences. A practical guide*. Oxford: Blackwell Publishing.

Rojon, C., McDowall, A. and Saunders, M. N. K. (2011) 'On the experience of conducting a systematic review in Industrial, Work and Organizational Psychology. Yes, it is worthwhile' *Journal of Personnel Psychology*, Vol. 10(3), pp. 133–138.

Rousseau, D. M. and Barends, E. G. R. (2011) 'Becoming an evidence-based HR practitioner' *Human Resource Management Journal*, Vol. 21(3), pp. 221–235.

Rousseau, D. M., Manning, J. and Denyer, D. (2008) 'Evidence in management and organizational science: Assembling the field's full weight of scientific knowledge through syntheses' *The Academy of Management Annals*, Vol. 2(1), pp. 475–515.

Tranfield, D., Denyer, D. and Smart, P. (2003) 'Towards a methodology for developing evidence-informed management knowledge by means of systematic review' *British Journal of Management*, Vol. 14(3), pp. 207–222.

Viswesvaran, C., Schmidt, F. L. and Ones, D. S. (2005) 'Is there a general factor in ratings of job performance? A meta-analytic framework for disentangling substantive and error influences' *Journal of Applied Psychology*, Vol. 90(1), pp. 108–131.

Wallace, M. and Wray, A. (2006) *Critical reading and writing for postgraduates*. London: Sage.

ANNOTATED FURTHER READING

Briner, R. B., Denyer, D. and Rousseau, D. M. (2009) 'Evidence-based management: Concept cleanup time?' *Academy of Management Perspectives*, Vol. 23(4), pp. 19–32.

Article illustrating the importance of systematic reviews in the context of a wider discussion around evidence-based management.

Denyer, D. and Tranfield, D. (2009) 'Producing a systematic review'. In Buchanan, D. and Bryman, A. (eds.) *The SAGE handbook of organizational research methods*. London: Sage, pp. 671–689. Book chapter offering a useful introduction to systematic review methodology and its application in the Management and Organization Sciences.

Petticrew, M. and Roberts, H. (2006) *Systematic reviews in the Social Sciences. A practical guide*. Oxford: Blackwell Publishing. A comprehensive and easy to read book on systematic review and how the methodology is utilized in the Social Sciences.

PART II

QUALITATIVE RESEARCH

6. Ethnographic research in HRD – managing a betrayal?
Dawn Langley

SUMMARY

The purpose of this chapter is to explore the distinct offer of ethnographic research to HRD practices. In so doing, I will consider the issue of field-work and the building of rapport between researcher and participants, an integral element of ethnographic research that can both create and challenge the research relationship.

INTRODUCTION

> THESE are the researches of Herodotus of Halicarnassus, which he publishes, in the hope of thereby preserving from decay the remembrance of what men have done, and of preventing the great and wonderful actions of the Greeks and the Barbarians from losing their due meed of glory; and withal to put on record what were their grounds of feuds.

Cited as the first ethnographer (Clair, 2003), as well as the father of history, these are the opening lines of 'Clio', Book One, from 'The Histories' by Herodotus (c. 484–425 BC). Herodotus wrote nine volumes in all as he explored the Middle East and documented its cultures and political history. Despite these early examples of ethnographic writing, the concept of 'ethnographie' was not raised until 1767, acquiring common usage among German scholars (Vermeulen, 2008) in the 1780s. The first Oxford English Dictionary reference to the term 'ethnography' (Dewald, 2004) did not appear until 1834, when it was cited in the Penny Cyclopedia (Vol. II: 97).

Ethnography is generally referred to as having emerged out of anthropology; sometimes the two terms are used interchangeably implying little difference. More recently it has been proposed that ethnography emerged in parallel to anthropology and was actually developed out of administrative studies. Some even argue that anthropology is an offshoot of ethnography (Vermeulen, 2008): 'better to regard academic anthropology as a specific instance of ethnographic practice than the other way around' (Salemink, 2003: 9). This suggests that ethnography developed out of history as a discipline, emerging as a new field of study from those empires that wished to document and understand their colonies. 'The early ethnographers were historians, geographers and linguists; the physical anthropologists were physicians and anatomists' (Vermeulen, 2008: 284).

Why bother delving so far back into the history of the approach? I would argue it highlights a number of issues that are worth bearing in mind if you are considering undertaking ethnographic research:

- Ethnography does not consist of a straightforward and universally agreed set of practices.
- How it is utilised as a research approach will depend on the philosophical and epistemological stance of the researcher.
- It locates ethnographic research within the field of organisations and organising from the earliest point of its development.

Ethnography has a well-established track record as a research approach in organisation studies. In the 1800s Reformists 'entered the workplace incognito to learn in more depth about the people they wished to help' (Zickar and Carter, 2010: 307). Charles Rumford Walker, on discharge from the army, worked in the steel mills and documented his experiences in the 1920s. Frances Donovan, originally a schoolteacher, waited on tables and worked in a department store and also published her accounts in the 1920s. She was connected to the 'Chicago School', which became an important influence on the development of participant observation in organisations.

In this chapter I will explore the relevance of ethnography to HRD practice by illustrating how it offers the ability to gain a deeper understanding of the ways people make sense of their organisations. Drawing on three examples of arts organisations that faced significant non-routine change as a result of financial crises, I will discuss the ethnographic process and how it offered insights into the cultures of the organisations involved that I might not otherwise have gained.

I then consider the relative strengths and limitations of ethnography in relation to HRD research. I will particularly highlight what it means to expose the lives of others and yourself in your research and writing. It is one thing to talk about your lived experiences; it is something quite different to see your words and world recorded in black and white. I conclude with some thoughts about the benefits of using ethnography within the HRD field and offer some alternative ways that you might engage with the 'spirit of ethnography' (Zickar and Carter, 2010) if a full blown ethnographic study is not feasible but you still wish to access some of its benefits.

CULTURE-STUDYING CULTURE

Becoming an Ethnographer

You have to learn how to do fieldwork
Fieldwork is a difficult subject

You have to learn how to write
Writing ethnography is difficult to learn

You have to learn who you are as a fieldworker, writer, self
Learning who you are is difficult

You have to learn how and where things are meaningfully connected
Learning to understand meaningful connections is difficult

The goal of fieldwork is to recognise patterns
The goal of writing ethnography is to express them[1]

Ethnography (Greek ἔυυος *ethnos* = people and γράφειυ *graphein* = writing) is based within a qualitative research tradition, and what makes the approach distinct is 'the matter of interpreting and applying the findings from a *cultural perspective.*' (Patton, 2002: 84). The researcher is therefore interested in taking a holistic view and understanding how people interact in their own environments. It 'bears a close resemblance to the routine ways in which people make sense of the world in everyday life' (Hammersley and Atkinson, 1995: 2) and takes as its guiding assumption that 'any human group of people interacting together for a period of time will evolve a culture' (Patton, 2002: 81). Ethnography could therefore be described as a 'culture-studying culture' (Spradley, 1979: 9).

The literal meaning of ethnography has been somewhat surpassed by two other meanings (Yanow, Ybema and van Hulst, 2012: 331). The second meaning comes in the form of ethnography being a set of methods or research strategy, often referred to as fieldwork. This aspect is generally associated with the role of the researcher as a participant-observer, a role that can range on a spectrum from purely observer to purely participant. The third meaning of the term derives from the general orientation of ethnography 'towards the social world – actors, (inter)actions, settings' (Yanow et al., 2012). My experience is that all three meanings give ethnography its characteristics:

a research process involving *fieldwork methods* engaging the extraordinary-in-the-ordinary with a particular sensibility towards often more hidden or concealed meaning-making processes, reported in a *particular form of writing* that places both author and reader at the scene, in the thick of things, through actor-centred and context-sensitive analysis and theorizing grounded in layered data. (Yanow et al., 2012: 332)

Ethnographic research can be conducted from either a realist–objectivist or a constructivist–interpretivist perspective. From a realist–objectivist position ethnographers can seek to discover what is 'really happening' in particular organisations or settings. In taking this perspective the researcher views themselves as an objective, independent observer. Alternatively, the researcher may regard reality as socially constructed and as such the research process becomes one of co-construction and interpretation; there is no single reality or truth to be uncovered and the researcher is not an objective distanced observer. Interpretive ethnography aims to surface what the researcher brings to the field socially, culturally, psychologically and politically, encouraging the ethnographer to make his or her work 'personal, interactive and self-reflexive' (Goodall, 2003). In adopting this interpretative approach, ethnography is concerned with an inductive rather than a deductive process.

IN THE THICK OF IT

My experience of ethnography involved researching three organisations over a three-year period. While I will explore the phases I experienced in doing ethnography (Figure 6.1), it is done so with a caveat: although there are a number of core elements, each experience will differ and as such this is not intended to be an n-step 'how to' guide. It is a sharing of my experience from which I hope you may gain some useful insights. Effectively the process moves from some initial sensitising concepts to the world of social experience that in turn shapes your final conceptual framework and the written artefact.

The starting point, as with other research approaches, is a clear research question; this will help shape the direction the research will take as well as providing a good test for whether ethnography is the right approach for you. The organisations I studied faced existence-threatening decline as a result of financial crises, and I was interested in exploring the culture of corporate turnaround and the nature of organisational learning in this context. Ethnography offered an approach that could take account of the collective experience of these organisations, 'the importance of understanding culture, especially in relation to change efforts of all kinds, is the cornerstone of "applied ethnography"' (Chambers, 2000).

In considering learning during an organisational crisis, what appeared

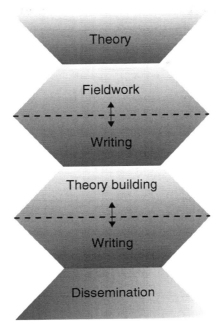

*Figure 6.1   Ethnographic research as a process of expanding and
contracting*

to be needed was an approach to investigating turnarounds that should
'aim to *unpack* the important elements of content, context and process'
(Pandit, 2000: 52).

Theory was a vexed question for me in relation to the early stages of
my research with regard to how much of a literature review I did before I
entered the field. As this will also be informed by your research perspective, it may be less of an issue if you are taking a realist–objectivist rather
than a constructivist–interpretivist position. As mine was an interpretive
study I researched some theory around insolvency and organisational
learning but regarded these as sensitising frameworks (Blumer, 1954) to
ensure they were held lightly while I was doing my fieldwork to safeguard
against them unduly influencing my observations.

Ethnography commonly calls for the researcher to undertake periods
of participant observation – to be there in the field and to be there long
enough to be able to understand the 'common sense, everyday, unwritten
and unspoken, tacitly known rules of engagement' (Yanow et al., 2012:
332). Negotiating access is something that can take time and may result
in a few false starts. This is usually done through a researcher's existing

networks, but it is worth bearing in mind that it may be possible for others to identify the organisation/s you study if they know you well, something to consider when you think about the dissemination of your research. My experience suggests that it is never too early to start writing: keep a journal, memos and fieldnotes from the very beginning – at the heart of the ethnographic approach is the writing.

Once you have agreed where your research will take place be ready for surprises when you enter the field. I found with one of my organisations that their office space was so compact that it was almost impossible for my presence to go unnoticed.

They also had an expectation that my research would include formal interviews, but there was nowhere in the building these could easily take place.

> We find our seats in the small café, and order our drinks. Coffee for him and cranberry juice for me. We have to meet here because the offices are too small and busy for a quiet conversation between the two of us. I produce my digital voice recorder and ask if he is comfortable if our conversation is recorded, he confirms it is okay. We chat casually as I set up the mic on the table. I am thankful for the advances in technology that allow the recorder and mic to be so small, smaller than an iPod.
>
> My experience from other interviews is that the devices will soon disappear from our awareness. We amiably catch up on recent events, common acquaintances and recent exhibitions, friendly and relaxed. The recorder goes on, it captures the arrival of our drinks, and we shift our positions slightly. A sign that we consider the 'proper' interview has begun.

Deciding how long to stay in the field can be difficult and may ultimately be determined by practicalities – how long the organisation is willing to grant you access, how much time you have available and so on. Although analysis is shown as a separate stage (Figure 6.1), it is likely this will also be occurring while you are still in the field; there will not necessarily be a clear division between the phases. You will be asking yourself questions in the field that are likely to inform the conclusions you draw later. Once you have left the field you will need to be systematic in dealing with the extensive data you have most likely gathered. This will also be the point when you return to theory in depth.

> I survey the dining room table, which is smothered with papers and books, with dismay . . . It was not the transcripts and the other documents themselves that bothered me so much as the complexities and contradictions I knew they contained. The voices of my participants chattered in my head.

Analysis can take many forms and will probably involve some form of coding; it can range from broad extrapolation to detailed computer aided analysis dependent on your approach. This is the point where you spot patterns and look to build themes from them, from which your theories will flow. A pattern can have a number of characteristics (Hatch, 2002):

- Similarities
- Differences
- Frequency
- Sequence
- Correspondence
- Causation

Inevitably, written representations of the ethnographic process appear neater and more orderly than you are likely to experience. The act of writing is smoothing in its nature; it is important not to underestimate the intertwined nature of the process and you may find yourself looping back or running stages in parallel. From my perspective this was one of the big challenges, but it was also part of its attraction: the dynamic interplay between practice and theory, data collection and analysis, and whether a written text could come close to representing cultures.

GAINING ON THE ROUNDABOUTS AND LOSING ON THE SWINGS

Thinking about ethnographic research in terms of its advantages and disadvantages frames this complex practice in terms of rational choices that do not necessarily sit comfortably with the experience of ethnography.

The relative value of ethnography will also be dependent on the sort of research question that you are trying to address; it may therefore be more productive to consider what it does well and less well and to reflect on how this relates to your own strengths and limitations as a researcher and the nature of your research.

Ethnography is unlikely to provide findings that can be generalised to a wider population. If this is your intention, other approaches will be more appropriate. This could be regarded as both one of its limitations and one of its strengths, as the notion of generalisation has attracted criticism from within social science: 'the approach of positivistic research to generalisation has been to abstract from context, average out cases, lose sight of the world as lived by human beings, and generally make the knowledge gained impossible to apply' (Greenwood and Levin, 2005: 55).

Through my research I endeavoured to open up the context and culture of the organisations I worked with, getting closer to the unwritten and unspoken and trying to build an 'understanding of the way things are done around here' (Levitt and March, 1988: 132). As such it is more relevant to think in terms of extrapolation and transferability than generalisability, where 'extrapolations are modest speculations on the likely applicability of findings to other situations under similar, but not identical, conditions' (Patton, 2002: 584). On this basis the work of transferability or 'naturalistic generalisation' (Stake, 1995) is left to the reader, whereby he/she takes on the narrative description to form vicarious experience that then works with 'existing propositional knowledge to modify existing generalisations' (Stake, 1995: 86).

In addressing issues of culture, a further strength of the ethnographic approach is that it encompasses 'not only language, acts and interactions, but also the "things" that are part and parcel of what we do, where we do it and about which we speak' (Yanow, 2012: 34). On this basis it does not privilege either discourse or materiality but acknowledges the importance of the settings in which our interactions take place. In my own research, the centrality of the buildings in which the artistic practices occurred became a core theme in understanding how the culture/s of each organisation had evolved and were enacted.

THE RESEARCHER–PARTICIPANT RELATIONSHIP – MANAGING A BETRAYAL

We sit around tables in a large hotel conference room that could be anywhere in the world. A densely patterned carpet, bland walls and generic hotel 'art'. It is not unpleasant just characterless. There are ten of us around the table, slightly lost in what is a very big space, eight PhDs and the two established academics guiding us. In a respectful manner we are turn taking, each outlining our research and getting feedback from the group. The young man next to me is further ahead than most of us. His fieldwork is done and he is well into his analysis. He tells us none too complimentary stories of the organisation that acted as his host. I wonder about what he is telling us and what his hosts might say if they heard his opinions. I ask naively, 'what did they say when you talked about your findings?' He looks me straight in the eye, apparently a little shocked, 'Oh I haven't been back there, I'm not going to be sharing any of this with them.' There is a short silence and someone asks another question.

Ensuring that research participants are fully aware in a 'comprehensive and accurate way' (Hammersley and Atkinson, 1995: 264) of the research in which they are involved, usually referred to as informed consent, is an important factor to consider in ethnography. In practice this is not easy, and like the research itself it is also grounded in the cultures of those involved. One of my research participants was visibly shocked when I suggested signing a research consent form. From her perspective the rapport we had built meant this was an unnecessary, almost insulting requirement.

It is this notion of rapport building that raises a number of issues in the writing of ethnography. A few years ago, during an ethnography course I attended, Gideon Kunda (2006; see also Kunda and Van Maanen, 1999) talked to us about his work as an ethnographer in organisational settings and, although I am now no longer sure he said this explicitly, I interpreted the essence of what he said as being 'ethnography is a relationship with betrayal built in'. That is, however hard we try, the relationship between researcher and research participants ultimately leads to a sense that the trust inherent in building rapport is broken. What he seemed to be referring to was the issue that at some point the relationships we build and conversations we have as researchers would be exposed in the writing up of the ethnography.

However much we prepare our participants for what is to come, and often we may not know ourselves until the writing is well underway, what emerges in the text and our participant's self-image may well not align. It can be the case that ethnographies arouse strong responses not because they are accurate but because they do not match the idealised views participants may hold of themselves and their communities (Warren, 1980). The residents of 'Plainville' developed a betrayal discourse around James West's book about their community; 'this enabled many of the people to admit that West's analysis was essentially correct and at the same time strongly criticize him and his book because the latter "didn't go far enough," that is, it did not include their own self-image' (Gallagher, 1964: 294).

Ethnographers would, I am sure, argue that they take a careful and considered approach to their writing up, but nonetheless it is not always possible to pre-empt the response of our participants to reading what has been re-presented.

Notwithstanding the debate on whether participants should be shown the final ethnographic writing in the first place, we cannot avoid the issue by assuming they will not read what is produced.

In their aptly named paper, 'But I thought we were friends . . .', Beech, Hibbert, MacIntosh and McInnes (2009) outline the requirement for a researcher to build a subjective connection with their participants, and therein is created a significant challenge; this leads us squarely to the fact that 'we must address the issue of writing "right" but doing wrong to those who host us' (Ellis, 1995: 69).

While many have written on the ethics of ethnography (Dingwall, 1980; Goodwin, Pope, Mort and Smith, 2003; Hammersley and Atkinson, 1995;

Murphy and Dingwall, 2007), and some have explored the implications of writing (Bettrell, 1996; Ellis, 1995), this notion of betrayal does not seem to have been covered. I have found it useful to turn to the field of life writing, as there seem to be some parallels with the challenges faced by ethnographic researchers and auto/biographical writers in dealing with the relationship implications of writing the lives of those around us. Mills (2004) makes her position on the dilemma clear: '. . . to be a friend is to stand in a relationship of trust, for the sake of one's friend; to be a writer is to stand ready to violate that trust for the sake of one's story' (Mills, 2004: 105).

DISCUSSION

> Examining areas of practice that are in need of greater understanding is vital to the continued effectiveness of HRD research and practice. (Torraco, 2004: 184)

HRD is arguably an applied discipline and as such it is in need of research that can address gaps along the applied and theoretical continuum (Torraco, 2004), that is, it calls for research that has the capacity to both contribute to knowledge and advance the profession. Ethnography is well placed to respond to this need in that it originates within practice in the field and then provides the capacity for theory building. From the deep qualitative insights gained in organisations ethnography allows for the development of theory that is arguably both accurate and tentative (Dyer and Wilkins, 1991).

While the rich description of ethnographic writing may not lead directly to generalisable results, it does offer the potential for pattern recognition, which, as Gregory Bateson (2002) put it, is the basis of all human communication – it 'requires the application of disciplined imagination to personal experience' (Goodall, 2000: 8). Ethnographic research is an approach that can recognise the cultural complexity of organisations and attempts not to uproot those complexities from their context as is the case with other methodologies.

The potential benefits of using an ethnographic approach will in part be determined by your perspective; from the realist–objectivist point of view ethnography allows you to impartially observe what is really happening in the field. To be able to see what people are actually doing as opposed to what they might say they are doing in the workplace, comparing espoused theory with theory-in-use. (Argyris, 1976). In taking a constructivist–interpretative perspective you will be able to explore meaning making and culture and consider the multiple viewpoints at work; how that culture is created symbolically and through discourse.

Undertaking ethnographic research in HRD does have a number of practical consequences, not least negotiating access and managing the sheer volume of data. I would suggest there are options that may help address these challenges while allowing you to still 'channel the spirit of ethnography' (Zickar and Carter, 2010):

- *Read ethnographies:* there are now a wide range of ethnographic studies in the HRD field and these may offer the 'vicarious experience' and adaptation of existing propositional knowledge as suggested by Stake (1995) in relation to the issue you wish to research.
- *Consider new methods – virtual ethnography:* this relies on the ethnographer being a virtual participant observer in chat rooms, group blogs, social networks and discussion boards. These can cover a whole range of workplace experiences from bullying and union membership through to redundancy and retirement. Although they still require a commitment over time, this may be a more accessible form for some researchers.
- *Collaborate with ethnographers:* if access, time or your epistemological preferences create difficulties you may wish to consider partnering with an ethnographer. This could also allow for the development of a more mixed methods approach.
- *Utilise the spirit of ethnography:* engage with people in the settings you are studying before you start other forms of research. Utilise your participant-observation skills when you are working with organisations, building your depth of insight and avoiding what I would regard as the dangers of becoming increasingly distanced from your participants.

While these alternatives cannot replace the rich experience of working in the field, I appreciate that for various reasons this is not feasible for everyone. Hopefully, these suggestions offer some other possibilities for benefitting from the strengths of ethnographic research.

[E]thnographers share a *common goal:* to learn from the people (the insiders) *what counts as cultural knowledge* (insider meanings). (Green, Skukauskaite and Baker, 2012: 309)

NOTE

1. Found poem based on Goodall (2000: 7–8). Found poems take existing texts and rework them into a form of literary collage. The words and their order generally remain true to the text but are then shaped according to the poet.

REFERENCES

Argyris, C. (1976). Theories of Action that Inhibit Individual Learning. *American Psychologist, 31*(9), 638–654.

Bateson, G. (2002). *Mind and Nature* (5th edn). Glasgow: Fontana/Collins.

Beech, N., Hibbert, P., MacIntosh, R. and McInnes, P. (2009). But I Thought We Were Friends? Life Cycles and Research Relationships. In S. Ybema, D. Yanow, H. Wels and F. Kamsteeg (Eds.), *Organizational Ethnography: Studying the Complexities of Everyday Life* (pp. 196–214). London: Sage.

Bettrell, C. B. (Ed.) (1996). *When They Read What We Write: The Politics of Ethnography*. Westport, CT: Bergin and Garvey.

Blumer, H. (1954). What Is Wrong with Social Theory? *American Sociological Review, 19*(1), pp. 3–10.

Chambers, E. (2000). Applied Ethnography. In N. K. Denzin and Y. S. Lincoln (Eds.), *Handbook of Qualitative Research* (pp. 851–869). Thousand Oaks, CA: Sage.

Clair, R. P. (Ed.) (2003). *Expressions of Ethnography: Novel Approaches to Qualitative Methods*. Albany, NY: State University of New York Press.

Dewald, J. (Ed.) (2004). *Europe 1450–1789. Encyclopedia of the Early Modern World, Vol. 2: Cologne to Fur Trade*. London: Thomson Gale.

Dingwall, R. (1980). Ethics and Ethnography. *Sociological Review, 28*(4), 871–891.

Dyer, W. G. and Wilkins, A. L. (1991). Better Stories, Not Better Constructs, to Generate Better Theory: A Rejoinder to Eisenhardt. *Academy of Management Review, 16*(3), 613–619.

Ellis, C. (1995). Emotional and Ethical Quagmires in Returning to the Field. *Journal of Contemporary Ethnography, 24*(1), 68–98.

Gallagher, A. Jr (1964). Plainville: The Twice-Studied Town. In A. Viditch, J. Bensman and M. Stein (Eds.), *Reflections on Community Studies* (pp. 285–304). New York: Wiley.

Goodall, H. L. Jr (2000). *Writing the New Ethnography*. Oxford: AltaMira Press.

Goodall, H. L. (2003). What Is Interpretive Ethnography? In P. Clair (Ed.), *Expressions of Ethnography* (pp. 55–63). Albany, NY: State University of New York Press.

Goodwin, D., Pope, C., Mort, M. and Smith, A. (2003). Ethics and Ethnography: An Experiential Account. *Qualitative Health Research, 13*(4), 567–577.

Green, J. L., Skukauskaite, A. and Baker, D. B. (2012). Ethnography as Epistemology: An Introduction to Educational Ethnography. In J. Arthur, M. J. Waring, R. Coe and L. V. Hedges (Eds.), *Research Methods and Methodologies in Education* (pp. 309–321). London: Sage.

Greenwood, D. J. and Levin, M. (2005). Reform of the Social Sciences, and of Universities through Action Research. In N. K. Denzin and Y. S. Lincoln (Eds.), *The Sage Handbook of Qualitative Research* (3rd edn, pp. 43–64). London: Sage.

Hammersley, M. and Atkinson, P. (1995). *Ethnography: Principles in Practice* (2nd edn). London: Routledge.

Hatch, J. A. (2002). *Doing Qualitative Research in Education Settings*. Albany, NY: State University of New York Press.

Kunda, G. (2006). *Engineering Culture: Control and Commitment in a High-Tech Corporation* (Revised edn). Philadelphia: Temple University Press.

Kunda, G. and Van Maanen, J. (1999). Changing Scripts at Work: Managers and Professionals. *The ANNALS of the American Academy of Political and Social Science, 561*(1), 64–80.

Levitt, B. and March, G. (1988). Organizational Learning. *Annual Review of Sociology, 14*, pp. 319–340.

Mills, C. (2004). Friendship, Fiction, and Memoir: Trust and Betrayal in Writing from One's Own Life. In P. J. Eakin (Ed.), *The Ethics of Life Writing* (pp. 101–120). London: Cornell University Press.

Murphy, E. and Dingwall, R. (2007). The Ethics of Ethnography. In P. Atkinson, A. Coffey,

S. Delamont, J. Lofland and L. Lofland (Eds.), *Handbook of Ethnography* (pp. 339–351). London: Sage.

Pandit, N. (2000). Some Recommendations for Improved Research on Corporate Turnaround. *M@n@gement*, *3*(2), 31–56.

Patton, M. Q. (2002). *Qualitative Research and Evaluation Methods* (3rd edn). London: Sage.

Salemink, O. (2003). *The Ethnography of Vietnam's Central Highlanders: A Historical Contextualisation 1850–1900*. London: Routledge.

Spradley, J. P. (1979). *The Ethnographic Interview*. Belmont, CA: Wadsworth Group/ Thomson Learning.

Stake, R. E. (1995). *The Art of Case Study Research*. London: Sage.

Torraco, R. J. (2004). Challenges and Choices for Theoretical Research in Human Resource Development. *Human Resource Development Quarterly*, *15*(2), 171–188.

Vermeulen, H. F. (2008). *Early History of Ethnography and Ethnology in the German Enlightenment: Anthropological Discourse in Europe and Asia*. Doctoral thesis, University of Leiden, the Netherlands.

Warren, C. A. B. (1980). Data Presentation and the Audience: Responses, Ethics, and Effects. *Journal of Contemporary Ethnography*, *9*(3), 282–308.

Yanow, D. (2012). Organizational Ethnography between Toolbox and World-Making. *Journal of Organizational Ethnography*, *1*(1), 31–42.

Yanow, D., Ybema, S. and van Hulst, M. (2012). Practising Organizational Ethnography. In G. Symon and C. Cassell (Eds.), *Qualitative Organizational Research: Core Methods and Current Challenges* (pp. 331–350). London: Sage.

Zickar, M. J. and Carter, N. T. (2010). Reconnecting with the Spirit of Workplace Ethnography: A Historical Review. *Organizational Research Methods*, *13*(2), 304–319.

ANNOTATED FURTHER READING

Goodall, H. L. Jr (2000). *Writing the New Ethnography*. Oxford: AltaMira Press. This book gives an overview of the creative processes involved in writing ethnography. It includes examples, advice and exercises to support the development of your ethnographic writing.

Wolcott, H. F. (2005). *The Art of Fieldwork*, (2nd edn), Oxford: AltaMira Press. Based on Wolcott's extensive experience, this is a very readable and open presentation of some of the core issues involved in undertaking fieldwork. It covers fieldwork as art and science, epistemology and technique.

Ybema, S., Yanow, D., Wells, H. and Kamsteeg, F. (Eds.). (2009). *Organizational Ethnography: Studying the Complexities of Everyday Life*. London: Sage. A comprehensive overview of the distinct contribution of the ethnographic approach to organizational studies.

7. In (re)search of the self: autoethnography in HRD research
Sally Sambrook

SUMMARY

Written as an autoethnography, this chapter examines how an HRD researcher can consider his/her own role, bringing personal insight and understanding to wider cultural, sociological issues associated with the complex context of higher education. The aim is to demonstrate, disseminate and celebrate the value of this controversial qualitative methodology.

INTRODUCTION

In this chapter I offer an innovative qualitative perspective on Human Resource Development (HRD) research, employing autoethnography. Autoethnography can be defined as 'research (graphy) that connects the personal (auto) to the cultural (ethnos), placing the self within a social context' (Reed-Danahay 1997: 145). The precise nature varies, depending on which of these elements is in focus (Wall 2006). I examine how an HRD researcher can consider his/her own role, bringing personal insight and understanding to wider cultural, sociological issues associated with the complex context of higher education, a site of HRD practice (Sambrook and Stewart 2010). My aim is to demonstrate, disseminate and celebrate the value of this controversial qualitative methodology. Cunliffe et al. (2009) warn that the more 'sophisticated' a qualitative methodology the more it courts a double marginalization . . . and risks telling its tales to itself' (p. 6). I tell my tales of autoethnography in HRD research to open up debate and resist such marginalisation.

The chapter is presented as an autoethnography, as I tell a personal story to illuminate one aspect of HRD practice in higher education – doctoral supervision. I offer evocative personal examples (from emails, conversations, articles and conference papers etc.), theorising my experiences in a 'narrative sandwich' (Ellis 2004: 98). First, I establish the research context (HRD in higher education) and articulate how I have experienced this. Next, I introduce autoethnography. It is beyond the scope of the chapter to offer a comprehensive exposition of this innovative qualitative method, but I share a personal narrative of my experiences and consider the advantages and disadvantages, for student and supervisor. I then share three ways in which we can better understand HRD research through telling, showing and doing autoethnography in doctoral supervision. Finally, as part of the discussion, I offer some conclusions.

HRD CONTEXT: DOCTORAL SUPERVISION AS HRD PRACTICE IN HIGHER EDUCATION

Let me begin with me – the auto! I am a former nurse, involved in training nurses, and now professor of HRD. I have always been curious to learn and understand my self in my research. My research interests include all aspects of supporting learning, and particularly learning within the doctoral supervisory relationship, which I argue is a form of HRD. This relationship is crucial (Sambrook et al. 2008; Doloriert et al. 2012), and an important – and often ignored – element is the psychological contract between student and supervisor (Wade-Benzoni and Rousseau 1998). Considering the psychological contract alerts students and supervisors to our implicit assumptions and enables us to start to explore our selves and our unwritten expectations and obligations.

Why am I telling you this? Because I'd like you to know that I am acutely aware of my role as supervisor, the potential power I have in this relationship (Doloriert et al. 2012) and my impact on doctoral students. I do this realising that I might be exposing my own shortcomings and you might think less positively of me for this. Indeed, Humphreys (2005: 852) notes it is 'unusual for academics to expose their doubts, fears and potential weaknesses'. But this is something absolutely necessary in autoethnography! I think it is also essential in doctoral supervision. Lee (2008: 269) states that, 'Postgraduate supervision has essentially been a private act between consenting adults, and pressure to open this to observation will raise hackles as well as ethical issues, but it could provide . . . very helpful data.' By opening up my experiences to external observation, and by exposing some of my own doubts, fears and possible weaknesses, I might help students and supervisors understand their own concerns, choices and impact on their research.

Of course, so far, I have been talking about my role as supervisor, but there is often more than one person 'in charge' of doctoral students (Powell and Green 2007: 4), with supervisory teams. 'Teams often operate on implicit assumptions about roles which are not openly addressed'

(Clegg 1997: 490), creating further possible complexities regarding obligations and expectations. So, I am arguing that I need to understand my self, your self and our selves in HRD research.

So enough of me – let's turn to the ethnos, the cultural context of HRD research. In the UK, HRD is usually located in business schools, unlike schools of education in North America, for example. This British business context tends to sustain a highly managerialist curriculum and positivist research agenda. If we look at HRD in particular, we see much teaching and research considerably shaped by the Chartered Institute for Personnel and Development (CIPD), with its performative orientation and discourse (Lawless et al. 2011), although there are growing pockets of resistance through critical HRD (Sambrook 2004, 2009; Sambrook and Willmott 2014). HRD academics face considerable challenges, similar to those of HRD practitioners, with increasing emphasis on work intensification and pressures to perform (Forrester 2011). As academics this includes pressures to 'publish or perish' to comply with the Research Excellence Framework (REF) in the UK (Willmott 2011). These pressures can impinge on doctoral supervision, emphasising the importance of completions and co-authored publications. Halse and Malfroy (2010: 79) note, 'A competitive higher education environment marked by increased accountability and quality assurance measures for doctoral study has highlighted the need to clearly articulate and delineate the work of supervising doctoral students.' This is why I think understanding our selves in doctoral supervision is so important and can be achieved through autoethnography.

Authoethnography is not without difficulty in this context. As Hawawini (2005: 774) observed, 'The typical business school course (undergraduate, graduate and, to a lesser extent, executive education) is designed to impart a large dose of quantitative management skills and techniques.' So there is limited space for doing and/or teaching qualitative research, and it is difficult to gain credibility for innovative approaches such as autoethnography. Many academics are uncomfortable with any attempt to 'dethrone the demons of modernism, positivism and managerialism' (Parker 2002: 118). I suggest this quantitative domination also pervades HRD. Yet, Lee (2001) proposes a 'becoming' ontology of HRD, and 'becoming' is an emergent, complex process, difficult to reduce to a few variables and correlations. Critical HRD challenges the positivist hegemony, calling for more innovative methodologies such as autoethnography. So, what is autoethnography?

METHOD: THIS IS WHERE I EXPLAIN HOW WE 'DO' AUTOETHNOGRAPHY

Tracing the history of this innovative qualitative approach, Hayano (1979) introduced the term 'auto-ethnography', proposing that the main focus of the study is the *ethnos*, with the *auto* being something extra. Reed-Danahay (1997) more closely aligned the *auto* and *ethnos* using the term 'auto/ethnography' suggesting various combinations, and then Ellis and Bochner (2003) offered 'autoethnography', positioning the auto as the main focal point. Ellis and Bochner (2003: 209) describe autoethnography as an 'autobiographical genre of writing and research that displays multiple layers of consciousness, connecting the personal to the cultural'. Autoethnography encompasses various different ethnographic techniques that embrace the 'self' or 'I' (Ellis 2004) of research and 'lets you use yourself to get to the culture' (Pelias 2003: 372). So, I suggest autoethnography can help our selves better understand HRD in academic and other work organisation cultures.

The higher education 'culture' offers a variety of opportunities for conducting autoethnographic research, with academics telling their personal tales as early career lecturers (Pelias 2003) and senior academics (Sparkes 2007). Autoethnography is emerging as a legitimate method for exploring aspects of management learning (Bell and King 2010; Kempster and Stewart 2010; Sambrook and Willmott 2014), but with limited consideration of HRD.

'Autoethnography is one of the approaches that acknowledges and accommodates subjectivity, emotionality, and the researcher's influence on research, rather than hiding from these matters or assuming they don't exist' (Ellis et al. 2011: 2). Autoethnography therefore draws upon the self as a source of data, to understand a social phenomenon or culture beyond the individual person through analytical writing. The author is seen and heard in the text, not marginalised in an attempt to promote objectivity, and Sparkes (2002) considers that this is rare. Hopefully, you can see and hear me in this text!

Ellis et al. (2011: 6) state that doing autoethnography involves 'aesthetic and evocative thick descriptions of personal and interpersonal experience . . . patterns of cultural experience evidenced by field notes, interviews and/or artefacts, and then describing these patterns using facets of storytelling (e.g. character and plot development), showing and telling, and alterations of authorial voice'. Ellis et al. (2011) argue that instead of trying to insist our and others' values should be minimised, they should be centre stage. This could be very useful in HRD research, where we are attempting to learn about (individual) learning, a very

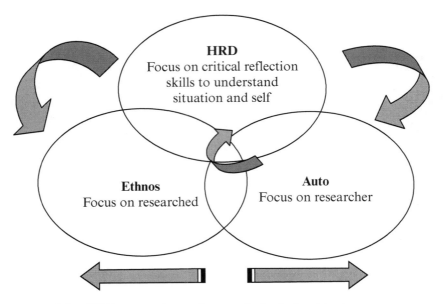

Figure 7.1   HRD, researcher and researched relationships in autoethnography

personal, subjective and value-laden activity within an organisational, cultural context.

Adapting earlier work (Doloriert and Sambrook 2009), HRD can be superimposed on the researcher–researched relationship to help the researcher and participants learn about themselves and their cultures, raising awareness of their roles and choices in decision-making and the impact of their actions in their organisations, whether in teaching, research or practice (Figure 7.1). This suggests a number of possible foci and combinations for HRD autoethnographies. For example, I consider my own role (auto) in doctoral supervision (HRD) within higher education (ethnos).

NOW I CONSIDER THE ADVANTAGES AND DISADVANTAGES OF AUTOETHNOGRAPHY

So, what are the debates and dilemmas surrounding autoethnography? Autoethnographies can be evocative (Ellis and Bochner 2006), analytic (Anderson 2006) or both (Learmonth and Humphreys 2012). Evocative autoethnographies stir our emotions and help us relate to particular social phenomena, such as the emotional struggles during doctoral research (Sambrook et al. 2008). Analytical autoethnographies rely more on precise analyses of cultural experiences, as encountered by participants and witnessed by the researcher themselves, such as integrating accounts of employee engagement in a case study organisation with the student's engagement with their doctoral research (Jones 2012). More recently, we can add radical-political autoethnographies (Holman-Jones 2005), which seek to expose inequalities and effect change, more aligned to critical HRD.

A key advantage of autoethnography is that it draws on various skills relevant to HRD, such as critical reflection (Reynolds 1999; Vince and Reynolds 2009), particularly reflecting on emotional and political dimensions of (experiential) learning and of HRD/managerial practice (Vince 1996), and reflexivity (Cunliffe 2002, 2009 a, b). These reflexive skills are pertinent to understanding our roles in facilitating all forms of learning and development and empathising with 'our' learners.

Autoethnography can help support attempts to introduce a more critical pedagogy in HRD education and research through encouraging more open dialogue and mutual learning between teachers and students, thereby opening up spaces to enable students to find and articulate their voice (Collin 1996). Autoethnography enables students to recollect and reflect on important events (often an 'epiphany'), either during their university studies and/or other cultural contexts, such as family, schooling and employment, for example. This provides opportunities to learn about themselves, about gender, power, illness, friendship, trust, conflict and other socio-cultural phenomena relevant to studying and practising HRD.

Much HRD research fails to acknowledge the role of the researcher in defining research questions, selecting research methods and analysing and interpreting data, and yet these all involve decisions, influenced by the researcher. There have been advances in our understanding of the role of the researcher's self, particularly in qualitative methods such as ethnography, although a crisis of representation still exists. To address this, some critical HRD researchers have developed autoethnographic approaches that explicitly include the researcher in the study, drawing on their own experiences to illuminate aspects of social phenomena under study and giving them voice in the research writing outputs (Lawless et al. 2012; Sambrook 2010).

Autoethnographic writing requires critical reflection and reflexivity, but these are not easily learned. Such reflective skills are important to HRD practitioners, but, in higher education, Armstrong (2008) notes how students often fail to contextualise their reflections in the wider socio-cultural, political and economic context and experience difficulty incorporating their self having been socialised to write in a more 'objective' way. Similarly, Crème and Lea (2008) advocate the need to put the 'I' back in academic writing. In my business school, students nervously question this style, 'but are you sure, is it really OK to use I', and I try to reassure them that yes, this *is* OK, but I can often see the apprehension, even incredulity, in their eyes. Inculcated with the dominant form of 'third person' writing, it is difficult to employ the first person, and confusion arises when different supervisors prefer different styles. This is where implicit assumptions and expectations should be made explicit to avoid ambiguity and/or conflict.

Fleming and Fullagar (2007) argue autoethnography offers supervisors a method to encourage students to write themselves into research and also make the reading–writing relations of knowledge production more transparent (Game 1991). The outputs are not 'anything goes' kinds of writing, or banal reminiscence, but a critically engaged and self-disciplined form of reflective analysis. Fleming and Fullagar (2007) also note that the process of supervising students using autoethnography is challenging because of the dual demands that creativity and rigour place on the creation of narrative. Autoethnography requires personal reflection and critical engagement while avoiding the trap of self-indulgent writing.

And perceived self-indulgence is our biggest enemy! Some deem autoethnography narcissistic (Coffey 1999; Delamont 2007), even academic 'wank' (Sparkes 2000). Atkinson (2006) argues autoethnography is merely a poor form of literary writing. Anderson (2006) claims it is nothing more than personal therapy for the researcher, whose stories are allowed to invade the spaces that should be occupied by others. These criticisms emanate from so-called authoethnographies that fail to connect the personal to the social, thus merely offering an anecdotal narrative with little or no contribution to sociological sense-making or theorising. This creates tensions for autoethnographers because our methodology does not fit within the conventional scientific mould (Doloriert and Sambrook 2011).

This raises the question of which criteria should be used to judge the quality of an autoethnography. Traditional qualitative criteria are often adapted from foundational ones for quantitative research, such as Lincoln and Guba's (1985) credibility, transferability, dependability and confirmability. However, Smith (1984: 390) states that 'what is clear . . . is that the assumptions of interpretive inquiry are incompatible with the desire for foundational criteria'. Bochner (2000) eschews positivist notions of quality and instead judges autoethnographies on the basis of key questions: is the work honest, does the author critique and show him/herself, is a sense of emotional epiphany gained and does the story enable the reader to understand and feel the experience it seeks to convey?

But can these satisfy university regulations (Doloriert and Sambrook 2011)? In the performative higher education culture, where there is pressure to publish in Association of Business Schools (ABS) 'top ranked' (usually positivist) journals and achieve PhD completions, autoethnography could be highly risky! Students might suffer conceptual broadsiding (Morse 2002) – moving away from the topic of study to some personal (self-indulgent?) issue(s). Their thesis might not be perceived to meet academic and/or autoethnography standards – whether by colleagues, examiners, journal editors or publishers. Can students persuade examiners that Bochner's criteria are appropriate to judge the doctoral thesis? From my experience, this is certainly possible (Sambrook 1998; Roberts 2007; Wainwright 2010, Jones 2012)!

Other issues concern the risk of harm to those identified (Ellis 2007), including the researcher's participants, the researcher and her family/ friends, who may all be (sometimes unintentionally) revealed. So, autoethnographic research is complex and difficult to master. Autoethnography can be learned from texts (such as Ellis 2004; Muncey 2010; Spry 2011), but none focus specifically on HRD, a gap I hope to bridge.

SO, SOME EXAMPLES OF HOW I'VE 'DONE' AUTOETHNOGRAPHIC HRD RESEARCH

I now illustrate the role for autoethnography in HRD research, drawing on evocative personal experiences and examples from my doctoral students. My own PhD was a reflexive thesis about HRD in the British National Health Service, but I struggled to find a way of writing it, as I 'confessed' in my doctoral narrative:

> I have searched for a term that could describe and explain my approach. . . . A review of the literature describing the 'reflective practitioner' . . . led me to the notion of myself as 'reflective researcher' – showing myself to myself. A further stage is showing myself to the reader . . . So in this thesis, I take a reflexive approach. (Sambrook 1998: 3)

Back then, I settled for terms such as 'reflective researcher' and 'reflexive approach', but felt that 'something' was missing. I only came to find this a few years later when I was teaching postgraduate research methods at the School of Nursing and stumbled upon autoethnography – which brilliantly captured that 'something' I was searching for. Soon afterwards, I had an uncomfortable incident with Clair, one of my 'business school' PhD students, at an HRD conference, and we worked through this problem employing autoethnography (Sambrook et al. 2008). I realised

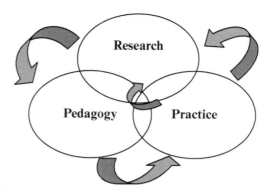

Figure 7.2   Three ways of using autoethnography in HRD doctoral supervision

how valuable autoethnography was in doctoral supervision. It was this painful experience that galvanised my appreciation of the important powerful and emotional relationship between student and supervisor. Not long after that, Delia, one of the nursing MSc students, embarked on a PhD exploring the psychological contracts of health and social care employees, which explicitly raised the notion of a psychological contract within our doctoral supervisory relationship – and thus became an autoethnography (Wainwright 2010).

I have come to realise there are opportunities for using autoethnography in doctoral supervision in three ways: telling (teaching the method = pedagogy), showing (examples of practice) and doing (research supervision), illustrated in Figure 7.2.

The first way is to explicitly teach autoethnography in doctoral training programmes (pedagogy), telling students about the method. Sometimes it is difficult to find 'space' in the curriculum, usually packed with positivist practices, but I have been fortunate to lead sessions on ethnography and introduce autoethnography as a more contemporary form. It's quite amusing to see some 'detached, objective' students' eyes glaze over as I ask them to consider their 'self' in their research!

As well as explaining various aspects of methodology, the PhD programme provides a second way of incorporating autoethnography, offering an opportunity to present more qualitative approaches and examples from HRD practice – to counteract the school's dominant positivist orientation – and showcase (or *show*) our own research. Here, I am not only using autoethnography but showing doctoral students personal and sometimes painful examples of revealing and reflecting on problematic aspects of research and academia (e.g. Humphreys 2005; Learmonth and

Humphreys 2012; Pelias 2003). Let's return to Delia and another 'incident' that could potentially wreck the supervisory relationship! I had been granted a sabbatical but had failed to fully consider and clearly articulate the implications for supervision.

> Well, a breach of our psychological contract? This is interesting! I did feel 'guilty' going on sabbatical, but I had earned it! D talked of me being busy/ crazy at work and just before I left, I thought I might have cracked! But, although I was going to be physically away, I always intended to retain regular email contact – and I thought I did. I counted up the number of emails I sent and it was a long list. My husband kept saying 'you're on sabbatical – you don't need to do this kind of work!' 'But I need to, I said I would and I feel I need to – it's only fair. She is my PhD student after all and that's legitimate work even when I'm on sabbatical'. (Sambrook 2010: 14)

I use this event to demonstrate to doctoral students some of the dangers of relying on only one supervisor, even when we have moved to team supervision. It also reveals the importance of talking through the implicit and dynamic supervisory contract, surfacing hidden expectations and assumed obligations from both student and supervisor perspectives.

The third way of employing autoethnography is through research supervision itself. Although I often suggest autoethnography to students, I am mindful of my powerful position and endeavour not to coerce students into adopting this approach. PhD students need to 'find' the intellectual idea for their autoethnography:

> Clair's study focussed on the interrelationships between corporate entrepreneurship and learning. Framing herself as a *knowledge entrepreneur* working in a large bureaucratic public sector organisation (her university), Clair wanted to use her journey of learning and innovation to better understand and enrich her study of other public sector *corporate entrepreneurs* and how they learned. She did not view herself and her role as distanced and detached from that of her research subjects. Like Sally, she saw her role and her interactions as subjective and reflexive. Clair recognised that her personal journey of knowledge discovery was inextricably interwoven with her research into entrepreneurship and knowledge discovery. (Doloriert and Sambrook 2011: 6)

Here, Clair clearly identifies the close link between her personal (auto) experiences and her participants' (ethnos). She is not privileging her own experiences (broadsiding her research topic), but using these to illuminate insightful aspects of the research culture.

When students embrace this approach, I am happy to work – and write – with them to craft collaborative (Sambrook et al. 2008) or co-produced (Kempster and Stewart 2010; Kempster and Izsatt-White 2013) autoethnographies. In collaborative autoethnographies, authors share

and synthesise experiences of some aspect of a mutual cultural phenomenon (e.g. Cohen et al. 2009; Bell and King 2010). For example, in my
incident with Clair, I turned to Jim Stewart (my own former doctoral
supervisor), and together we crafted our collaborative autoethnography.

> We each wrote our own narratives, individually. These were then collated and
> analysed, using thematic analysis, to identify any patterns in the 'data' and any
> similarities and differences. All three researchers had the opportunity to read
> each other's narrative and 'edit' these for this paper. An analysis of the ensuing
> three narratives provides insights into the complex, dynamic and, at times, dif-
> ficult nature of the supervisory relationship. (Sambrook et al. 2008)

In co-produced autoethnography, at least one writer/researcher is a
member of the organisational or management community of practice
(e.g. Kempster et al. 2008; Yarborough and Lowe 2007), but the story is
informed by dialogue with another author. For example, Orr and Bennett
(2012) employ an autoethnographic approach to explore the struggles they
faced in becoming co-researchers as academic and practitioner. I can also
offer an example from a collaborative autoethnography (Wainwright and
Sambrook 2009), written with Delia, who was exploring the psychological
contract of health and social care employees in her workplace. I had supervised Delia's MSc in Health and Social Care Leadership but it wasn't until
half way through her first year of her PhD that I emailed her:

> Hi D
> I've been thinking and wondered if there was a psychological contract in our
> doctoral supervisory relationship? This could run parallel with your study of
> the PC [psychological contract] at work and would make a fabulous autoeth-
> nography. (I can dig out some articles for you on this if you like.) Anyway just
> a thought . . .

> Hi Sal
> Interesting idea, I had actually thought about some of this when I was review-
> ing my reflexive notes I have been keeping about the whole research process. I
> have also been considering taking an autoethnographic approach. Please do dig
> out any articles that might be useful. I am reading the Ellis and Bochner book at
> the moment. Interesting stuff. (Wainwright and Sambrook 2009: 4)

Delia and I were collaboratively synthesising our mutual experiences
of the implicit contract within our doctoral supervisory relationship.
However, when Delia wrote about her psychological contract in her
own workplace, she engaged in dialogic learning with me to create a co-
produced autoethnography of a cultural phenomenon I had not experienced (Wainwright and Sambrook 2010).

Delia had actively and enthusiastically considered an autoethnographic approach. However, other students are not so eager! Natalie, one of my recent PhD students (co-supervised with Clair), provides a vivid example of palpable trepidation with the thought of autoethnography. When I suggested this approach early in our supervisory relationship, she quickly retorted, 'I don't want to get involved in any sort of that stuff'. However, her attitude slowly, silently shifted and after 18 months, as we met for our monthly supervisory meeting, she quietly enquired, 'I'm a bit confused – am I doing ethnography or autoethnography?' After briefly summarising the differences, and particularly the need to connect personal (auto) and ethnos aspects of her intellectual idea, she immediately replied, 'Oh, I'm definitely doing auto!' Her intellectual idea was employee engagement and Natalie could relate this to her own personal engagement (and disengagement) in her previous employment. Natalie then talked of including material from family conversations and was warned of the dangers of conceptual broadsiding (Morse 2002), the need to seek consent – procedural and relational (Ellis 2007) – and consider the ethics of 'I' (Doloriert and Sambrook 2009). In her successful thesis (Jones 2012), she shares an early excerpt from her research journal: 'I met with Sally and Clair today and they were going on about autoethnography again. If they think I'm going to indulge in all that navel-gazing again, they've got another think coming. They don't know me.' Yet, having now written her autoethnography, she has expressed the intense meaning acquired in connecting personal aspects of her former managerial role, deep troubles in her experience of doing doctoral research and her findings of the wider managerial issues associated with her research topic. Her examiners were also impressed with her honest, authentic story.

DISCUSSION

Conscious of the word limit, I now have to close. I hope I have made some contributions illuminating the uses and issues of autoethnography in HRD research. I've indicated a number of qualities and skills involved in doing autoethnography, such as the self-awareness and confidence to draw on self as a source of data, since this can be exposing; the ability to develop thick descriptions of personal and interpersonal experience from field notes, interviews and/or artefacts; and critical reflection and reflexivity, which are not easily learned, to produce self-disciplined accounts. To read more about the practicalities, refer to Ellis's (2004) *The Ethnographic I*, Muncey's (2010) *Creating Autoethnographies* and Spry's (2011) *Body, Paper, Stage: Writing and Performing Autoethnography*, which provide rich explication.

Here, I have shown and shared three ways of employing autoethnography at doctoral level, but these could equally apply in undergraduate and postgraduate HRD research. I have provided examples of autoethnography in HRD research to demonstrate its value to both students and supervisors. For students, this creates opportunities to learn more about themselves through writing about their study and work experiences, illuminating issues of power, gender and other socio-cultural phenomena, all relevant to studying HRD. For supervisors, this enables academics to engage in co-produced autoethnographies for publication, and reflect on supervisory experiences to provide rich examples to students (Doloriert and Sambrook 2011). I have exposed some of the challenges for students (such as writing in the 'strange' first person and presenting an autoethnography as a doctoral thesis) and supervisors (fighting for space in the curriculum and defending its validity, credibility and utility to colleagues). I enthusiastically support students who seek deep understanding of themselves and their HRD/management practices and am inspired by one manager who turned to postgraduate study and found autoethnography (Gockel and Parry 2004): 'My search for an authentic research mode to understand me as a manager, a mode that will enable me to grow professionally, and a mode that will enable me to perform to my greatest capacity had finally ended.' I hope this has helped in your search for yourself! To conclude, talking about autoethnography with John Van Maanen at an ethnography conference, I vividly remember him smiling and saying 'Good luck!'

REFERENCES

Anderson, L. (2006) Analytic autoethnography, *Journal of Contemporary Ethnography*, 35 (4), 373–395.
Armstrong, P. (2008) Toward an autoethnographic pedagogy, Paper presented at the 38th Annual SCUTREA Conference, 2–4 July, University of Edinburgh.
Atkinson, P. (2006) Rescuing autoethnography, *Journal of Contemporary Ethnography*, 35 (4): 400–404.
Bell, E. and King, D. (2010) The elephant in the room: Critical management studies conferences as a site of body pedagogics, *Management Learning*, 41 (4), 429–442.
Bochner, A. (2000) Criteria against ourselves, *Qualitative Inquiry*, 6 (2), 226–272.
Clegg, S. (1997) A case study of accredited training for research awards supervisors through reflective practice, *Higher Education*, 34, 483–498.
Coffey, A. (1999) *The Ethnographic Self*. London: Sage.
Cohen, L., Dubberley, J. and Musson, G. (2009) Work–life balance? An autoethnographic exploration of everyday home–work dynamics, *Journal of Management Inquiry*, 18 (3), 229–241.
Collin, A. (1996) The MBA: The potential for students to find their voice in Babel, in R. French and C. Grey (eds) *Rethinking Management Education*. London: Sage, 132–151.

Crème, P. and Lea, M. (2008) *Writing at University: A Guide for Students* (3rd edn). Maidenhead, UK: Open University Press.

Cunliffe, A. L. (2002) Reflexive dialogical practice in management learning, *Management Learning*, 33 (1), 35–61.

Cunliffe, A. L. (2009a) The philosopher leader: On relationalism, ethics and reflexivity – a critical perspective to teaching leadership, *Management Learning*, 40 (1), 87–101.

Cunliffe, A. L. (2009b) Reflexivity, learning and reflexive practice, in S. J. Armstrong and C. V. Fukami (eds) *The SAGE Handbook of Management Learning, Education and Development*, London: Sage, 405–418.

Cunliffe A., Linstead, S. and Locke, K. (2009) Telling tales: Guest Editorial, *Qualitative Research in Organizations and Management: An International Journal*, 4, 5.

Delamont, S. (2007) Arguments against auto-ethnography, qualitative researcher, Issue 4 (ISSN: 1748-7315). Available at: http://www.cardiff.ac.uk/socsi/qualiti/QualitativeResearcher/QR_Issue4_Feb07.pdf (last accessed 20 July 2013).

Doloriert, C. and Sambrook, S. (2009) Ethical confessions of the 'I' of autoethnography: The student's dilemma, *Qualitative Research in Organizations and Management: Conference Special Issue*, 1 (1), 27–45.

Doloriert, C. and Sambrook, S. (2011) Accommodating an autoethnographic PhD: The tale of the thesis, the viva voce, and the traditional business school, *Journal of Contemporary Ethnography*, 40 (5), 582–615.

Doloriert, C., Sambrook, S. and Stewart, J. (2012) The power and emotion of doctoral supervision: Implications for HRD, *European Journal of Training and Development*, 36 (7), 732–750.

Ellis, C. (2004) *The Ethnographic I.* Walnut Creek, CA: AltaMira Press.

Ellis, C. (2007) Telling secrets, revealing lives: Relational ethics in research with intimate others, *Qualitative Inquiry*, 13 (3), 1–28.

Ellis, C., Adams, T. A. and Bochner, A. P. (2011) Autoethnography: An overview, *Forum: Qualitative Social Research*, 12 (1), Art. 10, January. Available at: http://www.qualitative-research.net/index.php/fqs/article/viewArticle/1589/3095 (last accessed 25 March 2013).

Ellis, C. and Bochner, A. P. (2003) Autoethnography, personal narrative, reflexivity: Researcher as subject, in N. K. Denzin and Y. S. Lincoln (eds) *Collecting and Interpreting Qualitative Materials* (2nd edn). Thousand Oaks, CA: Sage, 199–258.

Ellis, C. and Bochner, A. (2006) Analyzing analytic autoethnography: An autopsy, *Journal of Contemporary Ethnography*, 35 (4), 429–449.

Fleming. C. and Fullagar, S. (2007) Reflexive methodologies: An autoethnography of the gendered performance of sport/management, *Annals of Leisure Research*, Special Issue on Graduate Student Research Edited by Richard Pringle and Ruth Sibson, 10 (3–4), 238–256.

Forrester, J. (2011) Performance management in education: Milestone or millstone? *Management in Education*, 25 (1): 5–9.

Game, A. (1991) *Undoing the Social: Towards a Deconstructive Sociology.* Milton Keynes, UK: Open University Press.

Gockel, R. E. and Parry, K. W. (2004) Self-reflective management learning: Toward an autoethnographic approach, Paper submitted to ANZAM 2004 Conference, University of Otago, Dunedin, 8–11 December.

Halse, C. and Malfroy, J. (2010) Retheorizing doctoral supervision as professional work, *Studies in Higher Education*, 35 (1), 79–92.

Hawawini, G. (2005) The future of business schools, *Journal of Management Development*, 24 (9), 770–782.

Hayano, D. (1979) Auto-ethnography: Paradigms, problems and prospects, *Human Organization*, 38 (1), 99–103.

Holman-Jones, S. (2005) Autoethnography: Making the personal political, in N. K. Denzin and Y. S. Lincoln (eds) *The Sage Handbook of Qualitative Research* (3rd edn). Thousand Oaks, CA: Sage, 763–791.

Humphreys, M. (2005) Getting personal: Reflexivity and autoethnograhic vignettes, *Qualitative Inquiry*, 11 (6), 840–860.

Jones, N. (2012) *Full Circle: Employee Engagement in the Welsh Public Service*, Unpublished PhD thesis, Bangor University.

Kempster, S. and Izsatt-White, M. (2013) Towards co-constructed coaching: Exploring the integration of coaching and co-constructed autoethnography in leadership development, *Management Learning*, 44 (4), 319–336.

Kempster, S. and Stewart, J. (2010) Becoming a leader: A co-produced autoethnographic exploration of situated learning of leadership practice, *Management Learning*, 41 (5), 131–145.

Kempster, S., Stewart, J. and Parry, K. W. (2008) Exploring co-produced autoethnography, Working paper downloaded from http://epublications.bond.edu.business_pubs/112 (accessed 21 July 2011).

Lawless, A., Sambrook, S., Garavan, T. and Valentin, C. (2011) A discourse approach to theorising HRD: Opening up a discursive space, *Journal of European Industrial Training*, Special Issue, 35 (3), 264–275.

Lawless, A., Sambrook, S. and Stewart, J. (2012) Critical human resource development: Enabling alternative subject positions within a master of arts in human resource development educational programme, *Human Resource Development International*, 15 (3), 321–336.

Learmonth, M. and Humphreys, M. (2012) Autoethnography and academic identity: Glimpsing business school doppelgängers, *Organisation*, 19 (1), 99–117.

Lee, A. (2008) How are doctoral students supervised? Concepts of doctoral research supervision, *Studies in Higher Education*, 33 (3), 267–281.

Lee, M. (2001) A refusal to define HRD, *Human Resource Development International* 4 (3), 327–341.

Lincoln, Y. S. and Guba, E. G. (1985) *Naturalistic Inquiry*. Beverly Hills, CA: Sage.

Morse, J. M. (2002) Writing my own experience. . ., *Qualitative Health Research*, 12 (9), 1159–1160.

Muncey, T. (2010) *Creating Autoethnographies*, London: Sage.

Orr, K. and Bennett, M. (2012) Down and out at the British Library and other dens of co-production, *Management Learning*, 43 (4), 427–442.

Parker, M. (2002) *Against Management*. Cambridge: Polity Press.

Pelias, R. J. (2003) The academic tourist: An autoethnography, *Qualitative Inquiry*, 9 (3), 369–373.

Powell, S. D. and Green, H. (eds) (2007) *The Doctorate Worldwide*. Buckingham, UK: Open University Press.

Reed-Danahay, D. (1997) *Autoethnography: Rewriting the Self and the Social*. Oxford: Berg.

Reynolds, M. (1999) Grasping the nettle: Possibilities and pitfalls of a critical management pedagogy, *British Journal of Management*, 9, 171–184.

Roberts, C. (2007) *Intraprelearning within Two Welsh Trusts: An Autoethnography*, Unpublished PhD thesis, University of Wales.

Sambrook, S. (1998) *Models and Concepts of HRD: Academic and Practitioner Perspectives*, Unpublished PhD thesis, Nottingham Trent University.

Sambrook, S. (2004) A critical time for HRD, *Journal of European Industrial Training*, 28 (8/9), 611–624.

Sambrook, S. (2009) Critical HRD: A concept analysis, *Personnel Review*, 38 (1), 61–73.

Sambrook, S. (2010) Get me out of there – I'm on sabbatical! 5th Annual International Ethnography Symposium, Queen Mary, University of London, 1–3 September.

Sambrook, S. and Stewart, J. (2010) Teaching, learning and assessing HRD: Findings from a BMAF/UFHRD research project, *Journal of European Industrial Training*, Special Issue, 34 (8/9), 710–734.

Sambrook, S., Stewart, J. and Roberts, C. (2008) Doctoral supervision: A view from above, below and the middle, *Journal of Further and Higher Education*, 32 (1), 71–84.

Sambrook, S. and Willmott, H. (2014) The rigor of management education and the relevance of human resource development – natural partners or uneasy bedfellows in management practice? *Management Learning*, 45 (1), 39–56.

Smith, J. K. (1984) The problem of criteria for judging interpretive inquiry, *Educational Evaluation and Policy Practice*, 6 (4): 379–391.

Sparkes, A. C. (2000) Autoethnography and narratives of self: Reflections on criteria in action, *Sociology of Sport Journal*, 17 (1), 21–41.

Sparkes, A. C. (2002) Autoethnography: Self-indulgence or something more? in A. P. Bochner and C. Ellis (eds) *Ethnographically Speaking: Autoethnography, Literature and Aesthetic*. Walnut Creek, CA: AltaMira Press, 209–232.

Sparkes, A.C. (2007) Embodiment, academics, and the audit culture: A story seeking consideration, *Qualitative Research*, 7 (24), 521–550.

Spry, T. (2011) *Body, Paper, Stage: Writing and Performing Autoethnography*. Walnut Creek, CA: Left Coast Press, Inc.

Vince, R. (1996) Experiential management education and the practice of change, in R. French and C. Grey (eds) *Rethinking Management Education*. London: Sage, 111–131.

Vince, R. and Reynolds, M. (2009) Reflection, reflective practice and organizing reflection, in S. J. Armstrong and C. V. Fukami (eds) *The SAGE Handbook of Management Learning, Education and Development*. London: Sage, 89–103.

Wade-Benzoni, K. A. and Rousseau, D. M. (1998) Building relationships around tasks. Psychological contracting in faculty–doctoral student collaborations, Technical Paper, Heinz School of Public Policy Carnegie Mellon University, Pittsburgh, PA. Available from: www.heinz.cmu.edu/research/19abstract.pdf (last accessed 25 May 2009).

Wainwright, D. (2010) *An Autoethnographic Study of the Psychological Contracts of Health and Social Care Employees in a Learning Disability Service*, Unpublished PhD thesis, Bangor University.

Wainwright, D. and Sambrook, S. (2009) Working at it: Autoethnographic accounts of the psychological contract between a doctoral supervisor and supervisee, 4th Annual International Ethnography Symposium, Liverpool University, August.

Wainwright, D. and Sambrook, S. (2010) The ethics of data collection: Unintended consequences? *Journal of Health Organisation and Management*, 24 (3), 277–287.

Wall, S. (2006) An autoethnography on learning about autoethnography, *International Journal of Qualitative Methods*, 5 (2), 1–12.

Willmott, H. (2011) Journal list fetishism and the perversion of scholarship: Reactivity and the ABS list, *Organization*, 18 (4), 429–442.

Yarborough, J. and Lowe, K. (2007) Unlocking foreclosed beliefs: An autoethnographic story about a family business leadership dilemma, *Culture and Organisation*, 13 (3), 239–224.

ANNOTATED FURTHER READING

Sambrook, S., Stewart, J. and Roberts, C. (2008) Doctoral supervision: A view from above, below and the middle, *Journal of Further and Higher Education*, 32 (1), 71–84. An example of a collaborative autoethnography about difficulties in doctoral supervision from the perspective of a student, her supervisor and her supervisor's former supervisor.

Wainwright, D. and Sambrook, S. (2009) Working at it: Autoethnographic accounts of the psychological contract between a doctoral supervisor and supervisee, 4th Annual International Ethnography Symposium, Liverpool University, August.

Wall, S. (2006) An autoethnography on learning about autoethnography, *International Journal of Qualitative Methods*, 5 (2), 1–12. An insightful exposition of learning to do autoethnography from a student's perspective.

8. Opening the visual methods toolbox
Kate Black and Russell Warhurst

SUMMARY

This chapter overviews the different approaches to using visual methods in HRD research, offering a 'toolbox' from which HRD-researchers might select according to their research needs. We explore the different traditions of visual research design and methods, with a specific focus upon their practical application within the HRD research context.

INTRODUCTION

One of the most discernible developments in the field of qualitative research over the past decade has been the increased interest in the use and analysis of visual data. Visual approaches comprise a vast and diverse field, with visual data encompassing a myriad of forms ranging from photos, video, sketches and diagrams engendered specifically for research purposes, to naturally occurring visual facets of the physical world such as advertisements, graphs, maps, cartoons, symbols, specimens, cyber-graphics and graffiti. We can also extend this beyond such 'capturing' of the world, to include the reading of the naturally occurring, visually experienced environment and encounters.

Despite this sea of images that surround us, methods using images have received very limited attention in the Human Resource Development (HRD) research literature when compared with other, more conventional, research methods. Indeed, very few guides to their use currently exist. Therefore, the aim of this chapter is to review visual techniques and to assess their potential for HRD research. Intentionally, we do not discuss the philosophical debates surrounding visual research, nor its theoretical underpinnings. Rather, our emphasis is upon practical application. The intention is to provide an overview, a 'toolbox' from which researchers might choose according to their personal research needs. Therefore, we anticipate that this chapter will be of particular interest to HRD-researchers new to visual research, and those wishing to extend HRD understanding and practice through visual approaches. We explore the different methodological traditions of visual research designs and methods, offering specific examples of their use within the HRD research context. We then proceed to discuss some of the many approaches to visual data analysis. The chapter concludes by addressing the main short-comings of these approaches in HRD research. Whilst a range of visual methods is outlined, focus is upon that holding the most potential in HRD research, namely imagery. A second chapter follows this current chapter, providing a far more in-depth examination of one specific visual approach: photo-elicitation interviewing. This technique uses photos and/ or images to stimulate reflection upon, and discussion of, the topic under consideration within the interview.

Learning processes, non-formal and implicit to work processes and relationships, often go unnoticed by both learners and researchers (Eraut, 2000). Visual methods provide a means to explore these hidden experiences helping to make tacit facets of our worlds more explicit. Significantly, visual data can be far more interesting and stimulating for the researcher, participant and research reader/user. For the *participant*, images provide a means of expressing self-understanding and emotions, whilst also offer-ing them a 'louder voice' in the research process, prioritising their way of seeing (Warren, 2005, p.864). In helping to bridge the experiences of the researcher and the researched, images assist the *researcher* to see what they might not otherwise see. Through fostering different types of responses to those secured through conventional approaches, images present facets that might otherwise have been overlooked, providing opportunities for exploring taken-for-granted assumptions held by either party. This encourages the generation of richer, more nuanced data that better com-municates understanding of how people think about themselves and experience their worlds. Finally, for the *reader/user*, visual data offers a more persuasive and inclusive articulation of reality: of the conceptions and relations being discussed and the multiple voices evoked. This helps the reader to 'see' what we, the researchers, have 'seen'. Yet it is not just the eyes that 'see'. Visual data invokes other non-rational thoughts in the viewer, offering a more emotional, aesthetic and sensory experience than that achieved through traditional text-based HRD research.

However, visual methods have played only a minor role within the pre-dominantly 'word-based' organisational research (Bryman, 2008). Indeed, their use within HRD research remains scant, especially when compared, for example, with educational research (Woolner et al., 2010; Wall et al., 2013) and marketing/advertising research (Schroeder and Zwick, 2004; Campelo et al., 2011). This scarcity can, in part, be attributed to the dominant positivist epistemological traditions that characterise the HRD field as it strives for ever more 'scientific' evaluations of learning interven-tions. Nevertheless, increasing attention is now being paid to the visual dimension of our social worlds. The ascendancy of visual techniques as reputable methods is marked by the emergence of bespoke journals such as *Visual Studies*, and through the setting-up of the Economic and Social Research Council (ESRC)-funded '*in*Visio' and thematic groups/Special Interest Groups within academic associations. Moreover, research findings derived from these methods now appear in mainstream management journals. This growth perhaps mirrors the predominance of imagery as a mode of communication in contemporary lives and of technological developments enabling the simple and cheap collection, manipulation and storage of visual data. It perhaps also reflects the increased use of 'art' (in its various guises) in workplace problem-solving and 'creative' training solutions.

METHODOLOGICAL APPROACHES USING VISUAL DATA

We now proceed to examine the main methodological traditions supporting the potential of visual methods for HRD research. The varied traditions from which visual research has emerged have rendered it a diverse and disparate field, characterised by a diversity of methodological and theoretical perspectives. Therefore, there is no 'one way' to work. We will consider the distinctions between the forms of visual data, their use and generation, before offering an overview of the visual methods used within these traditions. In doing this, questions will be raised over whose knowledge the images represent, for what purpose and for whom were the images made.

Early applications of visual methods understood images to capture 'accurate' records of reality. These provided a literal reading of a single event, action, communication or artefact, or recorded its longitudinal change. This positivist tradition typically used photos or film to document material, cultural and social practices, with the focus being upon the researcher's understanding of the content of the image (Collier and Collier, 1986). Buchanan and Huczynski (2004, pp.435–436), for example, report Gilbreth's use of still cameras and lights attached to workers' hands to capture their movements, for the purpose of work redesign. A similar approach was adopted at the turn of this century, using still photography to observe theatre delays within an NHS Trust, in efforts to re-engineer team scheduling (Buchanan, 2001).

However, this issue of 'photographic truth' is now heavily contested, with the debate over the authority that images hold forming a central theme within the visual research literatures. As Berger (1972) observed, the visual does not inherently mean the visible. As we view so all of our senses come into play. Thereby, visual data offers a 'window' to the socio-material, psychological or interior worlds of research participants. Through this, meanings emerge as social constructions, enabling us to better understand how other people see things. Consequently, this approach gives the participants' meanings prominence, enabling the researcher to experience their participants' subjective 'world' through their own eyes, providing far greater insights into the worlds that they are researching. In this modus, photos are not *taken* but rather are *made*. They cannot tell the story of how it 'is' or 'was', but offer an incomplete, fragmented and context-bound version of reality, with the image, and how it is framed, inextricably entwined with the cultures of the image-producer and image-reader (Berger, 1972).

However, Emmison (2011) questions whether aesthetics can really be captured in images. He argues that focusing upon only 'two-dimensional' representations is 'curiously short-sighted and unduly restrictive' (p.236). A third and divergent form of visual data focuses upon the spatial and visible facets of our social worlds: 'live' readings of the actual experienced environments and interactions. Data might include body language, temporal and spatial movements of individuals, their clothing and the communication of meaning through such material elements as buildings and public spaces. For HRD-researchers, these data might emerge through participant observation of, for example, interactions within a training session. They might examine how the architectural space, the appearance and layout of a training room, affects the learning that takes place: how the arrangements of chairs into lecture-room style rows might instil a very different understanding for the participants than if the session was conducted with chairs placed around small tables. Therefore, this visual data does not comprise representations of the room, rather the room itself: the actual objects that comprise the room and their layout within it.

RESEARCH DESIGNS USING VISUAL METHODS

Having decided upon their methodological approach, the visual HRD-researcher must consider the research design. This requires two further important decisions, informed by this epistemological perspective they have adopted. Firstly, they must decide upon the source of the visual materials: whether to use pre-existing visuals or to generate them for the purposes of the research. Secondly, they should consider how these visual materials would be used within the research process: as an aide memoir, illustrating other data, or as a data source in their own right. Each of these decisions poses practical and methodological issues.

The emphasis has, ordinarily, been upon the use of extant visual materials. These might include archival photographs, organisational charts, company reports, cartoons and advertisements. Although, the increasing use of social-networking sites and other websites to store and display images, especially 'personal' photos and videos, provides a wealth of opportunity to retrieve 'everyday' images of society. Meanwhile, simple diagrams, signs and maps offer information about, and a means to understanding, everyday custom-and-practice. Whilst, in the case of visual materials produced by organisations, it is important to remain cognisant of the persona and identity that they might be wishing to portray, they too provide an invaluable stock of data that might be used by the HRD-researcher.

More recently, visual materials have been produced specifically for the purposes of the research. Photos play an important role in this, although other techniques, notably diagramming, are being used increasing. However, when using images driven by the research, a fundamental decisions lies with who actually generates or provides the images: are they researcher-generated or participant-generated? Each of these draws upon divergent traditions and requires differing forms of analysis. Researcher-generated images might be used to encourage participants to discuss a subject based upon their interpretation of what is shown and/or to compare their own conceptions and experiences to this. This enables the HRD-researcher to both explicitly delimit the area of research interest whilst also assuring participants of the pertinence of their contributions. However, the images provided will inherently portray the researcher's construal of the research field, although these perspectives may, through participant questioning, be challenged.

By contrast, kindled by postmodern and feminist perspectives on the need to redress perceived power imbalances between researchers and participants, increased attention has been placed upon collaborative and participatory research methods. Participatory visual approaches, referred to by Wagner (1979) as 'native-image-making', invite the participants to create, generate, or locate images that portray their own experiences and understandings of phenomena in response to a specific assignment, rather than imposing the researcher's preconceptions upon the participants (Willig, 2008; Pauwels, 2011). Although Warren (2005) observes that these may tell the researcher more about the photographer/image creator than that which they have chosen to depict, they do, nonetheless, offer an invaluable opening into their worlds: its social, political and cultural elements.

The second research design hurdle confronting the visual researcher lies in determining the value or position that the visual holds within the research. These might be summarised into three broad categories:

1. Research approaches that use the visual as an aide memoir, to stimulate thought within interviews, for example in photo/visual-elicitation;
2. Studies that use visual illustrations, such as graphs and storyboards, in place of, or to supplement, other data forms, notably text;
3. Methodologies that understand images as a data source in their own right.

These are considered in more detail below, within the specific research methods that adopt these approaches.

VISUAL METHODS

Having settled upon a suitable research approach and design, the visual HRD-researcher must determine what actual method(s) to adopt. Table 8.1 provides an overview of a number of these methods, an explanation of their use in practice, suggestions of how they might be used in HRD research and, finally, evidence of their use, where known (to the best of our knowledge), by HRD-researchers. We will then examine in more detail five of these methods that have notable potential for HRD research. These are indicated by the shaded rows.

Graphic Mapping

Graphic mapping methods use participant-created illustrations to 'reveal how they think or feel about matters' (Wagner, 2011, p.55). These are created iteratively, typically before or during an interview with the researcher, encouraging the participants to reflect upon their perceptions of the phenomenon under study. A number of groups of techniques are identified in Table 8.1. As an example, mind maps might be used during an interview to help the HRD-researcher and/or participant to clarify their thoughts on, and understandings of, their informal workplace learning. This might identify the sources of this learning, and the tools and artefacts that have been utilised in this. In using the less well-established technique of personal maps, participants might be invited to develop a 'personal geography' of how they see their selves: their identities, attributes, feelings and ambitions; also people, places and events that have shaped their lives. Recent work by King (2013) used this approach to better understand academics' identity. This created maps, typically of islands or archipelagos,

Table 8.1 Overview of visual methods and their uses

Method	Brief overview	Possible use in HRD research	Evidence of use in HRD (where known)
Video, film and imagery to authenticate events, actions and emotions			
Film/video	The use of film or video either for recording events, or for reviewing perceptions of previously 'captured' and preserved events. This approach provides naturalistic access to the minutiae of behaviour and interactions that are unavailable through more traditional methods (see Heath et al., 2010)	Videos of training/coaching sessions to explore participants' perceptions of their effectiveness Using videos of workplace incidents to assess learners' understanding of them	Jubas and Knutson (2012)
Video dairies	A digitised diary collecting data on participants' lives over an extended time period. Participants conduct a daily camera session through which they share information, such as their thoughts, feelings, reflections, with the researcher 'audience'	To observe an apprentice 'learning the ropes' through weekly recordings in which they are asked to emphasise their workplace experiences and learning	Littlejohn et al. (2012)
Iconography	Illustrations, principally diagrams and photos, used to represent the social, cultural and political contexts within which they were developed	Use of images provided in annual reports, publicity and advertising materials to reveal perceptions of, and thereby illustrate areas for, workforce learning and development	Ardichivili (2006)

Behaviour: video tracking, eye tracking and motion analysis	Uses specialist technology-focused eye or motion tracking equipment to record participant behaviour	Examining non-verbal communication in developing customer relations. Examining use of workspaces to analyse task performance	Ross et al. (2005)

Diagramming and mapping

Participant-generated pictors (pictures)/doodles (graphic ideation)	Simple freehand drawings and doodles that help organise thoughts and ideas either in advance of, or during, interviews, offering a visual representation of how the participants view themselves, their social relationships and their social world. Might also be used by the researcher during the course of an interview to help clarify their understanding	To help participants explain their understanding of a specific workplace process following their attendance at a training session. To understand how participants feel that their learning and their relationships with others within the workplace are changing during a period of organisational change	
Graphic mapping	Participant created. Take various forms from ideas shared through sketches and maps to visual or spatial thinking tools (such as mind maps and concept maps) to develop concepts, organise and share ideas, articulate perceptions and promote reflection. May be developed prior to or within an interview within which they are subsequently explored	Asking participants to mind map their understanding of specific learning interventions. Asking participants to create a map to illustrate their perceptions of, and feelings about, their workplace learning journey	Daley et al. (2010) King (2013)

Table 8.1 (continued)

Method	Brief overview	Possible use in HRD research	Evidence of use in HRD (where known)
Diagramming and mapping			
Network mapping	Participants draw maps of interconnectivity (network maps) to illustrate the dyadic ties between the various actors that comprise their network(s). These can be used to identity local and external influential entities, and examine network dynamics	Examining whom participants interact with in the workplace and whom they learn from. Solid lines represent an interaction, whereas double lines between individuals might represent learning	
Process mapping	Participants (typically teams) 'process map' a common understanding of the current situation/system, reflecting not what should happen but what happens in reality.	Examining processes in place for decision-making within an organisation	Cameron et al. (2001)
Elaboration			
Photo/visual-elicitation	Using photos, drawings and artefacts (researcher or participant created) in interview to stimulate a response to the topics under examination	Examining how workspace configurations affect learning Examining how office architectures affect perceptions of workplace happiness/motivation Determining participants' perceptions of their workplace lives through images they provide to portray this	Warhurst (2013)

Diary-ing and story-ing

Photo diaries (Snap logs)	Participants take shots of actions, activities or events to help them explain their stories. The photos act as a log and also as stimuli in subsequent in-depth interviews. Reduces the problems of 'participant fatigue' associated with written diaries.	Tracking workplace novices (participants) information-seeking behaviour in the workplace. To understand informal workplace learning experiences: how/where systems and/or services promote or hinder learning processes. Examining participants' form of self-representation through the duration of these learning processes	Bramming et al. (2012)
Story/timelines	To recall participants' lived worlds and their meanings framed within a specified time period. Not intended to be chronological or linear but provide a visual representation of main events. May be prepared by the participant in advance of an interview, or may be a collaborative effort shared by the researcher and participant	Examining participants' career development, organisational development and learning journeys over a given time period with the intention of deepening and expanding their learning and performance	Mazzetti (2012)
Applied Drama and Theatre ('ethnodrama')	Using staged script and techniques of theatre production, dramatising participants' experiences and/or the researcher's interpretations of data	Assisting workplace educators to reflect upon their practice, and re-envisage how it could be changed and thereby enhancing their own personal development	Rae (2011) Pässilä et al. (2011)

Table 8.1 (continued)

Method	Brief overview	Possible use in HRD research	Evidence of use in HRD (where known)
Diary-ing and story-ing			
'Photomontage'	Juxtaposes multiple photo frames in order to capture a clearer sense of time, movement and narrative: an arrangement of images produces more vivid, complex stories	Manager's changing understanding of self through the course of a training programme	Shortt (2012)
Classifying			
Q-sort/Picture sort/Photosort	Participants organise images provided by the researcher according to guidelines provided. For example, classifying the images or telling a story from the pictures provided	Examining characteristics of managers considered important to managing workplace diversity	Eppler (2007)
Visual repertory grids	Participants provide images in response to the research purpose. They consider these images in randomly selected sets (typically three/time), identifying commonalities between pairs and differences with the third. This generates constructs. Images are presented until the constructs	Examining line managers' perceptions of team learning and creativity Participants' perceptions of the impact of objects on their workplace learning experiences Examining understanding of the characteristics of effective workplace coaching	Blundell et al. (2012)

	emerging are repetitive or until all possible combinations have been presented.	
Miscellaneous		
Blob Trees	Uses drawings of cartoon characters in different positions on a large tree. They are designed to enable participants to identify how they see themselves in a specific context (the tree) and in relation to others within it (other characters on the tree). This is with the intention of enabling them to articulate their own ideas with limited prompting, whilst also revealing hidden levels of consciousness	Examining participants' feelings and emotions before, and then after, a learning intervention · Talbot et al. (2009)
'Lego Serious Play'	Participants make visual representations using Lego	Building models to represent participants' workplace/occupational identity and/or learning · Gauntlett (2007)

119

with various geomorphic features, such as erupting volcanoes, or human features such as railway lines linking various facets of the self. These were overlaid and further annotated with 'post-its', images and photos. Participants were invited to explore these maps with the researcher through interviews.

Storylines

Storylines provide an invaluable means of invoking recollection and memories. This method can be especially useful where the researcher is looking to understand participants' perceptions and meanings of (periods of) their lived worlds (Cross and Barker, 1994). Importantly, storylines are not intended to be chronological, or indeed linear, but provide a visual representation of the main events within participants' lives framed within a specified time period. These may be prepared by the participant in advance of an interview, providing a stimulus for discussion. Alternatively, the construction of events along this storyline may be a collaborative effort between the researcher and participant, forming the focus of the interview. The HRD-researcher might use these storylines for portraying learning journeys. Such storylines offer participants an opportunity to reflect upon their experiences and events or activities they have encountered and then to relate these to how and what they have learned, for example the development of their leadership or team-working skills. Using these storylines as a stimulus for discussions might mean that the transcripts alone are used in the analysis, the storylines acting like a field memo. Alternatively, the researcher might also interpret the storylines themselves, examining the different elements depicted within them. These approaches to analysis are examined below.

Photo Diaries

Photo diaries provide a useful method for logging participants' activities, views and feelings over time. Within HRD research, participants might be requested to collate a series of photos or images that best illustrate how their thoughts and feelings change through the progress of a formal training programme. These images might then be used as stimuli for a subsequent interview to aid the participants' recollection. The photos may then act solely to support the interview. However, the photos and images may also be analysed separately to the text, with their interpretation 'grounded' within themes induced through the text analysis. Alternatively, the participant might be asked to provide the images supported by a written commentary of the story that they tell. The HRD-researcher might then both analyse the story, using suitable qualitative text analysis and also the images, or elements of them, independently generating themes identifiable within the image itself. This is examined further below.

Video

Video is a much neglected investigative tool (Heath et al., 2010), yet it provides a unique method of recording 'naturally-occurring', situated day-to-day actions as they happen. It offers an invaluable means of revealing the character and complexity of the mundane aspects of organisational activities, thereby addressing a range of phenomena and issues that remain largely unexamined. The minutiae of the embedded and embodied behaviours, also the tools, technologies and artefacts in use, can be scrutinised and dissected, time-after-time. This enables a far more nuanced analysis, offering 'multiple-takes' on the data, than is possible through more traditional methods (Heath et al., 2010, p.6). Video may be used by HRD-researchers to examine the effectiveness of training for professional–client interactions. Recordings might be made of staff activity prior to and post-training, with analysis scrutinising the changes in individuals' verbal and non-verbal behaviours. It might also be used to observe informal knowledge-sharing within collaborative teams, recording the verbal and non-verbal interactions and conduct between members. The HRD-researcher might analyse the video, or elements of it, and/or participants' explanations of the activity recorded within it.

Photo-elicitation

Photo-elicitation uses photos and/or other images to stimulate thought upon the topic/phenomenon under consideration within interview and/ or focus group discussion. This visual method is the focus of detailed examination in the subsequent chapter.

ANALYSIS OF VISUAL DATA

Analysis of the data generated through these different methods might take various forms. As visual data has gained acceptance within the social science research community, there has been increased demand for methods to organise and analyse visual data. In response, CADQAS (Computer Assisted Qualitative Data Analysis Software), notably NVivo10, ATLASti and MaxQDA, has been developed to provide a means of logging, tagging and annotating visuals. However, as Warren (2005) observes, the relationship between words and images remains 'uneasy and unclear'. Consequentially, many different approaches to analysis have been adopted. We will focus upon, and critically evaluate, two specific approaches appropriate to HRD research. Firstly, we will discuss how we might analyse the content of sets of images, using a simple content analysis. Secondly, we will consider the analysis and interpretation of single images, and/or elements within them, using a symbolic interpretation. These approaches are differentiated by the extent to which a literal reading is made of the conscious content – the actual image(s) portrayed – and to what extent account is taken of the unconscious also encapsulated within the images.

However, again, analysis poses a series of hurdles that the HRD-researcher must consider in advance. Firstly, s/he must decide upon the status that the visual data holds within the research findings. In some instances, visual representations are omitted from the subsequent reporting of research, the researcher suggesting that they hold the same status as field notes and therefore remain in the background of the study. Thereby, both the image and text are integrated into a whole. Other research presents visual data juxtaposed with text, each holding equal status. Significantly, visual data should be used to fulfil a unique and certain role that adds value to the research rather than being used solely to illustrate an idea that has been well crafted in words (Pauwels, 2011; Wagner, 2011). Secondly, as Wagner asserts, visual data can 'seem inherently messy . . . leaving the researcher with multi-dimensional records, artefacts and data sets . . .'. Whilst he notes that 'records can be wrestled into shape' through the normal process of coding, this involves a trade-off 'reflecting an abiding tension . . . between phenomenal fidelity and data reduction . . .' (pp.65–66).

Simple Content Analysis

For the realist HRD-researcher, focus is upon the coding of themes or content represented by the complete image or of elements identified within it. Crilly et al. (2006) identify four key properties: the actual objects that comprise the image; the attributes of these objects and what information this conveys about them; the relative arrangement of the objects; the meanings that might be conveyed through the actual arrangement of the objects within space (p.346). Thereby, this content may include such facets as whether the image is posed or natural, whether it incorporates people or artefacts and what these actually are and/or denote.

Symbolic Analysis

Symbolic analysis, developed from within the field of semiotics, examines images not to determine what they 'denote', but rather the 'connotations' contained within them, with the intention of decoding the messages, notably emotional states and relationships (Krampen et al., 1987). This approach also considers the social, cultural and political contexts within which the visual data were created. Where visuals form only a part of the data, supported by interview narrative, the HRD-researcher must consider the extent to which they should attempt to interpret what the images 'actually' mean and to what extent the interpretation should be grounded within supporting interviews, since it is for the participants to interpret what the images signify.

The application of both of these methods of analysis, with worked examples, is examined in the subsequent chapter.

DISCUSSION

We have, through the course of this chapter, provided a strong argument for the use of visual methods and data. However, it would be naïve to assume that this offers a panacea to the HRD-researcher. Whilst we have emphasised the significant benefits they offer over many conventional tools/methods, these methods are not without their shortcomings.

Perhaps the most significant problem is that the ease of collection means visual data grows uncontrollably. As Wagner (2011) identified, 'a downside is the cost in research time and attention to sorting through rivers of information when a small stream might suffice' (p.65). This, he suggests, is also exacerbated by a kind of 'commodity fetishism': the attractions of visual materials displacing attention to the phenomenon they are intended to represent (p.64).

Visual approaches are arguably favoured for their ability to generate naturalistic data. However, is not fully known to what extent the camera will influence the participants, and/or how/where the camera is positioned will impact upon the data generated, thereby questioning the trustworthiness of the data. Also, many of these methods involve the concurrent use of interview/discussion. The limitations of this approach are discussed in the following chapter.

Perhaps the most significant constraints for visual HRD-researchers lie in the ethical challenges associated with these tools. These challenges are discussed in detail in the next chapter; however, a brief synopsis is offered. Doubtless, most ethics committees will become concerned by the suggestion of cameras and recorders. It may also be difficult to gain permission from participants and/or organisations, and in some contexts the use of cameras, especially video cameras, may be practically problematic. Where the research requires images to be generated within the research context itself we advise the use of an incremental approach, building the fieldwork towards the use of visuals to develop the trust of the individuals/ organisation.

This chapter has provided an overview of the different approaches to visual research that might be considered by the HRD-researcher. Whilst the use of visual methods and visual data is, at present, limited in extent within HRD research, we assert that its use for capturing and expressing social meaning offers significant benefits. These benefits provide the researcher, the participant and the reader or user of the research interest and a more persuasive articulation of the research context and the meanings evoked.

REFERENCES

Ardichivili, A. (2006). Russian orthodoxy worldview and adult learning in the workplace. *Advances in Developing Human Resources, 8*, 3, 373–381.
Blundell, J., Wittkowski, A., Weick, A. and Hare, D. (2012). Using the repertory grid technique to examine nursing staff's construal of mothers with mental health problems. *Clinical Psychology and Psychotherapy, 19*, 3, 260–269.
Bramming, P., Hansen, B., Bojesen, A. and Olesen, K. (2012). (Im)perfect pictures: snaplogs in performativity research. *Qualitative Research in Organizations and Management: An International Journal, 7*, 1, 54–71.
Bryman, A. (2008). *Social Research Methods* (3rd edition). London: Sage.
Buchanan, D. (2001). The role of photography in organization research: a reengineering case illustration. *Journal of Management Inquiry, 10*, 2, 151–164.
Buchanan, D. and Huczynski, A. (2004). *Organizational Behaviour: An Introductory Text* (5th edition). Harlow, UK: Prentice-Hall.
Cameron, M., Cranfield, S. Valerie Iles, V. and Stone, J. (2001). *Making Informed Decisions on Change*. London: NCCSDO London School of Hygiene and Tropical Medicine. Available online at http://westminsterresearch.wmin.ac.uk/11233/ (accessed 28 January 2013).
Campelo, A., Aitken, R. and Gnoth, J. (2011) Visual rhetoric and ethics in marketing of destinations. *Journal of Travel Research, 50*, 1, 3–14.
Collier, J. and Collier, M. (1986). *Visual Anthropology: Photography as a Research Method*. Albuquerque: New Mexico Press.
Crilly, N., Blackwell, A. and Clarkson, P. (2006). Graphic elicitation: using research diagrams as interview stimuli. *Qualitative Research, 6*, 3, 341–366.
Cross, N. and Barker, R. (eds) (1994). *At the Desert's Edge: Oral Histories from the Sahel*. London: Panos.
Daley, B., Conceição, S., Mina, L., Altman, B., Baldor, M. and Brown, J. (2010). Concept mapping: a strategy to support the development of practice, research, and theory within human resource development. *Human Resource Development Review, 9*, 4, 357–384.
Emmison, M. (2011). Conceptualising visual data. In D. Silverman (ed.). *Qualitative Research* (3rd edition). London: Sage.

Eppler, M. (2007). An empirical classification of visual methods for management: results of picture sorting experiments with managers and students. *Proceedings of Information Visualization IV*. 11th International Conference (pp.335–341). Available online at http://ieeexplore.ieee.org/xpl/login.jsp?tp=&arnumber=4272002&url=http%3A%2F%2Fieeexplore.ieee.org%2Fxpls%2Fabs_all.jsp%3Farnumber%3D4272002 (accessed 28 January 2013).

Eraut, M. (2000). Non-formal learning and tacit knowledge in professional work. *British Journal of Educational Psychology, 70*, 1, 113–136.

Gauntlett, D. (2007). *Creative Exploration: New Approaches to Identities and Audiences*. London: Routledge.

Heath, C., Hindmarsh, J. and Luff, P. (2010). *Video in Qualitative Research*. London: Sage.

Jubas, K. and Knutson, P. (2012). Seeing and be(liev)ing: how nursing and medical students understand representations of their professions. *Studies in the Education of Adults, 44*, 1, 85–100.

King, V. (2013). Self portrait with a mortar-board: a study of academic identity using the map, novel and grid. *Higher Education Research and Development, 32*, 1, 96–108.

Krampen, M., Oehler, K., Posner, R., Sebeok, T. and Uexküll, T. (1987). *Classics of Semiotics*. New York: Plenum.

Littlejohn, A., Milligan, C. and Margaryan, A. (2012). Charting collective knowledge: supporting self-regulated learning in the workplace. *Journal of Workplace Learning, 24*, 3, 226–238.

Mazzetti, A. (2012). Evaluating visual timeline methodology for appraisal and coping research. Paper presented at *in*Visio Symposium: Advancing Visual Research in Organisational Studies, 28–29 November, University of Essex.

Pässilä, A., Oikarinen, T. and Vince, R. (2011). The role of reflection, reflection on roles: practice-based innovation through theatre-based learning. In H. Melkas and V. Harmaakorpi (eds). *Practice-Based Innovation: Insights, Applications and Policy Implications* (pp.173–191). Springer.

Pauwels, L. (2011). An integrated conceptual framework for visual social research. In E. Margolis and L. Pauwels (eds). *The Sage Handbook of Visual Research Methods* (pp.3–23). London: Sage.

Rae, J. (2011). A study of the use of organisational theatre: the case of Forum Theatre. Durham theses, Durham University. Available at Durham E-Theses, Online: http://etheses.dur.ac.uk/3268/ (accessed 8 February 2014).

Ross, A., King, N. and Firth, J. (2005). Interprofessional relationships and collaborative working: encouraging reflective practice. *Online Journal of Nursing Issues, 10*, 1, Article 3.

Schroeder, J. and Zwick, D. (2004). Mirrors of masculinity: representation and identity in advertising images. *Consumption, Markets, and Culture, 7*, 1, 21–51.

Shortt, H. (2012). Identityscapes of a hair salon. *Sociological Research Online, 17*, 2, May. Available online at http://www.socresonline.org.uk/17/2/22.html (accessed 8 February 2014).

Talbot, D., Bilsberry, J. and March, P. (2009). An exploratory study into the construction of employee fit and misfit. Paper presented at the British Academy of Management Conference Track: Organizational Psychology, Brighton, UK.

Wagner, J. (1979). *Images of Information: Still Photography in the Social Sciences*. London: Sage.

Wagner, J. (2011). Visual studies and empirical social inquiry. In E. Margolis and L. Pauwels (eds). *The Sage Handbook of Visual Research Methods* (pp.49–71). London: Sage.

Wall, K., Higgins, S., Remedios, R., Rafferty, V. and Tiplady, L. (2013). Comparing analysis frames for visual data sets: using pupil views templates to explore perspectives of learning. *Journal of Mixed Methods Research, 7*, 1, 22–42.

Warhurst, R. (2013). Learning in an age of cuts: managers as enablers of workplace learning. *Journal of Workplace Learning, 25*, 1, 37–57.

Warren, S. (2005). Photography and voice in critical qualitative management research. *Accounting, Auditing and Accountability Journal, 18*, 6, 861–882.

Widdance-Twine, F. (2006). Visual ethnography and racial theory: family photographs as archives of interracial intimacies. *Ethnic and Racial Studies, 29*, 3, 487–511.
Willig, C. (2008). *Introducing Qualitative Research in Psychology: Adventures in Theory and Method* (2nd edition). Buckingham, UK: Open University Press.
Woolner, P., Clark, J., Hall, E., Tiplady, L., Thomas U. and Wall, K. (2010). Pictures are necessary but not sufficient: using a range of visual methods to engage users about school design. *Learning Environment Research, 13*, 1, 1–22.

ANNOTATED FURTHER READING

Heath, C., Hindmarsh, J. and Luff, P. (2010). *Video in Qualitative Research*. London: Sage. Discusses a range of video-based projects in social sciences and also the ethical and practical issues that arise in generating video data.
Margolis, E. and Pauwels, L. (eds) (2011). *The Sage Handbook of Visual Research Methods*. London: Sage. A comprehensive handbook for HRD-researchers engaging with visual methods; however, it is possibly better suited to those researchers with some experience of visual methods rather than the complete novice.
Yau, N. (2013). *Data Points: Visualization that Means Something*. Indianapolis, IN: Wiley. Focusing upon many different techniques of data visualisation, this book uses photography, art, mathematics/statistics, cartography and various online links to explore both conventional and unorthodox thinking on data representation.

9. The use of photo-elicitation interviewing in qualitative HRD research

Russell Warhurst and Kate Black

SUMMARY

The chapter provides an overview of the as yet under-utilised tool of photo-elicitation interviewing. It examines the development of this method and its value to HRD research. A case of non-formal and expansive workplace learning of public sector professionals is offered to illustrate the application of this approach in HRD-research practice.

INTRODUCTION

Chapter 8 provided an overview of the potential for visual approaches in HRD research, offering a 'toolbox' from which HRD-researchers might select a visual method appropriate to their research needs. This chapter gives attention to one of these approaches offering the greatest potential within HRD research: the, as yet, under-utilised tool of photo-elicitation interviewing. Drawing upon an illustrative case of non-formal, expansive workplace learning of public sector professionals, we examine the efficacy of this research method, providing details of how the study was set up, how participant generated images were used to elicit dialogue and, finally, how the ensuing data was analysed.

OVERVIEW OF PHOTO-ELICITATION

Within the qualitative paradigm, interviews predominate as a data collection tool for gaining an insight into participants' subjective worlds. However, while they offer a flexible and 'powerful way of helping people to articulate their tacit perceptions, feelings and understandings' (Arksey and Knight, 1999, p.32), this approach relies upon the participants being able to verbalise these meanings and understandings. Where the phenomenon under study is complex or problematic, gaining this cognitive access can be challenging. Photo-elicitation interviewing offers a means of facilitating this access. As the previous chapter demonstrated, the provision of images is intended to act as a catalyst to help the participants talk about and expand upon difficult, perhaps abstract concepts, uninhibited by the constraints of speech alone (Pink, 2007; Gauntlett, 2007). However, similarly to other visual methods, very little has been written about the use and integration of images or photos into the interviewing process (Hurworth et al., 2005, p.52).

Photo-elicitation involves the simple idea of inserting a photograph into a research interview (Harper, 2002). Whilst most elicitation studies utilise photographs, as is the focus of this chapter, other visual images such as cartoons, adverts, paintings and graffiti may be used interchangeably within this technique (visual-elicitation).

The development of photo-elicitation interviewing may be traced back to Morin and Rouch's 'Chronique d'un été', an experimental film in which participants, who were filmed discussing culture and happiness in the working classes, examine the level of reality they thought the film secured. However, it was the anthropologist John Collier who first coined the term 'photo-elicitation' in his work on mental health and psychological stress undertaken in the 1960s (Collier and Collier, 1986). This work highlighted how using photos improved participants' memories and stimulated more comprehensive interviews. Nevertheless, within the traditionally 'word-based' field of social research, the use of photo-elicitation interviewing, as with other visual methods, remains 'sparse' (Ray and Smith, 2012) and has, until relatively recently, attracted only a small following. More recently we have witnessed the increased use of visual methods across various disciplines and participant-types, including education (Rasmussen, 2004), psychology (Salmon, 2001), housing (Suchar and Rotenberg, 1994) and nursing (Riley and Manias, 2003). Harper (1997, 2002, 2005), Banks (2001) and Pink (2004, 2007) offer significant contributions to the field. This rise in popularity perhaps mirrors the rise of imagery as the dominant mode of communication in today's society. Warren (2008, 2009) also notes how the rise of digital technology has made the collection, manipulation and storage of images simple and cheap. However, photo-elicitation interviewing still remains on the margins of research traditions.

DESCRIPTION OF PHOTO-ELICITATION INTERVIEWING

Conventional approaches to photo-elicitation use photos as an 'icebreaker' activity to develop a rapport with the participants. This approach encourages open discussion and acts as an aide memoir to stimulate thought and invoke memory within interview or focus group discussion. The photo, which is typically provided by the researcher and assumed to be meaningful to the participant(s), acts as a prompt to both 'mine' information from the participants and to encourage them to reflect upon what is depicted. This may trigger meanings and interpretations unseen by the researcher, thereby helping to expand their perspectives. By contrast, contemporary approaches place emphasis upon Hurworth's (2003) 'autodriving reflexive photography' and 'photovoice' which use participant generated images. Subsequent discussions are then 'driven' by the participants, empowering them 'to construct what matters to them' (Wang, 1997, p.382). Offering a 'bridge' between the researcher and participants' worlds, participant images enable the collaborative exploration of perceptions of difficult, often hidden, hard-to-access facets of their lives which might be otherwise overlooked (Widdance-Twine, 2006), while helping participants to express self-understanding and emotions. This approach generates a shared interpretation and understanding of experiences and practices as well as discussion about the broader significance and meaning of the images. Both the conventional and contemporary approaches to photo-elicitation interviewing, it is asserted, elicit richer data and extended personal narratives of the details of participants' everyday lives and experiences than conventional interview techniques (Pink, 2007; Ray and Smith, 2012). This chapter will specifically focus upon photos taken by the participants.

As can be drawn from the discussion above, photo-elicitation interviewing presents many opportunities for the HRD-researcher in exploring hard-to-access concepts such as learning. We now turn our attention to how data is actually generated, that is, elicited, through this technique. We propose that this process comprises three key stages.

ELICITING THE DATA IN PHOTO-ELICITATION INTERVIEWING

Initially, in adopting an 'autodriving' approach to data generation, participants are requested to produce a small portfolio of photos and/ or collected images (typically 3–6 photos or images) in advance of an interview that will help them to reflect upon and best explain the particular phenomenon/phenomena being researched. Typically the HRD-researcher will pose a couple of broad prompt questions to help the participants in compiling their portfolios. For example, 'what does . . . mean to you?'; 'how would you explain . . .?' However, care should be taken in suggesting examples of photos or images that they might provide for risk of failing to 'break the frame' of the participants' view (Harper,

2002, p.20); in other words, overly directing or shaping the participants' views. However, as is discussed below, to eliminate ethical concerns, clear guidance on the generation or collection of the photos and images should be provided to the participants at the outset. The photos and images act as prompts in the subsequent interview. Therefore, the interview may require little direction from the researcher, with the images providing both focus and structure. These interviews typically generate a more extended narrative than conventional interviews.

During the interviews, the researcher asks participants to explain what they have included within their portfolio and to talk around each photo or image, explaining the meaning that each holds for them. By taking this approach, the participants are able to lead the researcher into their worlds, to determine the order in which they tell their stories and to talk about the various topics from their perspectives. However, the researcher might also choose to ask the participant about the importance of specific objects or arrangements within a photo or image. This enables an understanding of the situation or phenomena to be co-constructed. Although within photo-elicitation interviewing it is intended that the researcher should act as a co-creator of meaning rather than director, s/he may choose to additionally use a series of pre-devised prompt questions. These questions may enable the examination of aspects of relevance to the research that are not directly addressed through the photos or images, to provide clarification of points raised. Researchers may choose to record the interviews, with participant permission, to enable the analysis of verbatim transcripts.

The final stage of photo-elicitation research comprises analysis of the data and consideration of the means by which both the interview transcripts and the visual data might be analysed. These processes are discussed further below.

An illustrative case is presented towards the end of this chapter. This provides further details of the actual process by which photo-elicitation interviewing might be undertaken with reference to a specific research aim. Before this we discuss some of the ethical and practical dilemmas surrounding the use of photo-elicitation interviewing beyond those typically associated with qualitative data generation. We then offer examples of analysis.

ETHICAL DILEMMAS ARISING FROM PHOTO-ELICITATION AND OTHER VISUAL RESEARCH

Ethical considerations should inform and underpin all approaches to, and methods of, social research (Robson, 2011). However, for visual research, especially using photos, this remains an under-developed, and indeed, hotly debated, area. Lapenta (2011) asserts that visual methods pose fewer ethical concerns than most qualitative methods because in essence the method is a participatory form of research, prioritising the voices of the participants, especially in the case of those from marginalised groups. Pauwels (2011) supports this position in advocating that through engaging individuals and communities in producing photos, this promotes participant empowerment, offering them *advance* control over what they photograph and discuss. Conversely, other scholars have asserted that photo data creates an additional level of complexity and challenge to existing ethical dilemmas facing qualitative researchers (Harper, 2005). Whilst within HRD research it might be argued that many of the concerns surrounding the use of images, notably the portrayal of children and vulnerable people, are unlikely to be of concern, attention should be drawn to two key ethical concerns.

Firstly, consideration should be given to the issue of informed consent. As Davies (2008) emphasises, participants may feel differently about providing consent for different images and may also wish to offer varied consent, according to the intended purposes, notably where dissemination is to extend to publication. This may especially be the case when photos hold particular sensitivities for the participants. However, in the case with 'found' images, and where individuals have been 'captured' within the background of a photo, it must be considered to what extent it is actually possible to trace the individuals either depicted within, or responsible for producing, them. The right to photograph the public without their consent, for research purposes, has not really been established, nor has the use of photos of public places and organisational 'spaces' without informed consent (Wiles et al., 2011). Whilst the UK Data Protection Act 1988 might consider the image of an individual to be personal data and therefore require consent to be obtained, the publishing of such images without this consent remains an everyday practice across print, web and broadcast journalism. In order to minimise risk, where images do include individuals, some researchers advocate concealing, pixelating or blurring to anonymise individuals (Wiles et al., 2008). However, others criticise such practice for de-humanising (Sweetman, 2008) and soliciting connotations of criminality (Banks, 2001).

Secondly, the HRD-researcher should be mindful of problems of distortion and falsification, whether intentional or unintentional, as images take on meanings, or are used to depict scenarios contradictory to those for which they were created.

In addressing these various concerns, the Economic and Social Research Council (ESRC) National Centre for Research Methods has published

Guidelines for Visual Research (Wiles et al., 2008), with Vince and Warren (2012) offering 'responsible photography' guidelines. When considering publication of empirical research containing visual data, journal and book publishers are now increasingly issuing guidelines for their use.

In conclusion, as Davies (2008) advises, the prudent and sensitive visual HRD-researcher will judge carefully who, both morally and legally, has the right to use photos and images, especially where there are practical barriers to seeking consent. This judgement will be based upon the researcher's own moral beliefs and upon their professional judgement. Ultimately, as with any research, the key aim should be to prevent exploitation and protect the vulnerability of the participants and the researchers.

RESEARCH VALIDITY USING PHOTO-ELICITATION INTERVIEWING GENERATED DATA

The significance of any research rests upon the credibility of its findings. Depending upon the epistemological approach adopted, the visual researcher must comply with the appropriate research standards. In undertaking photo-elicitation interviewing research, the HRD-researcher must take account of the central research standards underpinning the approach they have adopted. In the case of a positivist methodological approach, this concerns reliability, validity and generalisability, whereas the qualitative researcher is concerned with the trustworthiness and credibility, authenticity and relevance of the findings.

Reliability, the extent to which the data collection technique(s) will yield consistent findings and is not subject to error, is considered crucial in positivist research. However, reliability presents a key challenge in qualitative research, which applies the alternative standards of trustworthiness and credibility. Yet, trustworthiness and credibility presents one of the main challenges for visual researchers. As Goldstein (2007) asserted, 'all photos lie'. Therefore, are still and moving images an accurate rendition and truthful? Critics of visual approaches have exposed scams such as mock-ups, deceptions and manipulation of materials prior to or post 'capture'. Critics also assert the occurrence of bias and their use in propaganda but note how, to the qualitative analyst, such use provides invaluable data in itself.

Validity, for the positivist researcher, is concerned with whether the findings represent what they profess to do, that is, whether the data collection methods adopted accurately measured what they set out to measure (Bryman, 2008). In the case of visual research, concern is with internal validity, that is, the congruence between observations made and their reporting. Such validity is assured through the researcher's pre-existing experience within this research context and through the relatively extensive data collection period. However, for the qualitative researcher, greater concern is with authenticity and confirmability rather than validity. So, for example, the HRD-researcher must establish their neutrality in representing the participants' views.

The issue of whether we can, or should, generalise from qualitative data has been a topic of considerable discussion for many decades. However, the role of qualitative research is to interpret participants' meanings within social contexts, rather than measuring, explaining or predicting. Therefore, the visual HRD-researcher should ensure the quality of their research by demonstrating that s/he is portraying an honest representation of the data. The careful documentation of each stage of the research and analysis process will enable the research users and readers to make informed decisions regarding its relevance to other contexts. This approach should also enable the participants to determine the value of the research for extending their understanding of their social context and for understanding the views of others within it, while also assessing its value to the wider community for engendering change or improvement.

ANALYSING PHOTO-ELICITATION INTERVIEWING GENERATED DATA

As we examined in Chapter 8, many different approaches have been adopted in analysing visual data. We focused upon two specific approaches typically used: a simple form of content analysis and a symbolic semiotics-based interpretation. These approaches are differentiated by the extent to which a literal reading is made of the conscious content and to what extent account is taken of the unconscious facets also encapsulated within the images. We will now illustrate these two approaches by offering examples of their use in the analysis of photo-elicitation interviewing generated data. The research from which these examples are drawn aimed to understand managers' conceptions of their learning.

Figure 9.1 is an image of a motorbike, a Harley Davidson Sportster. This participant generated image was provided to illustrate his belief in the importance of continuous learning. He spoke of how this learning was critical to 'keeping the bike moving, lubricated . . . bringing in another part, replacing a part, changing the ways we do it when we've used the wrong spares . . . doing it differently to how we did it before'.

This image might also be interpreted in a very different way when adopting a symbolic perspective. Informed by Pirsig's (1974) *Zen and the*

*Figure 9.1   Participant-provided image of a Harley Davidson Sportster
(reproduced with permission)*

Art of Motorcycle Maintenance, it might be suggested that this research
participant understood lifelong learning to be down to attitude. That is,
that there is a need to have an approach to life and learning that is varied,
with the day-to-day routine of classical mastery potentially transformed
through creativity and intuition that come through (a Zen-like) being 'in
the moment'. Moreover, it might also be asserted that this participant
realised the foreseeable and unforeseeable dangers of riding this 'bike',
and of managerial work, and that he knowingly and freely accepted these
dangers.

Another research participant provided Figure 9.2 to illustrate her
need to have her own office away from the busy open-plan environment of the contact centre that she managed, in order to 'get her head
down to more conceptual and more strategic work'. The researcher
might also analyse this image at a symbolic level and speculate that
it was selected for conveying a sense of security, a meaning which
might have some veracity given the context of job cuts in this manager's
unit.

*Figure 9.2   Participant-provided image of her office door and lock
(reproduced with permission)*

CASE STUDY: USE OF PHOTO-ELICITATION INTERVIEWING IN ILLUSTRATIVE CASE OF NON-FORMAL AND EXPANSIVE MANAGERIAL LEARNING

In this final section we draw upon an illustrative case of non-formal and expansive manager learning to illustrate the use of photo-elicitation interviewing in HRD-research practice. In this case-study example we will provide details of how the study was set up, how participant-generated images were used to elicit dialogue and, finally, how the ensuing data was analysed. As explained above, this approach places emphasis upon the use of images, typically photos, for generating richer narratives than interviews alone.

The purpose of the empirical research was to examine how managers perceived the nature of their day-to-day management practice and the opportunities that this offered for workplace learning both for these individuals themselves and their teams. Taking a qualitative and largely inductive approach, the research focused upon a case study of MBA-educated middle-managers from within two English local authorities. Adopting an participatory approach to photo-elicitation, the 29 volunteer participants were requested, in advance of individual interviews, to create a portfolio of five images that helped them to answer the simple, but central, research question, 'what does being a manager mean for you?' Within the interviews, which lasted approximately one hour, these images acted as stimuli to help explore the participants' perceptions of being a manager. Additionally, the images acted as an aid to help the participants explore and express themselves. One participant presented a photo of his unit's staff meeting. Although this participant was the leader of this unit, he was sitting in a peripheral position at the table. Firstly, he used this image to explain how he believed that he delegated work, for example the chairing of the portrayed meeting, to members of his team to enable their development. Secondly, he spoke of how he coached staff, illustrating this through another member of the unit who was about to undertake a presentation and with whom he had spent time enhancing her presentation skills. A further participant, a youth social-work manager, provided a photo of an ice cream van with two of her team 'selling' ice cream cones (Figure 9.3).

Reflecting upon this image, she explained how, working with other professionals, notably those in education, health and the police, her team was charged with delivering various 'messages' to teenage kids during the school holidays. Following open discussions, facilitated by the participant-manager, the team had both condensed the elements of advice

Figure 9.3   Participant-provided image of her team 'selling' ice cream (reproduced with permission)

which they felt were most needed by teenagers in their area and identified an approach to directing that advice through ice-cream sales.

The researcher's questions typically took the form of simple requests for clarification around, or for further detail of, the images themselves. For example, one of the participants provided an image of herself and her friends on the shores of a lake in the English Lake District. She commented that, for her, this image meant two things: firstly, having a goal and achieving it – in this case the goal was the summit of the distant peak – and, secondly, the importance of work–life balance. The interviewer questioned her further about the first of these meanings, asking her, amongst other questions, whether she felt that she led from the front or allowed others to find their own way. The participant replied that in this instance, although she often walked the hills, she didn't know the area in the photograph particularly well and so, therefore, they were collectively finding their way together.

Qualitative content analysis of the interview transcripts was undertaken, with analytical codes induced from within the data (Silverman, 2011). These codes were refined and organised through the course of the analysis and through iteration with established theoretical understandings. Focus was also upon identifying codes emergent within the images themselves, but grounded within the interview data. For example, in illustrating the example offered above, the codes 'leadership as providing a goal' and 'leadership as enabling others' were induced. Participant validation, enabled though the participants being invited to comment on an initial draft of the findings, assured the credibility of the findings.

DISCUSSION

Photo-elicitation interviewing offers a number of advantages both for the HRD-researcher and his/her participants when used either as the primary method of data collection or as a secondary form. Perhaps its greatest advantage lies in its decentring of the authority of the researcher and empowering of the participants through overturning the power dynamics that prevail within standard interviews (Warren, 2005, p.867). With participant-generated photo-elicitation interviewing the participants themselves have far greater involvement throughout the process. Notably, their perspective is foregrounded so *they* act as 'guide' and 'expert' rather than being the *subject* of the interview (Winddance-Twine, 2006, p.496). They also have *advance* control over what they photograph and have opportunities to reflect upon the questions and the issues they raise in advance. This will help them to better understand how they think about themselves, rather than requiring them to provide an instantaneous verbal response (Walker and Weidel, 1985).

From the HRD-researcher's perspective, photo-elicitation interviewing holds many benefits. The use of images within interviews offers potential 'access' to what the researchers themselves cannot participate in: the contextual, emotional and cultural (Pink, 2007, p.88). This access provides opportunities for exploring phenomena and experiences which words are unable to capture, that participants are unable to verbalise, or that they overlook as inconsequential. As Harper (2002) asserts, they 'mine deeper shafts into . . . human consciousness,' offering 'new ways of seeing' (p.23).

From a theoretical perspective, photo-elicitation interviewing offers richness to potentially develop theory and knowledge within the field of study. Perhaps most notably the signs, symbols and perceptions offered present multiple perspectives and interpretations. This juxtaposes the fixed meanings offered through the dominant positivist approaches to examining social phenomena, such as those offered in statistics and charts, (Harper, 2000). As Becker (2002, p.11) concludes, 'what can you do with pictures that you couldn't do just as well with words? The answer is that I can lead you to believe that the abstract tale I've told you has a real flesh and blood life and is therefore to be believed'. Therefore, this approach presents a basis to move beyond existing studies to inductively develop the theorising in this field.

However, it is recognised that photo-elicitation interviewing is not without its shortcomings. Perhaps most significantly, the use of photos presents ethical concerns that might not be encountered through using more traditional methods of qualitative research. Moreover, interviews, in whatever form, are inherently limited by their being a contrived rather than naturalistic interaction, and as with conventional interviews, the researcher is unable to account for gaps between what the participants say and what they actually do in practice. Whilst the provision of photographs specifically depicting practice may help to alleviate this, they too present a 'staged and selected' account of reality in terms of what is selected and how it is framed (Widdance-Twine, 2006, p.502). With the participants themselves typically being absent from the photographs, their actual 'place' within this reality is omitted (Felstead et al., 2004). Photo-elicitation interviewing also assumes that the participants are able and willing, both cognitively and physically, to provide responses that are not merely socially desirable (King and Horrocks, 2010). Finally, from a purely pragmatic perspective, photos present issues of copyright, especially if the research is to be published. This requires a clear agreement over who owns the images before the research project commences.

This chapter has suggested that photo-elicitation interviewing is an invaluable alternative to the conventional, and arguably stale, methodologies of questionnaires and interviews typically favoured by HRD-researchers. The use of images enables the researcher to come far closer to the participants' lived realities than with conventional methods, generating far deeper, richer and more interesting data for the researcher, participant and reader and user of the research.

REFERENCES

Arksey, H. and Knight, P. (1999). *Interviewing for Social Scientists*. London: Sage.

Banks, M. (2001). *Visual Methods in Social Research*. London: Sage.

Becker, H. (2002). Visual evidence: a Seventh Man, the specified generalization, and the work of the reader. *Visual Studies, 17*(1), 3–11.

Bryman, A. (2008). *Social Research Methods* (3rd edition). London: Sage.

Collier, J. and Collier, M. (1986). *Visual Anthropology: Photography as a Research Method*. Albuquerque: New Mexico Press.

Davies, K. (2008). *Real Life Methods Toolkit #01: Informed Consent in Visual Research. Seeking Consent for the Use of Images Obtained in Photo Elicitation: Reflections from the Living Resemblances Project*. Available online at www.reallifemethods.ac.uk (accessed 12 January 2013).

Felstead, A., Jewson, N. and Walters, S. (2004). Images, interviews and interpretations: Making connections in visual research. In C. Pole (ed.), *Seeing is Believing? Approaches to Visual Research* (pp.105–122). Oxford: Elsevier Science.

Gauntlett, D. (2007). *Creative Exploration: New Approaches to Identities and Audiences*. London: Routledge.

Goldstein, B. (2007). All photos lie. In Gregory Stanczak (ed.), *Visual Research Methods: Image, Society and Representation*. London and Thousand Oaks, CA: Sage.

Harper, D. (1997). Visualizing Structure: Reading Surfaces of Social Life. *Qualitative Sociology, 20*(1), 57–77.

Harper, D. (2002). Talking about pictures: A case for photo elicitation. *Visual Studies, 17*(1), 13–26.

Harper, D. (2005). What's new visually? In N. Denzin and Y. Lincoln (eds), *The Sage Handbook of Qualitative Research* (3rd edition, pp.747–792). London: Sage.

Hurworth, R. (2003). Photo-interviewing for research. *Social Research Update, 40*(1), 1–4.

Hurworth, R., Clark, E., Martin, J. and Thomsen, S. (2005). The use of photo-interviewing: Three examples from health evaluation and research. *Evaluation Journal of Australasia, 4*(1), 52–62.

King, N. and Horrocks, C. (2010). *Interviews in Qualitative Research*. London: Sage.

Lapenta, F. (2011). Some theoretical and methodological views on photo-elicitation. In E. Margolis and L. Pauwels (eds), *The Sage Handbook of Visual Research Methods* (pp. 201–213). London: Sage.

Pauwels, L. (2011). An integrated conceptual framework for visual social research. In E. Margolis and L. Pauwels (eds), *The Sage Handbook of Visual Research Methods* (pp.3–23). London: Sage.

Pink, S. (2004). Visual methods. In C. Searle, J. Gumbrium and D. Silverman (eds), *Qualitative Research Practice* (pp.391–406). London: Sage.

Pink, S. (2007). *Doing Visual Ethnography: Images, Media and Representation in Research* (2nd edition). London: Sage.

Pirsig, R. (1974). *Zen and the Art of Motorcycle Maintenance*. New York: Morrow.

Rasmussen, K. (2004). Places for children – children's places. *Childhood, 11*(2), 155–173.

Ray, J. and Smith, A. (2012). Using photographs to research organizations: Evidence, considerations and application in field study. *Organizational Research Methods, 15*(2), 288–315.

Riley, R. and Manias, E. (2003). Snap-shots of live theatre: The use of photography to research governance in operating room nursing. *Nursing Inquiry, 10*, 81–90.

Robson, C. (2011). *Real World Research: A Resource for Social Scientists and Practitioner–Researchers*. Oxford: Blackwell.

Salmon, K. (2001). Remembering and reporting by children: The influence of cues and props. *Clinical Psychology Review, 21*(2), 267–300.

Silverman, D. (2011). *Qualitative Research*. London: Sage.

Suchar, C. and Rotenberg, R. (1994). Judging the adequacy of a shelter: A case from Lincoln Park. *Journal of Architectural and Planning Research, 11*(2), 149–165.

Sweetman, P. (2008). Just anybody? Images, ethics and recognition. In R. Leino (ed.), *Just Anybody*. Winchester School of Art: Winchester.

Vince, R. and Warren, S. (2012). Participatory visual methods. In C. Cassell and G. Symons (eds), *The Practice of Qualitative Organisational Research: Core Methods and Current Challenges*. London: Sage.

Walker, R. and Weidel, J. (1985). Using photographs in a discipline of words. In R. Burgess (ed.), *Field Methods in the Study of Education* (pp.1–24). Balcombe: Falmer.

Wang, M. (1997). Photovoice: Concept, methodology, and use for participatory needs assessment. *Health Education and Behavior, 24*(3), 369–387.

Warren, S. (2005). Photography and voice in critical qualitative management research. *Accounting, Auditing and Accountability Journal, 18*(6), 861–882.

Warren, S. (2008). Empirical challenges in organizational aesthetics research: Towards a sensual methodology. *Organizational Studies, 19*(4), 559–580.

Warren, S. (2009). Visual methods in organizational research. In A. Bryman and D. Buchanan (eds), *Handbook of Organizational Research Methods* (pp.566–582). London: Sage.

Widdance-Twine, F. (2006). Visual ethnography and racial theory: Family photographs as archives of interracial intimacies. *Ethnic and Racial Studies, 29*(3), 487–511.

Wiles, R., Clark, A. and Prosser, J. (2011). Visual ethics at the crossorads. In E. Margolis and L. Pauwels (eds), *The Sage Handbook of Visual Research Methods* (pp.685–706). London: Sage.

Wiles, R., Prosser, J., Bagnoli, A., Clark, A., Davies, K., Holland, S. and Reynold, E. (2008). *Visual Ethics: Ethical Issues in Visual Research*. National Centre for Research Methods, NCRM/011. Available online at eprints.ncrm.ac.uk/421/1/MethodsReviewPaperNCRM-011.pdf (accessed 12 January 2012).

ANNOTATED FURTHER READING

Pink, S. (2007). *Doing Visual Ethnography* (2nd edition). London: Sage. Offers a practical and accessible approach for HRD-researchers new to using visual methods, notably photo-elicitation interviewing.

Warren, S. (2009). Visual methods in organizational research. In A. Bryman and D. Buchanan (eds), *Handbook of Organizational Research Methods* (pp.566–582). London: Sage. Provides a useful introduction to the use of visual methods, especially photos in qualitative research.

10. Action research for HRD research
Rosalie Holian and David Coghlan

SUMMARY

This chapter explores the theory and practice of action research and how it may be utilized in HRD research. Action research's distinctive characteristics are that it addresses the twin tasks of bringing about change in organizations and in generating actionable knowledge, through focusing on real organizational problems or issues.

INTRODUCTION

In the context of management and organization studies, action research has been traditionally defined as an approach to research which is based on a collaborative problem-solving relationship between researchers and clients that aims at both solving a problem and generating new knowledge (Gummesson, 2001; Eden and Huxham, 2006; Greenwood and Levin, 2007; Shani, Mohrman, Pasmore, Stymne and Adler, 2008; Coughlan and Coghlan, 2009; Coghlan, 2011). It needs to be noted, at the outset of this chapter which explores the theory and practice of action research and how it may be utilized in Human Resource Development (HRD) research, that action research comprises a family of approaches with a wide diversity of practices. Raelin (2009) has described the family in terms of multiple 'action modalities'. The more common ones may be identified as action learning, action science, appreciative inquiry, clinical inquiry/research, cooperative inquiry, developmental action inquiry, intervention research and learning history, to name a selection. While these modalities may appear confusing to the reader who is new to action research, this chapter focuses on the broad characteristics of action research which may include particular modalities. The chapter is structured as follows. First, a definition of action research is provided and elaborated. Second, the congruence between action research and HRD is introduced. Third, the characteristics are applied to implementing action research in HRD research. Fourth, a case example is presented and reflected on in the light of the key characteristics. The chapter concludes with a discussion and some conclusions.

KEY CHARACTERISTICS OF ACTION RESEARCH

As the term suggests, action research combines both action and research, and it aims to contribute actionable knowledge, that is knowledge which is useful for practice and robust for scholars. The outcomes of action research are both an action and knowledge, unlike other research approaches which aim to create knowledge only. This chapter adopts Shani and Pasmore's definition that for us captures the essence of action research in the HRD context.

> Action research may be defined as an emergent inquiry process in which applied behavioural science knowledge is integrated with existing organizational knowledge and applied to solve real organizational problems. It is simultaneously concerned with bringing about change in organizations, in developing self-help competencies in organizational members and adding to scientific knowledge. Finally, it is an evolving process that is undertaken in a spirit of collaboration and co-inquiry. (1985: 439)

This definition locates our consideration of action research for HRD in the traditional action research approach that is historically grounded in the work of Kurt Lewin and the organization development (OD) tradition that developed from Lewin and associates' work (Burnes and Cooke, 2012; Coghlan, 2012). As a collaborative, interventionist form of research, it is grounded in Lewin's insight that it was not enough to try to explain things; one also had to try to change them (Schein, 1989). This insight led to the development of action research and the powerful notion that human systems could only be understood and changed if one involved the members of the system in the inquiry process itself. So the tradition of involving the members of an organization in the change process, which is the hallmark of OD, originated in a scientific premise that this is the way (1) to get better data and (2) to effect change. Action research was based on two assumptions, which are the cornerstones of OD. One is that involving the clients or learners in their own learning not only produces better learning but more valid data about how the system really works. The other is that one only understands a system when one tries to change it, as changing human systems often involves variables which cannot be controlled by traditional research methods. Action research used in OD is based on collaboration between the behavioural-scientist researcher and the client, where they collaborate on intervening in the organization (the action) and in exploring issues and generating data on the development of the organization (the research activity). They develop action plans to address the issues and implement them. Together they evaluate the outcomes of the actions, both intended and unintended. This evaluation may then lead to further cycles of examining issues, planning action, taking action and evaluation. Cyclical-sequential phases may be identified that capture the movements of collaboration through planning and action to evaluation and to knowledge generation. These activities may serve also to generate new behavioural science knowledge, which is fed into the depository of information for other behavioural scientists as general laws, types of issues or the process of consultant–client collaboration, thus addressing issues beyond the specific case.

Working from the above definition, we are identifying the critical themes that constitute action research: that as an emergent inquiry process it engages in an unfolding story, where data shift as a consequence of intervention and where it is not possible to predict or to control what takes place. It focuses on real organizational problems or issues, rather than issues created particularly for the purposes of research. It operates in the people-in-systems domain, and applied behavioural science knowledge is both engaged in and drawn upon. Action research's distinctive characteristic is that it addresses the twin tasks of bringing about change in organizations and generating robust, actionable knowledge, in an evolving process that is undertaken in a spirit of collaboration and co-inquiry, whereby research is constructed with people, rather than on or for them. Further characteristics are that it seeks to contribute to the realm of practical knowing, including decisions and actions by practitioners, in order to improve situations, and that it involves researching in the present tense. Accordingly, engagement in the cycles of action and reflection performs both a practical and philosophical function in its attentiveness and reflexivity as to what is going on at any given moment and how that attentiveness yields purposeful action.

Action research may be conducted by a 'full member' of an organizational system, rather than by one who enters the system as an external researcher or consultant and remains only for the duration of the research or project (Coghlan, Dromgoole, Joynt and Sorensen, 2004). Coghlan and Brannick (2014) explore how attention to the three core elements of insider inquiry – managing the tensions between closeness and distance (preunderstanding), organizational and researcher roles (role duality) and managing organizational politics – is critical to the development of effective action and the generation of actionable knowledge. The insider action research approach provides a methodological grounding for the growing prevalence of research by HRD practitioners, whether managers or internal HRD consultants.

Action research is a valid and rigorous approach for doing formal research and is particularly valuable for real world organizational and work-based research conducted collaboratively with existing stakeholders.

It differs from many other approaches used in business research in that it involves simultaneous mechanisms for taking action, learning and development while at the same time gathering information, making links between theory and practice, and seeking ways to address current practical problems or opportunities for improvement. The learning opportunities associated with being a member of an action research project include the development of a range of skills involved in identifying and 'diagnosing' areas in need of development; sourcing alternative options to address these; making collaborative decisions to choose each next step; monitoring progress and responding flexibly to emerging issues; and evaluating and reflecting individually and as a group on the outcomes in order to learn from the experience and be able to share this with others as actionable or usable knowledge.

HRD AND ACTION RESEARCH

The action research approach is congruent with the main directions of HRD theory and practice (Cho and Egan, 2009; Maurer and Githens, 2010). It has long been established in the field of OD (Coghlan, 2012). Our viewpoint on HRD is from a business and management perspective and includes both adult learning and organizational learning. Hamlin, Reidy and Stewart (1998: 275) describe their use of action research as a HRD method as 'neither novel nor innovative'. Based on their experience as HRD practitioners and HRD academics, they support the call for more 'professional partnerships' between organizations and universities to enhance rigorous HRD research beyond that generally found with service agreements and consultancy. Delahaye (2000) describes four stages of HRD – investigation, design, implementation and evaluation – which sit quite compatibly with an action research approach and Shani and Pasmore's definition that for us captures the essence of action research in the HRD context.

IMPLEMENTING ACTION RESEARCH IN HRD

Building on Shani and Pasmore's definition above, we now outline the key areas for engaging in action research in HRD.

Purpose and Rationale of the Research

An action research project has both a practical and an academic purpose. Its purpose is to change the organization or solve a problem, and to generate actionable knowledge in and through the action. Accordingly, HRD action researchers need to present the purpose and rationale of their action research piece of work, stating why the action chosen is worth doing for the organization, why it is worth studying and what it is that it seeks to contribute to the world of theory and of practice. It is critical for HRD researchers to make both a practical and an academic case for what they are doing. This is not just an argument for credibility but a formal effort to locate their work in both a practical and an academic context and articulate what the potential benefits for the co-researchers, members and organization are and what the potential contributions to knowledge and theory are.

Context

Context here refers to the business, social and academic context of the research and grounds its purpose and rationale. HRD action researchers need to describe the business and industry context in which the organization operates and the organization with which they are working. This would include some details of the competitive industry environment, an introduction to the organization and what it does (e.g., corporate, government, not-for-profit, SME, its size, location, purpose and functions), some historical background about the organization, its evolution and history with HRD efforts, if any, what its concerns are and what the issues in which it is engaging mean, and what is intended and hoped for out of the action research project. This description contains not only a presentation of the facts of the organization in its business and competitive setting but also contains a review of some of the relevant literature on the setting. Academic context is also important. Not only are the HRD action researchers reviewing the business context of their project, they also review and critique the research that has been done in that context and locate their action research in that tradition and so lay the ground for their hoped-for contribution to theory and to practice.

Methodology and Methods of Action and Inquiry

As in any research work, and particularly in one for academic accreditation, an introduction to methodology and methods of inquiry is required. This is a matter of providing some basic information on action research and an introduction to how it is to be used. As noted above, there are many different approaches within the broad field of action research, and the selection of any one, such as action learning, appreciative inquiry, clinical inquiry or others, would need to be articulated and positioned in relation to the specific purpose and context of the research.

Design

There needs to be a general plan of how learning mechanisms are designed both to address the practical issue and to generate knowledge and how ethical issues were considered (Shani and Docherty, 2003; Coghlan and Shani, 2005). For example, the design might be built around project teams that would meet to address the issues confronting the organization and which might work in an action learning mode to articulate their learning in-action. As the project proceeds in the present tense, ethical issues of obtaining consent, ensuring anonymity and confidentiality, and balancing conflicting and different interests are grounded in the cycles of planning, taking action and reflection (Walker and Haslett, 2002; Holian and Coghlan, 2013).

The action researchers also need to locate themselves in the project, that is as external or internal HRD consultants, senior or line managers. Here they introduce themselves in terms of their role regarding the project, and position themselves and the challenges they face. They need to be explicit about how they propose to deal with the challenges of preunderstanding, role duality and managing organizational politics (Coghlan and Brannick, 2014). Action researchers who act as external HRD consultants need to explain how the research role was negotiated, especially if the initial contract was more oriented towards helping than research (Schein, 1995).

Narrative and Outcomes

The heart of any action research paper is the narrative or story of what took place. This is the core of implementing the design as planned or as it evolves. The story needs to be told. The presentation of the story gives the evidence in a factual and neutral manner and includes how there may be multiple perspectives on what took place as the impact may be different for different groups or actors. Researchers' view of these events and their theorizing as to what these events are considered to mean should not be mixed in with the telling of the narrative. By separating the narrative from its sense-making, and by clearly stating which is story and which is sense-making, authors are demonstrating how they are applying methodological rigour to their approach. Combining narrative and interpretation leaves them open to the charge of biased storytelling, and it makes it difficult for readers to evaluate their work.

Reflection on the Narrative and Outcomes

Here the HRD action researchers present their understanding of the events of the story and their theorizing as to what these events and outcomes are considered to mean and what their judgements are about them. The outcomes, planned and intended, unintended and unwanted, are judged in terms of the intention of the project to address the organization's needs and the rigour, reflection and relevance of the collaborative processes in coming to judgements about the project's success or otherwise. These outcomes are also to be informed by literature and theory, and reflection on whether they are relevant or useful or not. If the project is established with an assigned time to report back on progress, the outcomes may be framed in terms of what has been learned about the issue, actions taken and outcomes of these to date.

Discussion/Extrapolation to a Broader Context and Articulation of Actionable Knowledge

One of the most common criticisms of action research presentations is that they lack theory. In other words, some action research accounts tell a story but do not address issues of emergent theory and so do not contribute to knowledge. Action research projects are situation specific and do not aim to create universal knowledge. At the same time, extrapolation from a local situation to more general situations is important. Action researchers are not claiming that every organization will behave as the one studied. But they can focus on some significant factors, consideration of which is useful for other organizations, perhaps like organizations or organizations undergoing similar types of change processes. They may also offer a contribution to methodology.

In terms of the framework of this chapter, HRD action researchers need to reflect on the purpose and rationale for action and inquiry in the context presented earlier, how the design and methods of inquiry were implemented and what outcomes emerged. For example, the discussion may reflect on the impact the context had on the project, especially if some change in the context had taken place during it. The discussion would reflect on the quality of the relationships between the action researchers and organizational members and how the relationships needed to be managed through trust, collaboration, dialogue, concerns for one another's interests, equality of influence, common language and so on. It would also reflect on the quality of the action research process itself – how the collaborative processes of shared inquiry and action worked. Finally the discussion would reflect on the outcomes of the project – what might be sustainable (human, social, economic, ecological) and the development of self-help and competencies out of the action along with the creation of new knowledge from the inquiry. It might also include a discussion of what the HRD action researchers learned about themselves and their ways of working.

The discussion on the action research process itself is central. HRD researchers work to help the organizational members to understand what is going on and to take action based on that understanding, and in the process they also develop their own skills (Coghlan, 2009). Through their interventions, both those to help take action and those to help generate knowledge, HRD researchers engage with organizational members, whether as clients or fellow organizational colleagues, to draw out their experience, their insights, their judgements and their actions in the settings where things change as a consequence of intervention, and where perceptions and meanings shift as people interact and enact strategies and actions for change. The focus is firmly on acts of knowing and doing in the present tense as the project unfolds. Hence, the discussion needs to show the integrity between the purpose of the research and action, how the context is assessed, the quality of the relationships, how the participants have engaged in cycles of action and reflection on a real-life issue, and how the outcomes are workable and that they generate actionable knowledge.

CASE EXAMPLE

As a senior HRD manager for a large national organization I was responsible for leading a development programme aimed at improving 'people management' skills for managers at all levels of the organization. The programme was delivered to all management teams through intact work groups, with first line supervisors, managers, directors and senior executives from the same division present in the same group. The facilitators were all in-house and had been selected to lead and deliver the development programme by seconding several hand-picked senior executives and directors to work with me (the HRD specialist). My role was to manage this team as well as the delivery of the programme, which included being hands-on at all of the workshops (which ran off-site for two days a month each month over six months for each work group).

I had been trained in action research previously as part of postgraduate university studies and had previously applied this approach for HRD activities associated with a major operational change in another (much smaller) national organization. I had endeavoured to incorporate collaborative and reflective practices that I had learned from action research into my normal everyday practices as a manager and HRD practitioner, and to share these as a way of working with others to enhance well-being as well as meet organizational goals. So for me it was a natural extension of normal practice to provide information about what action research involved and how we could use the principles in the way we worked as an HRD team charged with running a programme to improve organizational and individual (Human Resource Management (HRM) and HRD) practices as well as in the way we worked with our organizational clients and programme participants.

Purpose and Rationale for Action and Inquiry

There had been a high level organization decision that there was a need to improve 'people management' skills to help reduce the level of legitimate internal and external complaints about breaches in compliance with discrimination laws and regulations as well as internal organizational and HR policies. While we had already decided that this development programme would draw on the principles of action learning and action research, at the same time I also chose to enrol to undertake a PhD part-time concurrently with the organizational programme. My involvement in undertaking this study and the choice to use action research was supported by top management as well as the members of the HRD team I was working with to plan and deliver the programme. An added benefit of this was the introduction of concurrent access to academic advisers.

Context

The business context was a state office of a national organization in the finance sector. The local context included a recent history of avoidable complaints which had led to costly staff turnover as well as media reports which damaged the reputation of the organization.

Methodology and Method of Inquiry

The research involved group discussions within the following: the local HRD programme team, a separate learning circle of internal HRD senior executives and a group of members of a professional association of HRD/OD consultants. Data sources included internal documents, academic literature, observations of what happened on the programme and knowledge of broader organizational history and culture. Information gathering included individual interviews with HRM/HRD managers in other organizations. A personal reflective journal was kept for the duration of the project.

Design

The HRD programme design was adapted from an exemplar that had been successfully conducted in another large office in another state. Senior executives and HRD managers were brought together for an internal conference where the leaders of that programme passed on their plans and learnings from having undertaken the process. They provided learning resources, recommended instruments, and suggestions for facilitators, with an overall framework that could be delivered flexibly depending on local needs and workgroup dynamics.

The PhD project design included two major phases: (1) a 12 month study involving over 200 supervisors, managers and executives involved in the organizational programme, conducted by a team led by the researcher as part of her normal HRD work role, including producing documents, field notes, individual interviews and a personal reflective journal and (2) in-depth interviews with 30 managers (including 20 HRM professionals) from 32 different organizations (29 of these were in the private sector).

Narrative and Outcomes

The story of the experience of doing this work in this particular organizational context, the implementation of the HRD programme and outcomes was told in the PhD thesis, sometimes in quite graphic detail. There was no expectation at the time that more than a handful of academic readers would ever choose to access and look at the entire thesis.

Reflection on the Narrative in the Light of the Experience and the Theory

Reflections on what occurred and the reasons and lessons learned were included in the PhD thesis. A fairly reflective paper was published (Holian, 1999) about my experiences of doing action research in my own organization, some ethical dilemmas I had experienced and what I had learned so far from this that I thought could be useful to others planning to undertake a similar journey.

Extrapolation to a Broader Context and Articulation of Usable Knowledge

Academic journal articles were published which linked the findings to theory on management decision-making and ethics (Holian, 2002, 2006).

Applications to practice developed through working collaboratively with others undertaking and leading change in their own organizations(s), including part-time postgraduate students seeking to learn about and apply action research to their own practice and in their own organizations.

DISCUSSION

The choice to undertake action research is related to the challenges facing the organization, the imperatives to take action and the actionable knowledge that emerges from the action taken. It also incorporates the nature of the working relationship between the researcher and other people involved in the research processes and the quality of the processes of action and inquiry that take place. Action research is not necessarily suitable for all possible HRD research projects or researchers. It is particularly useful when there is a need to take action before there is a clear way to solve the problem, when issues are seen as important by the people involved, when there are effective working relationships and a supportive environment which allows experimental steps to be taken in a desired direction while remaining flexible to feedback, without the need for a detailed plan in advance. The process of undertaking action research is a developmental opportunity which incorporates learning how to do action research while at the same time concentrating on solving a practical problem.

Action research can be suitable for addressing a messy dilemma in a real world setting, where the problems may be difficult to define, other approaches have not worked and there does not seem to be a simple solution. There would be a group of key stakeholders who are or can be empowered to work collaboratively in order to generate options, make decisions, take action, reflect, and engage in an ongoing review of progress.

Doing action research with members of a group or organization differs from approaches where the researcher has an expert role to lead research involving participants and may be conducted on behalf of clients or organizational sponsors. While internal or external HRD practitioners may have expert roles in other settings, they may also choose to use an action research approach if this is suited to the specific context in which they are working. Under these circumstances it is advisable to consider the tasks and skills necessary to deal with the challenges of role duality outlined by Coghlan and Brannick (2014), to hold, to value and to manage the demands of both roles and the impact on the research and researchers. In putting aside their expert role within the action research project and team, HRD practitioners can attempt to look with fresh eyes and hear with fresh ears, temporarily suspending assumptions based on concepts and theories of the discipline, avoiding the use of jargon in preference for lay language and encouraging expressions about how people seem to be understanding their reality.

The methods of information gathering and analysis that are described in other chapters in this book may also be used in action research. These may range from sources of hard data derived using quantitative measures and descriptive statistics, through observable behaviours which can be recorded, while acknowledging that what is observed may be theory dependent, to ways of eliciting information about perceptions and interpretations, including interviews, storytelling and the use of images, sounds and metaphor. However, it needs to be noted that in action research data comes through engagement with others in the action research process. Therefore, it is important to know that acts which are intended to collect data are themselves interventions. So issuing a questionnaire or asking an individual a question is not simply collecting data but is also *generating* learning data for both the researcher and the individual concerned. Every action, even the very intention and presence of research, is an intervention and has political implication across the system. Accordingly, it is more appropriate to speak of data *generation* than data gathering.

Action research has a focus on current, practical issues, opportunities or problems in a real world setting. There is shared agreement that the research has the potential to address these issues and is worth doing. There is a joint willingness to work in a collaborative manner, as co-researchers. The action research team requires members with interpersonal facilitation and research skills in order to plan and implement the methods that are to be used for data generation and collection, analysis and making meaning of what is discovered, and to make decisions about the relative merit and value of options, desired outcomes, and the application and dissemination of results. The outcomes of an action research project include generation of knowledge, enhanced desired behaviours, improved relationships and confidence in individual capabilities. The findings can be presented to others within the research setting, written up as work in progress and aspects documented in formal internal reports, and may also make a contribution to practice and theory through presentations and publications made available to professional and academic colleagues.

This chapter has introduced action research as a valid and rigorous approach for doing HRD research that is particularly valuable for real world organizational and work based research because it is grounded in action. As we have explored in this chapter, its distinctive characteristic is that it addresses the twin tasks of bringing about change in organizations and in generating robust, actionable knowledge in an evolving process that is undertaken in a spirit of collaboration and co-inquiry. The action research approach is congruent with HRD theory and practice in its emphasis on improving organizational processes.

REFERENCES

Burnes, B. and Cooke, B. (2012) 'The past, present and future of organization development: Taking the long view'. *Human Relations*, 65: 1395–1429.

Cho, Y. and Egan, T. (2009) 'Action learning research: A systematic review and conceptual framework'. *Human Resource Development Review*, 8: 431–462.

Coghlan, D. (2009) 'Toward a philosophy of clinical inquiry/research'. *Journal of Applied Behavioral Science*, 45 (1): 106–121.

Coghlan, D. (2011) 'Action research: Exploring perspective on a philosophy of practical knowing'. *Academy of Management Annals*, 5 (1): 53–87.

Coghlan, D. (2012) 'Organization development and action research: Then and now'. In: Boje, D., Burnes, B. and Hassard, J. (eds.) *The Routledge Companion to Organizational Change* (pp. 47–58). Abingdon, UK: Routledge.

Coghlan, D. and Brannick, T. (2014) *Doing Action Research in Your Own Organization*. 4th edn. London: Sage.

Coghlan, D., Dromgoole, T., Joynt, P. and Sorensen, P. (2004) *Managers Learning in Action*. London: Routledge.

Coghlan, D. and Shani, A.B. (Rami) (2005) 'Roles, politics and ethics in action research design'. *Systemic Practice and Action Research*, 18: 533–546.

Coughlan, D. and Coghlan, D. (2009) 'Action research'. In: Karlsson, C. (ed.) *Researching Operations Management* (pp. 236–264). New York: Routledge.

Delahaye, B. (2000) *Human Resource Development: Principles and Practice*. Milton Keynes, UK: Wiley.

Eden, C. and Huxham, C. (2006) 'Researching organizations using action research'. In: Clegg, S., Hardy, C., Lawrence, T. and Nord, W. (eds.) *The Sage Handbook of Organization Studies*. Thousand Oaks, CA: Sage.

Greenwood, D. and Levin, M. (2007) *Introduction to Action Research*. 2nd edn. Thousand Oaks, CA: Sage.

Gummesson, E. (2001) *Qualitative Methods in Management Research*. 2nd edn. Thousand Oaks, CA: Sage.

Hamlin, B., Reidy, M. and Stewart, J. (1998) 'Bridging the HRD research–practice gap through professional partnerships'. *Human Resource Development International*, 1: 273–290.

Holian, R. (1999) 'Doing action research in my own organisation'. *Action Research International*, Paper 3, www.aral.com.au/ari/p-rholian99.html (accessed 6 March 2015).

Holian, R. (2002) 'Management decision making and ethics: Practices, skills and preferences'. *Management Decision*, 40 (9): 862–870.

Holian, R. (2006) 'Management decision making, ethical issues and "emotional" intelligence'. *Management Decision*, 44 (8): 1122–1138.

Holian, R. and Coghlan, D. (2013) 'Ethical issues and role duality in insider action research: Challenges for action research degree programmes'. *Systemic Practice and Action Research*, 26 (5): 399–415.

Maurer, M. and Githens, R. (2010) 'Toward a reframing of action research for human resource and organization development'. *Action Research*, 8 (3): 267–292.

Raelin, J.A. (2009) 'Seeking conceptual clarity in the action modalities'. *Action Learning Research and Practice*, 6 (1): 17–24.

Schein, E.H. (1989) 'Organization development: Science, technology or philosophy'. In: Coghlan, D. and Shani, A.B. (Rami) (eds.) *Fundamentals of Organization Development* (Vol. 1, pp. 91–100). London: Sage.

Schein, E.H. (1995) 'Process consultation, action research and clinical inquiry: Are they the same?' *Journal of Managerial Psychology*, 10 (6): 14–19.

Shani, A.B. (Rami) and Docherty, P. (2003) *Learning by Design*. Oxford: Blackwell.

Shani, A.B. (Rami), Mohrman, S.A., Pasmore, W., Stymne, B. and Adler, N. (2008) *Handbook of Collaborative Management Research*. Thousand Oaks, CA: Sage.

Shani, A.B. (Rami) and Pasmore, W.A. (1985) 'Organization inquiry: Towards a new model of the action research process'. In: Warrick, D.D. (ed.) *Contemporary Organization Development: Current Thinking and Applications* (pp. 438–448). Glenview, IL: Scott Foresman and Company. [Reproduced in Coghlan, D. and Shani, A.B. (Rami) (eds.) (2010) *Fundamentals of Organization Development* (Vol. 1, pp.249–260). London: Sage.]

Walker, B. and Haslett, T. (2002) 'Action research in management–ethical dilemmas'. *Systemic Practice and Action Research*, 15 (6): 523–533.

ANNOTATED FURTHER READING

Coghlan, D. and Brannick, T. (2014) *Doing Action Research in Your Own Organization*. 4th edn. London: Sage. This is an internationally popular and practical how-to-do-it book on action research with a particular focus on challenges for those engaging it in their own organization.

Greenwood, D. and Levin, M. (2007) *Introduction to Action Research*. 2nd edn. Thousand Oaks, CA: Sage. This is an important introduction to action research, with an emphasis on participatory action research.

Shani, A.B. (Rami), Mohrman, S.A., Pasmore, W., Stymne, B. and Adler, N. (2008) *Handbook of Collaborative Management Research*. Thousand Oaks, CA: Sage. Groundbreaking work on collaborative research between scholars and practitioners/insiders and outsiders conducted in an action research manner.

11. Critical action learning research: opportunities and challenges for HRD research and practice
Kiran Trehan and Clare Rigg

SUMMARY

This chapter presents a conceptual and empirical synthesis of critical action learning research and contributes to debates on criticality in action learning research. The chapter augments the need for more grounded approaches to the evaluation of research initiatives directed at HRD.

INTRODUCTION

The world of Human Resource Development (HRD) is awash with policy interventions offering myriad forms of support for performance improvement and advancement of human capital. Yet a common critique levelled at the field is a gap between HRD practice and research communities (Short et al., 2009). The debate calls for approaches to research that go beyond quantitative notions of 'impact'. For example, Gold and Thorpe (2008:399), with reference to small and medium-sized enterprises (SMEs), argue that serious attention needs to be accorded to 'the desires and aspirations of . . . managers, which can only be accessed from the inside'. In terms of the impact of research on practice, much HRD research in the 'expert' tradition, whilst it might enlighten a particular problem, often leaves participants ignorant and powerless in the face of ongoing issues (Cockman et al., 1999; Schein, 1998).

   This chapter responds to such calls by investigating how critical action learning research (CALR) can contribute to knowledge about and practice of HRD. We illustrate this by drawing from a five-year initiative that was run to support the development of a group of small business owners. The initiative was, in effect, an inquiry into the synthesis of CALR and HRD, which is an often neglected strand of evidence-based research in practical settings. We demonstrate how CALR was used to develop theoretical interest, at the same time as being a means of working with policy makers to change how they supported the development of business owners.

The chapter is organised as follows. We begin this presentation of CALR by positioning it in relation to its genesis in action learning and critical action learning (CAL). We develop this with reference to contemporary developments in action-orientated research and particularly action learning research (ALR); this is followed by an account of the implementation of CALR, comprising a discussion of an illustrative project and the interventions. Some conclusions from the outcomes of this experience for HRD research are offered in the final section.

CRITICAL ACTION LEARNING – AS HRD INTERVENTION AND RESEARCH APPROACH

Action learning is a familiar approach in HRD, traditionally employed to support the learning and development of professionals through their engagement in reflecting on their experiences as they attempt to address real issues and challenges within their work contexts. Defined by the equation $L = P + Q$ (Revans, 1982), action learning is underpinned by the central assumption that learning (L) derives from taking action. External expertise and theory (P) are considered insufficient, because, whilst it may be drawn from, existing codified knowledge may not suit the specific context of a particular problem. Hence asking insightful questions (Q) about burning problems, challenges or alluring opportunities facilitates change. In relation to philosophy of knowledge, action learning is based on praxeology, which essentially can be understood as a theory of practical knowing. Applied to HRD research, value is placed on knowledge, gained through action, and on the interplay between the researcher's developing self-knowledge and their growing organisational understanding (Prasad, 2005; Rigg, 2014).

Also based on praxeology, CAL is a contemporary development of action learning which holds that learning and organisational development can be advanced when the power and emotional dimensions of learning are treated centrally as a site of learning about managing and organising and learners draw from critical ideas to make connections between their individual and work experiences. The potential for criticality in action learning derives from the tensions, contradictions, emotions and power dynamics that inevitably exist both within an organisation context and in individual managers' lives. CAL is concerned that HRD be seen as a means for individual or collective transformation or emancipation and not simply a means of performance improvement. In terms of practical implementation, CAL has a number of distinguishing features, including drawing the attention of participants to the way that learning is supported, avoided or prevented through power relations within the organisational environment; applying questioning insight to reveal and understand the organisational significance of complex emotions, unconscious processes and relations; and a more active facilitation role than that implied within either traditional action learning or most other group-based HRD interventions. As an HRD approach, encouragement of critical reflection is central to CAL. Although reflection is integral to the classical principles of action learning, this is often interpreted to mean simply an instrumental encouragement of participants to think about their individual experience of action, to the exclusion of the emotional and political aspects of the learning process. Purely instrumental reflection neglects that action and learning are always undertaken in a context of power and politics, which inevitably carries potential for conflict, anxiety, and obstruction of learning. Critical reflection engages participants in a process of drawing from critical perspectives to make connections between their learning and daily work experiences, to identify the assumptions governing their actions, to locate the historical and cultural origins of their assumptions, question their meaning, and to recognise unquestioned norms held about organisational and personal practices. As an HRD practice, CAL helps participants develop alternative ways of thinking and acting, as through the process of critical reflection they come to interpret and create new knowledge and actions from their experiences. Herein also lies the potential of CAL as a research approach in that it blends learning through experience with theoretical and technical learning to form new knowledge constructions and insights as well as new behaviours.

CAL has evolved in recent years to emphasise learning and development through critical engagement in action and reflection. However, there has been no onus to contribute knowledge beyond those involved. CALR adds this further expectation, that knowledge is created for the wider world. In the terminology of Revans' original equation ($L = P + Q$), the focus of CALR becomes $P = L + Q$, in the sense that through research knowledge is codified (P) from the learning of participants (L) that comes from their particular critical inquiry (Q) context. In this sense CALR is part of the action turn in research.

THE ACTION TURN IN HRD RESEARCH

In organisation studies, including the field of HRD, frustration with positivist philosophy's separation between theory and practice, engagement and observation (action and research), has led to a variety of approaches concerned with actionable knowledge, that is knowledge that has both practicable use for those involved at the same time as contributing to the wider store of human knowledge or science. Known by varying terms, including Mode 2 research, collaborative research, practitioner research and action-orientated research,

> 'The new production of knowledge', as articulated by Gibbons and his colleagues (1994), is a network activity different from a model embedded in the expertise of isolated individuals operating from a top-down expert model. This network activity . . . is characterised by: knowledge that is produced in the context of application, transdisciplinarity, heterogeneity and organisational diversity, social accountability and reflexivity. (Coghlan and Coughlan, 2010:194)

ALR has been advanced as a related, yet distinctive form of collaborative learning and research activity (Coghlan and Coughlan, 2010) producing actionable knowledge. Our understanding of ALR is that it is research that involves engagement in action learning, whether by researchers as they inquire into their research practice or when employed as a method of organisation learning and change, for example, in the course of an action inquiry into an aspect of HRD. A CALR approach encourages critical reflection upon assumptions, contextual awareness, imaginative speculation and reflective scepticism. The relevance of CALR to action-orientated research is twofold. First, there is shared commitment to change and, second, a common value that knowledge should serve practice. Both abjure positivist approaches to research, instead valuing praxeology, with its high regard for practical knowledge derived from deliberation on and in the context of practice and for the systemic interconnections between an individual's learning about themselves, learning with others and learning about the wider organisation/society. Hence CALR is a process in which knowledge is generated through collaborative inquiry into the real life concerns and tensions of those involved. It resonates with the interest in pragmatist, constructionist and critical realist approaches to knowledge creation.

Building on the original epistemology of action learning, CALR is predicated on a theory of action in terms of a science of praxeology, comprising what Revans (1982) called systems alpha, beta and gamma. System alpha centres on the investigation of the issue/challenge/ problem, examining the external context, managerial values and available internal resources. System beta focuses on problem resolution, through decision cycles of negotiation and experimentation. System gamma concerns the participants' cognitive framework – their assumptions and prior understanding – and is concerned with the learning as experienced individually by each participant through their questioning and emerging self-insight.

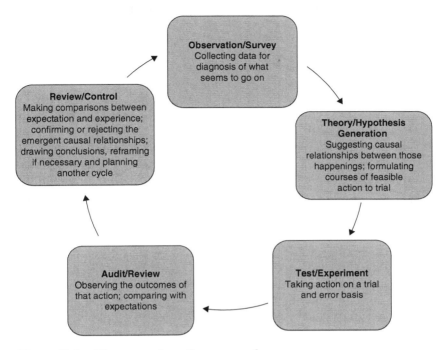

Figure 11.1   The system beta five-step cycle

The scientific method associated with system beta comprises a (continuously repeated) five-step cycle (Figure 11.1).

The three systems, alpha, beta and gamma, are not linear or sequential, but are perhaps best understood as a whole, with interlocking yet overlapping parts. Systems alpha and beta focus on the investigation of the problem whilst system gamma focuses on the learning. They overlap on important issues of learning, power and politics, as participants engage with the complexities of real issues. Criticality in the action learning cycles includes explicit attention to the process of decision selection and exclusion of solutions, involvement of other organisation stakeholders and questioning assumptions that underlie how the issue/problem is framed.

CRITICAL ACTION LEARNING RESEARCH AND HRD

A small but growing strand of literature is beginning to make the case for CALR in the formulation and implementation of research interventions.

CAL approaches to HRD pay particular attention to the goals of interventions, the importance of context and the exercise of power; yet their potential to enrich each other's perspectives has rarely been explored. The foregrounding of emotional and political dynamics is at the core of CALR; the proposed synthesis can therefore enhance both sets of debates. Within this form of inquiry, CALR addresses the criticism that many learning and HRD interventions are divorced from the prospective clients. CALR has the potential to overcome this problem because its starting point is participant-focused and requires the active engagement of practitioners involved in the research setting with political, social and emotional contexts internally and externally and moving beyond the instrumental necessity of 'getting things done' (Reynolds and Trehan, 2008; Vince, 2008).

PERSONAL EXPERIENCE OF USING CRITICAL ACTION LEARNING RESEARCH FOR HRD-BASED RESEARCH

The illustration presented in this chapter is based on a five-year inquiry involving the development of small business owners. We focus on how key elements of CALR were embedded in the design of the research project, illuminating the systematic documentation of the process in action which all too often remains implicit within extant HRD research. Implications for HRD research and practice are reflected upon.

The research project arose from discussions involving the researchers, the chief executive of a business support agency and a group of African-Caribbean entrepreneurs who were known to be running successful businesses. Our deliberations focused upon the nature of leadership development and business support for African-Caribbean businesses, a subject that had exercised us all in different ways. We (the researchers) had a longstanding research interest in human resource development (Trehan, 2007) and initiatives directed towards ethnic minority entrepreneurs (Ram and Jones, 2008). The entrepreneurs involved in our deliberations were keen on interventions that supported businesses like theirs and helped develop their leadership capabilities. The outcome of these interactions was an agreement to establish a network to develop African-Caribbean entrepreneurs. This action learning set comprised eight African-Caribbean entrepreneurs, the agency chief executive and two researchers. The next section recounts the approach and methods that were used to conduct the study.

Researching Power, Politics and Entrepreneurial Development

Our approach

The core elements of our research approach consisted of two key phases. The purpose of the first phase of the project was to facilitate the configuration of the group. It was important that the composition of the group was determined by the entrepreneurs themselves, because often in accounts of the research process, the formation of learning sets is presented as a largely procedural and unproblematic process.

Hence the start of the inquiry was collaborative and dialogical, involving engagement with a range of stakeholders. At first glance, this approach may appear to be consistent with other action research approaches. However CAL's influence is evident because, from the outset, assumptions about membership and organisation of the group itself were openly critiqued in order to surface the intricate social, political and emotional dimensions inherent in learning with and from the research group.

In the second phase, our main concern was to ensure that the research design procured active engagement by the participants with the emotional and political context in which the research intervention was embedded. This was crucial to the task of data gathering. In order to do this we, the researchers, adopted two mutually supportive roles in the inquiry: process consultant/facilitator; and researcher, researching the action learning process as it evolved over the life of the project. These roles transcend dichotomised positions in evaluation, which tend to separate investigators from participants. Equally, consistent with CAL, such an approach allows researchers to engage in a process of deliberation without necessarily compromising their commitment to the facilitation of the ALS. This is important because we, the researchers, offered perspectives (rather than prescriptions) that were sometimes at odds with group members' expectations. These were episodes of 'critical reflection' in which participants engaged in our involvement, this being the subject of considerable discussion.

We made it clear at the outset that we were not 'experts' on small business development, and that we would not be providing advice or guidance on such matters. This did not prevent repeated requests for inputs on leadership, marketing, the traits of successful entrepreneurs, and a whole series of other development related issues. The key elements of our role were as facilitators of the (critical) action learning process as it unfolded during the course of the initiative and as researchers with an interest in drawing broader lessons for policy makers, practitioners and academics. For example, in our research, discussions on recruitment to the group raised a number of issues, including size and type of business and aspirations of potential members; however, it soon became evident that the apparently fixed criteria relating to turnover and fast-growth were being relaxed. The ability to *fit in* and *get on* with existing group members appeared to be as, if not more, important. For us, this threw into sharp relief a tension between a philosophical commitment to the emancipatory ethos of CALR, and the realisation that its effect may be to reproduce inequality in respect of gender and leadership development. Our approach was to convey our concern and reinforce the message at appropriate points in time. Research in this vein values the active engagement of the researcher. Engagement involves promoting the fruits of the research to a diverse range of stakeholders whilst also ensuring that the different knowledge bases of researchers and practitioners are actively exploited; such interaction is more conducive to the generation of useful insights than either party working in isolation. Finally, our research design – in which the researchers themselves are participants – responds to Dover and Lawrence's (2011:305) exhortation to '"get dirty" – to move away from largely "hands-off" research approaches'.

Although an accurate presentation of the research design, the above account depicts an exceedingly sterile account of the actual research process. The way in which the research was conducted did not follow some goal-directed, linear path. Yet accounts of actual and 'messy' research are probably more useful than pristine prescriptions, because they provide valuable insights into a range of real issues that researchers face in the field and different ways in which they can be addressed. For new researchers entering the field, adopting a CAL approach requires a mix of different process skills. The role essentially involves the researcher developing relationships with the action learning group, observing, listening and asking critical questions. Learning happens through critical questions, investigation, experimentation and reflection, rather than through reliance on traditional interview techniques. This requires planned interventions in real time situations and a study of those interventions as they occur, which in turn forms further interventions. Thus, the researcher is involved in more than an exchange of information and ideas. Drawing on the tradition of process consultation (Schein, 1998), the researcher-as-facilitator helps the participants/group become aware of HRD processes and is concerned with passing on the approach, methods and values of CAL to participants. In this way the research strategy seeks to integrate the research activities with the participants' work and personal experiences and reflects the processual and situated nature of HRD research.

As Schein (1998) highlights, 'The processes we need to learn to observe and manage are those that make a demonstrable difference to problem solving, decision making, and organizational effectiveness in general' (p.28).

Methods

A variety of methods were used to record the interactions with the entrepreneurs. First, the formal action learning sets were tape-recorded and fully transcribed. Second, as a supplement to the tape-recording, we kept 'process notes' to document what we saw as the political and power-related dynamics that unfolded during these meetings. Third, each of the entrepreneurs was interviewed at the start of the inquiry and again two and four years later. This enabled detailed information to be gathered on the perceptions of development at an individual and business level. Finally, we reviewed company documentation and written material that the entrepreneurs generated during the inquiry (including minutes, emails and personal reflections). The data were analysed thematically in accordance with the key research themes, supplemented by categories that emerged during the course of the inquiry. Hence, all interactions were qualitatively analysed. Data analysis followed the sequence of reading and re-reading interview and inquiry transcripts, summarising, category formation (or thematising) followed by the description and analysis. However, as a qualitative study, the analysis was iterative rather than linear. This produced a rich set of data on the entrepreneurs' expectations, perceptions and responses to the inquiry at various stages; information has also been generated on the effects and impact of CAL as a model for individual, group, business and leadership development. As researchers we adopted the role of facilitators and investigated the action learning process as it emerged and evolved. Too often in accounts of CAL the intervention process is presented as a largely procedural and unproblematic process. In contrast, within this study, our position on facilitation was to recognise, surface and actively engage with the social, emotional and political processes associated with power relations, rather than simply 'managing them'.

In summary, we would highlight three distinctive aspects of this CALR approach. First, it facilitates a research process that critically reflects on power, politics and emotions in action. The research group itself is seen as a source of learning about business and leadership dynamics. Second, critical action research encourages collective reflection upon experience and active experimentation. Third, it links research to practice and contends that research is more than a technical exercise predicated on context-free evidence; as Ram and Trehan argue (2010), it is a process of argumentation that emerges from dialogue, interpretation, experience and prevailing power structures.

Research outcomes

The outcomes from this research project were threefold; first, the inquiry highlighted that CAL requires an authentic commitment to embed a research approach at the outset which ensures power relations are central to the design and implementation of HRD learning, both 'inside' and 'outside' of the organisation. By being 'critical by design', CALR throws into sharp relief the social and political dynamics that attend the process of HRD. As we have seen in the present study, this will have implications for the organisation of interventions. Second, research on HRD in small firms recognises that the business owner is embedded in a web of social and economic relationships which both enable and constrain his/her scope for development and action. Ram and Trehan (2010) highlight how the importance of this context involves extending one's gaze behind the often simplistic notion of the 'entrepreneurial individual'. CAL, with its heightened sensitivity to emotional and political context, is particularly well placed to elicit the complexity and multi-layered nature of HRD activity in small firms. Finally, CALR provides an interpretive counterpoint to the instrumentally driven research approaches which focus only on measurement and output rather than on impact and actionable knowledge. Explicit engagement with the concept of impact is central to researching HRD, as it facilitates a fusion of worlds of practice and research, with the aim of generating knowledge integration so they are no longer two separate domains. By adopting a CAL approach, researchers and practitioners can develop a detailed understanding of how entrepreneurs engage with the micro-political dimensions of HRD. As a result of these interactions, the participants were able to develop clearer understandings of the political and emotional processes that accompany business support systems when attempting to leverage resources and knowledge from policy makers, businesses intermediaries and academics. As the participants have evolved, these formal and informal interactions have been instrumental in prompting members to develop and, in many cases, re-appraise their business aspirations, as the following extracts highlight:

> It has been a rollercoaster of emotions since joining the group but I have learnt so much about myself and been exposed to different political environments. I am now more aware of the power dynamics in and outside of the group which has helped me develop, re-direct the business.

> It's turned me from an insular individual and has opened me up to share my business ideas, helped me to take advice, learn from others and challenges my opinions.

Furthermore, the participants have also developed their leadership capabilities and become more strategic, which has helped them access new markets for their products and services. Other outcomes included:

- Growth in turnover, profitability and employment;
- Advice on cost control and surviving the recession;
- Increased inter-trading;
- Personal development including building individual confidence;
- HR knowledge;
- Acquisition of new skills.

DISCUSSION: IMPLICATIONS FOR HRD RESEARCH AND PRACTICE

This chapter has illuminated how CALR has the potential to deepen our understanding of the emotional and micro-political processes of HRD practice. By combining ideas from debates on what HRD comprises, perspectives on CAL, and a critical research perspective, we offer new insights for fruitful research methods that enable the study of HRD in action.

However, a number of caveats need to be entered in respect of the issue of replicability. First, the research 'journey' is a long and uncertain process, with levels of interest waxing and waning according to the inevitable preoccupations and priorities of busy entrepreneurs. The longevity of this initiative is a testimony to the commitment of the participants. But the life of the project has also witnessed periods of apparent inactivity, which have, on occasions, prompted questions about the future of the research initiative.

Second, the research process is undoubtedly resource-intensive, and has been dependent on the commitment and goodwill of the participants for its sustenance. Third, the open-ended nature of the research process complicates the process of evaluation. There are certainly elements that can be measured. For instance, it is reasonably straightforward to quantify the number of meetings held, the types of input from facilitators and the findings from company assessments. It is much more difficult to assess the qualitative impact of the HRD and leadership process initiated by the group; yet it is precisely these intangible elements that appear to be the most influential.

A number of implications flow from the above conclusions. First, the context in which HRD research initiatives are introduced needs to be mapped out and understood. HRD research does not operate in a vacuum, but is fundamentally shaped by the context and power relations of the research setting. Accordingly, questions need to be asked about the nature and purpose of the research and the role of the researchers. In essence, it is important to explore, 'What works, for whom; and in what conditions?' This frames the possibility of moving away from research that only measures the easily measurable dimensions like expenditure, training days and qualifications, to research that can provide the basis of organisational change, on condition that the process of reflection, which is at its core, is in turn organisational, not individual. We argue strongly for this shift in perspective from individual to systemic whilst recognising the tensions that can result from this approach.

Finally, a mix of research skills and competencies are required for the effective implementation of such research initiatives. A CALR approach is ideally suited to the meshing together of diverse sources of expertise, since one of its key characteristics is a 'team-based' approach to investigation involving researchers and practitioners.

ACKNOWLEDGEMENT

This chapter draws on an earlier paper by Ram and Trehan (2009) published in *Action Learning: Research and Practice*.

REFERENCES

Cockman, P., Evans, B. and Reynolds, P. (1999) *Consulting for Real People: A Client-Centre Approach for Change Agents and Leaders*. London: McGraw-Hill.
Coghlan, D. and Coughlan, P. (2010) 'Notes toward a Philosophy of Action Learning Research'. *Action Learning: Research and Practice* 7 (2): 193–203.
Dover, G. and Lawrence, T. (2011) 'A Gap Year for Institutional Theory: Integrating the Study of Institutional Work and Participatory Action Research'. *Journal of Management Inquiry* 19 (4): 305–316.
Gold, J. and Thorpe, R. (2008) '"Training, It's a Load of Crap": The Story of the Hairdresser and His "Suit"'. *Human Resource Development International* 11 (4): 385–399.
Prasad, P. (2005) *Crafting Qualitative Research: Working in the Post Positivists Traditions*. Oxford: Routledge.
Ram, M. and Jones, T. (2008) 'Ethnic Minority Business: Review of Research and Policy'. *Government and Policy (Environment and Planning 'C')* 26: 352–374.
Ram, M. and Trehan, K. (2009) 'Critical by Design: Enacting Critical Action Learning in Small Business Context'. *Action Learning: Research and Practice* 6 (3): 305–318.
Ram, M. and Trehan, K. (2010) 'Critical Action Learning, Policy Learning and Small Firms: An Inquiry'. *Management Learning* 41 (4): 415–428.
Revans, R. (1982) *The Origins and Growth of Action Learning*. Bromley, UK: Chartwell-Bratt.
Reynolds, M. and Trehan, K. (2008) 'Leadership Pedagogies'. Research paper, Centre for Excellence in Leadership, University of Lancaster.
Rigg, C. (2014) 'Praxeology'. In D. Coghlan and M. Brydon-Miller (eds). *The Sage Encyclopedia of Action Research* (pp.651–653). London: Sage.

Schein, E. (1998) *Process Consultation Revisited: Building the Helping Relationship.* New York: Addison Wesley.

Short, D., Keefer, J. and Stone, S. (2009) 'The Link between Research and Practice: Experiences of HRD and Other Professions'. *Advances in Developing Human Resources* 11 (4): 420–437.

Trehan, K. (2007) 'Exploring the Relationship between Critical HRD and Psychodynamic Approaches to Development'. *Journal of Advances in Developing Human Resources* 9 (1): 73–82.

Vince, R. (2008) '"Learning-in-Action" and Learning Inaction: Advancing the Theory and Practice of Critical Action Learning'. *Action Learning: Research and Practice* 5 (2): 93–104.

ANNOTATED FURTHER READING

Ram, M. and Trehan, K. (2010) 'Critical Action Learning, Policy Learning and Small Firms: An Inquiry'. *Management Learning* 41 (4): 415–428. This paper presents a conceptual and empirical synthesis of 'critical action learning' and 'policy learning' (PL). The paper reflects upon an initiative that aimed to provide business support to an action learning set comprising entrepreneurs. The findings demonstrate how a synthesis of CAL and PL can enrich CAL by recognising the centrality of emotional and power relations, providing a vehicle to examine the tensions and dynamics that attend policy implementation and illustrating the merits of an experiential approach to evaluation (reflecting recent calls in debates on small-firm policy). We contribute to debates on criticality in action learning and the need for more grounded approaches to the evaluation of initiatives directed at small firms.

Rigg, C. and Richards, S. (2008) *Action Learning, Leadership and Organizational Development in Public Services.* London: Routledge. An edited collection in the Routledge HRD series, this book presents examples of action learning used across public service organisations as an approach that can simultaneously address individual, organisational and systemic development.

Trehan, K. and Rigg, C. (2011) 'Theorising Critical HRD: Complexities and Contradictions'. *Journal of European Industrial Training* 35 (3): 276–290. Empirical investigations that have systematically applied critical approaches to HRD are in short supply, and their potential to enrich HRD practice has rarely been explored. This paper contributes to addressing these gaps. First, it elucidates the concept of critical HRD; second, it demonstrates some of the intricacies and discrepancies within current theorising on critical HRD; third, it raises questions for the practical significance of tools and insights informed by critical HRD.

12. Facilitating learning using the Service Template Extended Process (STEP) within a process consultation framework

Mark N.K. Saunders, Paul Tosey, Claire Jones and Christine S. Williams

SUMMARY

In this chapter we consider the use and practical value of STEP, the Service Template Extended Process, to support applied HRD research in collaboration with practitioners. Used through a process consultation framework, STEP can surface values and underlying assumptions, thereby enabling both single and double-loop learning (Saunders and Williams, 2001).

INTRODUCTION

Applied management research is, invariably, concerned with learning about and understanding problem situations better in order to facilitate their improvement (Rynes, 2007). It therefore invariably involves the development of human resources. Yet, whilst such research often involves both practitioners and academics, attempts are less frequently made to span the academic–practitioner divide in which the academic researcher adopts a practitioner orientation, actively involving the practitioner in the research (and learning) process and embedding learning from findings in practice (Saunders, 2011; Gray et al., 2011).

Our experience of working with organisations over a number of years has highlighted how the groups involved in the situations we are researching as externals know, between them, far more that we as outsiders can ever hope to know. It has also highlighted the importance of time spent understanding each organisation's needs and ensuring that these have been understood, as intended by us as academic researchers. Whilst such issues have been recognised for many years (see, for example, Killman, 1986; Schein, 1999), they are still often relegated or ignored when researching organisations. As researchers we need to recognise that we are unlikely to understand the organisation and the problem situation as well as those involved on a daily basis. We therefore need to work with those practitioners, enabling them to learn about and better understand their own organisation relationships, and support them to develop solutions, in a manner similar to that of collaborators within action research (Coghlan and Brannick, 2010).

Process consultation offers what Schein (1999: 1) refers to as 'the key philosophical underpinning to organizational learning and development'. Like action research (see Chapter 10 in this volume) it involves close collaboration between researchers and practitioners. However, unlike action research, the researcher is not expected to be an expert in the problem area but the guardian of the research process. Consequently it is the creation of a relationship with a client (practitioner) that permits her or him to perceive, understand and act upon what is happening within both external and internal environments to improve a situation they have defined. Building on the assumption that on her or his own a researcher/consultant can never know enough about a particular problem situation and culture of an organisation to be able to make reliable recommendations for improvement, Schein emphasises the need for a helping process in which groups of people come together to learn about the situation and, where necessary, develop appropriate improvements for themselves. Within this, the focus is upon developing an effective helping relationship between the researcher/consultant and other participants in the problem situation so that all can work together to develop their understanding and develop appropriate solutions. Process consultation therefore offers a framework for Human Resource Development (HRD) researchers which emphasises firstly the importance of research being undertaken *between* and *with* those involved rather than *on* and *for* people; and, secondly, that research should lead to learning and not merely to description.

Process consultation enables values and norms held by one group to be challenged by another and, where necessary, modified. This may be necessary for real improvement to take place. Such 'double-loop' learning (Argyris and Schön, 1996: 21) involves taking into consideration the context within which the research occurs and seeing that context from new perspectives, rather than only looking within existing frameworks, norms, policies and rules. Double-loop learning has been characterised as the response to the question 'are we doing the right things?' (Romme and Witteloostuijn, 1999: 452) as opposed to the single-loop question 'are we doing things right?'

This chapter outlines the use of the Service Template Extended Process (STEP), to involve practitioners in applied research through employing a process consultation framework (Schein, 1999). Originally developed to better understand service relationships between service users and providers (Williams and Saunders, 2006), STEP offers a process which can surface values and underlying assumptions, thereby enabling both single and double-loop learning (Saunders and Williams, 2001).

We commence with a brief overview of the concepts of single- and double-loop learning. This is followed by a brief discussion of the development of STEP and an overview of the process within a process consultation framework. We illustrate this from our personal experiences, focusing particularly on an example of its use to learn about and improve an IT company's relationship with an alliance partner.

DOUBLE-LOOP LEARNING AND IMPROVING PROBLEM SITUATIONS

Many scholars observe that the concept of organisational learning often entails a dichotomy between types or orders of learning (Tosey et al., 2012). This has been expressed using a variety of terms – single-loop and double-loop (e.g. Argyris and Schön, 1996); lower-level and higher-level (Fiol and Lyles, 1985); first-order and second-order (Arthur and Aiman-Smith, 2001); incremental and radical (Miner and Mezias, 1996); and adaptive and generative learning (Senge, 1990) – although a reasonable consensus has been established that they refer to comparable learning processes and outcomes (Argyris, 1996; Arthur and Aiman-Smith, 2001; Miner and Mezias, 1996). In its basic form, single-loop learning is action-oriented, routine and incremental, occurring within existing frameworks, norms, policies and rules 'whenever an error is detected and corrected without questioning or altering the underlying values of the system' (Argyris, 1999: 68). However, where organisations are experiencing more profound problem situations, scholars argue that a qualitatively distinct, secondary form of learning is necessary. Such double-loop learning aims to correct mismatches by modifying the frameworks, norms, policies and routines underlying day-to-day actions and routines (Cope, 2003). It therefore involves reframing problem situations and learning to see them in new ways, something which few organisations have the capacity to undertake.

Implicit within double-loop learning is a desire for action to improve. For this to happen, differences in frameworks, norms, policies and routines between those involved and their associated perceptions and expectations in relation to the situation need to be made explicit. Once surfaced, such differences may challenge the underlying values of the system, helping to reframe the problem situation. Research in service relationships, such as those between a service user and a service provider, has illustrated the utility of such a disconfirmation approach to highlight such differences in the characteristics of a problem situation, thereby indicating a possible need for corrective action (Williams and Saunders, 2006). Making explicit these differences allows for potential reframing of the problem situation, providing a catalyst for ongoing open dialogue between those involved (Argyris et al., 1985). However, traditional data collection processes involve the person undertaking the research in making judgements about what is important, concentrating attention on those areas believed to be of critical concern (Foddy, 1994). S/he may filter or add her or his understanding to the language used and emphases placed by respondents. Consequently, differences in views regarding the characteristics of the problem situation and their relative importance may be missed; current 'theories in use' (Argyris and Schön, 1996) may go unchallenged. By contrast, double-loop learning results in a change in those values guiding the context in which the problem situation resides as well as changes to the strategies and assumptions made in the light of those modified values. This underscores the need to reinterpret the existing context (Jensen, 2005) and, based upon new understandings, modify the problem situation.

THE SERVICE TEMPLATE EXTENDED PROCESS (STEP)

Initially developed to highlight gaps in users' perceptions and expectations of those aspects of particular services they believed important (Staughton and Williams, 1994), research over the past two decades has focused upon extending the Service Template Process through a series of consultancy interventions into a process which can surface values and assumptions to enable double-loop learning. Although devised in response to concerns regarding the utility of generic, survey based, measures of service quality such as SERVQUAL (Parasuraman, 1995), and the need to learn about and understand the uniqueness of each service encounter, the process also has also been shown to have wider applications in organisational learning (Saunders and Williams, 2000; 2001). Its development, a full account of which is given in Williams and Saunders (2006), has been underpinned by two concerns: firstly, to ensure that the process can enable double-loop learning, and secondly, to ensure that it has real practical value to managers in both defining problem situations and deriving solutions. It focuses upon helping people in organisations learn about and improve specific problem situations, the goal being to increase their capacity for learning so that they can solve their own problems in the future.

Table 12.1   Use of STEP within process consultation

Process consultation	Service Template Extended Process
1. Initial contact	
2. Establish rapport and project ownership	
3. Select method(s) of working	
4. Use diagnostic interventions to gather data	I Participant selection II Characteristic identification and data validation
5. Use confrontational interventions to improve the situation	III Improvement agenda development
6. Reduce involvement and terminate	

Situations in which the STEP has been used include the provision of social housing, deliverers and users of IT services in a large electronics components firm, providers and users of automotive skills training, dissertation supervision in a new university and the author–publisher relationship in an international publishing house. However, it is only used to address a specific problem where all those involved agree that the purpose of the intervention is to ensure that they all perceive, understand and act upon the process consultation using an atmosphere of free and open enquiry.

Following initial contact within a process consultation, the preliminary tasks of the researcher/consultant are to establish rapport and project ownership and select jointly with the organisation involved the method of working (Table 12.1). Where STEP is selected as the method of working, the process incorporates three phases: (I) participant selection, (II) characteristic identification and data validation, and (III) improvement agenda development.

STEP allows each group in a specific organisational relationship to determine and collect separately data they believe are important. Represented visually as Templates, these data capture those characteristics each group identifies as important, perceptions and expectations for each being measured against a group-defined Likert-type scale anchored by 'ideal' and 'worst' descriptors (Figure 12.1). Following participant selection (Phase I), each of the groups involved generates their own (separate) visual representation (Templates) of the defined problem situation, these being a diagnostic intervention within the process consultation (Table 12.1). Subsequently, these Templates are used as catalysts for developing an improvement agenda (Phase III), this being structured as a confrontational intervention within the process framework (Table 12.1). This intervention enables each group to consider

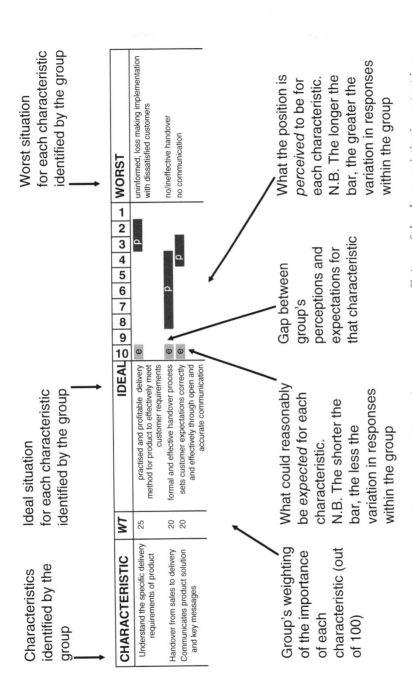

Worst situation for each characteristic identified by the group

Ideal situation for each characteristic identified by the group

Characteristics identified by the group

What the position is *perceived* to be for each characteristic. N.B. The longer the bar, the greater the variation in responses within the group

Gap between group's perceptions and expectations for that characteristic

What could reasonably be *expected* for each characteristic. N.B. The shorter the bar, the less the variation in responses within the group

Group's weighting of the importance of each characteristic (out of 100)

CHARACTERISTIC	WT	1	2	3	4	5	6	7	8	9	10	IDEAL	WORST
Understand the specific delivery requirements of product	25		p								e	practised and profitable delivery method for product to effectively meet customer requirements	uninformed, loss making implementation with dissatisfied customers
Handover from sales to delivery	20				p		p				e	formal and effective handover process	no/ineffective handover
Communicates product solution and key messages	20										e	sets customer expectations correctly and effectively through open and accurate communication	no communication

Figure 12.1   Annotated Template extract of IT production company staff views of the characteristics important in an alliance relationship

173

the appropriateness of their own underlying values and norms for that problem situation, as well as for the organisational context, and involves all groups in making well-informed choices regarding improvements (Saunders and Williams, 2000; 2001). STEP thereby facilitates learning beyond the single-loop.

In Phase I, *participant selection*, discrete purposive samples are drawn by the researcher/consultant in consultation with the client from each of the groups involved in the problem situation. Individuals are selected for each non-probability sample on the basis of their criticality to that situation, rather than to ensure statistical representativeness of those involved.

Characteristics identification and data validation (Phase II) allows each group to provide their own independent qualitative data from which logical rather than statistical generalisations can be developed. Together these represent the diversity of views regarding those characteristics the groups involved consider are important. As outlined by Williams and Saunders (2006), separate meetings of approximately two hours duration are organised with each group, the precise composition and number of participants (six to ten) in each group being informed by research on focus groups (Krueger and Casey, 2009). Each meeting is structured as a diagnostic intervention and managed by the researcher/consultant. Throughout this the situation being considered is displayed prominently on a flip chart to help maintain focus. The characteristics of the situation are elicited and displayed, on another flip chart in the order they emerge, by the process consultant using the group's words in a 'thought shower' type process. Clarification of meanings is sought to help ensure that group members have a similar frame of reference and the same understanding. Subsequently, the list is refined to typically between 20 and 30 characteristics and ideal and worst descriptors generated for the extremes of each characteristic (Figure 12.1). Perceptions and expectations of the relationship and variations within these are then measured and plotted for each characteristic relative to the extremes using a ten-point scale. The value ten represents the ideal and the value one the worst case. Longer bars (Figure 12.1) represent greater variation in responses within the group. The resultant Template is then discussed with participants to help confirm internal validity and the context. Finally, participants identify and weight, by allocating 100 points, those characteristics they consider most important.

In the final phase (Phase III), *improvement agenda development*, the groups who have generated their Templates meet. Joint exploration and testing and learning from others' views of the situation and the development of an improvement agenda are facilitated by the researcher/consultant. The composition of groups and the content of their discussions are determined by those involved to help maintain their ownership of the process. The Templates (created in Phase II) are used as visual catalysts to enable the groups to develop a shared understanding of each other's perceptions and expectations of the problem situation. Within this, participants are facilitated to explain and discuss which characteristics they consider important, the similarities and differences between the Templates and to explore possible reasons for this. This approach is based on the premise that people learn not only by acquiring new information (and techniques) but also by understanding the contexts in which these are effective (Roth and Kleiner, 2000). In this phase the process consultant adopts the role of confrontational inquirer (Schein, 1999), supporting the groups involved in understanding and challenging the norms and values upon which their own and others' understandings of the characteristics of the relationship are based. This also helps encourage ownership of the process and its outcomes by the participants, enabling the groups involved to understand and, where necessary, reconcile their own and others' views (Saunders and Williams, 2001). Finally, participants are asked to jointly agree an improvement agenda that assists modifications to improve the problem situation.

PERSONAL EXPERIENCE OF THE SERVICE TEMPLATE EXTENDED PROCESS IN HRD RESEARCH

We have worked with a range of organisations using STEP to learn about and address problem situations. Our experiences in undertaking these process consultations have highlighted the importance of capturing data independently with each of the groups involved so as not to contaminate views, the need to develop a shared understanding between groups, and how learning (both single and double-loop) can support improvements. Drawing on these experiences we now share our own learning.

Data Capture

Independent data capture of the views of each group within the problem situation requires both careful sample selection (within Phase I) and subsequent Template generation (within Phase II). We have found sample selection needs to include individuals who can, between them, account for and explain the extent and diversity of the situation. Within this, the number of groups and the number of participants within each group varies, reflecting potential differences regarding the characteristics that are likely to be important. For example, in a process consultation to improve a large organisation's reception service the receptionists' manager revealed that his presence in a group would constrain their responses, also indicating he was likely to have different ideas regarding what was crucial. Employee samples were therefore stratified into manager and receptionist groups to reflect this. In contrast, for work with an alliance partnership, discussion with the managers of the two teams involved emphasised a need to focus upon the overall alliance relationship. Consequently, the purposive samples from the product company and the solutions provider teams consisted of staff directly involved including the respective managers.

Within each group, Template generation allows identification and validation of those characteristics that are important visually (Figure 12.2 and Figure 12.3). Each Template explicitly represents the frequent variations within groups in their perceptions (p) and expectations (e) of the relationship being considered. In the alliance partnership, the product company's staff Template (Figure 12.2) highlights variations in perceptions. Perceptions for the characteristic 'Handover from sales to delivery' range from close to the ideal of 'formal and effective handover process' towards the worst of 'no/ineffective handover', this being represented by the long bar. In the Template produced by the solutions company's staff, on the other hand, there is clear agreement regarding both perceptions and expectations (Figure 12.3). We have found that participants are surprised but pleased that the process measures and records such within-group differences.

Within each group, we ask participants to clarify each Template characteristic's meaning and justify the recorded perception and expectation. This has often stimulated discussion and subsequent revision of the short description of that particular characteristic. It has also helped those within the group to develop a shared understanding of each other's perceptions and expectations. For example, the characteristic 'Understand the specific delivery requirements of product' (Figure 12.2) was explained in the context of the solution's company's perceived continual poor delivery performance. Where Templates show gaps between perceptions of current performance and expectations *and* these are weighted as less important, for example 'Customer referencing' (Figure 12.2), the relatively low weighting is also justified within group discussion. For 'Customer referencing' this was because the product company felt that as there were no successful product implementations to use in selling to other customers, there was nothing to share even if the solutions company was 'willing'.

CHARACTERISTIC	WT	IDEAL	10	9	8	7	6	5	4	3	2	1	WORST
Understand the specific delivery requirements of product	25	practised and profitable delivery method for product to effectively meet customer requirements	e								p		uninformed, loss making implementation with dissatisfied customers
Handover from sales to delivery	20	formal and effective handover process	e		p	p	p	p	p				no/ineffective handover
Communicates product solution and key messages	20	sets customer expectations correctly and effectively through open and accurate communication	e				p	p	p	p			sets customer expectations incorrectly
Pre-sales and sales communications	15	effective communication between two resulting in well-briefed pre-sales contribution to the sales process	e					p					no communication
Communication within Partnership	10	open and honest communications within Partnership, particularly when encountering and experiencing problem	e						p				complete breakdown of communication within Partnership
Customer referencing	10	willingness to share within product community	e								p		no sharing

Figure 12.2   Extract of Template showing the product company's view of the characteristics that were important to their relationship with the solutions provider

CHARACTERISTIC	WT	IDEAL	1	2	3	4	5	6	7	8	9	10	WORST
Up front client expectation setting (make product fit everything) by Product Company	20	client is clear that scope is limited and the implementation is part time and rapid		p								e	client believes they are getting a full tier
For Product Company team to work with Solutions Provider Sales/Pre-Sales Team	20	trusted relationship					p					e	no trust
Provide a professional and focused solution experience to our customers	15	customers see us as a top Product Company partner					p					e	customers see us as just another partner
Patching levels	15	know patches and consistent fit with product offering			p						e		constantly changing and incompatibility between product and applications patching levels
To be able to talk about ALL our customer experiences	10	able to use all customers for marketing and sales				p					e		use none
Project management time	10	sufficient project management time included to facilitate both project control and relationship management				p					e		relationship with client for whom experience is new suffers and escalations occur
Scope clarity	10	client's project staff have complete clarity of the scope of the project				p						e	client staff involved in sales are different from those involved in delivery
Consultants' part-time working	10	clients understand and focus on delivering their responsibilities				p				e			client does not understand and feels lost and helpless

Figure 12.3   Extract of Template showing the solutions provider's view of the characteristics that were important to their relationship with the product company

178

Developing a Shared Understanding

Phase III, improvement agenda development, provides the basis for all those involved to learn about each other's perceptions and expectations of the characteristics that are important, highlight differences and develop a shared understanding. Following assurances of confidentiality and anonymity, these joint explorations concentrate on the major differences and similarities of the high weighted characteristics and gaps between perceptions and expectations, rather than on the precise values suggested by the numbers on the ten-point scale.

For our alliance partnership example, joint exploration emphasised initial differences between the groups. The product company's theories in use related to the method of delivery and customer communication (Figure 12.2). The former emphasised the underlying assumption that the product company's prescribed method of product delivery was the right way to meet customer requirements and generate profit. The latter emphasised the importance they placed upon communication to the customer. In contrast the solutions provider highlighted concerns about the support they were receiving from the product company both in relation to the customer and internally alongside what they regarded as the gap between what the product company was claiming for the software and the reality of what could be achieved ('Patching levels', Figure 12.3). Through discussion between the two groups, understanding of each other's perspectives and goodwill were developed. This provided the basis for new joint understandings, which could lead to modifications in the ways the relationships operated. It is to these new understandings and possible new awarenesses and the associated implications for learning that we now turn.

Modifications to the Relationships and New Awarenesses

In our process consultations we have found that agendas for action created by the participants and subsequent discussions often reflect single-loop learning. Groups involved in the process consultation often recognise that prior to STEP they have considered only partially, if at all, the other group's perspective. Receptionists learned that, whilst they perceived that their knowledge of their organisation met customer expectations, this was not acknowledged by their users. These users were, as part of the process, able to specify those aspects where more knowledge was required. Similarly, after discussion of Templates, both groups to the alliance relationship recognised and agreed on the need to ensure that the solutions provider was kept up-to-date about product changes, something that had not been recognised previously as important by the product company.

Within the reception service process consultation, double-loop learning occurred when the receptionists' manager learned that the configuration of a joint reception service/switchboard was inefficient. Discussion in Phase III prompted him to explore alternative ways of organising the services, resulting in separation of the reception desk and switchboard. In contrast, in the alliance partnership it did not occur. In this partnership the product company's Template focuses on characteristics that highlighted shortcomings in the solutions provider's performance (Figure 12.2); the solutions company's Template focuses upon the product expectations set by the product company and the reality perceived by them and the end customer (Figure 12.3). Although this prompted a change in the way both groups understood the alliance and what was required, subsequent improvements focused on amending existing processes, suggesting learning was single-loop. Although double-loop learning appeared initially to be inhibited by the manager defending his own position through maintaining the status quo (Argyris, 2004), subsequent remedial interventions by solutions company senior management resulted in major changes to the way processes were managed and operated.

DISCUSSION

STEP's utility in enabling learning can be considered in relation to the use of Templates by organisations to improve problem situations (Saunders and Williams, 2000; Williams and Saunders, 2006). The process generates, tests and records independently those characteristics each group believes are important, offering a novel means of establishing and recording valid information. Subsequently, through confrontational enquiry, these Templates provide the basis for joint learning by the groups to that relationship and the opportunity to develop goodwill. Despite an apparent lack of similarity in the language used, there are often common elements in those characteristics considered important. These highlight where groups are operating using similar assumptions and norms. Where characteristics differ, this provides an indication of aspects where the assumptions and norms may also differ, which can be surfaced by the process consultant. By highlighting differences and similarities in the norms and values upon which such assessments are based, new and improved understandings, specific to the problem situation in question, are developed. The learning, understanding and ownership that are gained through these discussions, whilst considered beneficial in their own right by those involved, can also provide the precursor to meaningful actions.

However, whilst the STEP is able to provide a catalyst and content for single and double-loop learning, this does not necessarily mean that such learning will occur. Whilst it can enable aspects of the problem situation to be improved, in most instances this relates to doing the same things right. Other factors, such as an unwillingness amongst those involved to accept and act upon alternative and often critical views, as well as mismatch between the rhetoric and reality of their buy-in to the process, may prevent double-loop learning from occurring. This suggests that if such organisations are to move from doing the same things right to doing the right (different) things, more attention may be needed to help participants clarify what 'right' might mean in the context of possible new awarenesses emerging from the process.

The prevailing view in the literature is that learning is essential to business survival for the organisation (Senge, 1990; de Geus, 1997; Revans, 1998). Moreover, it is often believed that the higher the level of learning the better (Argyris and Schön, 1996; Romme and Witteloostuijn, 1999; Senge, 1990), although this assumption itself can be questioned on the grounds that higher is different in form rather than, necessarily, more desirable (Tosey et al., 2012). Nevertheless, in the absence of any routine learning, whether in the form of knowledge transfer or process improvement, even single-loop learning is an achievement, and one that is commonly gained through our use of the Template. It should not be forgotten that although single-loop learning only results in the changing of specific behavioural practices to achieve desired outcomes, achieving greater congruity between groups typically only occurs in approximately 30 per cent of adults (Torbert, 1999: 196).

Double-loop learning that changes the way in which problem situations are understood, defined and measured is even less frequent, occurring typically in approximately 10 per cent of adults (Torbert, 1999: 196). Consequently, organisations rarely develop this capacity to digest and respond to double-loop feedback such as that enabled through STEP. We consider STEP has the potential to support single- and double-loop learning and has wide application in promoting improvement and facilitating learning within organisational problem situations.

Within STEP the HRD researcher/consultant acts as guardian of the process rather than an expert in the problem situation. S/he facilitates using the process to enable those groups whom are party to the problem situation to learn. Each initial diagnostic intervention to create and validate a Template within a group forces that group to consider their own perceptions and expectations. During this they often learn that, even within their group, others view the problem situation differently. The subsequent confrontational intervention, where all groups involved share their Templates,

182   *Handbook of research methods on HRD*

forces them to learn about and understand the views of others. This learning informs their joint development of an improvement agenda. Yet STEP may not be appropriate to a process consultation or to better understanding of a problem situation. Whilst STEP can reflect the realities of those involved in an organisational relationship, it does not provide a statistically representative evaluation. Rather, it offers an additional research tool to the HRD researcher which, because predetermined scales are not used, is likely to be applicable without modification across a variety of relationships. Although time consuming, where agreement is reached to use STEP, those involved are made aware of and able to question and evaluate what they consider important and achieve a consistency of understanding. Integral to this is the need for discussion, learning, problem definition and developing joint ownership of agreed problem solutions. However, further research is needed to assess this and the process consultant role of the HRD researcher/consultant in other organisational contexts.

REFERENCES

Argyris, C. (1996). 'Unrecognized defenses of scholars: impact on theory and research', *Organization Science* 7: 79–87.
Argyris, C. (1999). *On Organizational Learning.* 2nd edn. Oxford: Blackwell.
Argyris, C. (2004). *Reasons and Rationalizations: The Limits to Organizational Knowledge.* Oxford: Oxford University Press.
Argyris, C., Putnam, R. and McLain Smith, D. (1985). *Action Science: Concepts, Methods and Skills for Research and Intervention.* San Francisco, CA: Jossey-Bass.
Argyris, C. and Schön, D. A. (1996). *Organizational Learning II: Theory, Method and Practice.* Reading, MA: Addison-Wesley.
Arthur, J. B. and Aiman-Smith, L. (2001). 'Gainsharing and organizational learning: an analysis of employee suggestions over time', *Academy of Management Journal* 44(4): 737–754.
Coghlan, D. and Brannick, T. (2010). *Doing Action Research in Your Own Organization.* 3rd edn. London: Sage.
Cope, J. (2003). 'Entrepreneurial learning and critical reflection: discontinuous events as triggers for "higher-level" learning', *Management Learning* 34(4): 429–450.
de Geus, A. (1997). *The Living Company.* Boston, MA: Harvard Business School.
Fiol, C. M. and Lyles, M. A. (1985). 'Organizational learning', *Academy of Management Review* 10(4): 803–813.
Foddy, W. (1994). *Constructing Questions for Interviews and Questionnaires.* Cambridge: Cambridge University Press.
Gray, D. E., Iles, P. and Watson, S. (2011). 'Spanning the HRD academic–practitioner divide: bridging the gap through Mode 2 research', *Journal of European Industrial Training* 35(3): 247–263.
Jensen, P. V. (2005). 'A contextual theory of learning and the learning organization', *Knowledge and Process Management* 12(1): 53–64.
Killman, R. H. (1986). *Beyond the Quick Fix: Managing Five Tracks to Organizational Success.* San Francisco, CA: Jossey-Bass.
Krueger, R. A. and Casey, M. A. (2009). *Focus Groups: A Practical Guide for Applied Research.* 4th edn. Thousand Oaks, CA: Sage.

Miner, A. S. and Mezias, S. (1996). 'Ugly duckling no more: pasts and futures of organizational learning research', *Organization Science* 7(1): 88–100.
Parasuraman, A. (1995). 'Measuring and monitoring service quality', *in* W. J. Glynn and J. G. Barnes (eds), *Understanding Services Management*. Chichester, UK: Wiley, 143–177.
Revans, R. W. (1998). *The ABC of Action Learning*. London: Lemos and Crane.
Romme, A. G. L. and van Witteloostuijn, A. (1999). 'Circular organizing and triple-loop learning', *Journal of Organizational Change* 12(5): 439–453.
Roth, G. and Kleiner, A. (2000). *Car Launch: The Human Side of Managing Change*. New York: Oxford University Press.
Rynes, S. L. (2007). 'Editor's afterword. Let's create a tipping point: what academics and practitioners can do, alone and together', *Academy of Management Journal* 50(5): 1046–1054.
Saunders, M. N. K. (2011). 'The management researcher as practitioner', *in* C. Cassell and W. J. Lee (eds), *Challenges and Controversies in Management Research*. London: Taylor and Francis, 243–256.
Saunders, M. N. K. and Williams, C. S. (2000). 'Towards a new approach to understanding service encounters: establishing, learning about and reconciling different views', *Journal of European Industrial Training* 24(2/3/4): 220–227.
Saunders, M. N. K. and Williams, C. S. (2001). 'Double loop learning and improving organisational relationships: the application of the Template process', *in* M. A. Rahim, R. T. Golembiewski and C. Lundberg (eds), *Current Topics in Management, Volume 6*. Amsterdam: Elsevier Science, 127–148.
Schein, E. H. (1999). *Process Consultation Revisited: Building the Helping Relationship*. Reading, MA: Addison-Wesley Longman.
Senge, P. (1990). *The Fifth Discipline*. London: Random House.
Staughton, R. V. W. and Williams, C. S. (1994). 'Towards a simple visual representation of fit in service organisations: the contribution of the Service Template', *International Journal of Operational and Production Management* 14(5): 76–85.
Torbert, W. R. (1999). 'The distinctive questions developmental action inquiry asks', *Management Learning* 30(2): 189–206.
Tosey, P., Visser, M. and Saunders, M. N. K. (2012). 'The origins and conceptualisations of triple loop learning: a critical review', *Management Learning* 43(3): 291–307.
Williams, C. S. and Saunders, M. N. K. (2006). 'Developing the service template process: from measurement to agendas for improvement', *The Service Industries Journal* 26(5): 581–595.

ANNOTATED FURTHER READING

Saunders, M. N. K. (2011). 'The management researcher as practitioner', *in* C. Cassell and W. J. Lee (eds), *Challenges and Controversies in Management Research*. London: Taylor and Francis, 243–256. This chapter offers insights and examples of the realities of working at the interface between academia and practice.
Schein, E. H. (1999). *Process Consultation Revisited: Building the Helping Relationship*. Reading, MA: Addison-Wesley Longman. This book builds on Schein's earlier books about process consultation, focusing on the interaction between consultants and clients and achieving a healthy and helpful relationship.
Williams, C. S. and Saunders, M. N. K. (2006). 'Developing the service template process: from measurement to agendas for improvement', *The Service Industries Journal* 26(5): 581–595. This paper provides an overview of the development of the Service Template Process and offers advice on how to use it within a process consultation, explaining how to operationalise each of the phases of STEP in reasonable detail.

13. Emergent discourses of learning and community formation: exploring social media for professional learning
Peter Evans

SUMMARY

This chapter explores how, using Actor Network Theory and Discourse Analysis, competing projections of power emerge and are 'processed' in a specific online environment to impact on community creation through the discursive practices of professional learning. It describes an investigation of the social practices and community-forming activities associated with professional development activities in social media environments, highlighting the usefulness and challenges of this research approach to the study of social media environments for learning.

INTRODUCTION

This chapter describes a research approach using Actor Network Theory and Discourse Analysis to analyse one of a growing number of regular Twitter discussion events for collaborative professional development activities. Twitter is described (Lerman and Ghosh, 2010) as 'a popular social networking site that allows registered users to post and read short (at most 140 characters) text messages, which may contain URLs to online content, . . . A user can also retweet or comment on another user's post'.

Discussion events on Twitter have become increasingly common in recent years (McCulloch et al., 2011; Bingham and Conner, 2010). These discussion events are organised through the convention of hashtags (#) in combination with a shortened name as an explicit ordering mechanism (Bruns, 2011). There are over a hundred regular professional events hosted on Twitter including: #ARchat (business analysts); #brandchat (branding); #edchat (education); #imcchat (integrated marketing communication); #pr20chat (PR and social media); #smbiz (small business); and #talentnet (recruitment industry) (see Gnosis Media Group, n.d.).

The events examined for this particular study were selected from the regular Twitter discussion events focused on Human Resource Development (HRD) and learning and development practitioners.

THE RESEARCH SITE

Each of the selected Twitter discussion events were organised around particular themes. Event 1 was on the use of metrics in learning and development, Event 2 was on crowd sourcing (the process of problem solving by outsourcing the activity to an undefined network of people, the 'crowd') and Event 3 was on skills and competence development for learning and development practitioners (Table 13.1).

As with many online research sites, the data boundaries of these events cannot be clearly prescribed. Schneider and Foot (2005: 158) use the term web sphere as 'not simply a collection of web sites, but as a set of dynamically defined digital resources spanning multiple web sites deemed relevant or related to a central event'.

The discussion event web spheres can be traced through emerging and expanding networks of digital resources and interactions. These include web pages providing the discussion questions and participants linking to other resources using URLs in their Tweets as well as posting reflections about the events on other websites and blogs.

Web spheres spread far beyond what is practical for a researcher to explore, and so conscious decisions are required from the researcher in bounding a 'manageable' research 'site'. This places an onus on the researcher to be sensitive to the implications of such decisions on what is included and excluded in the collection and analysis of the data.

Furthermore, the online research site is unstable and fluid (Fenwick and Edwards, 2010), and it is this interactive and dynamic nature of the research site that is key to understanding the selection of this approach for online research.

Table 13.1   Participants and Tweets for each event

	Number of participants	Number of Tweets in the event	Mean average Tweets per minute*
Event 1	54	922	10.2
Event 2	72	773	8.6
Event 3	68	518	8.6

Note: * Event durations varied.

DISCOURSE ANALYSIS

Discourse Analysis (DA) is concerned with studying 'language in use' (Nunan, 1993: 7). Heracleous (2006) identifies two levels of discourse: communicative action as interactions between individuals to, for example, share experiences or build inter-personal relations; and deeper discursive structures that 'guide' communicative actions. Discursive structures do not determine communicative actions but are 'drawn on' in the development and negotiation of the broader discourses within a group.

Bragd et al. (2008) argue that a discursive community forms through the generation of common meanings in discussion. So the focus of the research shifts from individual utterances to the overall discussion (Dennen, 2008), content and form. Discursive communities enable learning as sense-making that seeks to reinforce and re-produce common understandings among the members and highlight perspectives that differentiate members from 'others' outside the community (Bragd et al., 2008). These deeper discursive structures can also be understood as the legitimised discourses of professional practice (Fenwick et al., 2012) emerging from the stabilisation of the more fluid communicative actions.

Belnap and Withers (2008) developed the Framework for Contextualised Function (FCF) for the coding of unstructured educational group work interactions. They suggest categorising exchanges as nuclear (stand alone) or bounded within a sequence of exchanges. Bounded exchanges can be preparatory, to establish communication; embedded, to confirm uptake or repair a breakdown between exchanges; or dependent, to add to previous utterances or justify a response. Underpinning different exchanges are different speech functions (Fairclough, 2003) such as questions, statements, predictions, facts, evaluations and so forth that may require a specific response. A simplified version of the Belnap and Withers framework was adopted to analyse the conversational structures of the Twitter discussion events. This provided an entry point in identifying and analysing collaborative sense-making when looking at the discourse events as being distinctly learning orientated.

In this research, the focus of analysis was on identifying the processes whereby communicative actions stabilise as deeper discursive structures or resources. Such processes can be analysed through both the content and structure of the discourses in a form of dialogue analysis as suggested by Dennen (2008). From this, learning can be understood in terms of the re-production of these discursive resources as the legitimated professional practices of the learning and development practitioner.

THE RESEARCH FRAMEWORK

On seeking an appropriate theoretical perspective for the research, initial analysis of the discussion events found an exaggeration of many of the problematic features of unstructured discussions identified by Belnap and Withers (2008: 8): sequences extending over many exchanges; overlapping exchanges and sequences; short sequences being cut off prior to a conclusion; and sequences re-emerging later in discussions. The norms of participant interactions appeared to be under almost constant renegotiation. Also, non-human elements appeared to have an impact, suggesting more than passive mediation. Twitter apps such as Tweetdeck, which aggregates and organises Twitter 'streams', arguably shape how Twitter discussions are structured and 'consumed'. So the initial research 'site' was identified with complex interactions between language, collaboration, people, artefacts and control (Gherardi, 2000; Nicolini et al., 2003; Guzman, 2009; Geiger, 2009; Tuomi, 2000). The combination of inherent emergence, instability and ambiguity within a socio-material framework (Fenwick and Edwards, 2010) suggested that Actor Network Theory would provide a potentially insightful 'lens' to the analysis of the data gathered.

Actor Network Theory

This study made use of three key aspects of Actor Network Theory (ANT): translation, network assemblages and symmetry. ANT has been described as a sociology of translation (Latour, 2005) whereby translation refers to the interpretation and reinterpretation of knowledge or meaning as a means of enrolling actors into a particular network (Mitev, 2009). Translation works to generate as well as order and stabilise networks (Fenwick and Edwards, 2010: 9). ANT's interest in network assemblages is less concerned with the size of networks than with the dynamics of influence in and on networks underpinning a central concern of ANT with power as persuasion (Fox, 2005; McLean and Hassard, 2004). Finally, symmetry is the avoidance of subject–object dualism that privileges the human while avoiding technological determinism (Miettinen, 1997). So ANT understands 'actors' as being either human or non-human active participants within networks.

Ethical Considerations of Researching Online

Researching Twitter discussion events pose a number of ethical issues that need to be addressed under the rubric of doing no harm to others.

The Association of Internet Researchers (AoIR) 2012 policy, *Ethical*

Decision-Making and Internet Research, states: 'privacy is a concept that must include a consideration of expectations and consensus. Social, academic, or regulatory delineations of public and private as a clearly recognizable binary no longer holds in everyday practice' (AoIR, 2012: 7).

The Twitter discussion events are public events open to anyone with a Twitter account. The archives of each event require no more than internet access as these are kept on event websites and are accessible to anyone. However, it can be argued that such communities rely on aspects of mutual trust and respect that may be undermined by a 'lurking' researcher (Eysenbach and Till, 2001).

This research did not involve interventions or lurking in live events but rather used publicly available discussion archives that may be regarded as 'public domain' data (Androutsopoulos, 2008). As the research site was treated as in a public space, so individual explicit consent for participation was not sought, and participants have been made as unidentifiable as possible (Eysenbach and Till, 2001). In addition, the event organisers were contacted to inform them of the research and provide an opportunity to raise objections to it (AoIR, 2012).

Participant names have been altered, although their essential content, structure and capitalisation has been retained including where a corporate or name has been used as well as the gender indicated by that name. So, 'TrainingPete' is an anonymised Twitter name of a male participant who also demonstrated a clear professional label in that Twitter name. It does remain possible that an altered name is identical to a name of one of the over 200 million Twitter users worldwide (O'Carroll, 2012) but any similarities are coincidental.

A further difficulty arises in the treatment of quotations where anonymisation can be undermined by simple online searches to reveal the author. Furthermore, an anonymous quote may be seen as an infringement of the author's intellectual property (Eysenbach and Till, 2001). Mindful of the need for a pragmatic approach to anonymity in the context of a 'public space' research site, quotes from specific Tweets (although not from other articles or papers) have been altered through ellipses to retain both their meaning and the anonymity of the participant. However, it is acknowledged that some quotations will remain traceable.

THE RESEARCH

The following analysis attempts to demonstrate how ANT, operationalised through discourse or dialogue analysis, may provide a useful and insightful approach to our understanding of interactions in open online environments for learning. The research approach described here commences with an analysis of the discursive structure of the Twitter interactions, which provides the basis for exploring how community and identity issues are addressed in the course of the interactions. The effects of mediating technology as a non-human actor will then be explored.

Structure of the Discourse

The discussion events can be considered as cooperative learning events. Yet, as analyses of classroom discourses have tended to look for a sequence structure of *initiate–response–evaluation/feedback* (Bloome et al., 2005), so events that lack an explicit pedagogical focus tend to have a less clear structure (Belnap and Withers, 2008: 8). The functions of utterances lead to patterns of interactions that form traceable sequences of exchanges (Belnap and Withers, 2008). But, as different functions and participants become involved in such sequences, the structures of these sequences become less clear as a result of increasingly diverse patterns emerging in the discourses (Bloome et al., 2005).

Belnap and Withers (2008) provide 16 functional categories for moves in unstructured learning events. The categories of particular interest here are the building blocks of sequences: (a) suggestions directly addressing the dominant task and (b) propositions contributing to the development of the discussion. Moves and exchanges can be linked through the use of (c) modifications and (d) clarifications. The validity of statements can be addressed through (e) justifications, (f) invalidations, (g) confirmation, (h) qualifications, (i) restatements and (j) simple responses as basic acknowledgements of statements often used to indicate acceptance. Restatements (i) are often given as retweets and play an important function in Twitter discussions.

As can be seen in Table 13.2, sequences tend to build up over a number of short exchanges. The sequence is initiated by a question from the moderator, who subsequently receives only one direct suggestion. However, the initiating question also appears to provide an umbrella for a series of propositions contributing to the broader topic of the event that, in turn, generate further exchanges.

Proposition B2 initiates a new exchange of requests for information on the future progress of an organisational change initiative. This exchange of requests terminates when the original author of Proposition B2 confirms that further information would be posted to the event blog. However, the sequence commencing under Proposition D appears to terminate at a restatement (at 8:51:26).

The patterns of initiation, proposition, response, extension and

Table 13.2   Sequences

Time					
8:45:18	Initiation				
8:46:34	Suggestion A				
8:47:07		Proposition B			
8:47:32			Proposition C		
8:47:59				Proposition D	
8:48:13			Restate (Retweet)		
8:48:22			Restate (Retweet)		
8:48:36					Proposition E
8:48:50				Restate (Retweet)	
8:48:55		Extension/ qualification			
8:49:45				Simple response	
8:49:49				Restate (Retweet)	
8:50:34				Invalidation/ new proposition D2	
8:50:35	Restate (Retweet)				
8:51:06				Qualification	
8:51:26				Restate (Retweet)	
8:53:24		Qualification			
8:54:24		Extension/new proposition B2			
8:55:35					Restate (Retweet)
8:55:38					Extension
8:56:16	Restate (Retweet)				

qualification were replicated across the different Twitter events. Throughout the events, sequences are displayed in a fragmented manner co-terminously with other sequences, such that each exchange sequence becomes difficult to follow. Twitter is particularly difficult as the discussion event is often presented as a single chronological list of Tweets, so it is often difficult to identify whether a Tweet is part of an existing exchange or not. This difficulty may account for the seemingly short duration of each sequence 'run'.

These Twitter events appear to exaggerate many of the key problem features of unstructured discussions identified by Belnap and Withers

(2008: 8), including sequences extending over many exchanges; overlapping exchanges and sequences; short sequences; and sequences re-emerging later in discussions. This suggests a lack of event coherence and stability that should be more problematic, but participants appear to develop specific strategies to deal with this including adopting specific approaches to establishing conversational floors.

Simpson (2005) refers to conversational floors in terms of establishing cohesion and coherence in the discourse (2005: 338). The conversational floor performs the function of establishing the topic of the conversation. It is noticeable that Proposition B generates direct dialogue in the sense of an extension and qualification and goes on to generate further exchanges establishing a conversational floor as a translation of the initiating question. Such attempts to capture conversational floors may be to control the discourse direction or alternatively a means to stimulate discussions relevant to the formal topic of the event.

While the structures of these Twitter discussion events are generally limited, unstable, dynamic and fluid, there were patterns that tended to indicate some element of deeper discursive structure. The emergence of such discursive structures becomes more apparent through the analysis of the discourse content itself.

Community and Identity

Bloome et al. (2005) use a perspective of thematic coherence as establishing a discourse community that is a network assemblage of actors. Networks and communities emerge as actors seek the support of others by translating their perspectives and enrolling them into the network (Mitev, 2009).

For example, in discussing emerging skills and competence requirements for learning and development practitioners, participants appeared to assemble around a performative translation of HRD practice (Gold et al., 2010) (Table 13.3).

Tweets 1–3 (Table 13.3) place the emphasis on a performative discourse in terms of changes in professional practice. Tweet 1 translates this as a change of emphasis rather than a fundamental change of the practitioner discourse. Tweets 2–3 appear to suggest a mobilisation of the discursive practices of performance as the necessary means of addressing the challenges faced by practitioners. However, Tweet 4 can be seen as an attempt to position the discourse practice of performance as a legitimated professional knowledge and discursive resource (Mäkitalo, 2012) with alternatives being dismissed as 'a waste of time'.

Through the different events, particular perspectives became clearly dominant in the discourse. Alternative viewpoints were ignored by the

Table 13.3   Discussing emerging skills and competences

No.	Participant	Tweet
1	TrainingPete	. . . less focus on 'training' and more focus on 'performance support'. #. . .
2	JoanMar2	. . . Yes, . . . We need to [show] measureable ROI and performance improvement #. . .
3	TrainingPete	First thing is a new mindset [and by asking what is] the least intrusive way to address [a] performance issue? #. . .
4	ILPT	#. . . set performance . . . objectives . . . measure against those [do not] just track learning activity #wasteoftime

Table 13.4   Different perspectives in the discourse

No.	Participant	Tweet
1	jason_bean09	. . . tonight new drinking 'terms' Kirkpatrick and Level . . . #. . .
2	miranda0404	. . . I think that Kirkpatrick has a shot at the nobel prize too . . . #. . .
3	lknut	Levels 1–3 are for wimps #. . .
4	lknut	Can we have [a different] question [to avoid] wasting time burying Kirkpatrick? #. . .

wider community or explicitly dismissed rather than examined and discussed. For example, the Kirkpatrick approach to evaluation was rejected in the events to the extent that merely mentioning the model triggered indirect ridicule from participants arguably as a mechanism to block any discussion of why the model was deemed so inadequate (Table 13.4).

Tweet 4 presents an argument for directing the discourse based on an assumed legitimation from rejecting the Kirkpatrick model. The community of participants tended to seek consensus and bracket differences (Fairclough, 2003: 41–42) through dismissal or humour.

The communicative actions included using visual images to support discursive structures. For example, in mobilising a particular perspective on systematic learning design and off-the-job training as an ineffective approach to learning and development practices, Figure 13.1 was used.

The image is one of passive and un-engaging learning. The poor quality of the experience is replicated in and emphasised by the low quality of the image. The blurring of the pupils' faces appears to emphasise the

Figure 13.1   G. Rom. K1. 7598 'Romsey School, c 1910' used with permission of the The Cambridge Collection, Cambridge Central Library

impersonal and anti-individual nature of systematic learning design methods. The image suitably summed up this critique of the HRD discourses of formal and instructional training.

A more nuanced and complex discussion of the problems of HRD practice began to emerge in the discussions. So members of this discursive community were identified as understanding the need to change HRD practices. Yet there were implicitly 'other' HRD practitioners who were not able to move away from the formal and instructional practices of 'traditional' HRD through 'fear and ignorance'. So the event HRD community identified itself simultaneously as being part of the traditional HRD community failing to meet the needs of 'the business' but also as distinct from that HRD community as they present themselves as demonstrating aspects of newer and progressive HRD practices.

Therefore, these social media environments appear to mirror Billet's (2004) findings on workplace learning in terms of the tensions identified between established figures and newer participants as well as between perceived different institutionalised interests. It can be seen that such informal discussion events and communities can act simultaneously as sites for both 'restrictive' and 'expansive' learning reflecting similar discursive power relations specific to those found in other, more formal, learning environments (Fuller and Unwin, 2004). The dynamic nature of the negotiation of these tensions and relations could be understood in terms of the ANT concepts of translation, enrolment, network assemblages and obligatory passage points as a perspective of the process of elusive, diffuse and ever present power relations and dynamics of these Twitter discussion events.

Finally, the implications of the ANT notion of symmetry in research in open online discussion event will be explored.

Mediating Technology

The notion of symmetry in ANT explores the impact of non-human 'actors' actively participating in network assemblages such as the discussion events (Fenwick and Edwards, 2010). This goes beyond acknowledging that technology is necessary for these types of synchronous but dispersed social discussion events to actually take place (Irwin and Hramiak, 2010) but includes how the technological infrastructure itself translates discourses and has its own discursive structures and practices. For example, the way in which Twitter applications aggregate, organise and present Twitter 'streams' shapes how Twitter discussions are structured and 'consumed' as well as contributing to the inclusive and exclusive nature of the discussion exchanges and sequences (Fox, 2005) and so to the communicative actions and structures.

Fox's (2005) analysis of the role of newspapers illustrates the role of non-human actors in the generation and maintenance of the imagined community of the nation. Discussing the layout of newspaper front pages as consisting of a number of unrelated news stories, Fox asserts that (2005: 103):

> The regular reader thus keeps abreast of multiple narrative threads that weave the fabric of his or her imagined world. But this is not experienced as a simulated world but as the real world . . . By following the threads of news over time, the reader maintains a sense of a world known in common with distant, imagined others . . .

Fox concludes:

> In terms of 'symmetrical analysis', the non-human elements in the networks of 'print capitalism' made the 'imagined community' of the nation . . . a social and cultural reality.

Similarly, using a browser or specific applications such as Tweetdeck,[1] Tweets are co-visible to the participant in a single column stream in time

Figure 13.2   Screenshot of Tweetdeck used with permission of the author

order, enrolling individuals in making contributions across multiple sequences (Simpson, 2005).

Yet, the user may follow a number of different columns on the Twitter applications organised by specific search terms and hashtags (Figure 13.2).

A single Tweet included in the discussion event may appear in a number of columns: the main timeline; a 'mentions' column where Tweets that mention the specific user can be found; a column set up to follow the hashtag of the discussion event; and another column set up to search for specific key words or a different hashtag. As a result, the participant can experience a discussion event through different column 'threads' and different temporal frames. A single Tweet appearing in multiple columns may be consumed as indicative of the broader network of communities or networks that the user is enrolled in. Also, participants may be contributing to the discussion event through placing their contributions in a different network assemblage represented as a column in the software. So the available technology influences how these discussion events are understood by users.

DISCUSSION

The use of social media has become increasingly prominent in a range of organisational activities including learning and development, knowledge-sharing and employee engagement (CIPD, 2013) as well as being increasingly adopted as informal professional learning environments. So there is the need for research approaches appropriate to the practices associated with such technologies and environments where the main mechanism of practice is textual (Koole, 2010).

This chapter describes an approach to the research and investigation of open and informal learning events on the micro-blogging platform Twitter that used a DA within an ANT based framework. Through this research approach, the study found that these discussion events show high levels of instability and volatility, blurring distinctions between information producers, distributors and consumers (Androutsopoulos, 2008; Pata, 2009) within discursive communities. Furthermore, these network or community-forming learning events remain social practices with specific power relations operating within them and are not as informal and unstructured as they are often described. Rather, they are structured by the nature of the technologies used and by particular relations of power and interest mediated through the discursive structure of the community.

The research discussed in this chapter presents an approach to the study of the micro-political components of HRD practice (Vickers and Fox, 2010) through interactions between human and non-human actors. The micro focus of an ANT research approach may, for example, not just identify examples of restrictive learning (Fuller and Unwin, 2004), but also explain what practices generate such restrictive effects. The approach outlined in this chapter provides a way to research HRD as a social and discursive construct (Lawless et al., 2011), by studying the mobilisation of discursive resources in the practice of HRD (Francis, 2007). As such, ANT can be positioned as part of the 'practice-turn' in social research (Sørensen, 2009).

NOTE

1. Available via http://www.tweetdeck.com/.

REFERENCES

Androutsopoulos, J. (2008). Potentials and limitations of discourse-centred online ethnology. *language@internet, vol. 5*. Available at: http://www.languageatinternet.

de articles/2008/1610/index_html/?searchterm=None (Last accessed: 22 November 2010).

AoIR (2012). *Ethical Decision-Making and Internet Research 2.0: Recommendations from the AoIR Ethics Working Committee*. Available at: http://www.aoir.org/reports/ethics2.pdf (Last accessed: 2 March 2013)

Belnap, J.K, and Withers, M.G. (2008). Discourse Analysis: the problematic analysis of unstructured/unfacilitated group discussions. *Eleventh Conference on Research in Undergraduate Mathematics Education*, February, San Diego, CA.

Billet, S. (2004). Workplace participatory practices: conceptualising workplaces as learning environments. *Journal of Workplace Learning*, 16(6): 312–324.

Bingham, T. and Conner, M. (2010). *The New Social Learning*. San Francisco: Berrett-Koehler Publishers, Inc.

Bloome, D., Carter, S.P., Christian, B.M., Otto, S. and Shuart-Faris, N. (2005). *Discourse Analysis and the Study of Classroom Language and Literacy Events*. Mahwah, NJ: Lawrence Erlbaum Associates.

Bragd, A., Christensen, D., Czarniawska, B. and Tullberg, M. (2008). Discourse as the means of community creation. *Scandinavian Journal of Management*, 24(3): 199–208.

Bruns, A. (2011). How long is a Tweet? Mapping dynamic conversation networks on Twitter using Gawk and Gelphi. *Information, Communication and Society*, December, 37–41.

CIPD (Chartered Institute of Personnel and Development) (2013). *Social Media and Employee Voice: The Current Landscape*. Available at: http://www.cipd.co.uk/bina ries/6133%20SOP%20Social%20Media%20(WEB).pdf (Last accessed 23 July 2013).

Dennen, V. (2008). Looking for evidence of learning: assessment and analysis methods for online discourse. *Computers in Human Behavior*, 24(2): 205–219.

Eysenbach, G. and Till, G.E. (2001). Ethical issues in qualitative research on internet communities. *British Medical Journal*, November 10, 323(7321): 1103–1105.

Fairclough, N. (2003). *Analysing Discourse: Textual Analysis for Social Research*. London: Routledge.

Fenwick, T. and Edwards, R. (2010). *Actor-Network Theory in Education*. London: Routledge.

Fenwick, T., Jensen, K. and Nerland, M. (2012). Sociomaterial approaches to reconceptualising professional learning and practice. *Journal of Education and Work*, 25(1): 1–13.

Fox, S. (2005). An actor network critique of community in higher education: implications for network learning. *Studies in Higher Education*, 30(1): 95–110.

Francis, H. (2007). Discursive struggle and the ambiguous world of HRD. *Advances in Developing Human Resources*, 9(1): 83–96.

Fuller, A. and Unwin, L. (2004). Expansive learning environments: integrating personal and organisational development, in H. Rainbird, A. Fuller and A. Munro (eds). *Workplace Learning in Context*. London: Routledge, pp. 126–144.

Geiger, D. (2009). Revisiting the concept of practice: towards an argumentative understanding of practicing. *Management Learning*, 40(2): 129–144.

Gherardi, S. (2000). Practice-based theorising on learning and knowing in organizations. *Organization*, 7(2): 211–223.

Gnosis Media Group (n.d.) *TweetChat wiki*. Available at: http://www.gnosisarts.com/home/ Tweetchat_Wiki/By_Subject (Last accessed: 15 February 2013).

Gold, J., Holden, R., Iles, P., Stewart, J. and Beardwell, J. (2010). *Human Resource Development: Theory and Practice*. London: Palgrave MacMillan.

Guzman, G. (2009). What is practical knowledge? *Journal of Knowledge Management*, 13(4): 86–98.

Heracleous, L. (2006). A tale of three discourses: the dominant, the strategic and the marginalised. *Journal of Management Studies*, 43(5): 1059–1087.

Irwin, B. and Hramiak, A. (2010). A discourse analysis of trainee identity in online discussion forums. *Technology, Pedagogy and Education*, 19(3): 361–377.

Koole, M. (2010). The web of identity: selfhood and belonging in online learning environments, in L. Dirckinck-Holfeld, V. Hodgson, C. Jones, M. de Laat, D. McConnell and T. Ryberg (eds). *Proceedings of the 7th International Conference on Network Learning*, Aalborg, Denmark.

Latour, B. (2005). *Reassembling the Social*. Oxford: Oxford University Press.

Lawless, A., Sambrook, S., Garavan, T. and Valentin, C. (2011). A discourse approach to theorising HRD: opening a discursive space. *Journal of European Industrial Training*, 35(3): 264–275.

Lerman, K. and Ghosh, R. (2010). Information contagion: an empirical study of the spread of news on Digg and Twitter social networks. *Proceedings of 4th International Conference on Weblogs and Social Media (ICWSM-10)*. Available at: http://arxiv.org/abs/1003.2664 (Last accessed: 15 January 2013).

Mäkitalo, A. (2012). Professional learning and the materialities of social practice. *Journal of Education and Work*, 25(1): 59–78.

McCulloch, J., McIntosh, E. and Barrett, T. (2011). *Tweeting for Teachers: How Can Social Media Support Teacher Professional Development?* Pearson Centre for Policy and Learning.

McLean, C. and Hassard, J. (2004). Symmetrical absence/symmetrical absurdity: critical notes on the production of actor-network accounts. *Journal of Management Studies*, 41(3): 493–519.

Miettinen, R. (1997). *The Concept of Activity in the Analysis of Heterogeneous Networks in Innovation Processes*. CSST Workshop: Actor Network Theory and After, July.

Mitev, N. (2009). In and out of actor-network theory: a necessary but insufficient journey. *Information Technology and People*, 22(1): 9–25.

Nicolini, D., Gherardi, S. and Yanow, D. (2003). Introduction: towards a practice-based view of knowing and learning in organizations, in D. Nicolini, S. Gherardi and D. Yanow (eds). *Knowing in Organizations: A Practice-Based Approach*. London: M.E. Sharpe, pp. 3–31.

Nunan, D. (1993). *Introducing Discourse Analysis*. London: Penguin.

O'Carroll, L. (2012). Twitter active users pass 200 million. *The Guardian*, 18 December. Available at: http://www.guardian.co.uk/technology/2012/dec/18/twitter-users-pass-200-million (Last accessed: 10 February 2013).

Pata, K. (2009). Revising the framework of knowledge ecologies: how activity patterns define learning spaces? in N. Lambropoulos and M. Romero (eds). *Educational Social Software for Context-Aware Learning: Collaborative Methods and Human Interaction*. Hershey, PA: Information Science Reference, pp. 241–267.

Schneider, S.M. and Foot, K.A. (2005). Web sphere analysis: an approach to studying online action, in C. Hine (ed.). *Virtual Methods: Issues in Social Research on the Internet*. Oxford: Berg, pp. 157–170.

Simpson, J. (2005). Conversational floors in synchronous text-based CMC discourse. *Discourse Studies*, 7(3): 337–361.

Sørensen, E. (2009). *The Materiality of Learning: Technology and Knowledge in Educational Practice*. New York: Cambridge University Press.

Tuomi, I. (2000). *Internet, Innovation and Open Source: Actors in the Network*. SITRA, Finnish National Fund for Research and Development. 3 November.

Vicker, D. and Fox, S. (2010). Towards practice-based studies of HRM: an actor-network and communities of practice informed approach. *International Journal of Human Resource Management*, 21(6): 899–914.

ANNOTATED FURTHER READING

Fenwick, T. and Edwards, R. (2010). *Actor-Network Theory in Education*. London: Routledge. This book provides an overview of the breadth of ANT and how the concepts of ANT have been and could be applied in educational settings including vocational education as well as lifelong and workplace learning.

Journal of Education and Work, 25(1). Special Issue: Reconceptualising Professional Learning in a Changing Society. This special issue of the journal is focused on socio-material approaches (including ANT) to conceptualising and researching professional learning in practice.

14. And what kind of question is that? Thinking about the function of questions in qualitative interviewing
Paul Tosey

SUMMARY

This chapter explores qualitative interviewing, drawing from a project that investigated managers' metaphors of work–life balance, informed by a practice called 'Clean Language'. The chapter highlights the function of questions in interviews and considers how to design and ask questions in order to elicit data of good quality.

INTRODUCTION

Interviewing has become ubiquitous in the workplace, the media and research, to the extent that Atkinson and Silverman (1997) coined the term 'the interview society'. Some interviewers – for example the late Sir David Frost, and Oprah Winfrey – have achieved celebrity status.

Interviewing has become probably the most commonly used approach to data-gathering in qualitative research (King, 2004). Kvale and Brinkmann (2009, p.9) note the use of interviews in the social sciences by Freud and Piaget, and in the classic Hawthorne studies. Today, interviews are employed as a research tool across the range of social science disciplines, including anthropology, sociology, psychology and organizational studies, and within methodological approaches such as evaluation research, qualitative surveys, case studies, phenomenological studies and heuristic research. In Human Resources Development (HRD), since the inception of the journal *Human Resource Development International* (HRDI) in 1998, 52 articles have declared in the abstract that interviewing was used as a method of data collection (NB HRDI articles do not necessarily involve empirical research). This indicates at least that interviewing is common in HRD research, and, for example, Berings et al. (2006) assert that interviewing is, together with questionnaires, the most common choice of method for investigating on-the-job learning processes.

Interviewing offers several advantages as a method of data collection such as flexibility (since it can be used almost anywhere), the capacity to explore meaning in depth and a more personal engagement than with (for example) questionnaires, the relationship between interviewer and interviewee often being considered important (King, 2004). On the other hand, interviewing is time consuming and resource intensive, especially when it comes to transcribing and analysing data. Like any other method, interviewing may be more or less useful depending on its fit with the research aims and objectives.

Because interviewing involves an activity – conversation – that most people use every day, researchers may be lulled into believing that this method is unproblematic and requires little specialised knowledge. Guidance on interviewing is sometimes reduced to behavioural details such as how to put the interviewee at their ease and how to listen. This can ignore the need to consider theories of interviewing, and the decision to employ interviewing could represent 'an unthinking adoption of the current fashion' (Silverman, 2000, p.290).

Atkinson and Silverman (1997), among others, have advanced important critiques of the propensity to use interviewing in a naïve way that places unjustified faith in its capacity as a 'uniquely privileged means of access to the biographically grounded experiences and meanings of social actors' (Atkinson and Silverman, 1997, p.304). Such critique does not (in my view) mean that interviews are incapable of accessing personal experiences and subjective meanings. It does mean, however, that the researcher needs to assure themselves of the rigour and robustness of the way they plan to use interviewing, in theory as well as in practice.

Specifically, this chapter argues that approaches to qualitative interviewing often neglect to consider the function of questions, and so underestimate the need for questions to be designed and posed skilfully in order to elicit data of good quality. It focuses on a project which addressed that need by applying a practice called Clean Language to research interviewing (Tosey et al., 2014). The next section introduces Clean Language and the project.

CLEAN LANGUAGE

Clean Language is a practice that aims to facilitate exploration of a person's inner world through their own, naturally occurring metaphors. Its origins lie in the work of counselling psychologist David Grove in the 1980s (Grove and Panzer, 1991; Lawley and Tompkins, 2000), who discovered that by focusing on a client's naturally occurring metaphors, and enabling that client to become immersed in their inner symbolic world,

202 Handbook of research methods on HRD

spontaneous change could occur. Grove called this approach 'Clean Language' (Grove and Panzer, 1991, p.1) because of its intention to keep the practitioner's language 'clean' in the sense of being as free as possible from the practitioner's own metaphors, so that these do not influence or contaminate the client's metaphors. Clean Language has since been adapted for use outside a therapeutic context and can be learnt through commercially available training courses.[1] Today it has many applications in HRD, such as in coaching and consultancy (van Helsdingen and Lawley, 2012).

It is important to note that the conception of metaphor employed in Clean Language is informed by the work of Lakoff and Johnson, who defined its essence as '*understanding and experiencing one kind of thing in terms of another*' (Lakoff and Johnson, 1980, p.5: italics in original). These authors put forward the philosophical view that our conceptions of the world are fundamentally metaphorical, such that 'metaphorical thought is unavoidable, ubiquitous, and mostly unconscious' (Lakoff and Johnson, 2003, p.272). From that perspective, apparently innocent terms such as 'lie in' and 'put forward' (which I have used already in this section) are regarded as metaphorical. This means that it is both easy and common for an interviewer to embed their own metaphors inadvertently in their questions.

Grove identified a basic set of Clean Language questions (Box 14.1) and a syntax for their use (hence when used in practice each question is typically prefaced with 'and . . .'). Grove considered this set of questions to be the most minimal in terms of avoiding the introduction of the practitioner's constructs and metaphors.

Of course, presented in this way as a list, out of context, this set of questions can appear sparse and impersonal. The Clean Language

---

BOX 14.1   BASIC CLEAN LANGUAGE QUESTIONS

- Where/whereabouts is X?
- What kind of X is that X?
- Is there anything else about X?
- Is there a relationship between X and Y?
- That's X like what?
- When Y, what happens to X?
- What happens just before X?
- Then what happens/what happens next?
- Where does/could X come from?
- What would X like to have happen?

Source: Developed from http://www.cleanlanguage.co.uk/, accessed 17 July 2013.

practitioner's job is to select, pose and link these questions skilfully in order to facilitate a participant's exploration of their own 'metaphor landscape' (see, for example, the brief extract later in this chapter).

Through undertaking training in Clean Language myself, and due to an interest in innovative phenomenological methods (e.g. Tosey and Mathison, 2010), I was struck by its potential for research due to its systematic and rigorous way of exploring, and maintaining fidelity to, a person's own inner world. This led to a collaboration with a group of practitioners on a project that elicited the naturally occurring metaphors of a small sample of managers relating to the way they experienced work–life balance (WLB). The principal aim of the project was not to research WLB per se, but to learn about the viability and usefulness of Clean Language as a research method (Tosey et al., 2014). The full research team consisted of two academic researchers and four practitioners from, or affiliated to, a commercial Clean Language training organisation. The project was funded by a small pump-priming grant from my university, with matched contributions in kind from the training organisation.

Before describing the way this approach was used in the WLB project, I locate the approach taken in the WLB project within selected typologies of research interviews.

DEFINITIONS AND PHILOSOPHIES OF INTERVIEWING

A typical definition of an interview is 'a conversation with a purpose' (Berg, 1995, p.66), and Kvale (1983, p.174) describes the purpose as being 'to gather descriptions of the life-world of the interviewee with respect to interpretation of the meaning of the described phenomena'. However, it is important to note that not all qualitative interviews are the same. Numerous typologies of interviews exist, at a variety of levels. The first such level concerns the overarching philosophical position (Saunders et al., 2012), which affects the fundamental conception of the interview. King (2004), for example, describes three such philosophical positions, suggesting that these form a spectrum:

- *Realist*: assumes that 'the accounts participants produce in interviews bear a direct relationship to their "real" experiences in the world'.
- *Phenomenological*: the interview gathers data that enable the researcher to understand the structure and nature of the interviewee's subjective world.

- *Radical constructionist*: sees 'the account as a text produced in the specific setting of the interview, to be analysed in terms of the discursive strategies employed and resources drawn upon by the interviewee' (King, 2004, pp.12–13).

The WLB project adopted a phenomenological position, because it aimed to understand and represent interviewees' worlds authentically. Clean Language is highly compatible with the phenomenological principle of *epoche*, whereby a researcher aims to free themselves from using their own presuppositions and beliefs when exploring another person's subjective experience (Moustakas, 1994).

Turning to a second framework, Roulston (2010) describes six conceptions of the interview in qualitative enquiry, the assumptions they entail about knowledge production and their implications for judgements about quality. Roulston emphasises the need for congruence between the way in which interviews are used and the principles underlying a study's design. The Clean Language approach to interviewing most closely resembles (though does not completely match) Roulston's 'neo-positivist' conception (see also Alvesson, 2003), which assumes that 'the interview subject has an inner or authentic self . . . Which may be revealed through careful questioning by an attentive and sensitive interviewer who contributes minimally to the talk' (Roulston, 2010, p.204). According to Roulston, the neo-positivist approach is already widespread in published research. The distinctive, systematic approach offered by Clean Language could, however, address key criticisms of this conception of interviewing, especially that 'the researcher's subjectivities and beliefs may bias the data through the way questions are sequenced and formulated' (Roulston, 2010, Table 1 pp.205–206).

Both this neo-positivist conception and that which Roulston labels 'romantic' stand in direct contrast to alternative conceptions. For example, in a constructionist conception the prime focus of interest for the researcher is the way in which interview data are co-constructed in a social setting and produce situated accounts. Wang and Roulston (2007) criticise the tendency for HRD research specifically to employ in-depth interviews without attending to the co-constructed nature of interview data.

It is worth pausing here to reflect on how an approach to interviewing can be both 'phenomenological' and 'neo-positivist', since some might see a contradiction between a phenomenological emphasis on subjective experience and a neo-positivist interest in (for example) reducing bias. I would argue that this can be reconciled through the emphasis of Clean Language on rigorously eliciting the structure of the interviewee's inner, subjective world. Clean Language assumes that inner subjective worlds do have a structure, and that they can be elicited faithfully. Clean Language also acknowledges that the interviewer plays a significant role in that elicitation through directing the interviewee's attention. In other words, there is a sense in which accounts are co-constructed through the *process* of selecting and asking questions. At the same time, Clean Language aims to minimise co-construction of the *content* through the introduction of the interviewer's beliefs and constructs. Clean Language is therefore making a significant claim, to the effect that the criticisms of authors such as Alvesson and Roulston can be answered; and yet this is in complete agreement with those authors who believe that much qualitative interviewing is of suspect quality because the interviewer is inadvertently co-constructing the data whilst simultaneously claiming that the interview is neutral.

Briefly, there are two additional typologies in which to locate Clean Language interviews. First, they can be described as exploratory (King, 2004) – that is, typically having a predominance of open-ended questions (without predetermined responses) and focusing on situations and actions in the world of the interviewee rather than general opinions or abstractions – rather than semi-structured (topics and issues are likely to be outlined in advance but the question order and wording is decided by the interviewer during the interview) or structured (the interviewer uses a detailed schedule with specifically ordered questions, and the way the questions are asked is controlled as much as possible to avoid bias in the responses of different interviewees). Second, interview formats also vary by being conducted either with individuals or with groups and either face-to-face or remotely (e.g. via telephone, Skype or video link). Here the chosen format was individual interviews, one face-to-face, and a follow up by phone or Skype, with six UK managers – a relatively small, homogeneous sample chosen specifically for the purpose of testing the interview method.

CONCEPTUALISING QUESTIONS: CONTENT-CENTRED VERSUS EPISTEMIC

Patton recommends that in order to 'minimize the imposition of predetermined responses when gathering data . . . questions should be asked in a truly open-ended fashion' (Patton, 2002, p.353). Whilst many researchers might agree readily with Patton's prescription, it masks a significant issue. If the aim is to discover the interviewee's own words (bearing in mind that this will not be the aim in every philosophy of interviewing), *can* this be accomplished through using open-ended questions? If so, how?

The importance of questions is acknowledged within HRD in relation to facilitating reflection, for example in action learning (Harrison, 2006) and coaching (O'Connor and Lages, 2007, p.167). With regard to research interviewing, Gibson and Hanes (2003, p.190) emphasise that 'questioning in the interview is of utmost importance'. Yet despite Patton's assertion that 'The wording used in asking questions can make a significant difference in the quality of responses elicited' (2002, p.360), guidance largely emphasises the importance of asking open questions (e.g. Patton 2002, pp.355 *et seq.*).

Although research by Loftus (1975) has demonstrated how the wording of a question can influence an interviewee's recall and response, concern with the precise wording of questions and its impact figures mainly in discussions of how to standardise interviews for survey purposes (e.g. Dillman et al., 2009; Gobo, 2006; Kalton et al., 1978; Tanur, 1992). Treatments of interview questions typically comprise broad typologies of question types, based on distinctions between their form (e.g. open, closed, dichotomous, multiple and leading questions, and so on), or the type of content they are aimed at (e.g. Patton, 2002 identifies experience and behaviour questions; opinions and value questions; feeling questions; knowledge questions; sensory questions; and background/demographic questions), or their function (e.g. Kvale and Brinkmann, 2009, pp.135–136).

Crucially there are, I suggest, two very different ways of conceptualising the nature of questions. The standard way, which is reflected in virtually all research methods texts, is to focus on content, that is, to regard questions as a way of *eliciting data*. This is understandable because, of course, the purpose of a research interview is to collect data. However, this conception misses out a highly significant step in the process that leads from question to response. The alternative is to conceptualise a question as *epistemic* (Ikenuobe, 2001), in the sense of being concerned with *how* we know something rather than with what we know. From this perspective, asking a question is a way of *stimulating internal processing*. Hence all questions trigger *processes of knowing* (Tosey and Mathison, 2010), and Clean Language highlights this epistemic function in the sense that Clean Language questions are designed to direct the interviewee's attention to aspects of their inner world.

To illustrate the epistemic function of questions, read the following examples and pay attention to what you have to *do* in order to answer them:

1. What colour is your front door?
2. What is your favourite piece of music?
3. How did you get to work today?
4. How will you travel to work next week?
5. How might you be travelling to work in a year's time?

Even a question that sounds straightforward and factual, such as (1), is likely to have used internal processing, such as recalling a visual image of your front door. Responding to question (2) may have involved sorting through and selecting from alternatives, and perhaps hearing music. You may have noticed differences in processing according to whether a question concerned the past (3) or the future (4 and 5). Even though the content of your answer to questions (4) and (5) could be the same, it is possible that the process you went through to answer them was different. For example, there are likely to be subtle differences between 'will' and 'might', and between 'travel' and 'be travelling'. In addition, for each question you may have been aware of knowing when you had an answer ready.

Note that this is definitely *not* saying that the wording of a question determines the response. The way a question is asked, and the context in which it is posed, will also influence the interviewee's internal processing. Internal processing includes sense-making of the situation; therefore, a response can be influenced by a desire to present oneself in a particular light, or to please an interviewer – reflecting the interest of those who emphasise the situated, socially mediated nature of the research interview. Internal processing can also be out of awareness, such that interviewees can produce 'learnt' responses that are socially situated stock answers.

This epistemic perspective on questions is reflected in some fields of practice. For example, de Shazer's (1994) solution-focused brief therapy highlights the way in which the 'fateful first question' can direct the entire course of therapy towards problems or towards solutions. Barber (2005) compiles questions used by coaches, and Townsend et al. (2011) discuss an application of the 'miracle question'. However, there appears to be scarcely any literature on research methods that adopts this epistemic perspective. One example that does is a contemporary European development called 'psychophenomenology', which uses a method called the 'elicitation interview' ('l'entretien d'explicitation', Vermersch, 1994). This is a form of guided introspection that seeks to develop finely grained first-person accounts by using distinctions in language, internal sensory representations and imagery (Tosey and Mathison, 2010). Petitmengin et al. (2006) show the potential importance of this approach through the way it has been used to help epileptics to detect the onset of, and thereby better manage, seizures.

Even if not using Clean Language specifically, I suggest that it is useful for the interviewer to consider what a question *does*, or what kind of internal processing is likely to be stimulated. This enables the interviewer to refine their technique and to formulate questions that may stand a better chance of eliciting accurate and valid information. This is especially the case if the interview is concerned with understanding the interviewee's internal world.

CLEAN LANGUAGE AS AN APPROACH TO INTERVIEWING IN THE WLB PROJECT

Resuming the discussion of the potential contribution Clean Language can make to research interviewing, there are two obvious stages at which the standard qualitative research interview can be lacking. First, the interviewer can include their own constructs or metaphors in a question, which directs the interviewee's attention towards those constructs and metaphors and thereby influences the response. For example, the phrase 'work–life balance' entails the metaphor of 'balance'. Our project had to work out a way to discover an interviewee's own experience and metaphors relating to this issue without predisposing them to talk in terms of balance and imbalance. Considerable time and care was taken over deciding how to start the interviews, and especially how to introduce the topic of WLB. There was an argument for avoiding this phrase altogether; however, we took the decision to use the term at the start of the interview in order to introduce the topic in a way that the interviewee could easily understand. After the introduction the focus was firmly on the interviewee's own words. What this enabled us to do was to test the ability of Clean Language to elicit individuals' naturally occurring metaphors despite the existence of a conventional metaphor (Lakoff and Johnson, 1999) in the broad topic.

The second stage is that the interviewer can interpret or inadvertently misrepresent the interviewee's words when analysing and writing up the research. For example, Tosey et al. (2014) cite the example of an article by Berger (2004) which uses the metaphor of an 'edge of knowing' prominently in its findings, even though this does not appear to be present in the data. This is not a problem where a researcher *intends* to interpret their data and assesses the validity of their findings accordingly; it becomes a problem when a researcher claims to be portraying interviewees' own worlds authentically. These issues are compounded by the fact that the full detail of questions asked and responses received is rarely disclosed in published research, so that it is difficult for the reader to make their own assessment of the relationship between the questions asked, the data and the findings. Clearly there are constraints on space, but these matters are often assumed not to be problematic and not in need of being made transparent.

Applying the Clean Language approach involved several other issues relevant to the design and use of research interviews. Interviewing is acknowledged to be a powerful process, and the planning was informed fully by the institution's research ethics guidelines. Clean Language is often used to support personal change, for example in coaching or psychotherapy. In the WLB project the purpose was research, and so personal change was deliberately not pursued because it was not part of the contract with the participant. This also meant an adjustment to the way Clean Language was used, in that it is normally led by the participant's outcome (e.g. a desire for change, or a goal of behavioural improvement). In this project the reason for conducting the interview was to meet a research aim rather than to meet the participant's outcome. The project team nevertheless aimed to make sure that the interviewee would be likely to derive benefit for their participation through increased awareness of their experience of WLB, and this was made explicit when recruiting participants. It was interesting that in the follow-up interview, several participants reported that they had decided to make changes based on the awareness they gained through the first interview. From an ethical perspective it is also relevant to note that in a subsequent follow-up enquiry, all participants reported that they had found the interview beneficial, and no participant identified any disbenefits.

For any extensive use of Clean Language, for example in order to elicit metaphors or to explore the participant's inner world, the interviewer is likely to need to have undergone training in Clean Language. In the WLB project the interviewer was experienced in the method, and the project team included acknowledged experts in the field in the form of people who have delivered Clean Language training courses and used Clean Language in business consulting and psychotherapy.

An important difference between the Clean Language approach and a standard qualitative interview concerns rapport. It is typically assumed that rapport is a good thing, reflected for example in eye contact and congruent non-verbal behaviour. An effective Clean Language interview, however, requires the interviewee's attention to remain on their own inner world or metaphor landscape. Active attempts by the interviewer to establish eye contact would interrupt that inward attention and be counter-productive.

Finally, all the interviews were recorded and transcribed, then reviewed by the interviewer and other members of the project team in order to enhance validity. First, all the questions used by the interviewer were looked at it in terms of the extent to which they were 'clean', including whether they were confined to using the interviewee's own language. Any data following an 'unclean' question was scrutinised in case the interviewee had begun to use the interviewer's words. In this project the interviewer did remarkably well, with more than 95 per cent of questions being considered 'clean'.

A short extract from near the beginning of an interview in the WLB project is shown below as an illustration of a Clean Language interview. This extract uses two questions from the set listed in Box 14.1, 'That's X like what?' (twice) and 'Is there anything else about X?', and a third question, 'How do you know that . . .?', that is not in the above list but is still 'clean':

So, when your work–life balance is at its best, that's like what?

That's like what . . . that's like I suppose I'm getting good job satisfaction, I'm feeling that my employer is happy with my output and the quality of my output but also that my family life is also good and that I'm giving enough time to my husband and my children and the life outside work as well.

And when you're giving enough time to do the life outside work, how do you know that you're giving enough time?

Um, I suppose you know because you feel in control . . . and you feel happy about your life outside work.

And you feel in control that you feel happy about your life outside work, when you feel in control, is there anything else about feeling in control?

Um . . . in control . . . well I suppose it's easier to define it by when it . . . when it's not in control in a way, you know when it's not in control.

And when it's not in control that's . . . that's like what?

It's bad, it's you know, or it can be really bad and then . . . your stress levels go up and you're feeling pressure from other people that are part of your life outside work and then you're not happy I suppose as a consequence of that or you . . . you may be feeling unhappy, so I suppose work–life balance for me is really, really important.

(continues)

The second measure to enhance validity was that analyses of the interviews were reviewed by the team in order to confirm that they represented the interviewee's own metaphor landscape as faithfully as possible according to the data. Together these measures illustrate a potential advantage of Clean Language, which is that members of the project team were working to a common set of principles about the practice and can therefore debate both the questions and interpretations systematically. The detailed outputs from the analyses, comprising an individual profile of each interviewee's metaphor landscape, themes across the interviewees and implications regarding WLB, can be found in Tosey et al. (2014).

DISCUSSION

Clean Language represents a specific, innovative approach to research interviewing. Designed specifically for the elicitation of 'metaphor landscapes', Clean Language questions can nevertheless be incorporated into any interview and can therefore contribute to rigour and quality in the use of qualitative interviews (Kvale and Brinkmann, 2009) by minimising the risk of inadvertently introducing the interviewer's constructs, whether via their questions or their interpretations.

This discussion has three important implications for any HRD researcher intending to use qualitative interviews. First, it shows that philosophies of interviewing vary widely, and that the researcher proposing to use interviews needs to make an informed, aware choice. Second, it has highlighted the difference between content-focused and epistemic conceptions of questioning. Third, it has emphasised the importance of precision in designing and using research questions and in the subsequent analysis of data.

NOTE

1.   For example, http://www.cleanchange.co.uk/cleanlanguage/.

REFERENCES

Alvesson, M. (2003). Beyond neopositivists, romantics, and localists: A reflexive approach to interviews in organizational research. *Academy of Management Review*, 28(1), 13–33.

Atkinson, P. and Silverman, D. (1997). Kundera's immortality: The interview society and the invention of the self, *Qualitative Inquiry*, 3(3), 304–325.

Barber, J. (ed.) (2005). *Good Question! The Art of Asking Questions to Bring About Positive Change*. Great Britain: www.bookshaker.com.

Berg, B. L. (1995). *Qualitative Research Methods for the Social Sciences*, 2nd edition. Boston, MA: Allyn and Bacon.

Berger, J. G. (2004). Dancing on the threshold of meaning: Recognising and understanding the growing edge, *Journal of Transformative Education*, 2, 336–351.

Berings, M. G. M. C., Doornbos, A. J. and Simons, P. R.-J. (2006). Methodological practices in on-the-job learning research, *Human Resource Development International*, 9(3), 333–363.

de Shazer, S. (1994). *Words Were Originally Magic*. New York: W. W. Norton & Company.

Dillman, D. A., Smyth, J. D. and Christian, M. L. (2009). *Internet, Mail and Mixed-Mode Surveys: The Tailored Design Approach*, 3rd edition. Hoboken, NJ: John Wiley & Sons.

Gibson, S. and Hanes, L. A. (2003). The contribution of phenomenology to HRD research, *Human Resource Development Review*, 2, 181–205.

Gobo, G. (2006). Set them free: Improving data quality by broadening the interviewer's tasks, *International Journal of Social Research Methodology*, 9, 279–301.

Grove, D. J. and Panzer, B. I. (1991). *Resolving Traumatic Memories: Metaphors and Symbols in Psychotherapy*. New York: Irvington Publishers Inc.

Harrison, P. (2006). Questioning in action learning: Rhetoric or reality?, *International Journal of Management Education*, 5(2), 15–20.

Ikenuobe, P. (2001). Questioning as an epistemic process of critical thinking, *Educational Philosophy and Theory*, 33(3–4), 325–341.

Kalton, G., Collins, M. and Brook, L. (1978). Experiments in wording opinion questions, *Journal of the Royal Statistical Society, Series C (Applied Statistics)*, 27, 149–161.

King, N. (2004). Using interviews in qualitative research. In C. Cassell and G. Symon (eds.), *Essential Guide to Qualitative Methods in Organizational Research* (pp.11–22). London: Sage.

Kvale, S. (1983). The qualitative research interview: A phenomenological and a hermeneutical mode of understanding, *Journal of Phenomenological Psychology*, 14, 171–196.

Kvale, S. and Brinkmann, S. (2009). *InterViews: Learning the Craft of Qualitative Research Interviewing*, 2nd edition. Thousand Oaks, CA: Sage.

Lakoff, G. and Johnson, M. (1980). *Metaphors We Live By*. Chicago and London: University of Chicago Press.

Lakoff, G. and Johnson, M. (1999). *Philosophy in the Flesh: The Embodied Mind and Its Challenge to Western Thought*. New York: Basic Books.

Lakoff, G. and Johnson, M. (2003). *Metaphors We Live By*, Chicago: University of Chicago Press.

Lawley, J. and Tompkins, P. (2000). *Metaphors in Mind: Transformation through Symbolic Modelling*. London: The Developing Company Press.

Loftus, E. F. (1975). Leading questions and the eyewitness report, *Cognitive Psychology*, 7, 560–572.

Moustakas, C. (1994). *Phenomenological Research Methods*. Thousand Oaks, CA: Sage.

O'Connor, J. and Lages, A. (2007). *How Coaching Works: The Essential Guide to the History and Practice of Effective Coaching*. London: A & C Black.

Patton, M. Q. (2002). *Qualitative Evaluation and Research Methods*, 3rd edition. Newbury Park, CA: Sage.

Petitmengin, C., Baulac, M. and Navarro, V. (2006). Seizure anticipation: Are neurophenomenological approaches able to detect preictal symptoms? *Epilepsy and Behavior*, 9(2), 298–306.

Roulston, K. (2010). Considering quality in qualitative interviewing, *Qualitative Research*, 10(2), 199–228.

Saunders, M. N. K., Lewis, P. and Thornhill, A. (2012). *Research Methods for Business Students*, 6th edition. London: Pearson/Financial Times Press.

Silverman, D. (2000). *Doing Qualitative Research: A Practical Handbook*. London: Sage.

Sullivan, W. and Rees, J. (2008). *Clean Language: Revealing Metaphors and Opening Minds*. Carmarthen, Wales: Crown House Publishing House.

Tanur, J. M. (ed.) (1992). *Questions about Questions: Inquiries into the Cognitive Bases of Surveys*. New York: Russell Sage Foundation.

Tosey, P., Lawley, J. and Meese, R. (2014). Eliciting metaphor through Clean Language: An innovation in qualitative research, *British Journal of Management*, 25(3), 629–646.

Tosey, P. and Mathison, J. (2010). Exploring inner landscapes through psychophenomenology: The contribution of neuro-linguistic programming to innovations in researching first person experience. *Qualitative Research in Organizations and Management*, 5(1), 63–82.

Townsend, K., Wilkinson, A., Allan, C. and Bamber, G. (2011). All we need is a miracle:

Using a solution-based approach to human resource management in hospitals, *Asia Pacific Journal of Human Resources*, 49(2), 165–179.

van Helsdingen, A. and Lawley, J. (2012). Modelling shared reality: Avoiding unintended influence in qualitative research, *Kwalon*, 3, 1–7.

Vermersch, P. (1994). *L'entretien d'explicitation*. Issy les-Moulineaux, Paris: EDF Editeur.

Wang, J. and Roulston, K. J. (2007). An alternative approach to conceptualizing interviews in HRD research, *Human Resource Development Quarterly*, 18, 179–210.

ANNOTATED FURTHER READING

Kvale, S. and S. Brinkmann (2009). *InterViews: Learning the Craft of Qualitative Research Interviewing*, 2nd edition. Thousand Oaks, CA: Sage. A comprehensive text on research interviewing.

Roulston, K. (2010). Considering quality in qualitative interviewing, *Qualitative Research*, 10(2), 199–228. A very useful typology of six competing philosophies of interviewing.

Sullivan, W. and Rees, J. (2008). *Clean Language: Revealing Metaphors and Opening Minds*. Carmarthen, Wales: Crown House Publishing House. A popular introduction to Clean Language and how it can be used in everyday and professional contexts.

PART III

QUANTITATIVE RESEARCH

15. Using questionnaire surveys for within-organisation HRD research
Cinla Akinci and Mark N.K. Saunders

SUMMARY

This chapter provides an overview of the design and use of questionnaire surveys in Human Resource Development (HRD) research, focusing on the commonly occurring methodological issues and associated concerns. These are illustrated drawing upon personal experience of four projects within a large UK public sector organisation.

INTRODUCTION

Questionnaire surveys offer Human Resource Development (HRD) researchers an efficient tool for the collection of data on the same topic from a large number of respondents. As a general term, questionnaire refers to all data collection instruments in which each respondent is asked to answer the same set of questions in a predetermined order (deVaus, 2002). It therefore includes structured interviews and telephone questionnaires as well as those completed without an interviewer being present.

In this chapter, we focus on the use of questionnaires to gather data for within organisation HRD survey research. Following a brief overview of questionnaire surveys as a method for empirical research, we highlight a number of commonly occurring general methodological issues in using questionnaire surveys and outline how these might be addressed. An example of questionnaire surveys in HRD research is offered, exploring Mark Saunders' personal experience of a series of four applied research projects with a large UK public organisation. We conclude with a discussion in which we summarise key issues.

AN OVERVIEW OF QUESTIONNAIRE SURVEYS

Given the questionnaire survey's apparent ease and flexibility of use, compared to other methods of data collection (such as interviews and observations), it is not surprising that it is one of the most widely used methods within HRD research. Questionnaires collect data by asking people to respond to exactly the same set of questions in a predetermined order, collecting descriptive and explanatory data about opinions, behaviours and attributes from a large number of people. However, for some research questions and objectives, questionnaires may not be appropriate. For instance, questionnaires are, usually, not particularly suited to exploratory or other research that requires large numbers of open-ended questions. Use of a questionnaire is also affected by the available resources such as the time available to complete data collection; financial implications of data collection and, where not automated, of data entry for statistical analysis; and, for interviewer administered questionnaires, the availability and accessibility of interviewers.

Despite this widespread use, many authors (e.g. Bell and Waters, 2014; Oppenheim, 2000) argue that it is far harder to produce a good questionnaire than one might think. The researcher must ensure that the questionnaire will collect the precise data that are required to answer the research questions and achieve the objectives. We have found this is of paramount importance when using a questionnaire because, as researchers, we often only get one opportunity to collect data from our respondents, particularly those who wish to remain anonymous.

Once the use of the questionnaire survey method is agreed with the organisation, there are different types of questionnaires to choose from. The design of a questionnaire usually differs according to how it is delivered, returned or collected as well as the amount of contact with the respondents (Saunders et al., 2012). For example, *self-completed questionnaires* are usually completed by respondents without further input from a researcher. Such questionnaires may be sent using the Internet (*Internet-mediated* or *Web-based questionnaires*) or intranet (*intranet-mediated questionnaires*), posted to respondents, who may return them by mail after completion (*postal* or *mail questionnaires*), or delivered by hand to each respondent and collected later (*delivery and collection questionnaires*). Responses to *interviewer-completed questionnaires* (also referred to as *structured interviews*) are recorded for each respondent by an interviewer on the basis of their answers. Another type of interviewer completed questionnaire is the *telephone questionnaire*. Like other interviewer-completed questionnaires, this differs from semi-structured and unstructured (in-depth) interviews, as there is a defined schedule of questions (the questionnaire), from which the interviewer does not deviate.

Questionnaire design is influenced by a variety of factors related to the research questions and objectives such as the characteristics of the respondents from whom the data will be collected; importance of reaching a particular person as respondent; importance of respondents' answers not being contaminated or distorted; size of sample required for data analysis; types of questions to be asked in order to collect the necessary data; and number of questions required to be asked to collect the data (Saunders et al., 2012).

Longer questionnaires are often best administered as face-to-face structured interviews. They can include more complicated questions than telephone questionnaires or self-completed questionnaires (Oppenheim, 2000). The presence of an interviewer means that it is also easier to route different subgroups of respondents to answer different questions using filter questions. The suitability of different types of question also differs between research designs. Although a questionnaire can be the only data collection method used in a research study, it may be better to link it with other methods in a multiple or mixed methods research design (e.g. with secondary data such as personnel records or with in-depth interviews).

Saunders et al. (2012) note that the type of questionnaire chosen also affects the number of potential respondents who will actually respond. Interviewer-completed questionnaires usually have a higher response rate than self-completed questionnaires. The response rate, sample size and the way in which it is selected invariably have implications for the reliability of the data and the extent to which the findings can be generalised.

Quantitative research, such as that using questionnaire surveys, aims to develop knowledge by identifying variables and testing textual research questions and theories – often reflecting the epistemological stances of positivism and post-positivism (Johnson and Onwuegbuzie, 2004). According to these schools of thought, social science inquiry should be objective, suggesting that generalisations are desirable and possible, and the causes of social scientific outcomes can be determined reliably and validly. However, use of questionnaires is not only related to positivist and post-positivist philosophies. Where the key focus of choice of methods is to provide the best opportunity for answering the research questions and this necessitates using a questionnaire, it is likely that this will be within a pragmatist philosophy (Johnson and Onwuegbuzie, 2004). Questionnaires are used widely alongside qualitative methods in mixed methods studies. These studies often adopt a pragmatist philosophical stance.

In the next section, we reflect on some of the commonly occurring methodological issues and associated concerns we have encountered when using questionnaires in HRD research.

ISSUES AND CONCERNS WHEN USING QUESTIONNAIRE SURVEYS

Despite being a widely used data collection method, there are a number of issues (and associated concerns) related to using questionnaire surveys when undertaking empirical research. We now outline those that are most commonly experienced and their implications for HRD research.

Need for a Clear Research Question

In our experience, a common problem for HRD researchers, and organisations in general, is outlining the clear research question to be answered. This, we believe, is the most important step as it influences other choices such as the research method, including whether the use of a questionnaire survey is appropriate. As we have already alluded, questionnaires work best when asking standardised questions, where the researcher can be confident that the questions will be interpreted in the same way by all respondents (Robson, 2011). For this reason, questionnaire surveys mostly tend to be used for descriptive or explanatory research.

Once the research question and associated objectives are clarified, the next task is to establish precisely what data need to be collected in order to answer this question and meet the objectives. This is not as simple as it appears; organisations often ask to include additional questions that, whilst not directly relevant, they consider 'interesting'. Dillman (2009) distinguishes between three types of data variable that can be collected through questionnaires, which each influence the way questions are worded. These are *opinion variables* (how respondents feel about something or what they think or believe is true or false); *behavioural variables* (what people did in the past, do now or will do in the future); and *attribute variables* (respondents' characteristics such as age, gender, education, occupation). We have found it helpful, in designing each questionnaire question, to be clear whether we require data about respondents' opinions, behaviours or attributes and note how these data help explicitly to answer the research question.

Acting Ethically and Ensuring Anonymity

Whatever the questionnaire delivery method, organisational respondents need to be informed that their participation is voluntary. Employees often expect to remain anonymous when filling out the questionnaire and, where we have offered anonymity, we have needed to ensure this is preserved in our analysis and subsequent reporting of findings. Usually this necessitates removing identifying attributes of individuals (or organisations), for example tables of findings not reporting less than five responses from easily identifiable subgroups.

Development of the Questions

When designing the questionnaire, we consider the wording of individual questions before deciding the order in which they will be asked. Where appropriate we make use of questions, or sets of questions to measure a specific concept, that have already been developed and used by other researchers, referencing our sources. These questions have already been tested in organisations and found to work by other researchers and, in addition, their use allows us to compare our findings with those of others. Questions can be either open or closed, the former not prescribing answers whilst the latter asks the respondent to select the most pertinent answer from a predefined list. Being pre-coded, closed questions are easier to analyse, six common types being list, category, ranking, rating, quantity and matrix (for further details see Saunders et al., 2012). We also pay special attention to the flow and order of questions in our questionnaires, making sure that it appears logical to potential respondents. This is assisted by linking phrases (Figure 15.1) and filter questions that, dependent upon the answer given, direct respondents to the next relevant part of the questionnaire (Figure 15.2).

Consistency of Responses

Mitchell (1996) outlines three common approaches to assessing consistency. Although the analysis for each of these is undertaken after data collection, it helps if they are considered at the questionnaire design stage. Firstly, 'test re-test' estimates of consistency are obtained by correlating data collected with those from the same questionnaire collected

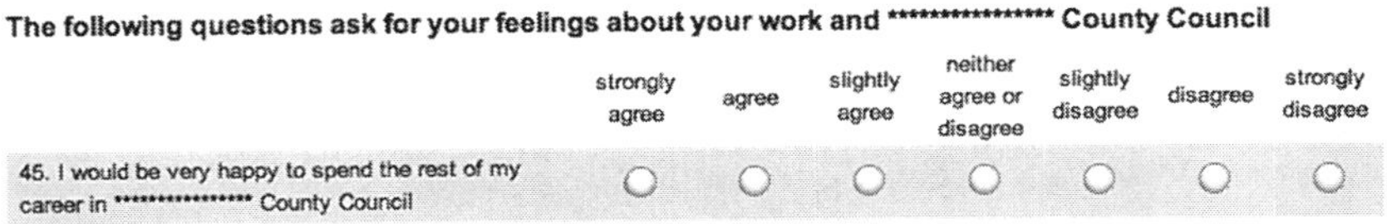

Source: Question layout created by SurveyMonkey.com, LLC (2014), Palo Alto, California. Reproduced with permission.

Figure 15.1   Link phrase and modified Likert-style question measuring an aspect of affective commitment

Your consent

Thank you for your interest in this research. Before you participate, we need to make sure you know what our research is about, what your involvement will be and that you consent to take part.

Please consider the following points before continuing:

• I understand that I am participating in a research study.
• I understand that I have been given an explanation of the research I am about to participate in and I know what is involved in my participating.
• I understand my participation in this research is voluntary and that I am free to withdraw at any time without giving any reason.
• I understand that my identity cannot be linked to my data and that all information I give remains anonymous.
• I understand that I have been given the name and email address of the researcher, Professor Mark Saunders (mark.saunders@surrey.ac.uk) to contact if I have questions about this research.

Do you agree to take part?

○ Yes

○ No

Source: Question layout created by SurveyMonkey.com, LLC (2014), Palo Alto, California. Reproduced with permission.

Figure 15.2   Request for consent to take part in a Web questionnaire and associated filter question

under as near equivalent conditions as possible. In HRD research this can cause difficulties as the questionnaire needs to be delivered and completed twice by the respondents, and it is difficult to persuade either employees or organisations to do this. It is also unlikely they will answer questions in exactly the same way. Secondly, internal consistency involves correlating the responses to questions in the questionnaire with each other. There are a variety of methods for calculating internal consistency, of which one of the most frequently used is 'Cronbach's alpha (α)'. This statistic measures the consistency of responses to a set of questions (scale items) that have been combined as a scale to measure a particular concept, such as employee commitment (Meyer and Allen, 1997). It calculates an alpha coefficient with a value between 0 and 1. Values of 0.7 or above are often taken to indicate that the questions within the scale are internally consistent. Thirdly, the 'alternative form' offers some sense of reliability within the questionnaire through comparing responses to alternative forms of the same question or groups of questions. This tends to be used with longer questionnaires through the use of 'check questions', which ask for the same information in a different way. For example, the check question for a respondent's length of service with an organisation would ask the year in which she or he started to work for that organisation.

Validity and Reliability of the Data

Valid and reliable data are needed to test a theory or theories. These theories are defined as relationships between variables, usually prior to designing the questionnaire. This requires the researcher to have reviewed the literature carefully, discussed their ideas widely and conceptualised their own research clearly prior to designing the questionnaire (Ghauri and Grønhaug, 2010). A valid questionnaire collects data that actually measure the concepts of interest, whilst one that is reliable means that these data will be collected consistently. Foddy (1994: 17) builds on this, emphasising: 'The question must be understood by the respondent in the way intended by the researcher and the answer given by the respondent must be understood by the researcher in the way intended by the respondent.'

Pilot Testing

For any research there is a temptation to skip the pilot testing. However, we would emphasise Bell and Waters' (2014) advice that no matter how pressed for time, it is well worth pilot testing the questionnaire as, without doing so, there is no way of knowing whether the questionnaire will work. Pilot tests help ensure that respondents will have no problems in understanding the questions and recording their answers. We ask a group of people drawn from the organisation that we are researching to complete the questionnaire prior to the main survey and to highlight those aspects with which they experienced difficulties. This provides us with a reasonable assessment, albeit rough and ready, of each question's validity and the likely reliability of the data that will be collected. Preliminary analysis using these pilot test data also allow us to check that the data collected will enable the research question to be answered (Saunders et al., 2012).

The number of employees with whom the questionnaire is piloted and the number of pilot tests conducted depend on the nature of the research questions, objectives, the size of the research project, the time and money resources available and how well the questionnaire is initially designed. For most small projects the minimum number for a pilot is 10 (Fink, 2009), and for large projects between 100 and 200 responses is usual (Dillman, 2009).

Response Rates

As HRD researchers we depend on the willingness and cooperation of employees to respond to our questionnaires. Whilst we aim to have as high as possible response rate, response rates of between approximately 35 per cent and 55 per cent are considered realistic (Baruch and Holtom, 2008). Low response rates increase the likelihood of statistical biases (Tomaskovic-Devey et al., 1994), there being general agreement that higher response rates lead to a higher probability of the sample being representative (Baruch and Holtom, 2008). Moreover, since response rate is an important factor in assessing the value of research findings, higher response rates provide greater credibility.

Data quality is also affected by nonresponse. Complete nonresponse occurs when employees fail to return the questionnaire, whereas partial response and abandonment occur if a partially completed questionnaire is returned (Saunders, 2012). Baruch and Holtom (2008) highlight two principal reasons for not responding: (1) failure to deliver the questionnaire to the target population (e.g. delivering to the wrong address, or being absent from work) and (2) the reluctance of people to respond. Whilst the former can be eliminated easily with thorough preparation (e.g. by obtaining up-to-date addresses and ensuring attendance when delivering in person), dealing with the latter is more challenging. Employees are often subjected to questionnaires in HRD research and, where these are numerous, it can result in fatigue and refusal to respond. Mode of delivery has also been shown to influence response rates, delivery and collection questionnaires being likely to result in the highest response rates, with mail delivered questionnaires generating more responses than Web delivered questionnaires (Baruch and Holtom, 2008). However, more recent research (Saunders, 2012) suggests a higher response rate for Web as opposed to mail delivered questionnaires within organisations.

Finally, questionnaires need to be introduced carefully to employees to ensure a high response rate. For self-completed questionnaires the introduction is often included in a covering letter, which explains the research purpose and why the employee should respond. For interviewer-completed questionnaires, the introduction is undertaken by the interviewer. We now illustrate the points made using Mark's personal experiences of using questionnaires for HRD research within organisations.

PERSONAL EXPERIENCE OF USING QUESTIONNAIRE SURVEYS WITHIN ORGANISATIONS

In this section we reflect on the use of questionnaire surveys within HRD research as part of a series of four applied research projects for one large UK public sector organisation undertaken by Mark and colleagues. This organisation was responsible for the provision of strategic planning, caring services, schools, roads and libraries to a predominantly rural English county. Each included the organisation's triennial employee survey in which a similar questionnaire was used to collect data on employees' attitudes, a minority of questions being altered for each project. The key objective remained constant across the four projects: to provide a position statement of employee attitudes to working for the organisation and, following the first research project, also enable comparisons to be made with previous projects. Mark was concerned, particularly, to provide valid and reliable data to inform a range of HRD policies and associated interventions relating to training, development and employee communication. These data were not used for academic publications, other than exploring the implications for questionnaire response of using Web as opposed to mail delivery methods (Saunders, 2012).

For each of the four research projects the questionnaire comprised over 100 Likert-style questions about employee attitudes. These included established scales devised and used widely by other researchers, questions developed specifically for the organisation to measure perceptions of other aspects of employee treatment and questions only included for that year's project. Organisation specific 'demographic' questions requested personal information including area of work, gender, length of service and broad salary band alongside a final open question, which provided an opportunity for comments on issues or areas of concern.

The established scales measured employees' commitment (Meyer and Allen, 1997), trust in organisations, perceived organisational support (Eisenberger et al., 1986) and the perceived fairness (justice) of treatment (Colquitt, 2001). Using all rather than just selected items (questions) from these scales allowed the findings to be compared with those from other studies published in academic journals as well as with the data from the other projects. To ensure such comparisons were realistic, only minor modifications to improve clarity were made to scale item wording. For example, in Meyer and Allen's (1997: 118) scale item 'I would be happy to spend the rest of my career in this organisation' (one of eight sub-scale items measuring the affective component of commitment) the phrase 'this organisation' was replaced by the organisation's name (Figure 15.1). More substantial amendments were not undertaken as these would have raised doubts as to whether the revised statements still represented the original measure. For the same reason, the possible responses were not altered, these being pre-coded. Consequently responses to all items measuring employee commitment were recorded on a seven-point scale with anchors labelled 'strongly agree' (code 7) and 'strongly disagree' (code 1), the magnitude of the code reflecting the strength of agreement.

For each applied research project, Mark and colleagues worked with the organisation to develop additional statements related to issues of particular concern at that time. These included employees' perceptions of leadership and of support for personal and career development. Where possible these questions were grounded in theory such as the psychological contract (Coyle-Shapiro and Kessler, 2002) and linked directly to the organisation's value statements expressed in their employee documentation. To minimise the need for data coding prior to analysis, only one open question was included: 'If there are any other areas or issues that concern you please feel free to comment below.' Whilst only 19 per cent of respondents answered this question, for one research project this still necessitated coding 264 responses with a mean length of 77 words (Saunders, 2012), the longest response being 589 words.

For both Web and mail versions, the questionnaire layout was designed to facilitate both the reading and answering of questions (Dillman, 2009). Questions were presented in a serif font on a white paper/screen background. For the Web questionnaire pale shading of alternative statements helped make reading across a screen easier. Scale anchors were repeated at the top of every screen/page, responses being collected using clickable response circles for Web and tick boxes for mail questionnaires. For the Web questionnaire, negative impact on response rates from scrolling was minimal as most sections fitted on one screen (Toepoel et al., 2009).

Based on previous experience, Mark adopted a two-phase pilot test of the questionnaire for each project. The first phase involved a group of eight potential respondents selected from the organisation completing the questionnaire in real time while Mark was present. Respondents were asked to note down which, if any, of the questions were unclear or ambiguous as well as those they felt uneasy about or had difficulty in answering. Subsequently they were asked to describe how they interpreted each of these questions and offer suggestions to, for example, improve clarity. After amended questions had been agreed, the questionnaire was revised. In the second phase of pilot testing, the paper version was delivered by mail, and the Web version by email with a Web link, to a purposive sample of 30 employees. These were selected to represent the variability of employees in terms of hierarchy and job type within the organisation. Following this stage only minor amendments to question wording were made.

Physical access to collect data using a questionnaire was granted as part of the applied research contract. However, Mark and colleagues still considered it important to gain direct support from employees for the research. Separate meetings to explain the research purpose and emphasise the independence of the researchers from the organisation were therefore held with employees' (Trades Union) representatives and senior managers. These involved a short presentation and a lengthy question and answer session during which the ways in which respondents' confidentiality would be maintained both during data collection and analysis were highlighted. Although for early projects the questionnaire was only delivered by post, for the most recent it was delivered both by mail and Web. This meant emphasising that as well as respondents not being asked to give their name, the Web questionnaire would not record respondents' IP (Internet protocol) addresses. For all four surveys it was emphasised that participation would be voluntary, this being highlighted in the letter/email accompanying the questionnaire. For the postal questionnaire, returning the questionnaire implied consent, whereas for the Web questionnaire consent was given if respondents answered 'yes' to the filter question 'Do you agree to take part?' (Figure 15.2).

With the organisation's agreement, Mark adopted Dillman's (2009) tailored design method for the delivery and collection of the questionnaires. Fortunately, within this organisation questionnaires had been used sparingly and so over-surveying was not a problem. General information about each forthcoming survey was provided by the organisation's normal communication method, the staff intranet. Subsequently each employee received four personal contacts in addition to the questionnaire. A pre-survey notification letter was delivered using the same method as that through which the respondent would receive the questionnaire. This explained the purpose of the research and offered assurances of both anonymity and Mark and colleagues' independence. This letter was signed by both Mark and the organisation's Chief Executive, the latter emphasising the support of the organisation's senior management team. The questionnaire was delivered with a cover letter/email. A week later, employees received a personal follow-up designed as an information sheet, reminding them to return the completed questionnaire by the prescribed date if they had not done so already. Two further reminders were posted on the staff intranet after the deadline for returns. These resulted in further returns, the impact of these for the most recent survey being illustrated in Figure 15.3. The overall response rate for the project using both Web and mail delivery and collection questionnaires was 41 per cent. Mark noted this was not dissimilar to that reported in Baruch and Holtom's (2008) analysis of response rates. However, in contrast to earlier research, response rates were significantly higher for the Web than the mail questionnaires (Saunders, 2012).

For each of the projects, Mark provided a report and presented the research findings to the organisation's management board. A separate presentation was given to middle managers and a two-page document

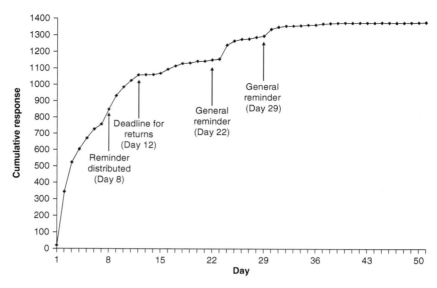

Source: Unpublished data; details of research in Saunders (2012).

Figure 15.3   Cumulative questionnaires returned

sent to all employees. In this document Mark summarised the findings, and the organisation's Chief Executive outlined the actions that would be taken in response. For the most recent project, these included improvements that would be made to communication processes and a range of new training programmes to ensure employees had the skills needed to embrace change.

DISCUSSION

This chapter has presented an overview of the design and use of questionnaire surveys in HRD research, with a particular focus on the commonly occurring methodological issues and concerns. We have illustrated these and ways of addressing them using an example of four projects with a large public sector organisation.

In summary, questionnaires collect data by asking a large number of people to respond to the same set of questions, selecting their answers from predefined choices. They are often used to collect descriptive and explanatory data about opinions, behaviours and attributes. The decision to use a questionnaire survey is influenced by the research question and objectives, and the resources available. The questionnaire design differs according to how it is delivered.

Prior to designing the questionnaire, it is important to know precisely what data need to be collected to answer the research question and meet the research objectives. Invariably the validity and reliability of the data collected and response rate achieved depend largely on the design of the questions, the structure of the questionnaire and the rigour of the pilot testing. When designing a questionnaire we recommend that the wording of individual questions is considered prior to the order in which they appear. Where suitable, we recommend that questions already in other existing questionnaires are used, subject to permission being obtained and suitable acknowledgement being given. In our experience we have found that, wherever possible, closed questions should be pre-coded on the questionnaire to facilitate data input and subsequent analyses.

Within questionnaire design, the order and flow of questions needs to be logical to the respondent. This can be assisted by filter questions and ensuring the questionnaire layout is easy to follow and responses are easy to fill in. Ethical issues need to be considered at the design stage to ensure confidentiality and anonymity where offered.

Consistency of the data should also be considered at the questionnaire design stage. Three common approaches are test re-test estimates, alternative forms of questions and internal consistency. Related to this is the internal validity and reliability of the data collected. A valid questionnaire enables accurate data, which measure the concepts; a reliable questionnaire enables these data to be collected consistently. Pilot testing the questionnaire is therefore of paramount importance to ensure that the respondents will have no problems in understanding the questions and recording their answers. Consideration of these factors at the design stage of the questionnaire is likely to improve response rates, helping the researcher to achieve a high response rate providing greater credibility to research findings.

REFERENCES

Baruch, Y. and Holtom, B. C. (2008) Survey response rate levels and trends in organizational research. *Human Relations*, 61, 1139–1160.

Bell, J. and Waters, S. (2014) *Doing Your Research Project* (6th edn). Maidenhead: Open University Press.

Colquitt, J. A. (2001) On the dimensions of organizational justice: A construct validation measure. *Journal of Applied Psychology*, 86(3), 386–400.

Coyle-Shapiro, J. and Kessler, I. (2002) Exploring reciprocity through the lens of the

psychological contract: Employee and employer perspectives. *European Journal of Work and Organisational Psychology*, 11(1), 69–86.
deVaus, D. A. (2002) *Surveys in Social Research* (5th edn). London: Routledge.
Dillman, D. A. (2009) *Internet, Mail and Mixed Mode Surveys: The Tailored Design Method* (3rd edn). New York: Wiley.
Eisenberger, R., Huntington, R., Hutchinson, S. and Sowa, D. (1986) Perceived organizational support. *Journal of Applied Psychology*, 71, 500–507.
Fink, A. (2009) *How to Conduct Surveys* (4th edn). Thousand Oaks, CA: Sage.
Foddy, W. (1994) *Constructing Questions for Interviews and Questionnaires*. Cambridge: Cambridge University Press.
Ghauri, P. and Grønhaug, K. (2010) *Research Methods in Business Studies: A Practical Guide* (4th edn). Harlow, UK: Financial Times Prentice Hall.
Johnson, B. R. and Onwuegbuzie, A. J. (2004) Mixed methods research: A research paradigm whose time has come. *Educational Researcher*, 33(7), 14–26.
Meyer, J. P. and Allen, W. T. (1997) *Commitment in the Workplace: Theory Research and Application*. Thousand Oaks, CA: Sage.
Mitchell, V. (1996) Assessing the reliability and validity of questionnaires: An empirical example. *Journal of Applied Management Studies*, 5(2), 199–207.
Oppenheim, A. N. (2000) *Questionnaire Design, Interviewing and Attitude Measurement* (new edn). London: Continuum International.
Robson, C. (2011) *Real World Research: A Resource for Users of Social Research Methods in Applied Settings* (3rd edn). Chichester, UK: John Wiley.
Saunders, M. N. K. (2012) Web versus mail: The influence of survey distribution mode on employees' response. *Field Methods*, 24(1), 56–73.
Saunders, M. N. K., Lewis, P. and Thornhill, A. (2012) *Research Methods for Business Students* (6th edn). Harlow, UK: Pearson Education.
Toepoel, V., Das, M. and Van Soest, A. (2009) Design of web questionnaires: The effects of the number of items per screen. *Field Methods*, 21, 200–213.
Tomaskovic-Devey, D., Leiter, J. and Thompson, S. (1994) Organizational survey nonresponse. *Administrative Science Quarterly*, 39, 439–457.

ANNOTATED FURTHER READING

Dillman, D. A. (2009) *Internet, Mail and Mixed Mode Surveys: The Tailored Design Method* (3rd edn). New York: Wiley. Although written for a general audience rather than HRD researchers, this book provides a vast amount of detail on how to design and administer questionnaires and the likely implications of various design choices.
Saunders, M. N. K. (2012) Web versus mail: The influence of survey distribution mode on employees' response. *Field Methods*, 24(1), 56–73. This paper offers insights on designing questionnaires for HRD research within organisations as well as an assessment of the impact of delivering questionnaires by the Internet (Web) rather than by mail.
Saunders, M. N. K., Lewis, P. and Thornhill, A. (2012) *Research Methods for Business Students* (6th edn). Harlow, UK: Pearson Education. Chapter 11 of this book provides useful insights into the use of questionnaire surveys in business research with numerous examples. Chapter 12 outlines how to prepare data (including that from questionnaires) for, and undertake, statistical analysis.

16. Now you see them, now you don't: using online surveys in HRD longitudinal research
Jim Stewart and Victoria Harte

SUMMARY

Online surveys are complex, with many factors affecting rates of response. Reasons for non-response are argued here to fall into three main categories: questionnaire design, personal motivation of respondents and distribution methods. The last category is particularly significant in relation to the assumed online preference of Generations X and Y.

INTRODUCTION

Questionnaire surveys are arguably ubiquitous. As citizens, most readers will have had the experience of being asked to complete a survey on a visited website. As employees, many will have experience of satisfaction and engagement surveys conducted by and/or on behalf of their employers. Or, as students or employees/learners, experience of being asked to complete a questionnaire as part of evaluations of learning programmes at some point after the programme ended. In addition, an unpublished analysis of academic research in Human Resource Development (HRD) published in journals sponsored by the United States based Academy of HRD (AHRD) shows that survey methods were used more than other methods in every year except one between 2003 and 2011; in 2006 quantitative and qualitative methods were equal. It seems therefore that, in all contexts of life, surveys are utilised as a favoured data collection method.

One direct HRD context where surveys are common is that of evaluation of learning programmes (Stewart and Rigg, 2011). Another is that of higher education (HE). This context may be debatable, but we accept the arguments of Sambrook and Stewart (2010) in support of accepting the premise that HE is indeed a site of HRD practice. This is relevant for three reasons. First, surveys of students in HE in the UK are now an integral part of policy, procedure and practice, for example the National Student Survey (NSS), internal institution surveys such as module and programme evaluations and the many local surveys that take place either by 'researching lecturers' or research units and centres within universities. Second, this chapter draws on a small scale research project conducted in an UK university, which examined reasons for attrition in a larger longitudinal study that utilised online surveys. Third, and as will be explained later in the chapter, that research project aimed to discover reasons for non-completion of the online survey.

As suggested by the examples mentioned earlier, use of web technologies for surveys is on the increase in all contexts (Greenlaw and Brown-Welty, 2009) and so also in all contexts and sites of HRD practice. Whether for identifying learning needs, evaluating learning programmes or measuring employee engagement, online surveys are likely to be an increasingly significant tool in HRD practice as well as HRD research. One reason for this is that in the so-called digital and technological age we have the ability to complete many transactions online. An additional reason is that 'X' and especially 'Y' generations, the latter born after 1982, are believed to be technologically driven and oriented and so immersed in and surrounded by technological equipment from such a young age that the expectation is they automatically engage in the use of web technologies (Oblinger, 2003). Members of these generations are current and future citizens, managers and employees, and so the assumption is that online completion is the natural and preferred method of conducting surveys, with sufficient or even high response rates a reasonable expectation. This though may be a false assumption.

There is, of course, a range of factors which affect response rates in all surveys. These include incentives, saliency, respondent burden and mode of administration. Three key and related components of the last of these are mode of delivery, completion and return. There is a range of options with respondent self-completion, online delivery and return being only one. But, according to the arguments just presented, this is supposed to be the favoured option for members of Generation X and Y and so a means of optimising response rates. Other factors favouring the option include speed, time and cost. These factors are seen as advantages for online surveys when compared with alternatives such as researcher face-to-face administered surveys or respondent completed paper based questionnaires delivered and returned by post. In a specifically HRD context of evaluating learning programmes, respondent self-completion through researcher hand delivered and collected survey instruments is common, that is, what are commonly referred to as 'happy sheets' completed immediately at the end of programmes. But, there are well-known drawbacks with that method (Stewart and Rigg, 2011), and evaluation studies also commonly include surveys at various time points post programme. Online surveys may well be attractive for reasons of time and cost in those circumstances.

The project we report and draw on here arose from an experience of using online surveys in an evaluation study in HE. The purpose of the chapter, therefore, is to raise questions about the efficacy of online surveys and to question whether they are in fact advantageous. Online surveys may be quicker and cheaper to administer than alternative modes of administration, but do they deliver adequate response rates? And, how can such response rates be facilitated and encouraged? We consider these questions in this chapter.

KEY ISSUES WITH ONLINE SURVEYS

Online surveys in HRD research and practice are undertaken in the general context of social research. Studies into that context are therefore relevant. Also relevant are studies which research the design and use of surveys in general. Factors that influence the efficacy of surveys per se will also have impact on online surveys. So, we review some of the key general and specific factors in this section. Our main focus is on response rates and what affects them, since that is clearly a significant issue affecting efficacy.

Incentives

Incentives in the form of a gift or money are often given to survey respondents in the hope that this might increase response rates (Laurie and Lynn, 2009). The aim of giving an incentive is to encourage respondents to view their participation in the research study as important and valuable. But, Sax and her colleagues (2003) found that respondents offered an incentive actually produced lower response rates than those offered no incentive. That said, Church (1993) found that for mail surveys incentives do have an effect and that monetary incentives have a greater effect than gifts. Church found that pre-paid monetary incentives increased response rates by 19.1 per cent as opposed to a 4.5 per cent increase where the monetary gift was conditional on completion. Furthermore, the follow-up response rates also increased when the monetary incentive amounts increased. There is an abundance of research available on the varying approaches to incentivised responses in research studies. What is clear is that no one way is the 'best' and varying approaches have yielded positive results in some research more than others.

Laurie and Lynn (2009) suggest that longitudinal surveys with repeated 'waves' of questionnaire completion constitute a high burden (see below) and that incentives are more appropriate the greater the burden to respondents. Just how and when incentives should be employed in longitudinal surveys is unclear, and there is little clear or firm guidance either from practice or in the literature. What is clear is that there is no simple relationship between incentives and response rates and so decisions on the use of incentives have to be weighed very carefully.

Saliency

Laurie and Lynn (2009) propose a 'topic saliency' concept, whereby importance is placed by respondents on the content of the questionnaire and the way it is introduced by researchers. The argument is that if the respondent is interested in the topic of the survey or believes that they or a group of importance to them might be advantaged by it, they enjoy the opportunity to exhibit their knowledge about the subject and are more likely to participate.

Greenlaw and Brown-Welty (2009) put forward the proposition that their high response rates were because the respondents in their study appeared to have a particular interest in the results of the survey, and so it was in their interests to participate. Though these are assumptions on their part, it appears a fairly plausible claim to make that saliency has a big part to play in response rates, and particularly in their study. Their participants were highly educated, employed and the average age was 35–45, and these factors too may have influenced response rates. A more likely explanation is perhaps the relationship between respondent factors and the focus of the study. Lynn et al. (2005) also report that surveys of high saliency to respondents are more positively received.

Modes of Administration

There is a general expectation that attrition will occur and non-response will increase in subsequent waves of longitudinal research (Burton et al., 2006; Porter and Whitcomb, 2005; Porter and Umbach, 2006), irrespective of the mode of administration. The only sure way of achieving and maintaining required response rates is to employ modes of administration which provide total control to researchers, something which is very rare. One example might be use of 'happy sheets' in HRD evaluation studies. Another might be in HE where completion of survey instruments is linked to assessment and so the 'incentive' is very salient.

In the case of online surveys, while online distribution, completion and return may be quicker and easier for respondents, it does not necessarily produce higher response rates. A study by Sax et al. (2003) found that offering an option of paper or online completion produced higher response rates than either as a single option. In another study, Greenlaw and Brown-Welty (2009) also found that offering a mixed-mode increased response rates, and to provide 'response method' choice is highly advisable. However, the issue of 'respondent burden' still remains a significant factor, with potential to interfere with response rates despite offering a 'response method' choice.

Respondent Burden

The issue of respondent burden can overlap with many other factors associated with non-response and attrition. Factors such as time to complete, length of questionnaire, saliency, accessibility (e.g. web based) and number of completions are all evidenced in the literature as influencing perceived burden. Online surveys may add to that depending on how the request to complete is distributed. An email with a URL link pasted into the message requires little effort for respondents to access the questionnaire and, given they are already online, access can be immediate. Other means of sending requests may, though, require more effort; for example, logging on to hardware and then opening a web page. And, of course, online surveys assume easy respondent access to necessary hardware and software, and this may not always be the case.

Lynn et al. (2005) propose in their research of methodologies pertinent to longitudinal surveys an 'opportunity costs' theory where respondents weigh up the costs and benefits in a survey. If the 'respondent burden' is too high relative to any benefits, the notion is they are likely to refuse the survey request (Groves and Couper, 1998; Groves et al., 2000). Other factors considered to have potentially significant negative impact in relation to respondent burden include length of questionnaire (Groves and Couper, 1998; Morton-Williams, 1993), complexity of questions (Baldinger et al., 1995; Meier, 1991; Sharpe and Frankel, 1983; Smith, 1995) and concerns about privacy and confidentiality (Cialdini et al., 1993; DeMaio, 1980; Frey, 1986; Goyder and MacKenzie Leiper, 1985; Olson and Klein, 1980; Singer et al., 1992; Singer, 1984).

Longitudinal studies add the additional burden of repeated completions of questionnaires. Lynn et al. (2005) found that there is an additional constituent to the questionnaire length: the impact of the perceived cost of future survey participation. Furthermore, Apodaca et al. (1998) found that the effect of the perceived longitudinal burden on survey participation resulted in a 5 per cent decrease in the response rate. Lynn et al. (1997), however, found that explicitly telling sample members that the survey was longitudinal, but only at a later wave, resulted in slight reduction in response at that wave, but an overall improved net response at subsequent waves.

Lynn et al. (2005) offer the suggestion that at second and subsequent waves sample members have information about the survey which they did not encounter at the beginning. This is because they have had experience of the survey at wave one and, potentially, find they have no interest and the topic has little or no salience. The opposite may be the case and, if so, response rates will be maintained in subsequent waves. This effect, though, only operates on those who complete the first wave. One effect that could be optimised at that point is physical presence of the researcher. This can often increase response rates, and so, if it can be arranged and there is confidence in a positive salience effect, a combination of paper completion with researcher presence at the first wave and online completion of subsequent waves could be an effective strategy in longitudinal studies.

PERSONAL EXPERIENCE: THE ATTRITION SURVEY

Our experience draws on a small scale research project which examined reasons for attrition in a larger longitudinal study which utilised online surveys. The larger project initially used paper based surveys and switched to online versions at the second wave. There are therefore three separate but related elements to the context. The first is a longitudinal study with a planned number of waves of paper based surveys. The second is a decision to change paper based to online surveys in that study after the first wave. The third is a small scale paper based survey to investigate reasons for attrition when the main project switched to online. This third element is the 'attrition survey' which provides some potentially useful lessons for use of online surveys in HRD longitudinal research.

Outline of Longitudinal Study

The purpose of the original longitudinal research was to explore the extent and nature of connection between a numbers of factors, that is the subject of enterprise; HE students; self-efficacy; and future career intentions. It was our intention to explore and examine the assumption that students are equipped to be more enterprising and/or that they may become more likely to pursue the desire/intention to become self-employed following study of enterprise focused modules. We planned to do this utilising a longitudinal approach over three years using a multi-method research design which consisted of a questionnaire and a series of semi-structured interviews. Our original research objective was: *'To explore the impact of*

enterprise modules in higher education on student's own perceptions of their
self-efficacy and their motivations towards particular career intentions.'

In our longitudinal study the response rate at the paper based first wave
(pre-test) in Semester 1 was n=189, but the follow-up response rate at the
online second wave (first post-test) was a disappointing n=13. This was a
key factor in our endeavours to determine reasons for non-response and
attrition.

Rationale for the Attrition Survey

Before we embarked upon our longitudinal study, the question of non-
response and attrition was discussed and featured in our research design.
Because the questionnaire consisted of one pre-test and two post-test
completions, an initial consideration to tackle attrition and non-response
was over-sampling to deal with any losses at the second and third waves.
A further design feature to deal with non-response and attrition, and following guidance in the literature as discussed above, was to use paper
based surveys initially and offer the option of paper or online surveys at
the second and third waves. However, when the second wave (first post-
test) was due, as a consequence of budgetary constraints, we were forced
to use the online distribution and completion method only, and the paper
based method was not included as an option. A major rationale presented
to us by budget holders and decision makers was the preference of the
population – that is, members of Generation X and Y – for web based
activity and so online means of completing surveys.

We believed the change to online distribution and completion and a
number of other factors had a negative impact on the respondents' desires
to participate, resulting in the high attrition and non-response noted
above. This became the focus of our attrition survey. We identified a
number of factors influencing attrition and non-response. These factors
were included in a short survey to determine reasons of attrition and
non-response.

Methods and Results

We decided to make the attrition questionnaire as simple as possible and
requiring little effort to complete. Respondents were presented with a list
of possible reasons for non-response to the longitudinal questionnaire
and were asked to select and rank the three reasons that most influenced
their decision not to respond. Additional comments were also sought in an
open-question section.

We returned to paper based and mail modes of distribution for this

Table 16.1   Analysis of responses

The reason I did not complete and return the questionnaire was:	SCORE	RANK
1 it was too long	29	1
2 the questions were too complex	12	4
3 the questions asked were too personal	6	8
4 the amount of personal information was too much	0	11=
5 I had concerns over privacy and confidentiality	3	9
6 I had concerns over third parties contacting me	1	10
7 I was required to complete the questionnaire 3 times	0	11=
8 my level of interest in the subject was low	18	3
9 I perceived no personal benefit	11	5=
10 the incentive to participate was not very attractive	11	5=
11 I was asked to complete it online	9	7
12 I was asked to complete it on paper	0	11=
13 I never received the letter in the post	27	2

survey. The envelope contained a covering letter, a copy of the first page of the original longitudinal questionnaire as a reminder/prompt, a reply paid envelope and a pen, to encourage and aid their participation. The sample size was approximately $n=290$, of which $n=61$ responses were received, a response rate of 21 per cent. It is interesting to note that the response to the attrition survey was higher than the second wave online version of the longitudinal survey. This is an additional indication from our projects that paper based distribution potentially delivers higher responses than online distribution and completion when used as a single mode of administration.

The results of respondents' rankings are presented in Table 16.1. We converted responses to produce an overall score and ranking for each reason by allocating a score of three to a ranking of one, a score of two for a ranking of two and a score of one for a ranking of three for each reason. These scores were then summed to give an overall score for each reason, and this overall score was used to arrive at a final ranking.

It is possible and useful to group the reasons for non-response and attrition into three broad categories. We suggest the following have some internal logic:

- Questionnaire design
- Personal motivation
- Distribution methods

Reasons 1 to 6 were to do with questionnaire design, reasons 8 to 10 personal motivation and reasons 11 and 12 covered distribution methods.

Reason 13 turned out to be somewhat of a 'red herring' and we disregarded that question. The question became irrelevant because we were unable to say whether this relates to the respondents receiving the request to complete the questionnaire online or due to physically not receiving the letter via postal mail due to non-delivery (e.g. respondent having moved address). On reflection, this is somewhat of a design flaw on our part. Reason 7 was a hybrid which could arguably be included in any of the categories. Given the intended use of the questionnaire in the longitudinal study, multiple completions could be considered part of questionnaire design. Alternatively, multiple completions could also be connected with the distribution methods, and especially in our project since they were changed between the first and second completions. Finally, non-response related to multiple completions also has a connection with the notion of 'respondent burden' under our category of personal motivation. At this point, and given the results shown in the table, multiple completions do not figure as a significant factor in the attrition rate we experienced. This is somewhat surprising. However, it does make potential sense because saliency possibly would be a factor over the number of completions. Here we are suggesting that the burden of the three completions would not matter if the subject was thought to be of interest and benefit to the respondent.

DISCUSSION

We look at the results in more detail in this section. We also include some of the respondents' comments to illustrate the general points that come from the quantitative rankings.

Disregarding item 13, the two highest ranked reasons come from the categories of questionnaire design and personal motivation. Taking personal motivation first, reasons associated with and included in this category were all of some importance and significance. Lack of personal interest was ranked third, and (lack of) perceived personal benefit was joint fifth (*I think if the purpose of the research were clearer – i.e. what good will come of it, for me or others – I may have been more motivated to complete it*) with lack of a personally attractive incentive (*No incentive to fill out the form*). These results indicate that personal motivation was a significant category of reasons for non-response in our longitudinal study and so a cause of high attrition. The most important of these reasons is that of personal interest, which suggests the need for a clear link to either exist or to be created and demonstrated to respondents if high response and low attrition are to be achieved. There are clear connections between this finding and writing on saliency (Greenlaw and Brown-Welty, 2009;

Lynn et al., 2005). However, respondent interests can be very diverse, and developing a strategy to secure saliency for questionnaire completion among heterogeneous populations would require an innovative approach.

The highest ranked reason for non-response was the length of the questionnaire. Other reasons in the category of questionnaire design are spread throughout the ranking: the complexity of the questions was ranked fourth and the personal nature of the questions was ranked eighth. The other reasons in this category, which are related to the amount of personal information, confidentiality and third party use, are the bottom three in the ranking – that is, the lowest in importance or significance for sample members choosing not to respond. It seems therefore that our respondents decided that questionnaire length and complexity of questions are the two main reasons for attrition in the category of questionnaire design. We are not surprised by this outcome as our main concerns for attrition did weigh heavily on questionnaire design, length being a main concern, and adds further weight to our postulations about the importance of saliency, as discussed above. We believe that had respondents had more interest in and higher perceived benefit from the questionnaire design, this may have affected attrition and non-response differently.

Finally, in the category of distribution methods relating to questions 11 and 12, there were no responses for the reason 'I was asked to complete it on paper' (Q12), but 'I was asked to complete it online' (Q11) was ranked as seventh. Though the responses to question 11 were low, there is some indication to suggest online completion was a reason for non-response whereas no respondent cited paper based completion as a reason. This fits with our hypothesis that respondents would have preferred paper completion and that many of the X and Y generation individuals are not as technologically driven as some might suggest. Furthermore, had we been given the opportunity of administering a multi-method response choice at the second wave, we would be in a much better position to be able to say which our sample preferred.

It is not possible to do even a simple ranking of the categories. We cannot therefore offer an 'objective' view on which was the most important in causing high attrition in our study. We can, however, state that our assumptions about the questionnaire seem to be correct, particularly the length, complexity of questions, saliency and perceived benefit.

Although simple in design and limited in size, our attrition survey does provide some empirical evidence. This evidence lends general support to reasons for non-response and high attrition as suggested in the literature, for example saliency, modes of administration, respondent burden and use of incentives. The evidence also suggests that the three categories we identified of questionnaire design, personal motivation and distribution methods are all significant in respondents' decisions on participation in surveys. Our three categories also seem to be potentially, at least, of equal importance and significance. We also suggest that the categories reflect factors previously and currently identified and discussed in the literature and so future research could usefully further investigate their utility. In summary, though, we suggest that use of online surveys needs to pay attention to the same factors as other approaches to survey research: questionnaire design, personal motivation of respondents and distribution methods. And, finally, use of online surveys should not work from an assumption that members of generations X and Y will have an inherent preference for online and web based approaches.

REFERENCES

Apodaca, R., Lea, S. and Edwards, B. (1998) The effect of longitudinal burden on survey participation. *1998 Proceedings of Survey Research Methods Section of the American Statistical Association*, 906–910. Available at http://www.amstat.org/sections/srms/proceedings (accessed 1 February 2009).

Baldinger, A., O'Neill, H.W. Wilson, W., Adams, C. and Borvers, D. (1995) The CMOR Respondent Co-operation Study, paper presented at the 1995 Market Research Association Conference.

Burton, J., Laurie, H. and Lynn, P. (2006) The long-term effectiveness of refusal conversion procedures on longitudinal surveys. *Journal of the Royal Statistical Society* 169(3), 459–478.

Church, A.H. (1993) Estimating the effect of incentives on mail survey response rates: a meta-analysis. *Public Opinion Quarterly* 57, 62–79. Cited in Laurie, H. and Lynn, P. (2009) The use of respondent incentives on longitudinal surveys, in P. Lynn (ed.) *Methodology of Longitudinal Surveys*, Chichester, UK: John Wiley and Sons, Chapter 12.

Cialdini, R.B., Braver, S.L. and Wolf, W.S. (1993) Predictors of non-response in government and commercial surveys, paper presented at the *4th International Workshop on Household Non-Response*, Bath, UK.

DeMaio, Theresa J. (1980) Refusals: who, where and why. *Public Opinion Quarterly* 44(2), 223–233.

Frey, J.H. (1986) An experiment with a confidentiality reminder in a telephone survey. *Public Opinion Quarterly* 50(2), 267–269.

Goyder, J. and McKenzie Leiper, J. (1985) The decline in survey response: a social values interpretation. *Sociology* 19(1), 55–71.

Greenlaw, C. and Brown-Welty, S. (2009) A comparison of web-based and paper-based survey methods: testing assumptions of survey mode and response cost. *Evaluation Review* 33(5), 464–480.

Groves, R.M. and Couper, M.P. (1998) *Non-response in Household Interview Surveys*. New York: John Wiley and Sons.

Groves, R.M., Singer, E. and Corning, A. (2000) Leverage-saliency theory of survey participation: description and an illustration. *Public Opinion Quarterly* 64(3), 299–308.

Laurie, H. and Lynn, P. (2009) The use of respondent incentives on longitudinal surveys, in P. Lynn (ed.) *Methodology of Longitudinal Surveys*. Chichester, UK: John Wiley and Sons, Chapter 12.

Lynn, P., Buck, N., Burton, J., Jäckle, A. and Laurie, H. (2005) A review of methodological research pertinent to longitudinal survey design and data collection. *Working Papers of the*

Institute for Social and Economic Research, Number 2005 29. Colchester, UK: University of Essex.

Lynn, P., Taylor, B. and Brook, L. (1997) Incentives, information and number of contacts: testing the effects of these factors on response to a panel survey. *Survey Methods Centre Newsletter* 17(3), 7–12.

Meier, E. (1991) Response rate trends in Britain. *Marketing and Research Today* 19(2), 120–123.

Morton-Williams, J. (1993) *Interviewer Approaches*. Aldershot, UK: Dartmouth Publishing.

Oblinger, D. (2003) Boomers, Gen-Xers, and Millennials: understanding the 'New Students'. *EDUCAUSE Review* 38(4), 36–40, 42, 44–45.

Olson, J.A. and Klein, R.E. (1980) Interviewers perceptions of reasons for participation refusal in a national longitudinal survey, 1979–1980. *1980 Proceedings of the Survey Research Methods Section of the American Statistical Association*, 552–557. Available at http://www.amstat.org/sections/srms/proceedings (accessed 1 February 2009).

Porter, S. and Umbach, P. (2006) Student survey response rates across institutions: why do they vary? *Research in Higher Education* 47(2), 229–247.

Porter, S. and Whitcomb, E. (2005) Non-response in student surveys: the role of demographics, engagement and personality. *Research in Higher Education* 46(2), 127–152.

Sambrook, S. and Stewart, J. (2010) Teaching, learning and assessing HRD [Special issue]. *Journal of European Industrial Training* 34, 710–734.

Sax, L.J., Gilmartin, S.K. and Bryant, A.N. (2003) Assessing response rates and non-response bias in web and paper surveys. *Research in Higher Education* 44(4), 409–432.

Sharpe, L.M. and Frankel, J. (1983) Respondent burden: a test of some common assumptions. *Public Opinion Quarterly* 47(1), 36–53.

Singer, E. (1984) Public reactions to some ethical issues of social research: attitudes and behaviour. *Journal of Consumer Research* 11, 501–509.

Singer, E., Hippler, H.-J. and Schwarz, N. (1992) Confidentiality assurances in surveys: reassurance or threat? *International Journal of Public Opinion Research* 4(3), 256–268.

Smith, T.W. (1995) Trends in non-response rates. *International Journal of Public Opinion Research* 7(2), 157–171.

Stewart, J. and Rigg, C. (2011) *Learning and Talent Development*. London: Chartered Institute of Personnel and Development.

ANNOTATED FURTHER READING

Denscombe, M. (2010) *The Good Research Guide*, 4th edition. Maidenhead, UK: McGraw-Hill Education. A useful general text on social research with helpful chapters on design and use of surveys and questionnaires in the context of general research principles and alternative methods.

Groves, R.M., Fowler, F.J., Couper, M.P., Lepkowski, J.M., Singer, E. and Tourangeau, R. (2009) *Survey Methodology*, 2nd edition. Hoboken, NJ: John Wiley and Sons. A detailed description, explanation and analysis of all the main methods, techniques and steps involved in survey research.

Sue, V.M. and Ritter, L.A. (2012) *Conducting Online Surveys*. London: Sage Publications Ltd. A text with a specific focus on design and use of online surveys, with much good advice and guidance on maximising responses and useable results.

17. Maximising telephone survey participation in international HRD research

Maura Sheehan, Mark N.K. Saunders and Catherine L. Wang

SUMMARY

This chapter provides an overview of the literature on improving survey response, focussing upon ways of tailoring the survey design to leverage potential respondents' decision to participate, and uses a case study to examine an application of leverage-saliency theory. Techniques likely to be effective in maximising telephone survey participation in HRD research are detailed.

INTRODUCTION

Telephone surveys offer Human Resource Development (HRD) researchers a valuable means of collecting data using an interviewer administered questionnaire to ask a large number of people the same pre-determined questions. Such surveys are particularly suited for collecting data from specified specialist target populations (such as people within organisations), providing they are accessible by telephone (Saunders et al., 2012). Where non-respondents differ systematically from respondents this may distort the data, resulting in 'non-response' bias (Couper et al., 1999) and a possible threat to validity. Although any rate of non-response can result in bias, there is a general consensus that higher response rates lead to a higher probability of those responding representing the entire sample and thus the population from which it is drawn (Baruch and Holtom, 2008). Conversely, low response rates increase the likelihood of not being able to generalise the findings of the study to the entire sample, undermining the conclusions drawn about the population. As with all surveys, there is a need to maximise participation from potential respondents to help ensure validity of their findings. Despite this need to maximise responses, researchers acknowledge an increasing problem since the late 20th Century of declining respondent participation in surveys, particularly those administered by telephone (Dillman, 2009; Wright and Marsden, 2010). Potential participants have not only become more difficult to contact, but once contacted are often reluctant to participate (Singer, 2010). This spectre of non-response, and the associated possibility of bias, raises two key issues for HRD researchers using this data collection method: first, the extent to which a range of factors influence response rates in various contexts and, second, what can be done to maximise participation in various contexts (Dillman, 2000; Roth and BeVier, 1998).

Within HRD survey research, there has also been considerable concern about the implications of the sample who respond and the effects of this for the reliability of findings (Gerhart et al., 2000). This becomes particularly important where an employee subgroup who are likely to rate things differently to other employees, or have privileged information on which to base their responses, are selected as respondents. For example, unlike some other employees, HR and HRD specialists may use industry standards to rate their own organisation's HRD practices, financial performance or competitiveness. In contrast, line managers and other employees may not have access to such industry information, resulting in very different responses and, ultimately, research findings (Sheehan, 2012b). Dependent upon the research being undertaken, there may be a need to ensure HR specialists, line managers and other employees are all selected and participate within a study (Guest and Conway, 2011; Mabey, 2008; Sheehan, 2012a and 2012b). Whilst the use of such 'multi-respondent' approaches can help to address low reliability of a single group's responses, as we shall illustrate later, it adds additional complexity when trying to generalise from responses.

Given the above, it is not surprising that a considerable amount of research has been undertaken regarding the importance of, and how to maximise, response rates. Much of this research is concerned with testing the effect of one factor (for example offering a particular incentive) with a specified group (for example employees) for a specified delivery type (usually by mail) (Groves et al., 2000). Although such analyses have increased our understanding regarding why the specified groups may respond to particular participation requests and the factors likely to increase their participation rates, the groups researched seldom include managers or senior executives. In addition, telephone questionnaires, despite their continued widespread use for special target populations such as clients and employees of organisations (Lavarakas, 2010; Wang and Saunders, 2012), are rarely considered in this discussion – notable exceptions being Anseel et al. (2010) and Baruch and Holtom (2008).

In this chapter we commence by providing an overview of the literature on improving survey response, focussing upon ways of tailoring the survey design to leverage potential respondents' decision to participate – an application of leverage-saliency theory. The practice of this is then explored using work undertaken by one of us, Maura Sheehan, to research the relationship between HRD and performance in United Kingdom (UK) owned subsidiaries. We conclude with those techniques likely to be effective in maximising telephone survey participation in HRD research.

LEVERAGING THE DECISION TO PARTICIPATE

Potential survey respondents' decisions to participate are, for all survey types, argued to be based on factors that are out of, and factors that are under, the researcher's control (Couper and Groves, 1996). Factors out of the researcher's control comprise the social environment, which creates the climate in which the survey is undertaken, and attributes of the sample selected to take part. Factors under the researcher's control include all aspects of survey design and each interviewer's characteristics. Although developed initially for household surveys, this framework has been subsequently revised in relation to telephone questionnaires (Wang and Saunders, 2012), to create a 'framework' for cooperation in (cross cultural) telephone questionnaires (Figure 17.1). It is this framework we now consider.

With regard to factors that influence participation outside the researcher's control, Couper and Groves (1996) and Lynn (2008) both argue that the social environment is likely to influence potential respondents' reactions to requests to participate. Within organisational and HRD research this includes attributes of the organisation and the sector as well as cultural, social and environmental norms and beliefs within which they operate (Wang and Saunders, 2012). For organisational research, the characteristics of the organisation members selected for the sample, such as their role within the organisation, are also influences (Anseel et al., 2010). Their knowledge of the research topic and its relevance to their work (Groves et al., 2004), their past experiences of involvement in questionnaires and their psychological predisposition to respond (Dillman, 2009) are also likely to affect participation.

Factors influencing participation which are under the researcher's control are wide ranging, relating both to the research design (Couper and Groves, 1996; Lynn, 2008) and, of crucial importance to telephone surveys, the interviewer (Schaeffer et al., 2010). With regard to research design, influencing factors include the perceived relevance of the topic to potential respondents, definition of the sampling frame and sample selection techniques used, use of advanced notice, the time of day administered,

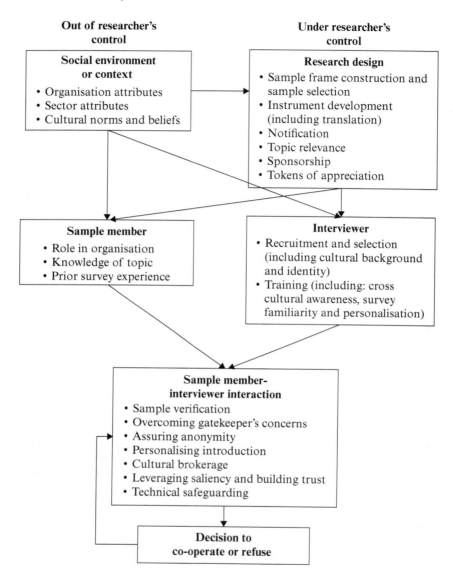

Figure 17.1   A framework for cooperation in telephone surveys

incentives to participate, assurances of anonymity, and external (university) sponsorship (Anseel et al., 2010; de Leeuw et al., 2007; Dillman, 1978, 2009; Saunders et al., 2012). Questionnaire design, including the length, will also influence participation, sample members being less likely to participate if questionnaires are long or administered at inconvenient times. Design features which are likely to increase participation in telephone surveys are summarised by Dillman (1978) in his 'Total Design Method', a forerunner of his (2009) 'Tailored Design Method' that focusses upon mail and web surveys. This incorporates careful survey design, including use of an advance letter (if possible) and a short introduction explaining who is calling, what is requested, why the respondent should take part and a conservative estimate of the time required. Dillman (1978) argues increased participation is enhanced by university sponsorship that emphasises the importance of the research. However, our research indicates that emphasising academic links or sponsorship by a university (Wang and Saunders, 2012) or an organisation such as the European Union (Sheehan, 2014) may not enhance responses in some contexts.

Telephone surveys necessitate using at least one 'interviewer' to ask the questions and record responses. Her or his cultural sensitivity and abilities, including where necessary foreign language skills, along with training, invariably impact upon subsequent interaction with potential participants. Prior to the start of the formal administration, s/he will need to establish contact with sample members, undertake screening and, where suitable, invite participation, introduce the research, offer assurance of anonymity and answer initial queries. Not surprisingly, clarity of the interviewer's voice and ability to read questions fluently are essential (Dillman, 1978). Although the introduction to telephone questionnaires is usually less than a minute duration, it is crucial in obtaining potential respondents' agreement to take part (Schaeffer et al., 2010). Response rates are likely to be enhanced where (experienced) interviewers are given freedom to personalise the questionnaire introduction, offering convincing assurances of anonymity and persuading the organisational member to participate (de Leeuw et al., 2007; Houtkoop-Steenstra and Van Den Bergh, 2000) in their own words, albeit from a specified agenda. The decision to participate is therefore based upon interacting influences, some facilitating and others constraining cooperation, thereby influencing response rates.

Leverage-saliency theory (Groves and Couper, 1998) argues that during this brief interaction where the interviewer requests a sample member to participate, the interviewer can observe the potential respondent's 'idiosyncratic concerns' (Groves et al., 2000: 299) and tailor the request to participate accordingly. Through tailoring, the interviewer attempts to heighten the salience or prominence of those aspects of the research judged likely to be most favourably received by each respondent. A specific research topic may have positive leverage for individuals who are generally interested in a topic and a negative leverage for those who are not (Groves et al., 2000). Features considered to have positive leverage as they make the questionnaire more appealing can be highlighted. Conversely, those features that make the survey less appealing have negative leverage and need to be neutralised. For example, an incentive such as a gift voucher might be judged to have positive leverage whilst a long interview is likely to have negative leverage.

Leverage-saliency theory assumes that a potential respondent has an expected utility for participating, only agreeing to participate if this expected utility is greater than other uses of her/his time and effort. Whether an attribute has a positive or negative salience will vary across sample persons. A telephone questionnaire may provide a financial incentive and appeal to civic duty (which could include, in the context of HRD research, a sense of responsibility to the potential respondent's employer). However, the interviewer may emphasise only one of these aspects, thereby increasing or decreasing its leverage, depending on the characteristics of the potential respondent and their idiosyncratic responses to the initial dialogue (Groves et al., 2000). Alternatively, research on an HRD topic such as the value of training to the organisation may have high topic saliency to both HR managers and specialists, whereas this may be low for other employees (also potential respondents) who are more concerned regarding the value to themselves. Tailoring the introduction to the research to each group by emphasising different aspects of the research is likely to increase participation. Leverage-saliency theory, therefore, provides a model of how interviewers may increase the likelihood of each potential respondent agreeing to take part (Maynard et al., 2010). It also emphasises the pivotal role of interviewers in telephone surveys, assessing how each respondent will be influenced by individual response enhancing techniques (Anseel et al., 2010) and customising their remarks accordingly.

We now consider the application of leverage-saliency theory to telephone surveys within HRD research. Within this we focus upon those aspects under the researcher's control: research design and the pivotal role of the interviewer; and the associated interaction between each sample member and the interviewer administering the telephone questionnaire.

PERSONAL EXPERIENCES OF LEVERAGING TELEPHONE SURVEY PARTICIPATION

In this section, we reflect on the use of a telephone questionnaire in a European Union funded study undertaken by one of us (Sheehan, 2012a).

This examined the relationship between HRD and organisational performance in the context of UK multinationals with subsidiaries in Poland, the Czech Republic and Hungary. Maura was concerned particularly with strategic management development, its diffusion within multinational corporations, and the performance of domestic and foreign subsidiaries. Using data collected through a large scale interviewer administered questionnaire, she explored the process of management development, in particular best practice and top management support, and its impact upon subsidiary performance. Her analysis tested whether the outputs of management development (such as line managers' perceptions of the importance and provision of management development) were associated with subsidiaries' performance (for example financial performance, employee turnover, innovation rates). We commence with research design issues, which were under Maura's (the researcher's) control.

Survey Design Issues

Sample frame construction and sample selection
Within HRD research involving both HR specialists and others there is, as highlighted in our introduction, the potential for a divergence of perspectives and, as a consequence, low reliability of responses are collected only from a single-rater group (Gerhart et al., 2000). For this reason a multi-respondent approach to data collection was needed, necessitating a sampling frame of UK owned subsidiaries within which data from HR Directors, HR managers and specialists, and line managers could be collected.

The population from which Maura selected her sample comprised Dun and Bradstreet's Global Reference Solution database. This is one of the most comprehensive and detailed sources for information on complex companies (Henriques, 2009). Initially, a purposive criterion based sample of 515 subsidiaries was drawn from the database using criteria relating to the 'global ultimate parent company'. Specifically, the parent company:

- was in the UK, thereby eliminating potential 'country of origin' effects;
- employed at least 200 people overall (thereby facilitating comparison with other large scale survey data that used this criterion, such as Cranet (Steinmetz et al., 2011);
- had a subsidiary in at least one of three study countries (i.e. Czech Republic, Hungary and Poland).

Within these subsidiaries, Maura gave priority to the 378 subsidiaries whose ultimate parent company also had a similar subsidiary in the UK.

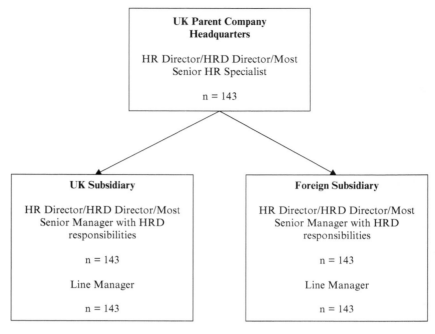

Figure 17.2   Study design and sample respondents

This, she argued, would ensure the data she collected from the headquarters and from the UK and foreign country subsidiaries were not affected by within company differences between the subsidiaries. Although this was time consuming, it was essential as HRD interventions within each company's subsidiaries were considered likely to vary according to the nature of work undertaken within a particular subsidiary.

The research design used critical case matched samples for each parent company and the UK and the foreign subsidiary (Figure 17.2), thereby allowing specific company-wide HR interventions to be assessed within their subsidiaries. Each matched sample comprised the HR or HRD Director or the most senior HR specialist in the parent company headquarters (1 person) and, for both the UK and the foreign country subsidiaries of that company, the HR or HRD Director or the most senior HR specialist and a line manager (two people in each).

Instrument development (including translation)
The telephone questionnaire, developed originally in English, allowed for a structured interview format for data collection (Saunders et al.,

2012). Although not the focus of this chapter, it is worth noting that the questions that Maura developed were influenced by previous research on the relationship between management development and perceived subsidiary performance. Research highlights that potential respondents are significantly more likely to respond to surveys in their native language (Harzing et al., 2012). Consequently, once questions had been developed and pilot tested, the English language questionnaire was translated into the native language of each foreign subsidiary to maximise linguistic saliency. Translation used a mixed techniques process involving translation and back translation by two independent native speaking translators with expertise in management related disciplines. Each translation was then adjusted by collaboration and interaction (Douglas and Craig, 2007) with practitioners to ensure that, within that foreign language version, conceptual and functional equivalence of meaning was maintained (Harpaz, 1996; Cascio, 2012). Reasons for any discrepancies that emerged were discussed and addressed.

Paper versions of the translated questionnaires were pilot tested initially on master's level students with HR/HRD and managerial expertise from each of the four study countries. These individuals subsequently participated in a focus group, where question wording was further adjusted to account for cultural, linguistic and organisational characteristics in each of the study countries. The telephone questionnaires were then pilot tested in three companies in each of the four countries. This pilot testing was undertaken by the interviewers employed for the research, and resulted in further minor amendments to question wording and order. It also provided a training opportunity for the interviewers.

The questionnaires used therefore ensured lexical, idiomatic and experiential meanings were consistent between the versions for the four countries. This was noted by the interviewers, who commented that the culturally specific nuances within the questions, reflecting the collaborative and interactive approach used in this survey's translation, helped them to enhance cultural bonding with their interviewees, especially the line managers.

Notification, Sponsorship and Tokens of Appreciation

Customised advanced survey notification was sent to each HR/HRD Director at corporate headquarters, in the main by email. Each advance notification included at least one personalised item of 'good news' about the parent company derived from that company's Annual Report or their web pages. The notification also emphasised relevance, in particular, how the organisation might use the study findings including effectively demonstrating the value added by the HR function, thereby leveraging salient issues. To further leverage participation, potential headquarters respondents were informed that they would receive a summary of the research findings and that a £50 donation would be made in their name to a charity of their choice. The notification acknowledged that the project was funded by the European Union; that the primary investigator was a Marie Skłodowska Curie Fellow; and that the research was supported by the UK Chartered Institute of Personnel and Development (CIPD).

Potential participants in each subsidiary received similar information in their notifications, although with differing emphases. Pre-survey consultation with line managers in subsidiaries had indicated that enriching and improving the relevance of HRD interventions was important (salient), so this was emphasised for these potential participants. For Polish subsidiary companies, Maura's Marie Skłodowska Curie fellowship was emphasised, highlighting Curie's Polish origins. In the overseas subsidiaries, European Union sponsorship seemed to have very positive leverage, although this did not appear to be so for the UK subsidiaries.

Response rates differed between those at company headquarters (52.6 per cent), HR personnel in the UK and foreign subsidiaries (45.6 per cent and 42.3 per cent respectively) and line managers in the UK and foreign subsidiaries (40.4 per cent and 38.2 per cent respectively). Despite this, telephone questionnaires were completed by all five respondents for 143 parent companies and their two subsidiaries, a response rate of 37.8 per cent. In addition to the 143 of these subsidiaries based in the UK, 57 were based in Poland, 46 in the Czech Republic and 40 in Hungary.

The Role of the Interviewers

Recruitment and selection
It is generally recognised that interviewer skills are instrumental in increasing response rates and generating reliable and valid responses for telephone surveys (Schaeffer et al., 2010; Wang and Saunders, 2012). Consequently, it is important that care is given to their recruitment and selection (Dillman, 1978). For Maura's research it was crucial that the interviewer had the necessary language skills and a high level of cultural awareness in relation to potential respondents (Harzing et al., 2012).

Within her research, Maura commissioned a professional research firm with vast experience of international telephone survey research to administer the telephone questionnaires using native speakers. This meant each questionnaire for a foreign subsidiary would be administered in that country's language by a native speaker who negotiated access to the respondent.

Training

All the professional research firm's interviewers were already experienced. Consequently, it was not necessary to train them in standard 'best practice protocol', other than ensuring each was familiar with the survey. Pilot testing of the questionnaires in each of the four countries (outlined earlier) allowed the interviewers to familiarise themselves with the survey in a 'real world' simulation. In addition, Maura briefed the interviewers about the objectives of her study, explaining the precise meaning of terminologies used, and tried to generate a sense of enthusiasm and importance for the survey amongst them, enhancing the leverage that these interviewers brought to the project themselves.

Sample Member–Interviewer Interaction

When accessing respondents, interviewers were pivotal in persuading 'gatekeepers' such as receptionists, personal assistants and administrators to allow access to potential participants. Where the respondent was too busy, an alternative time to telephone was agreed. If a call was initially unsuccessful, three follow-up telephone calls were made. Following best practice, interviewers already knew of the importance of speaking in a natural voice rather than reading verbatim (Dillman, 1987) and were given the freedom to personalise and request research cooperation in their own words. Having ascertained they were speaking to the right person, whilst working within the overall research agenda they also personalised the introduction to the research, taking into account the characteristics of the particular respondent (Schaeffer et al., 2010), for example by making reference to something pertinent in the respondent's country (for example a football match, an election, or weather).

Interviewers' language skills and cultural awareness were most significant at the point of introduction, where each interviewer personalised initial overtures regarding their request to participate according to the type of respondent and their initial responses. This helped, along with assurances of anonymity, to build trust. Although personalisation was used in the introduction, these interviewers were already aware of the need to read questions exactly as worded to ensure consistency across all interviews (Dillman, 1978). Their knowledge of the research from Maura's briefing ensured that interviewers understood the terms used in the questionnaire and could, where necessary, ensure that the meaning was understood correctly by participants.

The research company's quality-control assurances required interviewers to record the reasons for refusal. This allowed the research company to establish early on in the research any systematic factors causing negative

Table 17.1   Reasons for refusal

Reasons	Per cent
No explanation (including simply hanging up the phone)	59.2
Gatekeeper refused to put call through to target respondent, usually claiming that target respondent did not have an interest in completing the survey	19.3
No time to participate	10.0
Wrong contact name (and another suitable person in the company was not recommended)	1.5
Company policy of no survey participation	5.6
Survey too long	0.3
Named contact had insufficient knowledge about the survey topic (and another suitable person in the company was not recommended)	1.2
Concern regarding confidentiality of company information	2.3
Other (including an anti-European Union view)	0.6
Total (n=512)	100.0

leverage (such as length of the survey) or to identify if there is an absence of saliency (this would generally result in the introduction being re-scripted). None of these were observed in Maura's research, the patterns of reasons for refusal being similar to what they considered 'normal' (Table 17.1).

The overall impression gained from these data was that potential respondents lacked interest in academic research. Consistent with Wang and Saunders (2012) and Wenemark et al. (2010), amongst the stated reasons for refusal, 'no time to participate' (10.0 per cent) was the most common factor. Sponsorship by the European Union generated very negative responses from some potential respondents, all based in the UK. Refusals based on concern about company confidentiality were higher in the foreign subsidiaries (6.7 per cent) compared to the UK (1.3 per cent). Other than these differences and the gatekeeper issue, there were no other significant differences by respondent type or location amongst the non-respondents.

DISCUSSION

This chapter has presented our reflections on issues related to generating telephone survey responses using the example of multiple respondents across different countries for a study that focussed on the relationship between HRD and the performance of UK owned subsidiaries. Whilst our example is more complex than many HRD research projects that may adopt a telephone interview, it has allowed us to illustrate a wide range of factors under the researcher's control that can be leveraged to heighten saliency and maximise participation. Those tailoring methods we consider most effective are:

1. Notification – this involved informing potential participants in advance that they will be contacted by telephone and will be asked to take part in a survey.
2. Follow-up – contacting participants who had agreed to the survey but were not available at the pre-arranged time.
3. Emphasising the survey topic's relevance, or saliency, to the potential respondent and their organisation.
4. Personalisation of the introduction from the perspective of the potential respondent and their organisation.
5. Assuring the anonymity of the respondent and/or their organisation.
6. Emphasising sponsorship appropriate to the potential respondent such as that from the relevant professional organisation and institutions, such as the Chartered Institute of Personnel and Development (CIPD), Society for Human Resource Management (SHRM) (professional), the European Union, and the Kaufman Foundation (institutional).
7. Offering incentives to participate, such as charitable donations and, within an international context:
8. Use of native language.
9. Cultural awareness both in the introduction and throughout the telephone survey.

As suggested in the literature (Wang and Saunders, 2012), use of trained and experienced interviewers greatly facilitated participation. The competence and experience of interviewers appear to be critical for generating valid and reliable data from telephone surveys.

Telephone surveys can be an effective way to generate valid and reliable data, providing gatekeepers and respondents can be persuaded of the utility of the research. Telephone surveys offer a means of collecting data that overcomes geographical distance and enables an interviewer to leverage salient aspects and gain a higher response rate. Looking to the future, we have observed more generally that interviewees, including those at senior levels and in several national contexts, have been willing to participate in surveys using Skype and FaceTime. Whilst the utility of such technology is still relatively devoid of research, we would recommend its use to be considered, providing it is feasible and culturally acceptable to potential respondents.

REFERENCES

Anseel, F., Lievens, F., Schollaert, E. and Choragwicka, B. (2010) Response rates in Organisational Science, 1995–2008: a meta-analytic review and guidelines for survey researchers. *Journal of Business Psychology*, 25, 335–349.

Baruch, Y. and Holtom, B.C. (2008) Survey response rate levels and trends in organisational research. *Human Relations*, 6(18), 1139–1160.

Cascio, W. (2012) Methodological issues in international management. *International Journal of Human Resource Management*, 23(12), 2532–2545.

Couper, M.P., Blair, J. and Triplett, T. (1999) A comparison of mail and e-mail for a survey of employees in federal statistical agencies. *Journal of Official Statistics*, 15, 39–56.

Couper, M.P. and Groves, R.M. (1996) Household-level determinants of nonresponse. *New Directions for Evaluation*, 1996(70), 63–76.

De Leeuw, E., Callegaro, M., Korendijk, E., Hax, J. and Lensvelt-Mulders, G. (2007). The influence of advance letters on response in telephone surveys: A meta-analysis. *Public Opinion Quarterly*, 71(3), 413–443.

Dillman, D. (1978) *Mail and Telephone Surveys: The Total Design Method*. Chichester, UK: John Wiley and Sons.

Dillman, D.A. (2000) *Mail and Internet Surveys: The Tailored Design Method* (2nd edition). New York: John Wiley and Sons.

Dillman, D. (2009) *Internet, Mail and Mixed Mode Surveys: The Tailored Design Method* (3rd edition). New York, NY: Wiley.

Douglas, S.P. and Craig, C.S. (2007) Collaborative and iterative translation: an alternative approach to back translation. *Journal of International Management*, 15(1), 30–43.

Gerhart, B., Wright, P., Mcmahan, G.C. and Snell, S.A. (2000) Measurement error in research on human resources and firm performance: how much error is there and how does it influence effect size estimates? *Personnel Psychology*, 53(4), 803–834.

Groves, R.M. and Couper, M. (1998) *Non-response in Household Interview Surveys*. New York, NY: John Wiley and Sons.

Groves, R.M., Presser, S. and Dipko, S. (2004) The role of topic interest in survey participation decisions. *Public Opinion Quarterly*, 68(1), 2–31.

Groves, R., Singer, E. and Corning, A. (2000) Leverage-saliency theory in survey participation: description and illustration. *Public Opinion Quarterly*, 64, 299–308.

Guest, D. and Conway, N. (2011) The impact of HR practices, HR effectiveness and a 'strong HR system' on organisational outcomes: a stakeholder perspective. *International Journal of Human Resource Management*, 22(8), 1686–1702.

Harpaz, L. (1996). International management survey research. In Punnett, B.J. and Shenkar, O. (eds). *Handbook for International Management Research*. Cambridge, MA: Blackwell, pp. 37–62.

Harzing, A.W., Reiche, S. and Pudelko, M. (2012) Challenges in international survey research: a review with illustrations and suggestions for best practice [Online]. From: www. harzing.com. [Accessed: 14 June 2013].

Henriques, M. (2009) UK database, global linkage and global data collection. Internal Dun and Bradstreet (D&B) report on the representativeness and reliability of the Global Reference Solutions (GRS) database. Marlow, Buckinghamshire, UK: D&B UK Head Office.

Houtkoop-Steenstra, H. and Van Den Berg, A. (2000) Effects of introductions in large-scale telephone surveys. *Sociological Methods and Research*, 28(3), 251–280.

Lavrakas, P.J. (2010) Telephone surveys. In Marsden, P.V. and Wright, J.D. (eds). *Handbook of Survey Research* (2nd edition). Bingley, UK: Emerald Group Publishing, pp. 471–498.

Lynn, P. (2008) The problem of nonresponse. In de Leeuw, E.D., Hox, J. and Dillman, D.A. (eds). *International Handbook of Survey Methodology*. New York, NY: Lawrence Erbaum Associates, pp. 35–55.

Mabey, C. (2008) Management development and firm performance in Germany, Norway, Spain and the UK. *Journal of International Business Studies*, 39, 1327–1342.

Maynard, D.W., Freese, J. and Schaeffer, N.C. (2010). Calling for participation: requests, blocking moves and rational (inter)action in survey introductions. *American Sociological Review*, 75(5), 791–814.

Roth, P.L. and BeVier, C.A. (1998) Response rates in HRM/OB survey research: norms and correlated, 1990–1994. *Journal of Management*, 24, 97–117.

Saunders, M., Lewis P. and Thornhill, A. (2012) *Research Methods for Business Students* (6th edition). Harlow, UK: Pearson.

Schaeffer, N.C., Dykema, J. and Maynard, D.W. (2010) Interviews and interviewing. In Marsden, P.V. and Wright, J.D. (eds). *Handbook of Survey Research* (2nd edition). Bingley, UK: Emerald Group Publishing, pp. 437–470.

Sheehan, M. (2012a) Investing in management development in turbulent times and perceived organisational performance: a study of UK MNCs and their subsidiaries. *International Journal of Human Resource Management*, 23(12), 2491–2513.

Sheehan, M. (2012b) Devolvement of HRM and perceived performance within multinational corporations (MNCs). *European Journal of International Management*, 6(1), 101–127.

Sheehan, M. (2014) Human resource management and performance: evidence from small and medium-sized firms. *International Small Business Journal*, 32(5), 545–570.

Singer, E. (2010) Non-response bias in household surveys. *Public Opinion Quarterly*, 70(5), 637–645.

Steinmetz, H., Schwens, C. Wehner, M. and Kobst, R. (2011) Conceptual and methodological issues in comparative HRM research: the Cranet project as an example. *Human Resource Management Review*, 21(1), 16–26.

Wang, C.L. and Saunders, M.N.K. (2012) Non-response in cross-cultural surveys: reflections on telephone survey interviews with Chinese managers. In Wang, C., Ketchen, D. and Bergh, D. (eds). *West Meets East: Toward Methodological Exchange*. Bingley, UK: Emerald Group Publishing.

Wenemark, M., Frisman, G.H., Svensson, T. and Kristenson, M. (2010) Respondents satisfaction and respondent burden among differently motivated participants in a health related survey. *Field Methods*, 23(4), 378–390.

Wright, J.D. and Marsden, P.V. (2010) Survey research and social science: history, current practice, and future prospects. In Marsden, P.V. and Wright, J.D. (eds). *Handbook of Survey Research* (2nd edition). Bingley, UK: Emerald Group Publishing, pp. 3–26.

ANNOTATED FURTHER READING

Dillman, D. (1978) *Mail and Telephone Surveys: The Total Design Method*. Chichester, UK: John Wiley and Sons. Although published in 1978, this edition of Dillman's classic work offers the most depth of discussion of enhancing telephone survey response using the total design method. Later editions of the book focus more on mail and Internet rather than telephone surveys.

Saunders, M., Lewis, P. and Thornhill, A. (2012) *Research Methods for Business Students* (6th edition). Harlow, UK: Pearson. Chapter 11 provides a useful introduction to questionnaire design, including the use of telephone questionnaires.

Wang, C. and Saunders, M. (2012) Non-response in cross-cultural surveys: reflections on telephone survey interviews with Chinese managers. In Wang, C., Ketchen, D. and Bergh, D. (eds). *West Meets East: Toward Methodological Exchange*. Bingley, UK: Emerald Group Publishing. This chapter offers a useful discussion of leverage saliency as well as insights into undertaking telephone surveys in China.

18. Using Critical Incidents and Vignette Technique in HRD research to investigate learning activities and behaviour at work
Regina H. Mulder

SUMMARY

The Critical Incident Technique and Vignette Technique and their possible use in HRD research is explored. Examples of own research on informal learning and behaviour at work illustrate how challenges caused by the nature of the object of investigation and the complexity of the real work setting can be dealt with.

INTRODUCTION

Although there is a wide variety of views on what Human Resource Development (HRD) is, the following aspects seem to be widely acknowledged as important: the development of knowledge, skills and competences and the improvement of the effectiveness and performance of individuals, groups and organisations through formal and informal learning processes (e.g. Wilson 2012, pp. 7–8). In order to gain insight into the effectiveness of HRD, learning processes (being a prerequisite for individual development) and behaviour in organisations should be investigated. The aim of this chapter is to explore how the Critical Incident Technique (CIT) and the Vignette Technique (VT) can be used in HRD research.

CIT was developed to gather information on behaviour in a specific setting through observation (Flanagan 1954). 'By an incident is meant any observable human activity that is sufficiently complete in itself to permit inferences and predictions to be made about the person performing the act' (Flanagan 1954, p. 327). A critical incident is defined clearly in relation to the aim of the study, for example, a feedback incident in research on effects of feedback on learning activities at work (Mulder 2013). In contrast, the VT was developed to investigate beliefs, values and norms (Finch 1987). Vignettes are 'short stories about hypothetical characters in specific circumstances, to whose situation the interviewee is invited to respond' (Finch 1987, p. 105). Both techniques have a similar sequence: some kind of trigger (invitation to recall a critical incident or a vignette), one or more questions or instruction, and some form of answering mode.

CIT and VT are used in a variety of domains, and with a range of aims. CIT has, for example, been used in nursing, medicine, counselling, private industries, teacher education and service industries. Next to investigating behaviour, CIT was used for investigating beliefs and feelings alongside perceptions and critical thinking skills. For example, Ellinger and Bostrom (2002) investigated managers' beliefs about their roles as facilitators of learning, where 'beliefs' refers to closely held assumptions about the world that guide reasoning and action (Ellinger, cited in Ellinger and Bostrom 2002). Other examples are the investigation of values concerning leadership in different countries (Hamlin and Patel 2012), stress and coping at work, and motivation (Butterfield et al. 2005). Critical incidents are also used as an instructional method in learning organisations and in education, as vehicles that promote reflective learning (e.g. Branch 2005). VT was developed and used to investigate beliefs, values and norms (Finch 1987), originally in psychology laboratories (Shavelson, cited in Poulou 2001). Vignettes are used in the health care sector (Hughes and Huby 2002; Spalding and Phillips, 2007), for instance in nursing (Brauer et al. 2009), elder care nursing (Rahman 1996), and also in education (Miles 1990; Poulou 2001).

In this chapter the possibilities and limitations of these two techniques for investigating learning activities and behaviour in organisations are considered. There are two major issues that make this complex. First, the nature of the object of investigation; in addition, for HRD research we need to realise the relevance of context. What works in one organisation may not necessarily work in another, because of differences in characteristics of the context, the organisation, and also the employees. To foster employees' development, informal learning processes and subsequent behaviour need to be investigated, and insight is needed into the related conditions and determinants. Second, these measurement instruments have both possibilities and limitations in themselves and in relation to what and where can be investigated.

This chapter begins by describing how CIT and VT can be used in HRD research. Their development and use in HRD research, with examples of own research, will then be discussed. The selected examples deal with research on informal learning and behaviour at work. Both are difficult to investigate. Therefore, it considers challenges concerning the nature of the object of investigation and the complexity of the context, that is, a natural work setting. I describe how colleagues and I have taken up the challenge of using these methods for quantitative data analyses.

DESCRIPTIONS OF THE TECHNIQUES

In this section the CIT and VT are described. For both techniques their aims, their characteristics and the actions that need to be carried out are discussed.

Critical Incident Technique

CIT 'should be thought of as a flexible set of principles that must be modified and adapted to meet the specific situation at hand' (Flanagan 1954, p.335). There are five major steps to take when using this method. First, ascertain and make explicit the general objectives of the activity being studied; the situations observed and their relevance to the general objectives; and the extent of the effect on the general objectives, prior to collecting the data. Second, the persons who will carry out the research, as well as the behaviours to be observed, need to be defined. These phases are followed by collecting the data in an authentic setting; analysing and interpreting the data; and, finally, interpretation of and reporting the results (Butterfield et al. 2005; Flanagan 1954).

Data can be collected through observation, interviewing, group interviews and/or qualitative open-ended questions. The researcher needs to be competent in relation to all the mentioned research steps, which can be achieved through adequate training. An important aspect Flanagan (1954) mentions is the objectivity of the judgements of the researcher when s/he is evaluating the observations. This has to happen with reference to the aim of the study and the purpose of the activity in that context and should contain all the relevant details.

As Flanagan (1954) described the procedure, the data analysis is carried out inductively, and the focus is on the respondents' perspectives. A category system is devised, where the categories have operational definitions and self-descriptive titles. He argued that there are no simple rules to guide the researcher in making the categorisation and that this was more a subjective than an objective process. A classification system that has been developed for a specific type of critical incidents can be used to classify such incidents in the categories of the system. In this way we can achieve an acceptable degree of objectivity (Flanagan 1954). Later on, retrospective self-reporting was used for data collection. And in many studies the descriptions of the data analyses, which Flanagan considered important, are missing (Butterfield et al. 2005).

At first, CIT was used as a procedure for collecting certain important aspects of behaviour in specific and defined situations (Flanagan 1954), and CIT's potential for studying psychological states or experiences was not emphasised (Stano 1983, in Butterfield et al. 2005). Subsequently, the CIT was further developed into Critical Sequential Incident Technique (CSIT), in order to measure intended behaviour (having a picture in mind). Switching Path Analysis Technique (SPAT) represents a CIT variant. It was developed in research on customers switching service providers, in order to be able to make the process, with its dynamic character (of switching), understandable (Edvardsson and Roos 2001). A theoretical framework for Criticality CIT (CCIT) was developed which was a new way of approaching prediction of behavioural change without studying actual behaviour. Important aspects of this framework are the need to distinguish between positive and negative critical incidents (as they are dealt with differently), judgements concerning opinions or behavioural change, and the difference between working memory and long-term memory (Edvardsson and Roos 2001).

Vignette Technique

Vignettes include short descriptions of hypothetical persons or situations, which contain the information necessary for the respondents to base their judgements upon (Finch 1987). The background, referral or observation information is generally held constant, while the variables under study are allowed to vary (Huebner, cited in Poulou 2001). An important difference from CIT is that the episode is a vignette in the form of a hypothetical case or a scenario, and not an actual incident from the past experience of the respondent. The vignette needs to be carefully designed to depict a circumstance or represent a germane issue through which it is possible to elicit rich but focused responses. The technique requires questions or instructions and some kind of answering mode. These questions can be open-ended, seeking opinions and reactions to the content, or can involve fixed-choice responses (closed questions), or a combination of both (e.g. Finch 1987).

RESEARCH VALIDITY AND CAVEATS

This section considers how to develop the instruments, with an emphasis on aspects to take into account to optimise the quality of the research.

Critical Incident Technique

CIT is principally qualitative in nature, although Butterfield et al. (2005) note that it has been used in the early stages of quantitative research. Changes have occurred in how the method is used, especially in the way in which credibility or trustworthiness of the findings is established; thus Butterfield et al. (2005, pp. 484–490) highlight nine credibility checks.

One issue is that of theoretical validity. Researchers need to make explicit the assumptions underlying their proposed research and then scrutinise them in the light of relevant scholarly literature to see if these assumptions are supported. Flanagan (1954) suggested that the accuracy of the incident itself could be deduced from the level of full, precise details given by the respondent. For example, a vague general description can indicate that the incident is not well remembered and should be excluded. All variants of CIT are based on respondents' ability to recall incidents and make judgements based on these incidents (Edvardsson and Roos 2001). Time between the incident and the recalling of the incident plays a role in the quality of the answers. By asking for daily recall of incidents, twice as many incidents were recalled as by asking weekly, and about five times more than by asking two-weekly (Flanagen 1954). Also, asking for a similar incident to be recalled from earlier periods can help recall. Other psychological aspects influence recall, such as whether the respondent regards the incident as positive or negative. Therefore, knowledge about how to ask the questions and about the respondents and their stories is considered crucial (Butterfield et al. 2005).

Another important aspect of validity in relation to CIT is descriptive validity, which can be optimised through, for example, respondents' cross-checking (Butterfield et al. 2005). Alternatively, an expert in the CIT research method can be asked to listen to a sample of interview tapes (for example, every third or fourth) to check for interview fidelity. When the data are analysed quantitatively through categorising and coding answers, a comparison with the categories already formed in literature (empirical and or theoretical) can be made to see if there is agreement. However, a lack of agreement is not necessarily bad, because of CIT's exploratory nature. Indeed, Flanagan (1954) argues that categorisation is an inductive process and so more subjective than objective. It is important to describe the process of categorisation clearly: make clear the selected frame of reference, which depends on the aim of the study (for instance, input for training or for evaluations) and describing the decisions made on categories that are more specific versus more general behaviour (the first giving more specified information, the latter leading to fewer headings and leading to more generalisability) (Butterfield et al. 2005).

Vignette Technique

When using VT, the quality of the vignette is pivotal. Several quality criteria are important. Vignettes should be based on authentic, realistic situations that need problem solving (Finch 1987), are open (incomplete) and allow multiple solutions, and encourage independent thinking and unique responses (Jeffries and Maeder 2004). The content must be internally consistent (Finch 1987) and consist of a chain of context-specific events, in order to make it possible to infer causal influences (Miles 1990). The vignette should be a short story or narrative (50–200 words; Jeffries and Maeder 2004) that matches the reader's ability (Hughes and Huby 2004) so that the respondent understands the vignette (Finch 1987).

The vignette should be designed starting with the function, issue and topic (Richman and Mercer 2002), be based on literature (Wilson and While 1998) and be written in collaboration with professionals of the work context (Miles 1990). It should also be validated by professionals (Spalding and Phillips 2007), their credibility check determining the degree of realism in the vignette. Lincoln and Guba's (1985) general criteria for establishing the trustworthiness of qualitative research can also be applied: transferability, dependability and confirmability (Spalding and Phillips 2007; Wilson and While 1998). Transferability is the degree to which findings are relevant in other areas, determined with accurate contextual information. Dependability is achieved when it is clear that the findings would be similar if the research was replicated with information about the research process. Confirmability is accomplished when credibility, transferability and dependability are ascertained (Wilson and While 1998).

In research it is possible, by looking across several vignettes, to generalise about the dynamics of professional intervention, rather than merely to tabulate attributes, traits or skills (Miles 1990). Alternatively, it is possible to compare different groups (Renold 2002).

The use of open-ended questions can be comparable to projective techniques, where the meaning of the situation in question is defined by the respondent, and 'the closer the vignette comes to accurately portraying the individual's situation the more sensitively and accurately the instrument will perform' (Rahman, cited in Schoenberg and Ravdal 2000, p. 67). In conjunction with other methods (multiple or mixed methods), VT can be used as an icebreaker at the beginning of an interview about potentially sensitive subjects.

REQUIREMENTS OF VT AND CIT IN HRD RESEARCH

Using these techniques within HRD research requires two things to be taken into account: (1) the opportunities and limitations of the instruments themselves to investigate learning activities and behaviour at work and (2) the characteristics of the research objective and the HRD domain. In addition, what can or should be used should depend on the chosen scientific paradigms. Designs can be quantitative and/or qualitative. In both quantitative and qualitative designs, qualitative and quantitative methods (i.e. techniques) can be used (Niglas 2010). CIT and VT are techniques used in various scientific paradigms and in quantitative and qualitative research.

Validity, or accuracy, which is an important issue in every kind of research, is difficult to realise because of the nature of the topics investigated. For instance, when investigating learning processes at work, there are two important measurement problems. One is that, because learning processes can occur implicitly or explicitly (Eraut 2000; Mulder 2013), respondents might not be aware that they are learning or aware of how they learn. This makes, for instance, retrospective self-reports less valid. The second measurement problem is that, while behaviour is visible, learning processes or actual learning activities are partly overt and partly covert. Whereas so-called physical learning activities are overt, cognitive activities (e.g. decision making) are covert. Physical learning activities do not necessarily lead to cognitive learning (Mulder 2013). Depending on the object of investigation, the techniques used have different requirements.

In addition, these physical learning activities can happen individually or in social interaction at work in a non-organised manner, that is, outside formalised learning situations (Mulder 2013, p. 52). This implies that context characteristics are important for the actual development of employees, and these need to be taken into account.

This leads to another relevant validity issue, related to the generalisability and usefulness of the research results. High external validity means that the results of the research have meaning for the specific situation where the research is carried out and can be used in that HRD practice. On the other hand, because the relation with this context is so strong, the results are difficult to use as conclusions for other settings. In addition, high internal validity of research results, for instance in experiments in a lab, are not related to work context and, because of that, difficult to transfer to real contexts. This external validity can be high in both techniques, but especially the internal validity is difficult to realise.

In relation to validity it is important to be aware of a number of differences between CIT and VT. The validity of the CIT is higher, because these are real incidents that have happened, but the comparability of the answers in the VT is higher, because the same vignette is provided. A study in multiple domains may need CIT to reach high validity, because a vignette is context specific and cannot be authentic in, for instance, completely different jobs. For sensitive issues vignettes might be more appropriate, for instance in research on errors. Both techniques cater for realising objectivity. Objectivity and reliability are more likely to be realised with vignettes.

PERSONAL EXPERIENCE OF USING CIT AND VT IN HRD RESEARCH

In this section, examples of own research are discussed to show how the techniques can be used/handled, what the issues are and how to overcome certain challenges, with referencing to the earlier described credibility issues of the techniques. Sometimes intended, actual and/or expected behaviours are measured to find out how learning processes and development of workers take place. Insight can be derived on what the use of CIT and VT is for researching learning activities and behaviour at work.

CIT versus VT

I have used both techniques in work undertaken with a colleague to study learning from errors in nursing (Bauer and Mulder 2010). Half our respondents received vignettes and the other half were asked to write down critical incidents. One result was that the response rate for the CIT was very low. We argued, based on the situation at that time in the participating hospitals, that this could be due to the costs in terms of the time it takes the respondent to write down the critical incident. In addition, this might (partly) be caused by the recall problem mentioned earlier. In order to remedy this problem in a subsequent study with another colleague, in this case on innovative work behaviour in the automotive industry, the characteristics of a critical incident were described in great detail and the respondents were asked if they had experienced something similar. If they had not, a vignette was presented to the respondent (Messmann and Mulder 2012). This strategy can be used to compensate for respondents not having experienced critical incidents that are relevant to the research or help them to remember relevant critical incidents. This can increase the response rate.

Critical Incident Technique

With colleagues I have used CIT to measure the reactions to a specific incident that can be considered to be a trigger for learning. Potential triggers and subsequent reactions we researched are, for instance, the learning activities that followed after an error was made at work (Bauer and

Mulder 2010) and learning activities that followed a feedback incident (Mulder 2013). With another colleague I have used CIT to measure innovative work behaviour (Messmann and Mulder 2012).

In all research projects questionnaires were developed. The required steps of defining the aim and collecting the data in a natural setting were carried out. Questions to respondents were phrased depending on the objectives of the study. In relation to mentioned credibility checks, we used the following strategies. For theoretical validity, the assumptions underlying the proposed research were made explicit and then scrutinised in the light of relevant scholarly literature to see if they were supported. Working with colleagues, we tried to increase the accuracy of incident recall and of the subsequent answers by clearly stating what was meant by the specific construct, on the basis of a theoretical framework, and what characteristics (criteria) that construct has. In the case of the feedback incidents and errors, examples were given. In addition, this procedure increases the accuracy of the incidents selected and reported by the respondents. To get accurate incidents, it also helped to ask for something that had happened recently. This procedure also increased the comparability of the incidents selected. This goes also for the responses to the subsequent question.

What we did was ensure that the respondents understood what we meant by the critical incident, for instance in research on innovative work behaviour. The following is an example of domain-specific formulation of a critical incident, in this case innovation, to increase validity (Messmann and Mulder 2012, pp. 47–48).

> In modern work contexts it is increasingly necessary to develop new ideas that lead to a significant change. These ideas are either newly created or derived from other contexts. Usually, several people are involved. The goal of this questionnaire is to find out what people do, when they are an active part of such a process of change that has one of the following goals:
> - establishment of new routines,
> - simplification of work processes,
> - use of new materials and tools,
> - improvement of cooperation inside and outside the organisation and
> - creating new offers and services for clients.

Within this domain, that is, their work, the respondent had to think of such an incident and then answer questions, which were related to the aim of this study. For example, to measure actual past behaviour the question '*What did you do?*' was used. Respondents provided qualitative, open answers, which they wrote down. This was relatively time consuming for the respondents.

An alternative is to pre-code possible responses and request the respondent to tick the appropriate response, that is, to use a closed answering format which I used in another project (Mulder 2013). The objective of research in this study was to get insight into the relationship between feedback incidents and their subsequent informal learning activities (Mulder 2013). To avoid the possible negative effect of elapsed time and the problem of recall, respondents used a learning log. At the end of every day they wrote down a maximum of five feedback incidents they had experienced that day and the subsequent learning activities they had carried out. This procedure increased the number of (critical) incidents reported as well as the validity of the answers.

Vignette Technique

An important difference compared with CIT is that actual past behaviour cannot be investigated as well unless the vignette has actually happened. Sometimes intended behaviour can be investigated. Working with colleagues, we took care of the specific characteristics and demands of the VT. We developed vignettes that met the demands of context sensitivity, being realistic and familiar for the respondents and internally consistent. We made sure that the vignettes were authentic, such that all employees should have met a similar problem in their daily work that had characteristics that fitted our research aim, for example a certain amount of complexity. To check if the vignette is indeed realistic and authentic the respondents can be asked to give their impression after they have responded to the vignette. Colleagues and I have interviewed experts to elicit relevant cases on which to base the vignettes. To create the vignettes, we carried out semi-structured interviews as described in the following extract relating to the study of learning from errors (Leicher et al. 2013, pp. 212–213).

> In order to collect examples of error cases in elder care nursing, we conducted interviews with three experts on the domain. We considered the chosen participants as experts in elder care nursing, based on them having more than ten years of work experience and a supervisory function. Long experience is crucial for extensive knowledge about relevant errors that may occur in elder care nursing . . . The supervisory function was used as a criterion because it is part of a supervisors' role to have a critical perspective towards and an overview of their department. Moreover, the role of a supervisor implies a central position within a team, with a supervisor able to define what constitutes errors in a specific domain and to provide valid examples of errors.

To ensure the credibility of the vignettes, these interviews were conducted with experts (supervisors). During these interviews, authentic concrete examples were collected, and a deductive strategy to analyse the answers according to the definition of (types of) errors was applied. Situations that were mentioned most frequently, and about which rich information about dealing with errors was provided, were selected. Interviews were carried out until saturation was reached, that is, the last expert mentioned the same examples as the previous experts and no further examples of knowledge of rule-based errors were mentioned. Because we tried to identify the most frequent errors, saturation was reached. Following their development, the vignettes were checked with an additional expert interview and further refined.

As an additional credibility check on the potential severity of impact of the error cases on the participants' responses, we asked them to rate the authenticity and severity of the error cases and how well they could identify with them (using a six-point Likert-type scale with lower numbers indicating higher construct prevalence). The elderly care nurses could identify well with the error cases. Therefore, we determined that the developed error cases were relevant for the domain of elderly care nursing and appropriate for the combination with the questionnaire. An example of a vignette and answering mode is the following case of an error in planning of nursing activities (physical mobilisation; Leicher et al. 2013, p. 213).

It is your responsibility to assess a new resident's care planning. The dementia patient is in constant restlessness in the first days of his stay at the retirement home. He tries to dissolve the fixations and his safety bed rails. In order to counter this problem, you decide to plan a physical mobilization with a special mobilization chair. In this planning you don't determine the frequency and the length of time for the mobilization. Because of this inaccurate planning, your colleagues are not able to assess if the mobilization has been carried out. The result is that the planned mobilization is not implemented.

Participants were asked to imagine that they were experiencing one of the following error cases and rate how they would deal with this situation in relation to their engagement in social learning activities. To measure the intended past behaviour the question '*What would you do?*' was used. The answering mode to measure the learning process was quantitative. Respondents had to rate their engagement in learning activities on a six-point Likert-type scale. For instance, as part of the variable 'general cause analysis' the item 'discussing with my colleagues why I made this error' was an item they had to respond to, if they would do that in that specific situation.

In research on the effects of characteristics of the job task (in the IT sector), one major characteristic of job tasks that needed to be investigated was the complexity of the task. In this study my colleague and I chose to include this complexity of the task in the vignette; again, based on material collected in an interview study with experts, a high complex vignette and a lower complex one were conducted (Ketterl 2014; Ketterl and Mulder 2013). Half the respondents were given one vignette, the other half the other. The vignettes differed significantly in, for instance, the amount of relations between the constructs in the story. The vignette with high complexity is presented below:

> In the following, an authentic, but hypothetical example of your daily work is presented. Please, read it thoroughly. Try to imagine the situation.
>
> The producer of tools 'Toolmaster' would like to extend their enterprise. The product range comprises different tools of the renowned producer as well as possible equipment. You take employment to program the web-shop. The following features should be implemented:
>
> - Presentation of the goods, with appealing layout
> - Consumer basket
> - Suggestions of additional products
> - Payment, with the use of a third-party supplier (note: necessary for accepting credit cards, etc.)
> - Database for addresses, also for international customers, with plausibility check
> - Recognition of customers and list of recommendations on the basis of further purchases
> - Integration with stock system, including inventory audit and direct entry on stock
> - Possibility to contact
>
> During accomplishing the work task you detect a process that could not be integrated into the software concept. What would you do?

Answering Modes CIT and VT

The possibilities for questions (in relation to the objectives of the study) and the answering modes are similar for VT and CIT, and they can generate both quantitative and qualitative data. Closed, as well as open, questions were used to measure learning processes, learning results and behaviour. The answering mode we used in some studies was open (qualitative data were generated), and in others closed (generating quantitative data). Working with colleagues, categories were developed for these answers on the basis of a theoretical framework, sometimes inductively, based on responses to open questions (Bauer and Mulder 2010; Leicher et al. 2013), and sometimes before the construction of the vignette. In these situations the categories were based on the theoretical framework, clear definition of a construct and operationalisation, and were used as basis for the pre-coded answers (e.g. Mulder 2013). Mulder (2013) contains an example of a category system of informal learning according to the definition previously mentioned. For example, drawing on theory (e.g. Eraut 2000), cognitive, reactive, individual learning was defined as an activity that is not observable, is spontaneous and is carried out without social interaction. This formed the basis for the items representing aspects of informal learning activities that the respondents could tick in response to a question about what they did after a feedback incident. Examples of the informal learning activities in this case were: read professional journals, have a discussion with colleagues, ask a supervisor. Most importantly the qualitative data is transformable, through such coding, into quantitative data. In the case of qualitative data, the answers were categorised afterwards to make them suitable for quantitative analysis. Pre-coded answers were easier for comparison and data analyses.

DISCUSSION

CIT as well as VT can be used to investigate learning processes and behaviour at work in all kinds of organisations in all kinds of domains. It is important to realise that the techniques differ in appropriateness for measuring, for instance, actual behaviour or intended behaviour. In addition, these techniques are used in different research paradigms. They both can be used for collecting qualitative and quantitative data, and there are possibilities to quantify qualitative data. This also enables statistical investigation of the relationships between conditions and determinants with these learning processes, behaviour and performance.

Using the CIT and/or VT depends on the aim of the study, be it awareness, actual behaviour, performance or other relevant constructs for HRD. The first step is to decide upon the objective of the study. Deciding on the best technique for any given aim depends on the context, the sample and other research characteristics.

Both techniques have a structure starting with some kind of trigger, question or instruction and some kind of answering mode. In relation to the quality of the critical incident and the vignette, the importance of objectivity is emphasised by both techniques. And for both techniques many demands concerning validity/credibility are formulated. They need to be taken into account in all the phases of the use of the techniques: the development, data collection and analyses of the data. For the development of the trigger (vignette, demand for critical incident) the questions/instructions and the answering mode, the necessary steps for the two different methods have to be taken appropriately, and they have to be coherent. In addition, the interpretation and analyses have to fit (cf. Niglas, 2010). This chapter has offered examples of how critical incidents and vignettes can be developed and used in HRD research, and how they can conform to the demands of the techniques, such as context-boundedness, and authenticity.

Both techniques provide many opportunities and are rather flexible. This leads to many opportunities for application. However, there is the danger of not using them properly. Therefore, for both techniques, it is emphasised that competent researchers are required, which can be realised by training.

REFERENCES

Bauer, J and Mulder, RH (2010), 'In search of a good method for measuring learning from errors at work', in M Van Woerkom and R Poell (eds), *Workplace learning: concepts, measurement, and application*, Routledge, New York, pp. 111–128.

Branch, WT (2005), 'Use of critical incident reports in medical education', *Journal of General Internal Medicine*, vol. 20, no. 11, pp. 1063–1067.

Brauer, MP, Hanning, RM, Arocha, JF, Royall, D, Goy, R, Grant, A, Dietrich, L, Martino, R and Horrocks, J (2009), 'Creating case scenarios or vignettes using factorial study design methods', *Journal of Advanced Nursing*, vol. 65, no. 9, pp. 1937–1945.

Butterfield, LD, Borgen, WA, Amundson, NE and Maglio, AST (2005), 'Fifty years of the Critical Incident Technique 1954–2004', *Qualitative Research*, vol. 5, no. 4, pp. 475–497.

Edvardsson, B and Roos, I (2001), 'Critical Incident Technique: towards a framework for analysing the criticality of critical incidents', *International Journal of Service Industry Management*, vol. 12, no. 3, pp. 251–268.

Ellinger, AD and Bostrom, RP (2002), 'An examination of managers' beliefs about their roles as facilitators of learning', *Management Learning*, vol. 33, no. 2, pp. 147–179.

Eraut, M (2000), 'Non-formal learning and tacit knowledge in professional work', *British Journal of Educational Psychology*, vol. 70, no. 2, pp. 113–136.

Finch, J (1987), 'The vignette technique in survey research', *Sociology*, vol. 21, no. 1, pp. 105–114.

Flanagan, JC (1954), 'The Critical Incident Techniques', *Psychological Bulletin*, vol. 51, no. 4, pp. 327–358.

Hamlin, RG and Patel, T (2012), 'Behavioural indicators of perceived managerial and leadership effectiveness within Romanian and British public sector hospitals', *European Journal of Training and Development*, vol. 36, no. 2/3, pp. 234–261.

Hughes, R and Huby, M (2002), 'The application of vignettes in social and nursing research', *Journal of Advanced Nursing*, vol. 37, no. 4, pp. 382–386.

Hughes, R and Huby, M (2004), 'The construction and interpretation of vignettes in social research', *Social Work and Social Science Review*, vol. 11, no. 1, pp. 36–51.

Jeffries, C and Maeder, D (2004), 'Using vignettes to build and assess teacher understanding of instructional strategies', *The Professional Educator*, vol. 27, no. 1/2, pp. 17–28.

Ketterl, K (2014), *Informelles Lernen im Arbeitsprozess*, (PhD Thesis), Verlag Dr Kovac, Hamburg.

Ketterl, K and Mulder, RH (2013), 'Engagement in informal learning in relation to learning potential of the work task, social support and structural characteristics of the workplace', Paper presented at the EARLI conference, August, Munich.

Leicher, V, Mulder, RH and Bauer, J (2013), 'Learning from errors at work: a replication study in elder care nursing', *Vocations and Learning*, vol. 6, pp. 207–220.

Lincoln, YS and Guba, EG (1985), *Naturalistic inquiry*, Sage Publications, Beverly Hills, CA.

Messmann, G and Mulder, RH (2012), 'Development of a measurement instrument for innovative work behaviour as a dynamic and context-bound construct', *Human Resource Development International*, vol. 15, no. 1, pp.43–59.

Miles, MB (1990), 'New methods for qualitative data collection and analysis: vignettes and pre-structured cases', *International Journal of Qualitative Studies in Education*, vol. 3, no. 1, pp.37–51.

Mulder, RH (2013), 'Exploring feedback incidents, their characteristics and the informal learning activities that emanate from them', *European Journal of Training and Development*, vol. 37, no. 1, pp.49–71.

Niglas, K (2010), 'The multidimensional model of research methodology: An integrated set of continua', in A Tashakkori and C Teddlie (eds), Sage *Handbook of Mixed Methods in Social and Behavioral Research*, Sage Publications, Los Angeles, CA, pp.215–236.

Poulou, M (2001), 'The role of vignettes in the research of emotional and behavioural difficulties', *Emotional and Behavioural Difficulties*, vol. 6, no. 1, pp.50–62.

Rahman, N (1996), 'Caregivers' sensitivity to conflict: The use of the vignette methodology', *Journal of Elder Abuse and Neglect*, vol. 8, no. 1, pp.35–47.

Renold, E (2002), 'Using vignettes in qualitative research', *Building Research Capacity*, vol. 3, pp.3–5.

Richman, J and Mercer, D (2002), 'The vignette revisited: evil and the forensic nurse', *Nurse Researcher*, vol. 9, no. 4, pp.70–82.

Schoenberg, NE and Ravdal, H (2000), 'Using vignettes in awareness and attitudinal research', *International Journal of Social Research Methodology*, vol. 3, no. 1, pp.63–74.

Spalding, NJ and Phillips, T (2007), 'Exploring the use of vignettes: from validity to trustworthiness', *Qualitative Health Research*, vol. 17, no. 7, pp.945–962.

Wilson, JP (ed.) (2012), *International human resource development*, Kogan Page, London.

Wilson, J and While, AE (1998), 'Methodological issues surrounding the use of vignettes in qualitative research', *Journal of Interprofessional Care*, vol. 12, no. 1, pp.79–86.

ANNOTATED FURTHER READING

Butterfield, LD, Borgen, WA, Amundson, NE and Maglio, AST (2005), 'Fifty years of the Critical Incident Technique 1954–2004', *Qualitative Research*, vol. 5, no. 4, pp.475–497. This publication contains information on the origin of CIT, the method itself, its place within the qualitative research tradition and recommendations for use. It provides information on credibility/trustworthiness checks.

Finch, J (1987), 'The vignette technique in survey research', *Sociology*, vol. 21, no. 1, pp.105–114. This publication contains information on the characteristics of the VT, an example of how it is used, and strengths and weaknesses of the technique.

Flanagan, JC (1954), 'The Critical Incident Techniques', *Psychological Bulletin*, vol. 51, pp.327–358. This publication describes the background and the development of the CIT and contains detailed information on CIT and the procedure and how it is used.

Spalding, NJ and Phillips, T (2007), 'Exploring the use of vignettes: from validity to trustworthiness', *Qualitative Health Research*, vol. 17, no. 7, pp.945–962. The development and use of various forms of vignettes (portraits, snapshots and composites) in an action research case study is described, with specific emphasis on trustworthiness.

19. Accounting for complexity: structural equation modelling (SEM) in HRD research

Christoph König, Gerhard Messmann, Regina H. Mulder and Sven De Maeyer

SUMMARY

The interdependence between organizations and their members confronts HRD with complex research problems. Structural equation modelling (SEM) offers a useful tool to account for this complexity. Using examples, this chapter illustrates and discusses the possibilities, limitations and caveats of using SEM in HRD research.

INTRODUCTION

Workplace learning, be it formal or informal, is a constituent component of Human Resource Development (HRD). In order to improve theory and practice of HRD, it is necessary to shed light on the development of individuals in organizations. In their Delphi study, McGuire and Cseh (2006, p. 663) identified the 'balancing [of] the needs of employees, organizations and societies when responding to organizational issues' as a key challenge for HRD theory and practice. This interdependence between organizations and their members confronts research with complex problems (Camillus, 2008). For example, changes in employees' perceptions of the organizational feedback culture may lead to changes in their innovative work behaviour (IWB). IWB is considered increasingly important for organizational effectiveness (Messmann and Mulder, 2014). The development of IWB may, for instance, be influenced by the leadership style of the managers. While IWB is an individual attribute of the employee, perceived culture in relation to feedback is a characteristic of the organization and the leadership style is a characteristic of teams. In order to investigate the relationship between IWB, feedback culture, leadership style and organizational effectiveness, it is necessary to integrate individual, team and organizational-level data into a coherent statistical model. To understand development, be it individual or organizational, it is necessary to investigate changes over time; for example, investigating change in perceived feedback culture requires longitudinal data. An adequate understanding of reactions to changes in the hypothetical perceived feedback culture requires a careful identification and measurement of potential influencing factors, outcomes and consequences, and mediating constructs on different levels and over time. Regression analysis is only of limited use for these kinds of complex research problems, because it does not allow integration of multiple dependent constructs into a single model.

Against this background it is not surprising that Calver et al. (2013, p. 97) identify 'the failure to demonstrate a return on investment on activities' as a main characteristic of current HRD research. There are two overarching analytical requirements to identify reliably the value added by HRD. First, the constructs have to be selected and developed with maximum care for validity and reliability. This includes controlling for and minimizing measurement error. Second, the statistical approach must be flexible enough to allow the specification of constructs at different levels (individual, team and organizational) as well as changes in these constructs over time. Such a combination of both multilevel and longitudinal aspects allows for the investigation of contextual effects and behavioural change. This, in turn, enables researchers to conduct more in-depth evaluations of training and of the consequences of formal and informal learning (Calver et al., 2013; Grossman and Salas, 2011).

SEM and its extensions offer a useful tool to investigate such complex research problems (Jöreskog, 1973). SEM allows the control of measurement error, the specification of multiple levels, the specification of change over time and the testing of direct and indirect relations between constructs that are relevant for HRD. The structure of this chapter follows the two requirements mentioned above: (1) the measurement and development of constructs and (2) the integration of individual and organizational constructs which change over time. The chapter provides readers with an overview of the foundations and possibilities of SEM in HRD research as well as recommendations and caveats.

DESCRIPTION OF THE METHOD

SEM has its roots in factor analysis (Spearman, 1904) and path analysis (Wright, 1921). Factor analysis is commonly used to investigate correlations of observed variables (indicators) in order to identify an underlying unobservable (latent) construct. Latent constructs are empirical phenomena that cannot be observed directly, for example work motivation, organizational culture, or learning processes. They are measured by sets of observed indicator variables. These observed indicator variables can be derived from a variety of sources such as scores on a performance test or questionnaires with Likert-scaled items (e.g., the Multifactor Leadership scale; Bass and Avolio, 1995). Path analysis is used to investigate directed relations between sets of observed variables. SEM combines these approaches in an integrated analytical framework. In the measurement part of the model, latent constructs are related to their observed indicator variables. In the structural part of the model, the latent constructs are related to each other (Jöreskog, 1973).

SEMs have several advantages over regression analysis. First, contrary to regression analysis, it is possible to investigate multiple dependent constructs simultaneously. For example, researchers may include organizational effectiveness and efficiency as dependent constructs in a single model. Second, it is possible to investigate direct and indirect effects between independent and dependent constructs. Thus, more complex hypotheses can be tested (for example, the relation between perceived organizational feedback culture and IWB, mediated by the leadership style of the managers). Third, modern software packages for SEM such as Mplus (Muthén and Muthén, 2013) provide a variety of estimators to handle non-normal data such as censored and categorical variables or combinations of those. Another advantage of SEM over regression analysis is the possibility to take into account explicitly error in the measurement of the latent constructs and in the hypothesized relations between them. This is important for the careful development of latent constructs as well as for an exact evaluation of effects between them. Consider, for instance, the simple SEM depicted in Figure 19.1. In this the latent constructs are surrounded by ellipses, and the direction of their relationships with their observed indicator variables (surrounded by rectangles) is

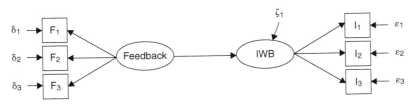

Note: F_1–F_3 are observed indicators measuring the independent latent variable feedback. I_1–I_3 are observed indicators measuring the dependent latent variable IWB. δ and ϵ are measurement errors of the indicators. ζ is the error in the prediction of IWB by feedback.

Figure 19.1   A simple structural equation model illustrating a direct effect of feedback on IWB

shown by arrows. These relations constitute the measurement model. This can be used to answer the question of how well the latent constructs are measured by their observed indicator variables.

Modelling Complex Constructs – the Measurement Model

The measurement model relates the latent constructs to their observed indicator variables. It describes how well the latent construct is measured by its observed indicator variables. In order to be able to estimate measurement models with one latent construct, three indicators are necessary. For models with more than one latent construct, at least two indicators are necessary for each latent construct (Kline, 2010). In principle, the number of indicators per latent construct is only limited by sample size. Depending on the objectives, researchers use three to five indicators per latent construct. If more indicators are available for a single latent construct, item parcels can be formed by averaging scores of substantially correlated indicators (Little et al., 2002). The links between observed indicators and latent constructs are called factor loadings (which can be interpreted as regression coefficients). Each indicator is associated with a specific error term called residual variance. This error term is denoted by the Greek letter ε (epsilon) and represents the measurement error. In principle, it describes variance in the indicators that is not explained by the latent construct. The amount of this residual variance indicates the adequacy of the indicators for measuring their associated latent constructs.

The basic procedure to build measurement models is called confirmatory factor analysis (CFA). A factor represents a latent construct or a dimension of a multidimensional latent construct. In CFA, the factor structure, that is, the number of factors underlying a given set of indicators, has to be specified before the actual analysis. It is, however, possible to compare measurement models with a varying number of factors (for example, 1-factor, 2-factor, or 3-factor models). In order to decide which measurement model is adequate, global and local fit indices are available. These describe if and how well a (measurement) model fits the data. A model that fits, however, does not imply that a researcher has found the correct model (Jöreskog, 1973). Rather, to assess if the model is the correct or best model, researchers have to assess the plausibility of the model parameters, that is, the local fit of the model. Local fit is determined by the magnitude, the sign and the significance of the model parameters (e.g., the factor loadings). Most SEM programs automatically compute the significance of model parameters with two-sided *t*-tests.

Global indices give information about the model as a whole, that is, about all the relations specified in a given model. The most common is the

χ^2 (chi square) test statistic. A non-significant χ^2 test ($.05 < p < 1.00$) indicates that the model fits the data. This test compares the covariance matrix found in the sample with the covariance matrix implied by the specified model. χ^2 values can be further used to compare models with varying numbers of factors. With the degrees of freedom of compared measurement models, a χ^2 difference value is computed. If this value is significant, there are substantial differences in the specified relations of the models. In most SEM programs χ^2 difference tests are implemented.

Other global fit indices are the root-mean-square error of approximation (RMSEA) and the standardized root-mean-square residual (SRMR). Like the χ^2 test, these indices describe deviations of the sample covariance matrix from the covariance matrix of the specified model. The higher these deviations are, the worse is the fit of the model, good model fit being suggested by RMSEA and SRMR values of .05 or lower (Byrne, 2012; Heck and Thomas, 2009).

Furthermore, when researchers want to compare different models, comparative fit indices, such as the comparative fit index (CFI; Bentler, 1990) and the Tucker-Lewis index (TLI; Tucker and Lewis, 1973), can be used. In principle, these indexes compare models with fewer parameters with a model with more parameters (which means that they are nested). Good model fit is indicated by CFI and TLI values of .95 or higher (Heck and Thomas, 2009). Literature suggests reporting the χ^2 value and the corresponding test result as well as the CFI, TLI, RMSEA and SRMR values as indicators of model fit (Beauducel and Wittmann, 2005). Further fit indices are described in Byrne (2012). In the case of our example (Figure 19.1), good model fit can be interpreted as meaning that the relations between the two latent constructs feedback and IWB and their indicators are specified correctly.

Analysing Complex Relationships at the Individual Level

After the specification, estimation and evaluation of the measurement model, the next step in SEM is the specification of the structural model. The structural model relates latent independent constructs to latent dependent constructs by a specification of directional paths between them. These paths represent specific hypotheses about the relations between latent constructs and are interpreted as regression coefficients. The accuracy of the prediction of the latent dependent construct by the latent independent construct can be evaluated by the magnitude of a specific error term (ζ; zeta). This error term is called 'disturbance' and indicates the variance in the latent dependent construct that is not explained by the latent independent construct. This error term allows for an assessment of how well a given latent independent construct predicts a latent dependent construct. The combination of measurement and structural model is called the structural equation model. The fit of the structural equation model to the data is also assessed with the indices described in the previous section.

Moreover, the use of SEM is not limited to the investigation of direct effects (such as the directional path from feedback to IWB represented by the arrows in Figure 19.1). SEM can also be used to analyse mediation effects, indirect effects and moderation effects (such as the directional paths represented by the arrows from perceived social support to intrinsic motivation, and further from intrinsic motivation to idea generation in Figure 19.3). In principle, the complexity of a model is only limited by the size of the available sample. Sample size is also a prominent challenge in multilevel models that include individual, team, or organizational-level data simultaneously. In order to obtain correct parameter estimates and standard errors, large sample sizes are required.

Analysing Complex Relationships between Individual, Team and Organizational-Level Data

When investigating processes within organizations, there is often the need to incorporate data situated at different levels. Such multilevel problems involve populations with a hierarchical structure, for instance, when employees are nested within teams, which are nested within organizations. Under these circumstances, individuals and individual observations are not independent from each other. In addition, depending on the sample design, there are differing probabilities for individuals who are nested within teams within organizations being selected for the sample. Neglecting these aspects leads to incorrect estimations of standard errors and estimates. SEM software packages allow researchers to include information about the sample design.

If single-level analyses are applied to such data structures, parameter estimates are less accurate due to either aggregating or disaggregating individual or contextual information. Moreover, neglecting the hierarchical structure leads to theoretically poor models. Besides losing important information due to aggregation procedures, this also leads to biased estimates. Multilevel SEM accounts for the nested data structure and the dependence of individual observations. It decomposes the variance of constructs into two parts: first, the variance of a given construct which is associated with differences between individuals within an organization and, second, the variance of a given construct which is associated with differences between organizations. Thus, multilevel SEM enables researchers to investigate phenomena that may be due to differences within and between organizations.

From a HRD perspective, a relevant question is whether there are contextual practices which affect individuals; for instance, whether leadership styles affect IWB. Such questions can be investigated by specifying cross-level interactions (more information on cross-level interactions can be found in Heck and Thomas, 2009). Another relevant question is whether there are constructs that have different effects at different levels. This is called compositional or contextual effect and is defined as the difference in the size of the organizational-level and individual-level effect (Raudenbush and Bryk, 2002). Multilevel SEM allows researchers directly and easily to estimate such effects, because, contrary to multilevel regression, constructs can be specified simultaneously at the individual, team and/or organizational level.

A critical issue in both single-level and multilevel SEM is sample size. Maximum likelihood estimation of model parameters usually assumes large samples. This is problematic, especially in the multilevel case, where samples of organizational units are usually small. Unfortunately, a large sample size at the individual level does not compensate for a small sample size at the organizational level. With increasing sample sizes at both levels, estimates become more accurate as the size of the standard errors declines. Rules of thumb range from 30 groups with 30 individuals in each group for estimating simple models to 50 groups with 20 individuals in each group for estimating cross-level interactions (Hox, 2010).

Analysing Longitudinal Data in a Multilevel Framework

The basic multilevel SEM can easily be extended to investigate change and development of individuals or organizations over time, for instance, the development of IWB due to a change in leadership styles. Such models, referred to as growth models, have an additional level, which evolves from observations at different points of measurement that are nested within individuals. This means the first level of this kind of model contains the successive observations of individuals' IWB, that is, its development over time. The second level consists of individual-level predictors such as gender, attitudes, or socioeconomic status. Constructs at this level can be used to explain variance in the initial status of IWB and its development. The third level consists of organizational-level predictors of IWB such as feedback culture. By adding this third (organizational) level, it is possible to examine variation in the development of individuals' IWB within organizations as well as differences in the development of IWB between organizations. Depending on the number of points of measurement, it is possible to model linear, quadratic and cubic developments of IWB. For estimations of linear growth, two or three points of measurement are required; for estimations of quadratic and cubic growth, at least four observations are needed. Duncan, Duncan and Strycker (2008) offer an easily understandable and thorough introduction to such longitudinal models.

PERSONAL EXPERIENCE WITH SEM IN HRD RESEARCH

This section illustrates how SEM can be used to specify, estimate and evaluate relations between latent constructs and their observed indicator variables as well as relations between latent constructs. The basis of these examples is a study on facilitators of IWB which, as outlined earlier, play a considerable role in HRD. In the first step, a measurement model of IWB is illustrated (Messmann and Mulder, 2012). In the second step, the specification of a structural model is explained, in which potential facilitators are tested with respect to their influence on IWB. Direct and indirect effects among multiple dependent and independent latent constructs are illustrated (Messmann and Mulder, 2014).

SEM as a Psychometric Tool: Modelling IWB

The first aim of this study was to construct a Likert-scaled self-report questionnaire for measuring IWB as a dynamic, context-bound construct. The development of the instrument was based on a definition of IWB as 'the sum of physical and cognitive work activities carried out by employees in their work context, either solitarily or in a social setting, in order to accomplish a set of tasks that are required to achieve the goal of innovation development' (Messmann and Mulder, 2012, p.45). The questionnaire was based on existing instruments but sought to enable the measurement of authentic work activities carried out by employees during the development of an innovation in their work context. Each work activity that was assessed was associated with one of the five dimensions (or latent constructs) of IWB. That is, opportunity exploration (questionnaire item: 'Keeping oneself informed about the organization's structures and processes'), idea generation (item: 'Suggesting improvements on expressed ideas'), idea promotion (item: 'Convincing others of the importance of a new idea or solution'), idea realization (item: 'Testing evolving solutions for shortcomings when putting ideas into practice') and reflection (item: 'Assessing the progress while putting ideas into practice'). Altogether, 30 items had to be rated on a six-point Likert scale from 1 ('does not apply') to 6 ('fully applies') regarding how adequately each described the respondent's behaviour. Prior to the main study, undertaken in vocational colleges, the instrument was validated using a pilot study in an automotive supply company. These work contexts share several relevant characteristics, such as knowledge intensity, and were therefore considered comparable.

In both studies, the aim was to determine whether IWB really consists of the aforementioned theoretically assumed latent constructs. By means of an exploratory factor analysis, several theoretically sound, yet competing factor models were identified: a five-factor model (as theoretically postulated), a four-factor model (with idea realization collapsed into two other latent constructs) and a one-factor model (in line with previous studies on IWB).

The second step of the construct validation procedure was the confirmation of these explorative results. The objective of the main study was to determine which of these competing models was most appropriate. Hence, three different measurement models, namely, a five-factor, a four-factor and a one-factor model, were specified. These models differed in the relations between the latent constructs (opportunity exploration, idea generation, idea promotion, idea realization and reflection) and their observed indicator variables. These models were then estimated and compared regarding their local and global fit indices. First, the χ^2 test statistic was evaluated for each of the competing models regarding its significance. Second, the RMSEA, SRMR, CFI and TLI values were evaluated to further examine the global fit of each of the competing models. Third, differences in the χ^2 test statistics of the models were computed to find out whether the results of the models were significantly different from each other. Based on these steps, it was found that the four-factor model of IWB fitted the main study data best. Furthermore, results of the analysis showed that IWB could be modelled as consisting of four separate, correlated factors, or as a latent second order construct with the four factors as latent indicators. Second order models are a special case of measurement models, where latent constructs are used as indicators for another, superior latent construct. As a further aim of the study was to find out which factors facilitate opportunity exploration, idea generation, idea promotion and reflection, the measurement model of IWB containing these four separate, correlated factors was chosen for further analysis (Figure 19.2).

SEM as a Tool to Model Complex Relationships: Analysing Individual and Contextual Facilitators of Innovative Work Behaviour

Based on gaps in previous IWB research, the second aim of the main study was to investigate how the different dimensions of IWB can be facilitated.

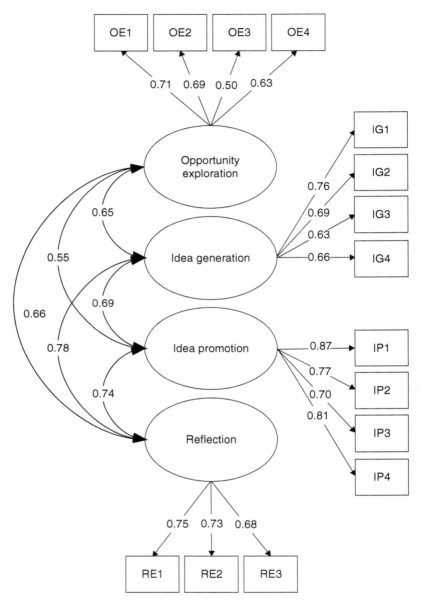

Note: Model fit: $\chi^2_{(84)}$ = 86.71, p = .40; *RMSEA* = .01 with 90% confidence interval (CI) .00–.01; *SRMR* = .04; *CFI* = .99; *TLI* = .99.

Figure 19.2   Standardized estimates for the multidimensional measurement model of IWB

To this end, the effects of perceived impact at work, perceived supervisor support for innovation, perceived supportive climate for innovation and intrinsic motivation for innovation on opportunity exploration, idea generation, idea promotion, and reflection were tested. In order to specify the respective structural model, it was hypothesized that perceived impact at work would only have an effect on opportunity exploration, because both constructs are related to a preparatory stage of realizing an innovation. Furthermore, it was hypothesized that perceived supervisor support and perceived supportive climate for innovation would have a positive effect on idea generation, idea promotion, and reflection, as all of these constructs are closely related to the realization of an innovation. Moreover, since there was hardly any insight into relationships between these constructs, possible indirect effects were also tested. In particular, it was hypothesized that intrinsic motivation for innovation would mediate the effects of perceived impact, perceived supervisor support and perceived social climate on idea generation, idea promotion, and reflection.

Since intrinsic motivation, perceived impact at work, perceived supervisor support and perceived supportive climate were also latent constructs, a measurement model for the four independent constructs was specified. For this purpose, the items of the respective measurement scales were used as manifest indicators of each latent construct. Based on thorough data screening, item parcels were formed to make the measurement models more parsimonious. Furthermore, intercorrelations among independent constructs were investigated in order to avoid problems with multicollinearity, that is, high correlations among the independent constructs which may lead to estimation problems. These intercorrelations indicated that two of the constructs, namely, perceived supervisor support and perceived supportive climate, had a correlation of .60, which would cause such problems. Based on theoretical considerations, it was decided that these two constructs could be specified as latent indicators of a second order factor (i.e., perceived social support for innovation).

In the next step, the measurement models of all latent constructs under consideration were integrated into a full measurement model. The full measurement model consisted of opportunity exploration, idea generation, idea promotion, and reflection as latent dependent constructs as well as perceived impact, perceived social support and intrinsic motivation as latent independent constructs. For this measurement model, the χ^2 test statistic, the RMSEA, SRMR, CFI and TLI values indicated good fit.

The final step of the analysis was to specify the structural model. For this aim, we specified directional paths from every latent independent construct to each latent dependent construct based on our hypotheses. Each directional path represents one specific hypothesis and is interpreted as a regression coefficient. Furthermore, a directional path from perceived impact and perceived social support to intrinsic motivation for innovation was specified. Hence, it was possible to test whether perceived impact and perceived social support had indirect effects on opportunity exploration, idea generation, idea promotion, and reflection via intrinsic motivation for innovation as a mediating construct. The structural model is illustrated in Figure 19.3.

The estimation of the structural model mainly supported the outlined hypotheses: the model showed that intrinsic motivation for innovation had a significant effect on opportunity exploration, idea generation, idea promotion, and reflection. That is, all four innovative behaviours required a sufficient amount of intrinsic motivation for the overarching task of developing an innovation. Also in accordance with the hypotheses, perceived impact at work had a significant positive effect on opportunity exploration. And perceived social support had a significant effect on idea generation, idea promotion, and reflection. That is, the general perception of one's influence at work had an effect on opportunity exploration, which refers to a general search for possibilities to innovate. By comparison, specific social support for innovation influenced the generation and promotion of ideas, as well as innovation-specific reflection, which were all directly related to the development of innovative products and processes at work.

Moreover, the model showed marginally significant indirect effects of perceived impact at work ($\beta = .06 - .08$, $p < .10$) and significant indirect effects of perceived social support ($\beta = .08 - .11$, $p < .05$) on opportunity exploration, idea generation, idea promotion, and reflection. That is, intrinsic motivation for innovation mediated the effect of one's perception of impact at work and of the perception of social support for innovation on IWB.

Further Directions: SEM as a Tool for Modelling Multilevel and Longitudinal Data

In this section, the use of SEM for dealing with hierarchically clustered and longitudinal data is illustrated by a hypothetical extension of the example described in the previous sections. The research question is as follows: what is the relation between intrinsic motivation, IWB and leadership styles and perceived social support for innovation as organizational characteristics over time? Thus, a hierarchical data structure is assumed in which individuals are nested within organizations with different leadership styles and different perceived social support for innovations. It is furthermore assumed that IWB (i.e., the manifestations of opportunity

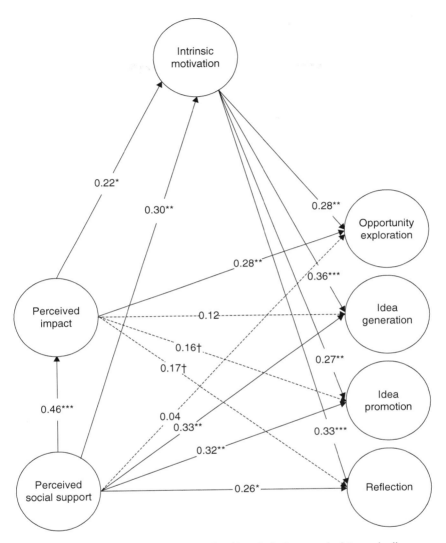

Note: Solid arrows depict significant relationships, dashed arrows depict marginally significant ($p < .10$) and insignificant relationships. $^\dagger p < .10$, $^*p < .05$, $^{**}p < .01$, $^{***}p < .001$. $N = 239$. All factor loadings are statistically significant at $p < .001$. Model fit: $\chi^2_{(382)} = 455.45$, $p = .01$; $RMSEA = .03$ with 90% CI .02–.04; $SRMR = .05$; $CFI = .97$; $TLI = .97$ (adapted from Messmann and Mulder, 2014).

Figure 19.3   *Standardized estimates for a model of individual and contextual facilitators of IWB (measurement part omitted)*

exploration, idea generation, idea promotion, and reflection) change over time. Hence, data are collected at four points of measurement. In order to consider this longitudinal nature of the data, SEM is used to analyse the data in a single multilevel framework.

An excerpt of the model to be estimated is shown in Figure 19.4. In contrast to the single-level model illustrated in the previous section, this model has an additional level. Since IWB and intrinsic motivation are individual-level constructs, they are specified at the individual level of the model (the lower half). Similarly, leadership style and perceived social support for innovation are treated as organizational characteristics. Thus, these constructs are specified at the organizational level of the model (the upper half). IWB is specified at both the individual and the organizational level, in order to be able to investigate effects of the organizational-level constructs on IWB. At the organizational level, IWB represents the innovativeness of an organization. Multilevel SEM allows for such a detailed specification of the constructs while simultaneously accounting for the hierarchical structure of the data.

As already mentioned, IWB data would be collected at four points of measurement, therefore requiring a longitudinal SEM. These points of measurement are illustrated by the four rectangles labelled IWB 1–4. Changes in IWB over time at the individual level are captured by the two ellipses labelled 'intercept within' and 'slope within'. The first, 'intercept within', represents the initial status of IWB, that is, the characteristic of IWB at the first point of measurement. The second, 'slope within', represents the change in IWB over the four time points, that is, the individual development of IWB. The paths from 'intercept within' and 'slope within' to the four measurement occasions can be interpreted as factor loadings. Since IWB is specified both at the individual and the organizational level, a similar specification of intercept, slope and IWB is found at the organizational level. Models where the dependent latent construct is only specified at the higher (e.g., organizational) level are also possible. Accordingly, the within and between models do not need to be exactly alike.

To answer the aforementioned (longitudinal) research question, the initial status of IWB and change in IWB are then regressed on intrinsic motivation at the individual level as well as on leadership styles and perceived social support for innovation at the organizational level. The first step is to specify and test the measurement models of the respective latent constructs. The second step requires estimating a model without the individual and organizational predictors (called unconditional model), in order to establish a baseline change in IWB. The third step involves specifying and testing directional paths between the initial status of IWB, the change in IWB, and intrinsic motivation (as individual predictor) at the

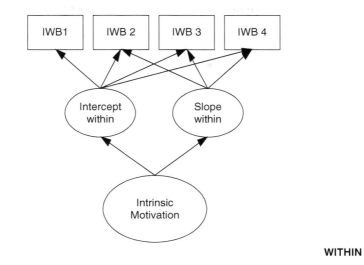

Figure 19.4 *A longitudinal SEM within a multilevel context investigating the influence of intrinsic motivation, leadership styles and perceived social support on individual and organizational IWB*

individual level as well as and between the initial status of IWB, the change in IWB, and leadership styles and perceived social support for innovation (as organizational predictors) at the organizational level. In order to investigate effects of IWB on further constructs, the model can easily be extended to include latent constructs that are fostered by IWB, such as performance or efficiency.

DISCUSSION

This chapter has outlined how the SEM enables researchers to tackle complex problems found in HRD research. SEM offers a useful and flexible tool to answer research questions related to the measurement of complex, unobservable constructs and to analyse complex relationships among such constructs. Moreover, hierarchical and longitudinal data structures can be handled. Consequently, SEM can be used to provide answers to research questions which aim at uncovering developmental processes. SEM is an advantageous statistical approach compared to regression analysis, both with regard to the modelling of constructs and the explicit consideration of measurement errors as well as with respect to the possibility of modelling multiple dependent constructs.

It is important to note that the field of SEM is rapidly evolving. The method itself and the respective software packages are constantly under development. A prominent example is Bayesian data analysis (Gelman, Carlin and Stern, 2003). The Mplus software, for instance, allows researchers to use Bayesian estimation of structural equation models. This kind of estimation is especially suited for the investigation of models with small sample sizes. Given that the requirements of SEM with respect to sample size are relatively strict, Bayesian estimation offers a valuable alternative that further enhances the flexibility and utility of SEM within the context of HRD research. Furthermore, in addition to commercial software packages such as Mplus, free open source software, such as the lavaan package for R, are under constant development (Rosseel, 2012).

Other possible applications of SEM, not discussed in this chapter, include the investigation of the equivalence of latent constructs across different cultures (measurement invariance analysis), cross-country comparisons (multi-group analysis) and the identification of different subgroups or types of individuals and organizations based on a given set of characteristics (latent class analysis).

SEM is not limited to questions regarding formal training but also allows the investigation of informal learning. The characteristics and flexibility of SEM make it possible to directly address developmental aspects of HRD. The value of such HRD research depends on its ability to provide answers to questions about the relationship between the development of employees and organizational characteristics such as (the effects of) professional training or both formal and informal learning opportunities. Moreover, the relevance of such HRD research for practice heavily depends on researchers' ability to address their research questions with a rigorous statistical approach. In this respect, the multiple possibilities offered by SEM enable researchers to demonstrate the return on investment of HRD measures and, thus, provide an adequate basis for improving organizational practice and policy.

REFERENCES

Bass, B. and Avolio, B. (1995). *MLQ Multifactor Leadership Questionnaire*. Redwood City, CA: Mind Garden.

Beauducel, A. and Wittmann, W. W. (2005). Simulation study on fit indices in confirmatory factor analysis based on data with slightly distorted simple structure. *Structural Equation Modeling, 12*, 41–75.

Bentler, P. M. (1990). Comparative fit indexes in structural models. *Psychological Bulletin, 107*, 238–246.

Byrne, B. M. (2012). *Structural equation modeling with Mplus*. New York: Routledge.

Calver, J., Cuthbert, G., Davison, S., Devins, D., Gold, J., Hughes, I. and Tosey, P. (2013). HRD in 2020: A hop-on, hop-off city tour. *Human Resource Development International, 16*, 94–105.

Camillus, J. C. (2008). Strategy as a wicked problem. *Harvard Business Review, 86*, 98–106.

Duncan, T., Duncan, S. and Strycker, L. (2008). *An introduction to latent variable growth curve modeling* (2nd edn). London: Taylor and Francis.

Gelman, A., Carlin, J. B. and Stern, H. S. (2003). *Bayesian data analysis* (2nd edn). Boca Raton, FL: Chapman and Hall.

Grossman, R. and Salas, E. (2011). The transfer of training: What really matters. *International Journal of Training and Development, 15*, 103–120.

Heck, R. H. and Thomas, S. L. (2009). *An introduction to multilevel modeling techniques* (2nd edn). New York: Routledge.

Hox, J. (2010). *Multilevel analysis: Techniques and applications*. New York: Routledge.

Jöreskog, K. G. (1973). A general method for estimating a linear structural equation system. In A. Goldberger and O. D. Duncan (Eds.), *Structural equation models in the social sciences* (pp. 85–112). New York: Seminar Press.

Kline, R. B. (2010). *Principles and practice of structural equation modeling* (3rd edn). London: Guilford Press.

Little, T. D., Cunningham, W. A., Shahar, G. and Widaman, K. F. (2002). To parcel or not to parcel: Exploring the question, weighing the merits. *Structural Equation Modeling, 9*, 151–173.

McGuire, D. and Cseh, M. (2006). The development of the field of HRD: A Delphi study. *Journal of European Industrial Training, 30*, 653–667.

Messmann, G. and Mulder, R. H. (2012). Development of a measurement instrument for innovative work behaviour as a dynamic and context-bound construct. *Human Resource Development International, 15*, 43–59.

Messmann, G. and Mulder, R. H. (2014). Exploring the role of target specificity in the facilitation of vocational teachers' innovative work behaviour. *Journal of Occupational and Organizational Psychology, 87*, 80–101.

Muthén, L. K. and Muthén, B. O. (2013). *Mplus user's guide* (7th edn). Los Angeles, CA: Muthén and Muthén.

Raudenbush, S. W. and Bryk, A. S. (2002). *Hierarchical linear models* (2nd edn). Newbury Park, CA: Sage.

Rosseel, Y. (2012). lavaan: An R package for structural equation modeling. *Journal of Statistical Software, 48*, 1–36.

Spearman, C. (1904). General intelligence objectively determined and measured. *American Journal of Psychology, 15*, 201–293.

Tucker, L. R. and Lewis, C. (1973). A reliability coefficient for maximum likelihood factor analysis. *Psychometrika, 38*, 1–10.

Wright, S. (1921). Correlation and causation. *Journal of Agricultural Research, 20*, 557–585.

ANNOTATED FURTHER READING

Byrne, B. M. (2012). *Structural equation modeling with Mplus.* New York: Routledge. Introductory-level book illustrating the basic concepts of SEM using the Mplus software and covering factor, multilevel and longitudinal data analysis.

Hancock, G. R. and Mueller, R. O. (Eds.) (2013). *Structural equation modelling: A second course* (2nd edn). Charlotte, NC: Information Age Publishing. Intermediate-level book including chapters on current developments in SEM, for instance, exploratory factor analysis, measurement invariance analysis, multigroup analysis and Bayesian SEM.

Heck, R. H. and Thomas, S. L. (2009). *An introduction to multilevel modeling techniques* (2nd edn). New York: Routledge. Introductory-level book describing the use of multilevel modeling, including a comparison with ordinary multilevel regression analysis, longitudinal multilevel models and models with non-normal data.

20. Using systematic content analysis to establish theory–practice links in HRD literature
Rob F. Poell

SUMMARY

This chapter provides an overview of systematic content analysis (SCA) as an approach to analysing qualitative data. SCA aims to summarise the meaning of (textual) communication. The chapter looks briefly at its history, main characteristics, advantages and disadvantages. Its use is then illustrated presenting an empirical HRD study and discussed.

INTRODUCTION

Systematic content analysis (SCA) is a quantitative approach to the analysis of qualitative data, which aims to summarise the meaning of texts or other forms of communication. Bryman and Bell (2011, p. 302) offered the following definition: 'Content analysis is an approach to the analysis of documents and texts (which may be printed or visual) that seeks to quantify content in terms of predetermined categories, and in a systematic and replicable manner.' Placing more emphasis on its desired outcomes, Riffe, Lacy and Fico (1998, p. 22) defined quantitative content analysis as 'the systematic and replicable examination of symbols of communication, which have been assigned numeric values according to valid measurement rules using statistical methods, in order to describe communication, draw inferences about its meaning, or infer from the communication to its context, both of production and consumption'. SCA has a long history going back way before the behavioural and social sciences emerged in the first half of the last century.

In the context of this handbook on research methods in Human Resource Development (HRD), the purpose of this chapter is to provide an overview of SCA as a research method, or more specifically, as an approach to analysing qualitative data. After taking a brief look at the history of using SCA, its main characteristics will be described, together with its advantages and disadvantages. For illustration purposes, the chapter will also offer an account of how I used SCA with a number of colleagues in an empirical study into the theory–practice links emerging from the HRD literature.

A BRIEF HISTORY OF THE USE OF SCA

According to Krippendorff (2004, p. 3), 'empirical inquiries into the meaning of communications date back to theological studies in the late 1600s, when the Church found the printing of nonreligious materials to be a threat to its authority'. Although the notion of 'content analysis' was not used as a term in the English language until 1941 (Krippendorff, 2004, p. 3), its ways of summarising texts or other forms of communication in a systematic manner clearly have a long history. German sociologists, including Max Weber, hinted at the idea in the beginning of the 20th Century; however, no empirical studies were conducted at the time. This changed as Schools of Journalism were founded in the United States, leading to quantitative accounts and comparisons of newspaper articles.

The emergence of behavioural and social sciences in the 1920s and 1930s led to an increased acceptance of, and need for, empirical methods of doing research, thus paving the way for a proliferation of studies employing content analysis. Before World War II, content analysis was applied to propaganda messages in an attempt to isolate potential 'propagandists' and to prevent their ideas from spreading. After World War II, the use of content analysis further proliferated to fields as diverse as anthropology, psychology, history and computer science (among others). Today SCA has become a mainstay in the field of communications research and a supporting technique in many other disciplines (Krippendorff, 2004).

DESCRIPTION OF THE SCA METHOD

In a comparison of various approaches to SCA, Hsieh and Shannon (2005) concluded that they usually require a similar analytical process consisting of seven steps, which will be described and illustrated below.

Formulating the Research Question(s)

As in most other research methods, formulating an appropriate (set of) research question(s) is a crucial precondition before collecting and analysing data. If a research question is not clear or specific enough, one runs the risk of making inappropriate design decisions pertaining to sample selection, building a coding scheme, actual coding and analysing the results.

Wasti, Çakar and Poell (2008), for example, were interested in divergence versus convergence with respect to the underlying science and practice orientations in the US and European academic HRD literatures. This research question gave them a clear sense for their SCA of which journals and which articles to sample, which variables and categories to include in their coding scheme and which analytic steps to take in order to answer it (see below).

Selecting the Sample to be Analysed

Sampling is a set of techniques aimed at drawing conclusions about a larger population (of people, or in this case, of texts) without having to study the whole population. As most authors do, Bryman and Bell (2011, pp. 185–203) distinguish between probability and non-probability samples.

Probability samples are either randomly chosen from the population (simple random sample) or randomly selected groups within the population (stratified random sample). Alternatively, one may choose texts systematically using a random list (systematic sample; for example, picking every seventh entry from an unordered list) or work in several stages: first select randomly a number of relevant clusters within the population, from which texts are then sampled randomly (cluster sample). As these are all random samples, the assumption is that their contents can be generalised to a wider population with a limited amount of error.

Non-probability samples are less useful for statistical generalisation. They include choosing texts (or people) because they are available (convenience sample), using already selected texts to find other relevant texts (snowball sample) and non-randomly sampling a population in terms of the relative proportions of texts in different categories, for example, academic versus practitioner journals (quota sample) (Bryman and Bell, 2011, pp. 185–203).

To answer their research question (see above), Wasti et al. (2008) first selected the most relevant journals for inclusion in their sample: the two most established academic HRD journals on both sides of the Atlantic, *Human Resource Development Quarterly* (HRDQ) and *Human Resource Development International* (HRDI), and a larger number of both macro- and micro-oriented high-impact organisation studies journals published in the United States and Europe. They then decided to start sampling from January 1990 (marking the emergence of HRDQ as the first journal devoted specifically to HRD). Finally, article sampling was conducted by means of a keyword search in several major scholarly databases, focusing on those articles dealing primarily with HRD. Non-refereed articles (book reviews, letters to the editor or editorials) and those dealing with non-work settings were excluded. All authors checked the remaining articles' reference information to ensure content adequacy. This selection procedure combines the characteristics of a stratified random sample and a multistage cluster sample.

Defining the Categories to be Applied

In this step the variables that are central to the research question are operationalised. The key constructs are broken down into measurable units that can be coded by the raters at a later stage. One might go about this in a more inductive or deductive manner. If the variables have already been well researched it is more likely that a deductive approach to establishing coding categories will yield relevant results; in this case, existing literature will most often enable the researcher to put forward a useful set of (sub)categories for each variable. If, however, the topic to be investigated is under researched or even completely new, a more inductive approach will be much more in place; in that case, the researcher needs to engage in a process of open coding in one (sub)sample before being able to apply the ensuing list of 'sensitising' categories in a fuller sample.

Wasti et al. (2008) employed a mostly deductive approach. First, a number of general coding categories were selected: source (journal), date, authors' institutional affiliation (country/academic unit), primary HRD topic and single-country versus comparative study. Consistent with the research question, two main categories were chosen: the article's underlying practice and science orientations.

Practice orientation consisted of many different coding subcategories, only one of which will be illustrated here because of space limitations. So, for example, to evaluate the adoption of a humanist versus a managerialist position in an article, raters were to code whether a 'soft' or a 'hard' perspective was put forward with respect to people. If an article emphasised the quantitative, calculative and business strategic aspects of developing the headcount resource, this was considered indicative of a hard approach. If the article endorsed employees as valued assets, a source of competitive advantage through their commitment, adaptability and high quality, it was coded as adopting a soft approach. Some articles were expected to show indicators of both perspectives.

Science orientation also comprised many subcategories, intended to evaluate articles' methodological approach and rigour. For instance, each article was coded for its primary research strategy, broadly speaking differentiating between non-empirical and empirical pieces, and among the latter group, between qualitative versus quantitative strategies. One aspect of methodological rigour involved was authors' concern for construct validity, which was evaluated by reference to whether reliability and validity information was provided regarding the measurement of key constructs.

Outlining the Coding Process and the Coder Training

After the aforementioned key decisions about texts to be sampled and coding categories to be included have been taken, in line with the research question(s), the coding process can be further outlined. Essentially, this involves the development of a coding schedule and a coding manual (Bryman and Bell, 2011, pp. 311–315). The coding schedule is a form (later often turned into a spreadsheet type of file) into which all the data (i.e., codes) relating to the relevant (sub)categories are entered. The coding manual contains the instructions to coders that specify which codes can be entered for each (sub)category and when to choose which code. The aim of a coding manual is to provide enough detailed information about each of the (sub)categories and possible codes, so that the latter can be assigned consistently. It is usually still necessary to provide coder training to make sure that all coders interpret the (sub)categories and possible codes in the same way and as intended by the researchers. Inter-rater reliability needs to be established and guaranteed before the actual coding process can start.

The coding manual in the Wasti et al. (2008) study ran to a 13-page document outlining the codes to be attributed to 29 different subcategories. While some subcategories had only two possible codes to be assigned, others had up to 13. Before the main sample of 267 articles could be coded, however, two research assistants coded eight articles selected to represent different journal origins and types; and so did all three authors. This served as a training session for the research assistants but also allowed the authors to identify patterns in any discrepancies. The coding manual was jointly revised to reflect shared agreement regarding the meaning of codes for each subcategory. Then, to assess the reliability of the coding system, 30 articles were chosen at random as a pilot sample and each article was coded independently by both research assistants and at least one author. The codes for the 30 articles were compared and the per cent agreement was calculated for each subcategory as an assessment of inter-rater reliability (Riffe et al., 1998).

Implementing the Coding Process

Most of the work usually goes into the actual coding process, although a good coding manual and good coder training can help immensely to speed things up. If all previous steps have been taken diligently, and preparation in terms of research questions, sampling and coding categories has been dealt with meticulously, the actual coding process is a matter of systematically applying the coding manual to the sample of texts, making sure all codes are entered into the right spot within the coding schedule.

For the Wasti et al. (2008) study, before actual coding could start some final decisions had to be taken on the basis of the assessed inter-rater reliability in the 30-article pilot sample. Although per cent agreement was acceptable (> 70 per cent) for the vast majority (25 out of the 29) of coding subcategories, agreement was marginally lower on four of them. The authors and the research assistants discussed all discrepancies at length, particularly focusing on the four problematic dimensions. After finalising the coding guidelines, the remainder of all articles were randomly distributed to one of the two coders. Each article was then coded independently, and a final data file was compiled by merging the two separate sets of article codes.

Determining Trustworthiness

The key to ensuring trustworthiness really is in all the steps taken before. In doing SCA, regardless of the nature of one's research question(s), broadly speaking internal validity comes from explicitly basing one's coding subcategories and codes on previous literature and discussions with experts in the field; external validity comes from employing a probability sampling strategy to the best extent possible; and reliability comes from having well-trained coders use a meticulously prepared coding manual. There are obviously more specific criteria by which trustworthiness can be established as well as other ways to improve it; however, in the context of this chapter, there is no scope for a full account of these.

Although Wasti et al. (2008) did all of the above, there were still some limitations that might lessen the trustworthiness of the outcomes in some respects. One of them concerns the fact that the European HRD articles in their study turned out to be predominantly comprised of scholars from the United Kingdom. As previous reviews of the European management and social sciences literature had typically observed that the United Kingdom forms a unique cluster in terms of research paradigm, distinct from both the United States and Continental Europe, all the analyses were rerun across these three clusters. What emerged was a similarity between the

United Kingdom and the Continent with respect to their practice orientations, while the United States and the Continent clustered closer in terms of their science orientations. These generalisability limitations may arise from the fact that only English language articles were sampled, which could be resolved by expanded sampling of journals or topics in the future.

Analysing the Results of the Coding Process

The final step in doing a SCA is analysing the data entered into the coding schedule (usually a data file for statistical analysis). The exact types of analysis and how to go about them are obviously a function of the research question(s) that started the process in the first place. Descriptive and inferential statistics can normally be applied quite well to typical data files from a SCA, while for some more advanced procedures other ways of data collection might be needed. Ultimately, the findings that come out of the analysis need to do justice to the text materials that were sampled and then coded. As mentioned at the outset of this chapter, SCA aims to summarise the meaning of texts (or other forms of communication); hence its main added value lies in bringing back vast numbers of text pages to a meaningful overview of core themes. Comparisons and correlations among various themes from the texts can contribute to an even better understanding, provided they follow logically from the research questions.

Wasti et al. (2008) used simple frequency calculations and cross-tabulations of variables to answer their research questions. While space prevents a more detailed account of the findings in the present chapter, the main conclusions from their SCA were as follows. In contrast to its European counterpart, the US literature on HRD was observed to be more practice oriented while at the same time adhering firmly to the natural science paradigm. The European HRD literature showed a greater likelihood of endorsing critical perspectives and more theoretical studies as well as a smaller concern with adhering to methodological standards derived from the natural science paradigm and with providing prescriptive conclusions.

Research Validity and Caveats for SCA

Some remarks have already been made in the above about validity issues associated with SCA. When the seven steps advocated by Hsieh and Shannon (2005) are followed as outlined in the first part of this chapter, SCA will achieve high levels of internal and external validity. Nevertheless, several potential disadvantages of doing a SCA can be distinguished besides its obvious benefits (Bryman and Bell, 2011, pp. 318–321). Both categories will be elaborated upon below.

To start with the advantages of SCA, not only does it allow for summarising large amounts of text into a manageable number of topics, it can also provide information about their relative importance (based on frequencies). The fact that SCA uses explicit sampling and coding procedures makes it into a highly transparent research method amenable to replication and (longitudinal) follow-up studies. Moreover, SCA is a flexible research method that can be used for a broad array of unstructured types of information. Finally, it is a largely unobtrusive measure that will allow researchers to derive information even about organisational actors that are hard to get access to using other ways.

Nevertheless, there are also some disadvantages associated with the use of a SCA. Of course, the quality of a SCA ultimately depends on the quality of its contents, which strengthens the importance of good sampling criteria. Another potential problem is in devising a coding manual that is as independent as possible from personal interpretations by the coders. This issue plays out all the more when attempting to code for inferred meanings rather than objective content, and it also points to the relevance of good coder training. A further limitation is that SCA cannot very well provide answers to why?-type questions as opposed to what?- and how?-type questions. Finally, there is a risk of SCA becoming too a-theoretical (i.e., data driven) when coding categories are not derived from previous literature at least in part. These potential caveats should be taken into account when deciding on whether or not to employ a SCA (Bryman and Bell, 2011, pp. 318–321).

PERSONAL EXPERIENCE USING SCA: EXPLORING THEORY–PRACTICE LINKS IN HRD LITERATURE

The 267 articles included in the Wasti et al.(2008) study constituted only the academic journals part of the total SCA. Another 312 articles were sampled from HRD practitioner journals from both sides of the Atlantic using the same methods as the ones described above (Poell, 2009).[1]

The starting point for including both academic and practitioner journals was my observation that HRD as a field seems to find itself caught in between two different logics. On the one hand, the requirements of practical relevance to organisations force HRD to focus on developing applied knowledge directly useful in organisational practice. On the other hand, the need for HRD to be regarded as a serious academic discipline drives researchers to producing context-independent and generalised knowledge.

As a result, HRD practitioners complain about the lack of utility of HRD research, whereas HRD researchers sneer at practitioners for ignoring the results of their empirical studies. According to Cohen (2007), researchers seek general explanations for everyday phenomena that occur, whereas practitioners look for practical solutions to their own daily problems. As a result, the worlds of researchers and practitioners are not well attuned, which may lead to a disconnect between theory and practice.

Although this theory–practice gap has been studied in various fields related to HRD, review studies about the development of HRD as an academic discipline have paid little attention to the practical relevance of the academic work in HRD (Poell, 2009). For a practice-based discipline like HRD, it is vital to gain insight into the extent to which theory and practice are linked. Hence, this particular study aimed to show how HRD research and practice (fail to) interact in their quest to produce relevant HRD knowledge.

Anderson, Herriot and Hodgkinson (2001) distinguished among four types of science, based on the two dimensions of practical relevance and methodological rigour: pragmatic science (high on relevance and rigour), popularist science (high on relevance, low on rigour), pedantic science (low on relevance, high on rigour) and puerile science (low on relevance and rigour). In their own field of study (industrial, work and organisational psychology), they observed a shift from pragmatic science to pedantic and popularist science onto puerile science.

Applying the model developed by Anderson et al. (2001) to the HRD field, the following research questions were investigated in this particular study:

1. To what extent are HRD articles published in academic and practitioner journals indicative of pragmatic, popularist, pedantic or puerile science?
2. To what extent is the type of science related to various theory–practice links within an article?

Theoretical Framework of the Study

Anderson et al. (2001) developed a fourfold typology of research, based on the two dimensions of practical relevance and methodological rigour, as indicated in Figure 20.1. This typology will be elaborated upon below.

The first type is referred to as pragmatic science, which is high on both relevance and rigour. Research studies belonging to this type of science investigate practically relevant issues in a methodologically rigorous way. Besides Anderson et al. (2001), Tranfield, Denyer and Smart (2003) also

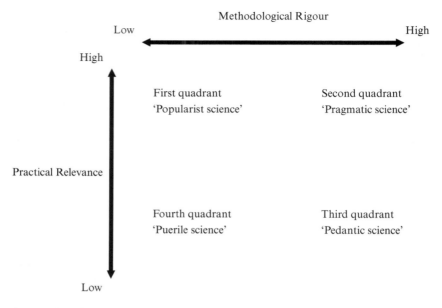

Source: Based on Anderson et al. (2001).

Figure 20.1 Four types of research

deemed this way of doing research to be the preferred one in scientific disciplines. All academic studies should therefore fall into this category, according to Anderson et al. (2001).

The second type of research pictured in Figure 20.1 contains so-called popularist science, which is high on relevance but low on rigour. The topics investigated in this type of studies are important to practice; however, their lack of methodological rigour implies that the findings presented should be viewed as unreliable.

In the third quadrant of Figure 20.1, studies are represented with low relevance and high rigour, resulting in pedantic science. The designs used in this type of research are demanding and analytically complex; however, the practical relevance of the topic that these studies deal with is either not clear or plain absent.

The fourth type of science is labelled as puerile science, characterised by low practical relevance as well as low methodological rigour. The topics studied here are irrelevant to practice and the findings are unreliable at the same time. According to Anderson et al. (2001), this type of studies has a detrimental effect both on practice and on the reputation of scientific research.

As indicated above, Anderson et al. (2001) observed a shift from pragmatic science to pedantic and popularist science onto puerile science. According to them, the resulting divergence between academics and practitioners will likely lead to irrelevant theory as well as untheorised and invalid practice. Their plea is for more synergy between practical relevance and methodological rigour to reduce the theory–practice gap.

The literature is clear about the criteria required for sound scientific research, and there is consensus about the desired dominance of the pragmatic type of science as well (Anderson et al., 2001; Tranfield et al., 2003). There are obvious advantages of linking theory closer to practice (Rynes, Bartunek and Daft, 2001). For example, managerial decisions are better if they are based on the most recent scientific insights (Rousseau and McCarthy, 2007). Also, the best academic results are obtained if researchers sustain the answers to their scientific questions with empirical data (Rynes, McNatt and Bretz, 1999). Nevertheless, the academic world takes an ambiguous stance to the desirability of academic–practitioner collaborations (Rynes et al., 2001). There is fear that such collaborations might narrow down the academic output to limited, short-term and commercial studies (Murphy and Saal, 1990).

Based on normative idea(l)s, in the absence of previous empirical research into this matter, it is hypothesised in the present study that HRD articles in academic journals will be mostly indicative of pragmatic science and HRD articles in practitioner journals of popularist science. Furthermore, we expect the type of science to which an HRD article belongs to be related to various theory–practice links in the article.

Research Methods

Procedures were conducted as described in the Wasti et al. (2008) study. A total of 579 HRD articles published in 20 HRD and mainstream (Management and Organisation, Organisational Behaviour, Human Resource Management) academic and practitioner journals between 1990 and 2003 were content analysed. Table 20.1 presents the number of articles per journal included in the analysis.

To represent the academic literature, in addition to the above mentioned HRDQ and HRDI, two specifically learning and development-oriented SSCI-accredited journals were included: *Adult Education Quarterly* from the United States and *Management Learning* from Europe. Also, both macro- and micro-oriented organisation studies (OS) journals published in the United States (n=6) and Europe (n=6) were selected, as Table 20.1 shows.

The four practitioner journals included in the analysis were two HRD-oriented journals, *Training and Development* from the United States and

Table 20.1   Journals selected for the study and number of HRD articles included

Journals	Number of Articles
* Academic	308 ****
– Human Resource Development	176 –
• Human Resource Development Quarterly	105
• Human Resource Development International	31
• Adult Education Quarterly	7
• Management Learning	33
– Organisation Studies	43 –
• Academy of Management Journal	11
• Journal of Management Studies	14
• Administrative Science Quarterly	9
• Organisation Studies	9
– Work and Organisational Psychology	30 –
• Journal of Applied Psychology	15
• Journal of Occupational and Organizational Psychology	3
• Personnel Psychology	10
• Journal of Organizational Behavior	1
• Organizational Behavior and Human Decision Processes	1
– Human Resource Management	59 –
• Personnel Review	34
• International Journal of Human Resource Management	10
• Human Resource Management	15
* Practitioner Journals	271 ****
– Human Resource Development	257 –
• Training and Development	175
• Personnel Management	82
– Organisation Studies	14 –
• Management Today	11
• Across the Board	3
Total	579 ****

Personnel Management from Europe, as well as two OS-oriented journals, *Across the Board* from the United States and *Management Today* from Europe. These journals were selected based on their inclusion in previous review studies (e.g., Wasti and Robert, 2004) and consultation with colleagues.

As for measures, *practical relevance* was deemed low if an article did not (or only superficially) pay attention to prescriptive implications of the findings; it was scored as high if the article devoted at least a separate paragraph to these. *Methodological rigour* was measured using five indicators: a non-speculative research strategy, random or population sampling, specification of response rate, attention to reliability and/or validity, and clear procedures for data analysis. *Theory–practice links* were operationalised using five dichotomous indicators for practitioner journals (interviews with academics, explicit references to specific organisations providing 'best practices', to textbooks, to academic journals, and to universities or the content of academic programmes) and five dichotomous indicators for academic journals (explicit references to specific organisations providing 'best practices', to specific companies, to practitioners, to consultants and to practitioner journals).

Results

Analysis for the first hypothesis was conducted using cross-tabulations. Results (displayed in Table 20.2) show that 32 per cent of all 308 HRD articles published in academic journals qualified as 'pedantic science' and 31 per cent as 'pragmatic science' ('puerile' 22 and 'popularist' 16). In terms of the 271 HRD articles published in practitioner journals, 64 per cent qualified as 'popularist science' and 36 per cent as 'puerile science' (none were 'pragmatic' or 'pedantic'). The 'academic' part of the first hypothesis, therefore, needs to be rejected, whereas the 'practitioner' part is supported.

The second hypothesis was analysed using Spearman correlations. In terms of the five indicators for theory–practice links, 43 per cent of all 308 HRD articles published in academic journals showed none at all, 43 per cent had one (predominantly references to practitioner journals),

Table 20.2   HRD articles rated pragmatic, popularist, pedantic and puerile science (n=579)

Type of Science	Percentage of Articles in	
	Academic Journals	Practitioner Journals
Pragmatic	31	0
Popularist	16	64
Pedantic	32	0
Puerile	22	36
Total	100	100

Table 20.3   Percentages of HRD articles containing theory–practice links (n=579)

Number of Links	Articles Published in	
	Academic Journals	Practitioner Journals
Zero	43	63
One	43	23
Two	11	12
Three	4	2
Four	0	1
Five	0	0
Total	100	100

11 per cent had two, 4 per cent had three and none had four or five. As for the five indicators for practice–theory links, 63 per cent of all 271 HRD articles published in practitioner journals showed none whatsoever, 23 per cent had one (mostly references to best practices), 12 per cent had two, 2 per cent had three, 1 per cent had four and none had five, as Table 20.3 indicates. No correlations could be established between type of science and theory–practice links either for academic journals (p=.43) or for practitioner journals (p=.50). Therefore, the second hypothesis was rejected.

Conclusions

The above findings provide, all things considered, strong indications of a disconnect between practice and academia in the HRD field. The field of HRD, however, is not alone in this respect. Anderson et al. (2001) made similar observations about the discipline of industrial, work and organisational psychology; Cohen (2007) concluded the same about the field of Human Resource Management; and Rynes et al. (2001) did likewise about the broad management discipline. Apparently, in many social sciences the studies that are conducted do not combine high practical relevance with methodological rigour. Anderson et al. (2001) even saw a shift occurring from pragmatic science to pedantic and popularist science onto puerile science, that is, away from the ideal towards far less desirable ways of doing research. The data set used for the present study does not allow for any longitudinal analyses; however, further research should investigate whether a similar shift may be occurring in the field of HRD.

Contrary to expectation, no relationships were found between the type of science and the theory–practice links in an article. Apparently, although academics and practitioners do collaborate in producing knowledge (Rynes et al., 2001), this has no bearing on the ways in which practical relevance and methodological rigour are sought. One explanation for this finding is that academic literature is rather ambiguous about the sheer desirability of bringing together theory and practice (Murphy and Saal, 1990). Shrivastava and Mitroff (1984) offered another explanation: in their view, the paucity of links between theory and practice is down to different ways of thinking about what constitutes knowledge between academics and practitioners. Cohen (2007) seemed to allude to these differences as well when she referred to researchers seeking general explanations for everyday phenomena and practitioners looking for practical solutions to particular problems.

DISCUSSION

The empirical study presented in the previous section illustrates the potential power of carrying out a SCA. Thousands of pages of journal articles can be summarised into a manageable number of tables, which allow for scientifically and practically relevant conclusions to be drawn. Obviously, a great deal of work goes into conducting a decent SCA, especially in the preparation of the sample and the coding manual. A certain inner desire to do things systematically is a definite plus for a researcher contemplating the use of a SCA. On the other hand, the requirements of reliability urge the researcher to be able to work with (other) raters in terms of drawing up the best possible coding manual and engaging in the actual coding process. Potential rewards come in the shape of elegant Tables containing enormous amounts of work executed diligently but presented in a heavily stripped down yet meaningful summary.

Two recent examples of SCA in the field of HRD illustrate the potential of this method to summarise large amounts of relevant information elegantly. Jeung, Yoon, Park and Jo (2011) did so by selecting the top 20 Academy of HRD journal articles most frequently cited in research articles published in other journals. This non-probability sample was used to identify how HRD research had contributed to knowledge building in related disciplines. Based on the analysis, the authors were able to put forward three core research themes in which this was the case: (1) training transfer and evaluation; (2) learning in organisations; and (3) knowledge sharing/creation. Compared to the SCA conducted by Wasti et al. (2008), which attempted to capture all relevant HRD research published in a particular time frame, Jeung et al. (2011) deliberately chose a limited number of high-impact texts to draw conclusions about the field as a whole.

The second recent example (Sun and Wang, 2013) investigated HRD research on the basis of citations to papers published in the four Academy of HRD journals since 2005. Google Scholar was used to collect data and then compare these journals on the basis of commonly reported SSCI indices (e.g., h-factor). The authors conclude that HRD journals have made considerable research impact, although there is still substantial scope for quality improvement. This Sun and Wang (2013) study is different from Jeung et al. (2011) in that it focuses on citations and analyses quality through generally accepted indices. Compared to Wasti et al. (2008), Sun and Wang (2013) have a rather more limited sample; yet they usefully show different aspects related to the status of the field.

These three relatively recent examples (Sun and Wang 2013; Jeung et al. 2011; Wasti et al. 2008) each make different choices in designing and conducting SCA; thereby they manage to paint different yet complementary pictures of where HRD is at in terms of its academic stature. Hopefully readers will be inspired by this chapter to build on the aforementioned examples and to further enrich the field of HRD through SCA.

NOTE

1.   The study reported in this chapter was funded in part by a UFHRD research honorarium. The author would also like to thank Arzu Wasti, Bram Metsers, Nigar Demircan Çakar and Lutz Remer for their contributions.

REFERENCES

Anderson, N., Herriot P. and Hodgkinson G. P. (2001). The practitioner–researcher divide in industrial, work and organizational (IWO) psychology: Where are we now, and where do we go from here? *Journal of Occupational and Organizational Psychology, 74*, 391–411.
Bryman, A. and Bell, E. (2011). *Business Research Methods* (3rd edn). Oxford: Oxford University Press.
Cohen, D. J. (2007). The very separate worlds of academic and practitioner publications in human resource management: Reasons for the divide and concrete solutions for bridging the gap. *Academy of Management Journal, 50*, 1013–1019.
Hsieh, H. and Shannon, S. E. (2005). Three approaches to qualitative content analysis. *Qualitative Health Research, 15*(9), 1277–1288.
Jeung, C. W., Yoon, H. J., Park, S. and Jo, S. J. (2011). The contributions of human resource development research across disciplines: A citation and content analysis. *Human Resource Development Quarterly, 22*(1), pp. 87–109.
Krippendorff, K. (2004). *Content Analysis: An Introduction to Its Methodology* (2nd edn). Thousand Oaks, CA: Sage.
Murphy, K. and Saal, F. E. (1990). Psychology in organizations: Integrating science and practice. In K. Murphy and F. E. Saal (Eds.), *Series in Applied Psychology* (pp. 49–66). Hillsdale, NJ: Erlbaum.

Poell, R. F. (2009). Are practice and academia in HRD disconnected? Evidence from a content analysis of 579 journal articles. Paper presented at the Tenth International Conference on HRD Research and Practice across Europe, Newcastle, UK, 10–12 June.

Riffe, D., Lacy, S. and Fico, F. (1998). *Analysing Media Messages: Using Quantitative Content Analysis in Research*. Mahwah, NJ: Erlbaum.

Rousseau, D. M., and McCarthy, S. (2007). Educating managers from an evidence-based perspective. *Academy of Management Learning and Education, 6*, 84–101.

Rynes, S. L., Bartunek, J. M. and Daft, R. L. (2001). Across the great divide: Knowledge creation and transfer between practitioners and academics. *Academy of Management Journal, 44*, 340–355.

Rynes, S. L., McNatt, D. B. and Bretz, R. D. (1999). Academic research in organisations: Inputs, process and outputs. *Personnel Psychology, 52*, 869–898.

Shrivastava, P. and Mitroff, I. I. (1984). Enhancing organizational research utilization: The role of decision makers' assumptions. *Academy of Management Review, 9*, 18–26.

Sun, J. and Wang, G. G. (2013). How is HRD doing in research and publications? An assessment of journals by AHRD (2005–2011). *European Journal of Training and Development, 37*(8), 696–712.

Tranfield, D., Denyer, D. and Smart, P. (2003). Towards a methodology for developing evidence-informed management knowledge by means of systematic review. *British Journal of Management, 14*, 207–222.

Wasti, S. A., Çakar, N. D. and Poell, R. F. (2008). Oceans and notions apart? An analysis of the U.S. and European human resource development literature. *International Journal of Human Resource Management, 19*(12), 2155–2170.

Wasti, S. A. and Robert, C. A. (2004). Out of touch? An evaluation of the correspondence between academic and practitioner concerns in IHRM. In J. L. C. Cheng and M. Hitt (Eds.), *Managing Multinationals in a Knowledge Economy: Economics, Culture and Human Resources* (pp. 207–239). London: JAI Press.

ANNOTATED FURTHER READING

Hsieh, H. and Shannon, S. E. (2005). Three approaches to qualitative content analysis. *Qualitative Health Research, 15*(9), 1277–1288. This article delineates analytic procedures specific to three SCA approaches: conventional, directed and summative approaches.

Krippendorff, K. (2004). *Content Analysis: An Introduction to Its Methodology* (2nd edn). Thousand Oaks, CA: Sage. A theoretical as well as practical introduction to SCA, dealing with its history, core principles, conceptual and methodological aspects, and practical protocols.

Riffe, D., Lacy, S. and Fico, F. (1998). *Analysing Media Messages: Using Quantitative Content Analysis in Research*. Mahwah, NJ: Erlbaum. Another useful handbook, which provides step-by-step instruction on conducting SCA and looks specifically at issues around measurement, sampling, reliability, data analysis, validity and technology.

PART IV

METHODOLOGICAL CHALLENGES

21. The competing interests of paradigm and praxis in critical HRD research: incorporating quantitative methods to enact critical practice
Jamie L. Callahan and Gary Connor

SUMMARY

In this chapter, we challenge the hegemonic notion that the underlying values of critical paradigms necessitate qualitative research. We argue that a solitary focus on epistemological underpinnings is counterproductive to achieving critical social transformation. We offer an example of the interplay of quantitative and qualitative research toward addressing a Critical Human Resource Development (CHRD) issue.

INTRODUCTION

H. L. Mencken is reputed to have said, 'There is always an easy solution to every human problem – neat, plausible, and wrong' (Bartleby.com, n.d.). Current thinking with regard to the conduct of critical (Human Resource Development – HRD) research is that the underlying philosophy of critical theory necessitates qualitative research – a simple response to what is rarely a simple issue. Research is not a Weberian ideal type; from the investigative impulse through to the implementation of the research project, the reality of engaging in research is complex. HRD research done from a critical perspective may be even more complex because accomplishing its aims of social change may require dissonance with its informing philosophical foundations.

A critical theory perspective of HRD, called Critical HRD (CHRD), is beginning to occupy a significant place in theory, practice and research associated with the field. To address this emerging interest, HRD scholars are beginning to question *how* to conduct CHRD research. Although research using a critical theory perspective in general has been explored (e.g., Kincheloe and McLaren, 1994), the field of HRD has not substantively explored what it means to conduct CHRD research.

CHRD emerged from other fields applying a critical theory perspective, such as critical management studies (CMS) and critical pedagogy (CP). Sambrook (2004) notes that the critical component within HRD calls for 'challenging contemporary practices, exposing assumptions, revealing illusions and questioning' tradition (p. 614). But HRD professionals face a challenge in that they serve both 'dominant social structures (usually organisations) and the individuals within those structures' (Callahan, 2007, p. 78). Thus, HRD scholars must be creative with the ways in which they ply their trade through both research and practice. And it is this distinction that will be addressed in this chapter. We contend that the nature of CHRD research differs depending upon whether the researcher applies the critical concept to the 'paradigm' of critical research or to the 'purpose' of the research outcomes.

In this chapter, we challenge the taken for granted notion that the underlying values of critical paradigms necessitate qualitative research, making qualitative methods the dominant technique used to explore critical concepts. We argue that a solitary focus on these epistemological underpinnings of critical theory may be counterproductive to achieving the ends of critical social transformation. To begin, we explore what CHRD is that it can be studied and how epistemology relates to CHRD research. Because we challenge the hegemonic use of qualitative methods in CHRD research, we also offer an example of the interplay of quantitative and qualitative research toward addressing a CHRD issue. We conclude with recommendations for engaging in CHRD research.

CRITICAL RESEARCH METHODS – PARADIGM OR PRAXIS?

Guba and Lincoln (2005) argue that critical theory, like positivism, is a paradigm that has particular affiliated epistemologies and methodologies. A researcher using a critical paradigm is a 'criticalist' (Kincheloe and McLaren, 1994) whose work serves as social or cultural criticism. Criticalists contend that such work is necessarily dialogic and dialectical (Guba and Lincoln, 2005) and, as such, inherently qualitative in nature. Indeed, some would even suggest that quantitative techniques are antithetical to the underlying values of critical theory (Kincheloe and McLaren, 1994).

Others (e.g., Alvesson and Willmott, 1996), however, contend that critical theory is inherently interparadigmatic and cannot be reduced to a singular paradigm. Clegg (2005) suggests that creating a narrative of 'quantitative is bad and qualitative is good' for critical research is antithetical to the aims of 'challenging dominant power-knowledges' (p. 418). The aim of critical research is to transform the power inequalities of social structures through advocacy and emancipation (Guba and Lincoln, 2005). To do so, 'Critical Theorists . . . have kept alive the Enlightenment idea that critical reason can be mobilised to transform society' (Alvesson and Willmott, 1996, p. 60). Historically, radical change in society, to include civil rights and gender equity policies, has been enacted in response to evidence that is both qualitative AND quantitative in nature (Clegg, 2005).

The claim that quantitative data and analyses are based wholly in assumptions of objectivity and positivism (and, therefore, cannot be used within a critical perspective project) privileges paradigm over praxis. Such a claim confounds epistemology with technique. Frankenstein (1992) notes that, 'People's *misconception* [emphasis added] that statistical knowledge is objective and value-free closes off challenges to such data' (p. 251). While much quantitative research is grounded in the values of positivism, there is a rich history of quantitative research supporting the values of critical theory (Miner-Rubino and Jayaratne, 2007). A critical purpose can be achieved with any number of techniques for collecting 'data'; it is time for the field to explore how quantitative (and qualitative) methods can be employed to enact a CHRD.

CHRD

In one of the earliest presentations proposing a CHRD, Elliott and Turnbull (2002) challenged the performative emphasis of the field at the conference for the primary professional association for HRD scholars, the Academy of Human Resource Development. Rigg et al. (2007) argued that HRD has typically been seen as 'technocratic development of effective practitioners' (p. 3) whereby the economic desires of the organisation take precedence over the needs of the people who work in the organisations. They highlight the underlying assumption that workers are resources 'from whom more value can be extracted' (p. 4) if they are developed and, as an added benefit, those workers become more adept at exploiting other resources (to include people). In other words, traditional HRD tends toward the notion of humans as capital (i.e. human capital theory), in whom investment is warranted because a well-trained workforce is perceived as more economically productive (Baptiste, 2001).

And, yet, Trehan and Rigg (2011) note that traditional HRD 'has often failed to supply the performative promises' (p. 277). CHRD scholars have begun to challenge the perspective that the value of the field lies in its ability to deliver increased performance for organisational gain. Others (e.g., Perriton, 2009) have suggested that the desire to appeal to dominant organisational interests through the use of 'business cases' results in the reproduction of inequalities instead of the desired social changes. Rigg et al. (2007) contend that a CHRD orientation is necessary to challenge assumptions of power in organisations and learning contexts, and to enact social change.

To do this, CHRD professionals must begin by questioning assumptions. Callahan (2007) argues that the essence of CHRD is to question whose interests are being served by their interventions, while recognising that they serve two masters – both the organisation and the individual. By extension, we contend, the reality is that HRD professionals serve stakeholders even beyond an organisation and the individuals that comprise the organisation in which our interventions are applied. A CHRD would uncover biases and assumptions associated with institutional sexism, racism, ableism, heteronormativism and other 'isms' that privilege some and oppress others. Accomplishing this, though, requires openness to employing whatever enquiry methods will achieve an outcome of democracy, justice, equity, freedom, self-determination and empowerment.

CHRD RESEARCH

If one focuses on the practical end of the research (i.e., how it can be used to actually transform social structures), then the *means* of enlightening those who can make productive changes to structures of oppression is secondary. Because HRD is an applied field, it is important to engage 'critical constructionist' (Callahan, 2007) techniques that privilege critical action. In other words, the purpose of the research is critical, although the methods may be contrary to the paradigmatic perspectives of many critical scholars.

Quantitative research has been used effectively for both policy and cultural change by revealing and documenting social inequalities (Harnois, 2013). Quantifying these inequalities can be powerful, because, '[w]hen most people hear these statistics, they are in some way affected. And more often than not, these numbers convey in stark terms the social injustices' (Miner-Rubino and Jayaratne, 2007, p. 294) that confront the oppressed.

Because this critical purpose of quantification is not commonly accepted in CHRD research, we will offer an example of a study that incorporated both qualitative and quantitative analytic methods to expose power differences and create a more equitable evaluation within a learning environment.

CRITICAL CONSTRUCTIONIST RESEARCH: A MIXED METHODS EXAMPLE

There is a taken for granted assumption in the vast majority of UK business schools that students are assessed via a written format only. Verbal assessments are generally restricted for use in subjects such as language, medicine, architecture and law; some business schools across Europe are known to utilise verbal exams, but they are the exception, not the rule. Yet, research undertaken at a Higher Education (HE) institute in the UK identified that international (non-UK/EU students) performed better in verbal exams than they did in written exams. Results of the study we describe here showed that international student assessment scores for verbal examinations showed no significant difference from home/EU students' scores, while written reports and written exams were significantly lower than home/EU students' scores in a repeated measures Analysis of Variance (ANOVA) between the two groups in the three assessment types (F1.9.100.4=3.27, p=0.044). These quantitative data suggested that, contrary to popular belief, international students performed better when given the opportunity to have a conversation about their knowledge. Thus, in this section, we explore the nature of this research project that employed both qualitative and quantitative methods with a CHRD intent to enact change in university assessment methods to avoid marginalising international students.

The example we present here has implications for HRD, and CHRD, on several levels. Just as organisations engage in evaluation of employees, so these assessment mechanisms for graduate students can (and perhaps should, we argue) emulate more organic processes of evaluation that occur in the workplace. In many cases, graduate students in the field of HRD either have work experience or are currently working adults, taking their degree part-time. A graduate degree may serve as an intensive training and development programme for organisations; in some cases, organisations will pay tuition and fees for an employee to attend courses. Thus, these programmes represent an extension of the various means of operationalising training and development for an organisation. Because this study highlights how evaluation mechanisms can result in unfair disadvantage to certain groups, the study may be instructive to CHRD professionals.

The module leader conducted an analysis of his students' mark sheets for those who had failed, under-performed or excelled in the written assessments typically used in the majority of Human Resource Management modules. This relatively informal observation revealed that students with surnames that appeared to be of a non-EU or non-UK origin had in the majority failed or under-performed. Many of those who had failed came knocking on the office door; the majority of these students were originally from India, Africa and China. Discussions with these students revealed that they too had expected to perform better in assessment, particularly the written exam. These individual meetings reinforced the perception that the students had more than enough knowledge, acumen and academic ability to have passed the module assessments easily. In general, they were able to discuss the subject to a standard expected at a master's level, but were unable to communicate their knowledge in the written form in an examination environment. This experience served as the investigative impulse to devise a formal study that combined qualitative and quantitative methods to find an assessment modality that more adequately reflected the knowledge, skills and abilities of students from all backgrounds.

The first step taken to systematically explore this apparent lack of relationship between ability and performance was to hold interviews with stakeholders (students, colleagues and administrators) regarding the possibility of introducing verbal exams. The vast majority of students and staff clearly preferred written assessments and were strongly opposed to verbal exams. From the perspective of a pure criticalist, the preferences from the qualitative voices of the marginalised other are likely to have had a significant impact on any future assessment choice, and verbal exams would not have been pursued. However, the quantitative data seemed to suggest that a trial of verbal exams was warranted.

Armed with data analysed through written assessment mechanisms (written report and exam) across two groups of students (home/EU and international), and the resulting evidence that verbal testing could likely be fairer, the module leader approached the administration and gained authorisation to change the format of assessments to include verbal examinations. Briefly, a 10-minute verbal exam and an in-class one hour written exam were substituted for a three-hour written exam in a HRM postgraduate module. The 10 minutes was decided upon due to it taking 10 minutes to say what can be written in 60 minutes. The verbal exam was replacing a section of the written exam whereby students were given 60 minutes to write their answers. A sample of past written exam papers were analysed by simply timing how long it took to read what had been written. The reading out loud was done in a manner meant to replicate how a student would verbally have answered (i.e., with gaps for thinking, pausing and the occasional silence).

The verbal exam was designed to replicate a typical workplace situation; for that purpose, the exam was designed to be interactive. The examiner can stop the student from digressing, ask additional questions and confirm meaning of responses. The exam is intended to measure the student's subject acumen, not their exam technique.

Specific learning outcomes are aligned to the verbal exam; students must prepare themselves for a range of questions covering these subject matters. However, the verbal exam is designed such that the examiner asks only one key question; the student at the commencement of the exam chooses this blindly. The marking criteria follow those of written assessments, allowing for consistency in student exam preparation.

In addition to students academically preparing themselves, the verbal exam is a catalyst for improving much needed business oral communication skills (e.g., Applebome, 1995). Furthermore, the exam adds to the list of social settings required to increase their level of transferring skills (Bridges, 1993). Finally, business graduates require experience and instruction in verbal communication to avoid being disadvantaged in a range of business settings, for example negotiation, informal conversations, team meetings and promoting their own strengths (Freihat and Al-Machzoomi, 2012).

For the purpose of analysis, students were categorised as Home/EU or international, in line with student records held by the university. After the assessments had taken place, detailed SPSS analysis of written and verbal assessment results was performed. Results clearly identified a significant relationship between demographic of student and mode of assessment – marginalised student populations fared significantly better when the verbal exam was incorporated into the assessment, resulting in a fairer process. Before results of the assessment were released, students were interviewed about their experience with the verbal exam. Unlike their initial reaction prior to experiencing the verbal exam, the vast majority of students now preferred the verbal exams and enquired why verbal exams were not included in all modules. This preference for the verbal exam was displayed by all demographics.

This trajectory suggests that, in this case, a traditional criticalist research approach of privileging only qualitative methods (i.e., stopping at point 2 in the below table) would have resulted in an outcome that did not create a new system that was fairer to all students. A summary of the trajectory of the process can be seen in Table 21.1.

CHRD research will undoubtedly encounter participants who have differing 'truths'. Additionally, there will be other interested parties who would be affected by any action following the CHRD research. All parties are stakeholders, all of whom have varying levels of power, interest, support and influence. Relevant stakeholders to the verbal exam research include students, teaching staff, employers, business school management and university registry.

From the perspective of the research on verbal exams, and a requirement of CHRD research, to transform power inequalities in social structures

Table 21.1   Implications of divergent approaches

	Assumed Paradigm	Methodology	Methods	Conclusion	Implications
Investigation prior to introduction of verbal exam					
1	Pre-paradigm stage	Mixed Methods	Comparison of predictive result and actual result	Little relationship shown between predicted and actual results	Question the taken for granted
2	Critical	Qualitative	Interviews with colleagues and other stakeholders on introducing verbal exam	Stakeholders against introduction of verbal exam	Do not question the taken for granted
Investigation post introduction of verbal exam					
3	Critical	Qualitative	Informal interviews with students prior to assessment	Students prefer written exam	Do not question the taken for granted
4	Positivist	Quantitative	Analysis of student results including the verbal exam	Statistically significant with regard to mode of exam	Question the taken for granted
5	Critical	Qualitative	Informal interviews with students after verbal assessment	Students prefer verbal exam	Question the taken for granted

(Guba and Lincoln, 2005), issues of power and interest need to be analysed as they relate to each stakeholder. Additionally, for CHRD research, the mode of data collected and analysis should also be investigated. Trying to change university assessment policy at management level would surely be better achieved using quantitative data; while this contradicts the taken for granted assumptions of critical research, if those with power demand quantitative data, then this is what should be presented. The objective of change should override the paradigm of enquiry and its suggested research methods (Miner-Rubino and Jayaratne, 2007).

Figure 21.1 is a simple stakeholder map that outlines where each stakeholder for the verbal exam presented here sits within the map. The map highlights that university management and graduate employers are key with regard to implementing change. These stakeholders hold the power to change and would generally respond more favourably to quantitative data. Students and teaching staff have a high level of interest, but less

Interest

	Satisfy	Manage
High	Registry: Mixed data	Management: Quantitative data Employers: Quantitative data
	Monitor	*Inform*
Low		Students: Mixed data Teaching staff: Mixed data

Power (vertical axis, left)

| **Low** | **High** |

Interest

Figure 21.1   Stakeholder map for the verbal exam intervention

power. It is envisaged that these stakeholders would require mixed data to encourage a change in assessment strategies. Registry hold little interest, but have the power to negate change; it is then imperative they are satisfied with the research process and can assess a mixed methods view of data. Stakeholder mapping and presentation of suitable data is subjective. For this example, it is considered that all stakeholders have at least some interest or power; however, this is not always the case. The context of the research will determine the matrix of power, interest and suitable mode of data required to encourage the questioning of the taken for granted.

DISCUSSION

The research we have presented here does not disagree with the theoretical arguments that qualitative and quantitative methods can have unique philosophical foundations. However, it demonstrates that the approach taken must not be slave to those philosophical foundations at the expense

Table 21.2   Consideration Factors in CHRD Research

Factors	Description
Identifying stakeholders	Who are those who stand to gain or forfeit from the research? Who needs to be convinced that change (if any) is warranted?
Assessing interests • Procedural • Practical	For each stakeholder, determine what procedures (qualitative or quantitative) would best facilitate a critical outcome (procedural interests). Also determine what practical changes (if any) each stakeholder would seek (practical interests). Analyse points of emphasis to balance procedural and practical interests around which to collect data to facilitate change. How can you alternatively use different methods to meet the procedural interests of each stakeholder while seeking to meet ethical practical interests?
Obtaining and evaluating data	Using the outcome of the interest assessment, use qualitative and/or quantitative methods to obtain and evaluate data.
Catalysing value outcomes	Enact findings that serve a critical interest.

of other factors – to include stakeholder expectations, the nature of access to data, the process of the research journey, the authenticity of stakeholder expectations or the sentiment of doing no harm in the results of our interventions. Each of these factors holds implications for our choices of technique in conducting HRD research with a critical orientation (see Table 21.2).

As the map above suggests, there are multiple stakeholders in any research project. Some stakeholders have significant power over others; some stakeholders stand to gain significantly more than others depending on the outcome of a research project. Further, not all stakeholders will be participants in a given study that affects them; even key stakeholders may not be participants, for a variety of reasons beyond the control of the researcher. As a result, critical researchers must first assess who their stakeholders are for any given object of study, and they must also assess the procedural and practical interests of those stakeholders in determining methodological techniques. Simply put, procedural interests are those that would best facilitate a critical outcome for a particular stakeholder. For example, as noted above, and as a number of critical quantitative scholars argue (e.g., Frankenstein, 1992; Miner-Rubino and Jayaratne, 2007; Harnois, 2013), senior level decision makers are most likely to be swayed initially by quantitative data. Practical interests refers to the nature of practical change a particular stakeholder would want to see, even if it is not critical in nature – financial, political, strategic, cultural and so on. To enact change, these procedural and practical interests must be acknowledged and perhaps taken into account for methodological consideration.

The power held by some stakeholders may need to be incorporated into a critical researcher's design in order to enact change, much like Lewin's force field analysis. In the end, the research needs to suit the question at hand *and* it needs to provide the type of data that will be relevant to effecting change.

Nevertheless, accessing the type of data necessary to effect critical change may be difficult. On the one hand, qualitative data provides the rich narrative that can emotionally move stakeholders toward change; on the other hand, accessing qualitative data requires more intrusive access to the organisation and deeper trust from the participants. And, similarly to qualitative data, on the one hand, quantitative data may be simpler to obtain and more concise to present; on the other hand, quantitative data masquerades as value-free (Callahan and Reio, 2006) and enables decision makers to ignore the emotions that facilitate change. Regardless of how the data is obtained, it is gathered through the people who take part in our studies. Craib (1984) notes that the language and words we use are not our words, but those of the society and culture to which we belong (Matthews, 2003). If responses from participants are simply a regurgitation of a discourse, then deconstruction of the narrative used throughout the research process (to include our qualitative and quantitative instrumentation all the way through to the response data we receive) will need to take place to understand the discourse and power relations existing within.

Like any other researcher, CHRD researchers must sometimes pursue interests by finding ways to best utilise the data to which they have access. This is the issue of reality outweighing rhetoric when it comes to research design. The 'reality' of research requires that scholars critique the forms of data collection they choose to use, never taking for granted that any type of finding is 'truth'. This is relevant for quantitative researchers who may well consider that there *is* a truth that can be found, and only found through numerical data. But it is also important for critical researchers who may be inclined to 'believe' the results of qualitative methods over quantitative methods. As our example here demonstrates, such a misplaced 'belief' may lead to outcomes that continue to privilege the already privileged at the expense of the 'other'.

It is toward those outcomes that CHRD researchers must be mindful. Unlike traditional research, which is distinguished from evaluation by its focus on supposedly value-free reporting of data, critical research is inherently evaluative. It is fundamentally connected to 'valuing' ethical outcomes. CHRD researchers must be ever mindful to claims of authenticity of these ethical outcomes. Interventions associated with issues such as public relations, branding, marketing or employee relations may frequently appear to be critically oriented, but are enacted for political or financial performative gain as the primary priority. For example, as Callahan (2007) observes, arguing that onsite day-care centres promote more family time is misleading as these centres increase employee time at work while not substantially increasing family time. Nevertheless, such centres are often much more convenient for a parent, thereby serving a *different* interest of the employee. Another example is the 'golden handcuffs' of smart mobile devices paid for by the organisation, which have the consequence of making the employee 'on call' at all times. These may seem to be authentic attempts at offering more privilege to workers or creating more equitable workspaces when, in fact, such interventions are frequently in the performative interests of the organisation. CHRD researchers must strive to be transparent in their claims and hold the powerful to do the same.

In the end, CHRD researchers seek to correct unfairness and inequity toward liberating and empowering employees, and organisations, in a climate of democracy and justice. The hallmark of a critical researcher is the desire to facilitate such change and to being open to using whatever research methods will achieve those ethical ends – whether qualitative or quantitative. Ironically, critical scholars easily dichotomise qualitative and quantitative while simultaneously decrying the inappropriate dichotomisation of so many other constructs – male versus female, emotion versus reason, black versus white, gay versus straight. The desire to remain philosophically pure has a negative consequence of potentially reinforcing the inequities a critical scholar hopes can be changed. Thus, instead of focusing on 'critical' as purely a paradigm, we contend that, unlike other paradigms, it derives its research methods of use by praxis instead of philosophy. The purpose of CHRD research is to facilitate a critical practice – praxis. As Miner-Rubino and Jayaratne (2007) and other feminist quantitative researchers note, it is not about your method, it is about your outcome; mixed methods may well be the most effective means to facilitate valued outcomes, as demonstrated in our example of the verbal exams more effectively representing international students' knowledge.

CONCLUSION

> To deny the importance of subjectivity in the process of transforming the world and history is . . . to admit the impossible: a world without people. . . . On the other hand, the denial of objectivity in analysis or action . . . postulates people without a world . . . [and] denies action itself by denying objective reality. (Freire, 1970, pp. 35–36)

Most would acknowledge that Freire was the epitome of critical theory in action. His comments illuminate the point that epistemological purism is not likely to lead to the radical change that is supposedly the aim of critical theory. Our ability to engage in the praxis of critical theory is impaired by purist conformism.

To eschew quantitative approaches that may offer the emancipatory catalyst necessary to create more democratic, equitable or fair work spaces because quantification is perceived as contradictory to the values of critical theory seems counterproductive to the very essence of critical claims. Realising the kinds of changes sought by critical scholars requires that researchers do not privilege paradigm over purpose – praxis is the paramount consideration. Researchers need to acknowledge that qualitative and quantitative are not, in fact, incommensurable. Both operate together to create a picture of our phenomena of exploration. As Miner-Rubino and Jayaratne (2007) so bluntly put it, 'Whether we like it or not, people respond to quantitative data' (p. 296). The research example we provided here further demonstrates the validity of such an argument.

REFERENCES

Alvesson, M. and Willmott, H. (1996). *Making Sense of Management: A Critical Introduction.* Thousand Oaks, CA: Sage.

Applebome, P. (1995). Employers wary of school systems: Survey finds broad distrust of younger job aspirants. *New York Times*, pp. A1, A13.

Baptiste, I. (2001). Educating lone wolves: Pedagogical implications of human capital theory. *Adult Education Quarterly, 51*(3), 184–196.

Bartleby.com (n.d.). Respectfully Quoted: A dictionary of quotations [online], available from http://www.bartleby.com/73/1736.html (accessed December 2013).

Bridges, D. (1993). Transferring skills: A philosophical perspective. *Studies in Higher Education, 18*(1), 43–51.

Callahan, J. L. (2007). Gazing into the crystal ball: Critical HRD as a future of research in the field. *Human Resource Development International, 10*(1), 77–82.

Callahan, J. L. and Reio, T. G. (2006). Making subjective judgments in quantitative studies: The importance of using effect sizes and confidence intervals. *Human Resource Development Quarterly, 17*(2), 159–173.

Clegg, S. (2005). Evidence-based practice in educational research: A critical realist critique of systematic review. *British Journal of Sociology of Education, 26*(3), 415–428.

Craib, I. (1984). *Modern Social Theory: From Parsons to Habermas.* Brighton, UK: Harvester Press.

Elliott, C. and Turnbull, S. (2002). Critical thinking in HRD – a panel led discussion. In T. M. Egan and S. A. Lynham (Eds.), *Proceedings of the Academy of Human Resource Development.* Honolulu, HI.

Frankenstein, M. (1992). Critical mathematics education: An application of Paulo Freire's epistemology. In K. Weiler and C. Mitchell (Eds.), *What Schools Can Do: Critical Pedagogy and Practice*, pp. 237–265. Albany, NY: State University of New York Press.

Freihat, S. and Al-Machzoomi, K. (2012). The Picture of workplace oral communication skills for the ESP Jordanian business graduate employees. *International Journal of Business, Humanities and Technology, 2*(1), 159–173.

Freire, P. (1970). *Pedagogy of the Oppressed.* New York: The Continuum International Publishing Group, Inc.

Guba, E. G. and Lincoln, Y. S. (2005). Paradigmatic controversies, contradictions, and emerging confluences. In N. K. Denzin and Y. S. Lincoln (Eds.), *The Sage Handbook of Qualitative Research*, 3rd edn. pp. 191–216. Thousand Oaks, CA: Sage.

Harnois, C. E. (2013). *Feminist Measures in Survey Research.* Thousand Oaks, CA: Sage. http://dx.doi.org.ezproxy2.library.drexel.edu/10.4135/9781452269955.n1.

Kincheloe, J. L. and McLaren, P. L. (1994). Rethinking critical theory and qualitative research. In N. K. Denzin and Y. S. Lincoln (Eds.), *The Sage Handbook of Qualitative Research*, pp. 138–157. Thousand Oaks, CA: Sage.

Matthews, P. H. (2003). *Linguistics: A Very Short Introduction.* Oxford: Oxford University Press.

Miner-Rubino, K. and Jayaratne, T. E. (2007). Feminist survey research. In S. N. Hesse-Biber and P. L. Leavy (Eds.), *Feminist Research Practice*, pp. 292–326. Thousand Oaks, CA: Sage. http://dx.doi.org.ezproxy2.library.drexel.edu/10.4135/9781412984270.n10.

Perriton, L. (2009). A reflection on the significance of numbers. *Management Learning, 40*(4), 393–399.

Rigg, C., Stewart, J. and Trehan, K. (2007). *Critical Human Resource Development: Beyond Orthodoxy.* Essex, UK: Pearson Education Limited.

Sambrook, S. (2004). A 'critical' time for HRD? *Journal of European Industrial Training, 28*(8/9), 611–624.

Trehan, K. and Rigg, C. (2011). Theorising critical HRD: A paradox of intricacy and discrepancy. *Journal of European Industrial Training, 35*(3), 276–290.

ANNOTATED FURTHER READING

Fenwick, T. (2005). Conceptions of critical HRD: Dilemmas for theory and practice. *Human Resource Development International, 8*(2), 225–238. This article provides additional depth and understanding of what constitutes a *Critical* HRD from both theoretical and practical perspectives.

Sprague, J. (2005). *Feminist Methodologies for Critical Researchers: Bridging Differences.* Lanham, MD: AltaMira Press. This book provides a comprehensive critique of both qualitative and quantitative methods used in critical research and provides practical strategies for engaging in critical research in such a way that research findings can effectively catalyse change.

Valentin, C. (2006). Researching human resource development: Emergence of a critical approach to HRD enquiry. *International Journal of Training and Development, 10*(1), 17–29. Arguably the first scholarly publication to explicitly explore the nature of CHRD enquiry – a seminal work.

22. Mixed methods in HRD research: theory and practice from a study of Hong Kong SMEs

Steven Tam and David E. Gray

SUMMARY

Mixed methods design can contribute great value to academic research. The purpose of this chapter is to share with readers an empirical HRD study which used both quantitative and qualitative methods as part of the research design. It discusses how the research was designed and implemented, why mixed methods suited the study and what critical insights emerged from the research.

INTRODUCTION

Social and behavioural research has been dominated by positivist schools of thought on the one hand and interpretivist approaches on the other, often generating division and hostility between the two. One negative result of this is that researchers have often felt it necessary to ally themselves to one school or another and to accept the view that quantitative and qualitative research are mutually exclusive. Thankfully, this situation appears to be changing, with some scholars, including some within the practice of Human Resource Development (HRD) (Jayanti, 2011; Cameron, 2009) advocating the linking of qualitative and quantitative research designs to produce mixed methods studies.

This chapter provides an example of such an empirical study in the context of HRD research, by looking at workplace learning practices in Hong Kong small and medium-sized enterprises (SMEs) at different life-cycle stages. The quality of the SME workforce is significant to the economy in Hong Kong, especially within the context of the knowledge economy (Hong Kong Trade and Industry Department, 2011), one reason why the study explored it from a workplace learning perspective to understand how SME employees *learn* at work.

The research design involved two consecutive phases of data collection. Phase 1 identified the life-cycle stage (namely inception, high-growth or maturity) of the firm through theoretical sampling using an Organisational Life Cycle (OLC) questionnaire. Phase 2 then adopted a mixed methods design to explore the workplace learning practices (categorised by learning levels) in those SMEs at each life-cycle stage through a quantitative online Learning Practices Questionnaire (LPQ) as well as qualitative semi-structured interviews with four SMEs identified at each stage through snowball sampling. The qualitative data were used to validate, deepen and enrich the quantitative results. The study described here will attempt to illustrate how a mixed methods design fits the research aims and promotes the credibility of research findings, with the whole (integrated data collection and analysis) being greater than the sum of the parts (quantitative or qualitative results).

WHAT ARE MIXED METHODS?

According to Greene, Caracelli and Graham (1989), mixed method designs are those that include at least one quantitative method and one qualitative method. In the past, the two methods would not have mixed because they come from different epistemological paradigms. For example, an ethnographic study that incorporated both qualitative data from participant observation but also quantitative data from a survey would be considered inappropriate because most ethnographers would see quantitative data as incompatible with the epistemology of ethnography – quantitative and qualitative approaches typically embrace different philosophical assumptions about the nature of the world. However, in recent years this hard divide has started to break down. Indeed, some researchers are now referring to mixed methods as a 'third methodological movement' (Johnson, Onwuegbuzie and Turner, 2007), with quantitative methods the first and qualitative methods the second (Teddlie and Tashakkori, 2010).

Not all researchers see mixed methods as legitimate. Rossman and Wilson (1985) provide an overview of three different schools of thought on the issue, namely the *purists*, the *situationalists* and the *pragmatists* (Figure 22.1). These schools can be viewed as lying on a continuum, with the purists and pragmatists at opposite ends and the situationalists positioned somewhere in the middle. For the purists (the traditional school), quantitative and qualitative methods are mutually exclusive, because they stem from different ontological and epistemological stances about the nature of research and the world. Quantitative and qualitative methods should never be mixed. Situationalists, however, hold that while both methods have value, certain research questions lend themselves more to quantitative approaches and others to

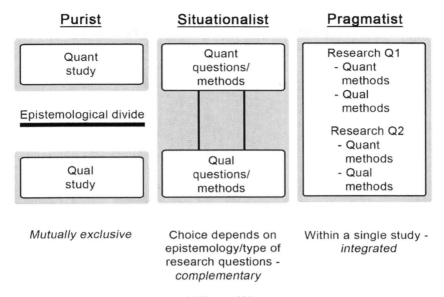

Purist   Situationalist   Pragmatist

Source: Adapted from Rossman and Wilson (1985).

Figure 22.1   Mixing or not mixing methods: purist, situationalist and pragmatist

qualitative. So while both methods would be used, they would complement each other but not be combined. Pragmatists, however, recommend integrating the two methods within a single study, utilising the strengths of both. Rather than come at a research problem from a position of epistemological purity, researchers should begin with their research questions and select the most appropriate method(s) (Teddlie and Tashakkori, 2010).

There are, of course, different ways of using mixed methods. As Gray (2014) explains, quantitative and qualitative methods can be used independently or interdependently (and in a range of different sequences) and can focus on the same research questions or on different questions. The key is selecting the combination of methods that can bring an added dimension to the research. Figure 22.2 offers three examples of typical mixed methods design. Design 1 can be used when relatively little is known about the subject. The first phase comprises a qualitative exploration of themes – for example, the use of a focus group, through which concepts are explored. This may assist the second, quantitative, phase, where, for example, a questionnaire

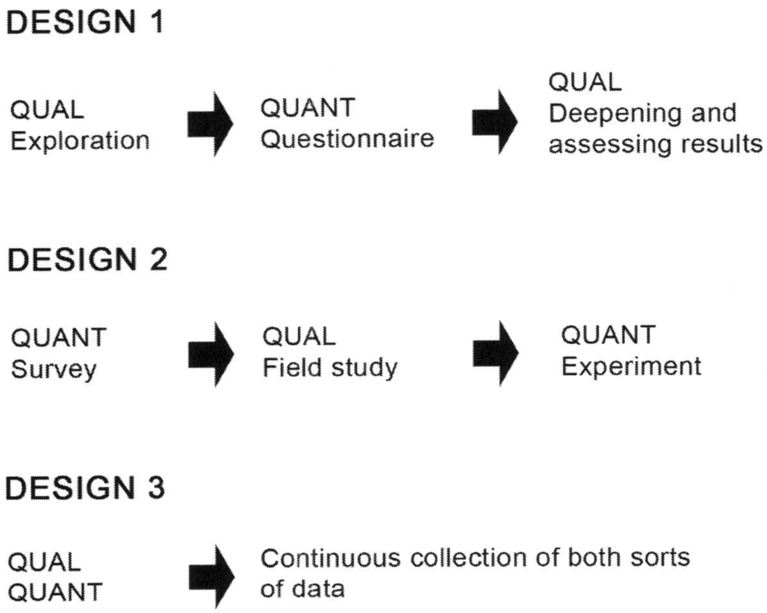

DESIGN 1

QUAL
Exploration   ➡️   QUANT
Questionnaire   ➡️   QUAL
Deepening and
assessing results

DESIGN 2

QUANT
Survey   ➡️   QUAL
Field study   ➡️   QUANT
Experiment

DESIGN 3

QUAL
QUANT   ➡️   Continuous collection of both sorts
of data

Figure 22.2   Three typical mixed methods models

is designed. The third stage is qualitative, where some of the themes identified in the questionnaire are explored and deepened – for example, through case studies and interviews. So say, for example, an organisation is interested in knowing more about bullying in the workplace. A focus group on this emotive subject might elicit some themes that the researchers were unaware of. Using some of the academic literature on workplace bullying and the analysis of focus group data allows researchers to construct a questionnaire about the subject. Given that some respondents to the questionnaire admit to being bullied and tick a box to indicate they are willing to be contacted, researchers are able to follow up the survey with some detailed, qualitative case study interviews. At the report writing stage, the qualitative data are used to supplement and reinforce the themes identified in the survey, an example of data triangulation.

In Design 2 a quantitative survey is used in the first phase of the research, often in circumstances where the main parameters are already known, because there is already a body of research in this field. During the second phase, fieldwork is undertaken to enrich the quantitative findings. A quantitative experiment is then designed to test, perhaps, some competing hypotheses that have emerged from the fieldwork. So, for example, a staff survey might discover deficiencies in morale and a lack of confidence in management. These themes are followed up by fieldwork involving covert observations and focus groups. As a result, a major staff development programme is designed and launched. The quantitative phase is used to measure how effective the programme is in changing attitudes.

In Design 3, both quantitative and qualitative methods are used, not sequentially as in designs 1 and 2, but concurrently and in an integrated fashion. This often occurs when quantitative and qualitative methods are addressing different research questions which are part of the same study. So, for example, an organisation wishes to measure the impact of its new mentoring programme aimed at improving diversity by nurturing the career progression of women managers. It conducts a (quantitative) survey each year for three years among its women managers, measuring their levels of self-efficacy and confidence. During this period, the organisation also interviews a random sample of 20 employees to elicit detailed opinions on how the mentoring programme can be improved. Hence, the quantitative part of the research design measures impact, while the qualitative element explores how the programme can be developed, both elements continuing in parallel.

The study in this chapter is presented from a perspective that combines elements of both the pragmatist and situationalist approaches, with some research questions being addressed using both quantitative and qualitative methods (pragmatist – RQ-1 and RQ-3) and some purely using one method (situationalist – RQ-2 and RQ-4). This suggests that in the mixed methods model, presented in Figure 22.1, some studies can combine elements of more than one model (see Table 22.1). Let us now look at the study itself.

Table 22.1 The approach(es) against each of the research questions

Research Questions	Approach(es)	Respondents	Research Instruments
RQ-1	Quantitative; Qualitative	SME employees	An online questionnaire; Semi-structured interviews
RQ-2	Qualitative	SME employees	Semi-structured interviews
RQ-3	Quantitative; Qualitative	SME employees	An online questionnaire; Semi-structured interviews
RQ-4	Qualitative	SME employees	Semi-structured interviews

THE MIXED METHODS CASE STUDY: HRD PRACTICES IN HONG KONG SMEs

The Research Questions of the Study

The purpose of the study was to examine the workplace learning practices in Hong Kong SMEs at different life-cycle stages and was guided by four research questions (RQs):

RQ-1: How do SME workplace learning practices differ between life-cycle stages?

RQ-2: What are the common organisational factors that may explain the different workplace learning practices at different life-cycle stages?

RQ-3: How important do SME employees view the workplace learning practices at different life-cycle stages?

RQ-4: Do the workplace learning practices become more structured with firm growth? If so, how?

These research questions addressed either the 'how' or 'why' perspective on workplace learning practices and life-cycle stages. It is sensible to assume that RQ-1 and RQ-3 were better tackled quantitatively (via an online questionnaire in this study) to be able to reach a larger population for statistical analysis, while RQ-2 and RQ-4 were to be approached qualitatively (through semi-structured interviews in this study) to gain deeper insights as required. With mixed methods, data triangulation was made possible since semi-structured interviews would also collect the information about RQ-1 and RQ-3. As such, the data from both the online questionnaire and interviews for RQ-1 and RQ-3 could be compared to validate and strengthen the overall findings. Table 22.1 maps the approach(es) against each of the research questions.

The Empirical Case Study

The study adopted the case study method. Yin (2003) points out that a case study is favourable if the researcher is exploring how and/or why something happens. Gray (2014) also comments that the case study method is ideal when a 'how' or 'why' question is being asked about a contemporary set of events over which the researcher has no control. In this study, all the research questions focused on the 'how' and the 'why' about the differences in workplace learning practices by SMEs across different life-cycle stages. Mason (2002, p. 1) similarly claims that the case study method is good for examining 'how things work in particular contexts'. Specifically, the type of case study design is termed as multiple cases/holistic in nature (Yin, 2003; Gray, 2014). That is, the study used a single, holistic unit of analysis (workplace learning practices) and replicated the findings over multiple cases (SMEs within each life-cycle stage) for comparison until a common pattern could be found.

The research design for this case study

In theory, no fixed number of SMEs (cases) in the sample were assigned, nor the number of participants within each firm. Theoretical sampling was adopted to classify SMEs into different life-cycle stages, and snowball sampling was exercised in interviewing employees within a firm until data saturation was reached with a consistent pattern of workplace learning practices (Glaser and Strauss, 1967; Mason, 2002; Patton, 2002; Teddlie and Yu, 2007). There were two consecutive phases:

> *Phase 1 – OLC*. Each SME in the sample was classified into one of three life-cycle stages (namely inception, high-growth or maturity) using a self-declaring OLC questionnaire. The questionnaire featured the stage characteristics described by Smith, Mitchell and Summer (1985). Its context was similarly used by Born (2000) and had further been pilot-tested by a group of SMEs in this study to ensure validity. It was intended that the number of SMEs at each life-cycle stage would be equal or very close. If the sample was exhausted and there were significantly few firms at a stage, new SMEs would be added until a comparable number of SMEs was found for each stage (Mason, 2002).

> *Phase 2 – Workplace Learning*. The SMEs at each of the three life-cycle stages were provided access to an online LPQ for their employees to share their learning practices in the workplace. The LPQ questionnaire had been pilot-tested by a group of SMEs before use. In addition, four SMEs at each life-cycle stage were identified (from among all those at that stage) for semi-structured interviews to compare and understand their workplace learning practices in detail. Data were gathered through snowball sampling until data saturation was reached (i.e., a consistent pattern of workplace learning practices was noted) (e.g., Patton, 2002; Teddlie and Yu, 2007).

As indicated, the case study consisted of two distinct phases: Phase 1 classified the SMEs in the sample into three different OLC stages, and Phase 2 explored SME employees' workplace learning practices at each

Phase 1 -
Organisational Life Cycle

Phase 2 -
Workplace Learning

Purpose: To classify SMEs into one of three life-cycle stages.
Sampling Strategy: Theoretical sampling based on Smith *et al.'s* (1985) OLC framework - Inception, High-Growth, and Maturity.
Instrumentation: An OLC questionnaire (adapted from Born, 2000).
Nature: Quantitative.

Purpose: To explore the workplace learning practices in those SMEs at each life-cycle stage.
Sampling Strategy: Multi-case comparisons and snowballing until data saturation reached.
Instrumentation: (1) An online learning practices questionnaire; (2) Semi-structured interviews.
Nature: Mixed methods of quantitative then qualitative.

Figure 22.3   The two phases of research design for the study

of these stages. Phase 1 adopted a single quantitative instrument, the OLC questionnaire, to satisfy the purpose. For Phase 2, the type of mixed method design was 'quantitative then qualitative' (Gray, 2014), in which the findings from the online questionnaire (LPQ) were seen to be helpful in identifying the qualitative interviewees in SMEs to follow up and deepen the data. In addition, data triangulation made it possible to compare and verify both sets of findings for credibility. Figure 22.3 illustrates the two phases of research design for this study.

The sampling frame of the study
There are approximately 299,000 SMEs in Hong Kong, representing over 98 per cent of all local enterprises and employing about 50 per cent of the workforce in the private sector (Hong Kong Trade and Industry Department, 2011). The major divide falls between industry and services, of which SMEs in the import/export trade and wholesale sector and retail sector add up to more than 50 per cent of the total SMEs in Hong Kong (Support and Consultation Centre for SMEs, 2011). Sectors of professional and business services as well as social and personal services are also deemed to be significant (Support and Consultation Centre for SMEs, 2011). According to the Hong Kong Yearbook (2010, p. 106), SMEs are defined as 'those manufacturing businesses in Hong Kong employing fewer than 100 people, or non-manufacturing businesses with fewer than 50'.

As this study adopted the case study method, the target population were a non-probability quota sample of Hong Kong SMEs. To help the representativeness, the distribution of SMEs in the sample was selected from the sampling frame to map the actual distribution of SMEs in Hong Kong in terms of activity and sector. The researchers searched appropriate SMEs through contacts until the distribution (quota) requirement (by industry/sector) was met. Out of nearly 100 contacts, 30 suitable SMEs were prepared for the sample. This sample was also considered final since the number of firms classified into each life-cycle stage in Phase 1 was comparable.

In an SME, all the employees, regardless of managerial or non-managerial status, were the key informants of this study. It was intended that the study explored what learning opportunities were offered by the firms for their employees in the workplace. Therefore, the data collection process started from the owner/manager or the person who formulated the policies for people development in the firm (as the workplace learning provider) before contacting other employees (as the workplace learning user).

Data collection

Phase 1: Classifying the life-cycle stages of SMEs The first phase identified the life-cycle stage of each SME in the sample using a quantitative OLC questionnaire to invite SME owner/managers to self-declare their firm's life-cycle stage by answering ten specific questions about their current business operations. The self-declaring approach has been used for identification of life-cycle stages of firms in numerous studies (e.g., Smith, Mitchell and Summer, 1985; Kazanjian, 1988; Born, 2000; Moy and Luk, 2003).

Phase 2: Exploring the workplace learning practices in SMEs The second phase of the study examined the workplace learning practices among the three identified groups (inception, high-growth and maturity) of SMEs. Given the SMEs were at different stages, consistently different patterns of workplace learning practices were sought to identify different learning practices and also to explain why they might occur. Mixed data collection methods used in this phase were a quantitative online LPQ and qualitative semi-structured interviews:

LPQ. This online instrument was developed by the researchers. LPQ addressed the different learning practices that SMEs would use, based on multiple sources in the literature to ensure content credibility (Huang, 2001; ENSR, 2002; Clifford and Thorpe, 2007; CIPD, 2008).

The LPQ was also reviewed by two experienced researchers and two SME owner/managers to address inter-judge reliability, a measure that compares the consistency of observations when more than one person is judging (Gray, 2014). It was then piloted online by a group of SMEs for further improvements. LPQ sought information about employees' learning practices in the workplace (which are made available by the organisation). It used a five-point Likert type scale (5 = Strongly Agree; 4 = Agree; 3 = Neutral; 2 = Disagree; and 1 = Strongly Disagree) and an additional option of 'Approach Not Available' to collect the learning approaches provided/supported by the organisation and measured employees' opinions about their workplace learning practices. The learning approaches in the questionnaire were categorised under the four different levels of learning (individual, group, organisational and inter-organisational) according to the organisational learning framework for SMEs suggested by Jones and Macpherson (2006).

Semi-Structured Interviews. Yin (2003, p. 89) stresses that 'one of the most important sources of case study information is the interview'. Interviewing facilitates deeper information collection and is powerful for tackling research questions with dimensions of 'why' and 'how' (e.g., Mason, 2002; Yin, 2003; Gray, 2014). In this study, each interview was executed in a one-to-one setting (one of the researchers and the SME worker) without interruptions. English was used as the language of communication, and all the interviews lasted an average of 75 minutes. Interviews were audio-recorded, and probing questions were posed when appropriate to supplement the interview question schedule. The sampling strategy used was snowballing, subsequent interviewees within each firm being selected on the basis of 'an interviewee nominates the next interviewee' fashion until data saturation was reached or a consistent pattern of data was noted (Patton, 2002; Teddlie and Yu, 2007). This particular approach is useful where there are difficulties in obtaining useable sampling frames (Eland-Goossensen et al., 1997). Snowball sampling was repeated in other selected SMEs at each OLC stage.

Data analysis
Data analysis involved the integration of both quantitative (the OLC and LPQ questionnaires) and qualitative (individual in-depth interviews) data. With this mixed instrumentation, descriptive statistics were applied to the questionnaires and content analysis to the interviews. The following discusses each part of the data analysis process.

Quantitative points system On the OLC questionnaire in Phase 1, a points system (1, 2 or 3) was allocated to the answers of the first nine questions in relation to the life-cycle stages (inception, high-growth or maturity) respectively. Based on the responses by an SME, a mean score of the total points from these nine questions was computed using SPSS to represent the firm's life-cycle stage. Upon obtaining all the mean scores from the firms in the sample, k-means cluster analysis was conducted to classify the data set into firms of three different life-cycle stages. The final open narrative question specifying the general nature of each life-cycle stage for the firm highlighted what they regarded as their own life-cycle stage directly to safeguard a situation in case the k-means cluster analysis failed to identify three significant clusters (Born, 2000). It also allowed for validation of the k-means results if these self-selected results were the same – which in each case they were.

On the LPQ in Phase 2, the five-point Likert scale represented the responses numerically for each available workplace learning practice in an SME. Each of the four levels of workplace learning (individual, group, organisational and inter-organisational) had multiple questions of practices, and the mean score of a respondent's responses to these questions *at each learning level* was sought. This resulted in four separate mean scores (one for each learning level) per respondent. With these mean scores for *each respondent*, four overall means (one for each learning level) could be calculated. In the end, three sets of such means (one set for each life-cycle stage) were obtained. The one-way ANOVA (Analysis of Variance) was conducted to compare the means of these three different life-cycle stages (i.e., three different groups of SMEs) on each level of workplace learning. Four separate one-way ANOVAs were computed. Post hoc multiple comparisons – the Tukey Honest Significant Difference test or the Games-Howell test – followed to determine the source of the mean differences if the ANOVA F was significant. From the results, it was expected that statistical significance on the four levels of workplace learning practised by SMEs at different life-cycle stages would be noted. Moreover, the responses for 'Approach Not Available' would reveal the specific learning approaches that were *not* provided/practised by SMEs at a particular life-cycle stage.

Qualitative coding process Semi-structured interviews produce rich, unorganised textual information from interviewees, which can be coded for categorisation/content analysis to explore meanings (Mason, 2002; Patton, 2002). As Patton (2002, p.453) states, '[content analysis is] qualitative data reduction and sense-making effort that takes a volume of qualitative material and attempts to identify core consistencies and meanings'.

Qualitative researchers call such 'core findings' patterns or themes. In this study, three major steps were taken in the coding process, as supported by Mason (2002) and Patton (2002), from capturing the raw interview data to developing the meaningful common themes:

1. *Capture the data.* The interviewer (one of the researchers) wrote down the interviewees' responses (quotes and information) for the questions on an interview worksheet. Interviews were audio-recorded to allow for subsequent reviews.
2. *Categorise the data.* The interviewer reviewed the data carefully (and repeatedly) to identify any emerging themes and linked/sorted them into different categories.
3. *Analyse the emerging themes.* The interviewer interpreted the different categories, refined them and synthesised similar kinds into the final common themes.

This qualitative coding process generated the patterns of workplace learning practices in SMEs at different life-cycle stages.

DISCUSSION – RESULTS AND INSIGHTS FOR HRD RESEARCHERS

The study compared multiple cases – 30 suitable SMEs with 718 employees in Hong Kong – using the mixed methods design of collecting data quantitatively and qualitatively in two distinct phases. While the results are beyond the scope of this chapter for detailed discussion, four major findings emerged (Tam, 2012), as shown in Table 22.2 below.

The study provides three essential points, which should be borne in mind by HRD researchers. Firstly, research questions help determine whether mixed methods should be part of the research design and, if so, what kinds of mixed methods are valid. For example, while RQ-2 and RQ-4 required the use of qualitative interviews, both RQ-1 and RQ-3 required the use of a quantitative online questionnaire and interviews, combined.

Secondly, the study helps to demonstrate that quantitative and qualitative methods can be used in a variety of different phases. In this study it was quantitative then qualitative (Gray, 2014), with the qualitative interviews being used to add substance and depth to the quantitative findings. However, mixed methods can be used in other combinations – for example qualitative (such as focus groups to explore concepts needed in a study) then a quantitative survey to measure responses to these concepts. Or

Table 22.2   The four major findings of the study

Item	Description of the Major Findings
1	The *individual level* of workplace learning is important at all life-cycle stages but most important at inception
2	The *group level* of workplace learning is more important at high-growth than it is at maturity
3	The *organisational level* of workplace learning is more important at high-growth and maturity than it is at inception
4	The *inter-organisational level* of workplace learning is high at all life-cycle stages and there is no significant difference between stages

Source: Tam (2012).

mixed methods can be used in parallel with both quantitative and qualitative data being collected within the same time frame, with triangulation of method strengthening the validity of the findings.

Thirdly, in this study the quantitative phase helped to focus the qualitative phase. In other words, it was not merely a matter of the quantitative and qualitative phases complementing each other. By undertaking the online quantitative study, it was possible to identify the kinds of themes and issues that were significant and relevant for the later qualitative study. Hence, the quantitative method assisted in the construction of the qualitative interview schedule.

Hopefully, by presenting this case study on HRD practices in Hong Kong SMEs, we have shown that mixed methods research can be a valuable and powerful design in empirical research, provided their use can be justified in relation to research aims. While there is generally an absence of exemplars of mixed methods studies (Bryman, 2007), there is a growing acceptance of mixed methods in research, of which this chapter is an example.

REFERENCES

Born, C. C. (2000). *Nonprofit Board of Director Attributes at the Stages of the Organizational Life Cycle*. PhD Thesis, California School of Professional Psychology, Los Angeles, CA.

Bryman, A. (2007). Barriers to Integrating Quantitative and Qualitative Research. *Journal of Mixed Methods Research* 1 (1), pp. 8–22.

Cameron, R. (2009). A Sequential Mixed Model Research Design: Design, Analytical and Display Issues. *International Journal of Multiple Research Approaches* 3 (2), pp. 140–152.

CIPD (The Chartered Institute of Personnel and Development). (2008). *Who Learns at Work? Employees' Experiences of Workplace Learning*. London: CIPD.

Clifford, J. and Thorpe, S. (2007). *Workplace Learning and Development: Delivering Competitive Advantage for Your Organization*. London: Kogan Page.

Eland-Goossensen, M. A., van de Goor, L. A. M., Vollemans, E. C., Hendriks, V. M. and Garretsen, H. F. L. (1997). Snowball Sampling Applied to Opiate Addicts Outside the Treatment System. *Addiction Research* 5 (4), pp. 317–330.

ENSR (European Network for SME Research). (2002). *ENSR Enterprise Survey*. European Commission.

Glaser, B. G. and Strauss, A. L. (1967). *The Discovery of Grounded Theory: Strategies for Qualitative Research*. New York: Aldine de Gruyter.

Gray, D. E. (2014). *Doing Research in the Real World*. 3rd edn. London: Sage.

Greene, J. C., Caracelli, V. J. and Graham, W. F. (1989). Toward a Conceptual Framework for Mixed-Method Evaluation Designs. *Educational Evaluation and Policy Analysis* 11 (3), pp. 255–274.

Hong Kong Trade and Industry Department. (2011). *Support to Small and Medium Enterprises*. [Online]. Hong Kong Government. Available at: www.tid.gov.hk (accessed 16 October 2012).

Hong Kong Yearbook. (2010). *Chapter 5: Commerce and Industry: Small and Medium Enterprises*. [Online]. Hong Kong Government. Available at: www.yearbook.gov.hk (accessed 17 October 2012).

Huang, T. C. (2001). The Relation of Training Practices and Organizational Performance in Small and Medium Size Enterprises. *Education + Training* 43 (8/9), pp. 437–444.

Jayanti, E. B. (2011). Towards Pragmatic Criteria for Evaluating HRD Research. *Human Resource Development Review* 10 (4), pp. 431–450.

Johnson, R. B., Onwuegbuzie, A. J. and Turner, L. A. (2007). Toward a Definition of Mixed Methods Research. *Journal of Mixed Methods Research* 1 (2), pp. 112–133.

Jones, O. and Macpherson, A. (2006). Inter-Organizational Learning and Strategic Renewal in SMEs: Extending the 4I Framework. *Long Range Planning* 39, pp. 155–175.

Kazanjian, R. K. (1988). Relation of Dominant Problems to Stages of Growth in Technology-Based New Ventures. *Academy of Management Journal* 31 (2), pp. 257–279.

Mason, J. (2002). *Qualitative Researching*. 2nd edn. London: Sage.

Moy, J. W. and Luk, W. M. (2003). The Life-Cycle Model as a Framework for Understanding Barriers to SME Growth in Hong Kong. *Asia Pacific Business Review* 10 (2), pp. 199–220.

Patton, M. Q. (2002). *Qualitative Research and Evaluation Methods*. 3rd edn. Thousand Oaks, CA: Sage.

Rossman, G. B. and Wilson, B. L. (1985). Numbers and Words: Combining Quantitative and Qualitative Methods in a Single Large-Scale Evaluation Study. *Evaluation Review* 9, pp. 627–643.

Smith, K. G., Mitchell, T. R. and Summer, C. E. (1985). Top Level Management Priorities in Different Stages of the Organizational Life Cycle. *Academy of Management Journal* 28 (4), pp. 799–820.

Support and Consultation Centre for SMEs. (2011). *Distribution of SMEs in Hong Kong*. [Online]. Hong Kong Trade and Industry Department. Available at: www.success.tid.gov.hk (accessed 16 October 2012).

Tam, S. (2012). *Connecting Workplace Learning Practices and Organisational Life Cycle: A Case Study of Hong Kong SMEs*. PhD Thesis, Surrey Business School, University of Surrey, UK.

Teddlie, C. and Tashakkori, A. (2010). Overview of Contemporary Issues in Mixed Methods Research. In: Tashakkori, A. and Teddlie, C. (eds). *Handbook of Mixed Methods in Social and Behavioral Research*. 2nd edn. Thousand Oaks, CA: Sage.

Teddlie, C. and Yu, F. (2007). Mixed Methods Sampling: A Typology with Examples. *Journal of Mixed Methods Research* 1 (1), pp. 77–100.

Yin, R. K. (2003). *Case Study Research: Design and Methods*. 3rd edn. Thousand Oaks, CA: Sage.

ANNOTATED FURTHER READING

Gray, D. E. (2014). *Doing Research in the Real World*. 3rd edn. London: Sage. This research book is comprehensive and filled with helpful examples, providing readers with excellent knowledge and practices in academic research. A great tool book for every researcher.

Saunders, M., Lewis, P. and Thornhill, A. (2012). *Research Methods for Business Students*. 6th edn. Harlow: Pearson. A classic research book on the global stand, which is complete with research wisdom and solutions. A great companion for every researcher who wishes to excel in doing research.

Tashakkori, A. and Teddlie, C. (eds) (2010). *Handbook of Mixed Methods in Social and Behavioral Research*. 2nd edn. Thousand Oaks, CA: Sage. A useful handbook with a good collection of chapters discussing mixed methods in research from a variety of perspectives.

23. Key issues for gender research in HRD: a Multi-Stakeholder Framework for analysing gendered media constructions of women leaders
Sharon Mavin and Jannine Williams

SUMMARY

This chapter outlines key issues for gender researchers. It introduces the importance of women leaders and gender aware HRD and a range of issues in gender research. The key issues in practice are presented and illustrated through research that operationalizes a Multi-Stakeholder Framework for analysing gendered media constructions of women leaders.

INTRODUCTION

Gender research can be a highly political process with significant impact, positively or negatively, on the researcher(s) and research participants. As a result there are key issues for consideration when preparing to undertake gender research in Human Resource Development (HRD). Gender research in HRD requires a mature level of researcher reflexivity in terms of personal understandings of gender; individual researcher values, philosophical positions and standpoints on gender; motivations for research; and awareness of how gender research may construct researchers in their own professional settings and how research participants may respond to gender research. We contend that a process of researcher reflexivity, in critically reflecting upon and reviewing individual assumptions and standpoints, is essential *before* beginning gender research. Gender is a significant dimension of personal life, social relations and culture: an arena where we face difficult practical issues about justice, identity and even survival; where there is much prejudice, myth and falsehood; and where social sciences gender research is producing a relatively new form of knowledge (Connell, 2009).

This chapter outlines key issues for gender researchers illustrated through research into gendered media constructions of women leaders.

We introduce the importance of women leaders and gender aware learning and HRD and outline understandings of gender; diverse advances in gender research; consistency, harm, pleasure and power; participant–research relationships; and the researcher's position in gender research, by drawing upon our previous studies. We then present the key issues in practice, through our operationalization of a Multi-Stakeholder Framework for analysing gendered media constructions of women leaders. We utilize a mixed method design (Saunders, 2012) of statistical analysis of secondary data on women in senior positions in a UK region (geographies of gender); analysis of three Supplements of the Top 500 Influential Leaders via discourse analysis; a semi-structured interview with a media producer; group and individual interviews with selected aspiring and current women leaders; and stages of ongoing researcher reflexivity and accountability. We conclude with reflections on the constraints and possibilities of the Multi-Stakeholder Framework approach.

WOMEN LEADERS AND HUMAN RESOURCE DEVELOPMENT

We follow Bryans and Mavin's (2003) contention that much of what we know about learning and development has been based on the masculine norm and that management, organizing, learning and development have been historically viewed as gender neutral concepts where women's experiences are ignored. An example of this comes through education and development in UK business and management higher education settings, where curricula and leader development interventions are argued 'to collude with the status quo; simply repeating existing management theory and practice' which is gendered (Mavin and Bryans, 1999: 99). In terms of HRD, our assumption is that women's leadership experiences and strategies for learning leadership should be integrated into management and leader development, thus placing gender on the agenda, problematizing traditional perceptions of manager and leader as men and supporting the move to disrupt and 'dismantle sex role stereotypes in the organisations to which the students (will) belong' (Mavin and Bryans, 1999: 99). While there are an increasing number of studies investigating the gendered nature of leadership, management and learning research, subsequent models and frameworks (e.g., Bryans and Mavin, 2003; Elliott and Stead, 2008) and investigating empirically into women, gender management, learning and leadership (e.g., Kelan, 2013; Stead, 2013), there are few studies examining social contexts and processes which influence and 'shape the development of leadership practice' (Kempster and Stewart, 2010: 208).

The research we outline in this chapter advances contexts and processes impacting on leadership by exploring how women leaders are gendered through media representations and reporting.

UNDERSTANDINGS OF GENDER

As gender researchers we see gender as 'socially produced distinctions between male and female, masculine and feminine' (Acker, 1992: 250) and acknowledge that understandings of gender have progressed from traditional essentialist concepts of male–masculine, female–feminine as ascribed individual traits to recognizing 'gendering processes', so that gender is constantly redefined and negotiated by individuals in everyday practices (Poggio, 2006). The way we each, as individuals, continually redefine and negotiate gender against the binary divide categories of male–female, feminine–masculine is socially constructed. We know these processes as 'doing gender' (West and Zimmerman, 1987), which involves a 'complex of socially guided perceptual and interactional and micropolitical activities that cast particular pursuits as expressions of masculine and feminine "natures"' (West and Zimmerman, 1987: 126). Underpinning their concept of doing gender, West and Zimmerman (1987) analytically distinguish between sex, sex categorization and gender. There are ongoing debates about the value of identifying a clear distinction and a causal link between sex (biologically based) and gender (culturally based), recognized as a useful tactic for feminist sociologists. However, the contribution of physiological differences to social behaviour is not yet settled (Acker, 1992), and any gender research requires researchers to identify their assumptions and positioning within this debate. For example, Kelan (2010) argues that people are already categorized by their sex (biology) when they 'do gender', therefore the body is not neutral. '"Doing gender" is the process through which the gender binary is enacted' (Kelan, 2010: 182). Amongst gender researchers, some argue this binary divide can be 'undone' by ignoring or not referring to it. Others argue that the binary divide can be destabilized through research positions that question the naturalness of the gender binary or disturb it through different and confusing readings of the binary (Butler, 1990, 2004). However, Kelan (2010), Messerschmidt (2009) and West and Zimmerman (2009) argue that undoing gender is really not undoing gender but re-doing or doing gender differently (Mavin and Grandy, 2013).

Our understanding of gender, which shapes this chapter and our own lifelong gender projects, is that gender can be done well and differently through simultaneous, multiple enactments of femininity and masculinity

(Mavin and Grandy, 2012, 2013). In this way women and men can do gender well (in congruence with sex category, e.g., women doing femininities and men masculinities), while simultaneously re-doing or doing gender differently (e.g., women doing masculinity and men femininity) (Mavin and Grandy, 2013). We explicitly incorporate sex category (feminine–masculine) into our understanding of doing gender, as we believe it cannot be ignored in experiences of doing gender. While gender binaries can be challenged or unsettled, the binary divide continues to shape how men and women do gender. Through gender stereotypes, women and men continue to evaluate themselves and others and are evaluated against the femininity–masculinity binary divide in organizations (Mavin and Grandy, 2012, 2013).

DIVERSE ADVANCES IN GENDER RESEARCH

Beyond HRD, gender research has a longer history, and as gender researchers we should remain cognizant of the ever advancing nature of the study of gender from multi-disciplinary perspectives. Gender research enables the possibilities of reaching out to other fields to advance existing knowledge within business, management and organizational studies and to contextualize our specific research questions in appropriate literature and research methods. As gender researchers we should also keep abreast of the diverse advances for gender research within HRD. For example, a contemporary issue for management and organization studies is the need to be sensitive to the potential for geographical differences (Billing, 2011; Connell, 1987, 2009; Connell and Messerschmidt, 2005) within explorations of the complexities and contradictions in how women experience gender and management. Further, there are growing debates which draw upon intersectionality to highlight the salience of other social categories for gender relations, such as class, race and disability (Acker, 2000; Holvino, 2010; Valentine, 2007; Williams and Mavin, 2012) and whether gender research can produce valuable knowledge if gender is the sole conceptual frame. Within business and management studies this poses challenges because, as Broadbridge and Simpson (2011) point out, certain developments that run alongside gender research (e.g., diversity, masculinities and men in management, meritocracy and choice) occur at the expense of gender, diluting gender in the process. This is not to say that diversity or meritocracy have no place in gender in management; nor is it to say that such discussions are less important than gender. It is suggested that the foci of gender in management should be "'gender with [. . .]" rather than the more equal footing of "gender and [. . .]" race, class, age and/or other key categorizations' (Broadbridge and Simpson, 2011: 473). We recognize that gender is grounded in relationships of power and the body, which, when including other social categories, can surface different dynamics (Hassard and Holliday, 2001). This suggests a heterogeneity for women and men, as different bodies are coded and read as inferior in relation to social categories such as disability, race, age and sexual orientation, for example, experiences of women of colour are qualitatively different to white women (Crenshaw, 1991).

CONSISTENCY, 'HARM AND PLEASURE' AND POWER IN GENDER RESEARCH

It is important for gender researchers to establish their own understandings of gender and to be consistent in how this is reflected in research methods and positioning of gender within findings and conclusions. This is manifested most clearly in whether gender is treated as a key variable in research, where findings are re-presented against the gender binary unreflexively, or whether gender is considered a co-construction between the researcher and the researched, where power relations and inequalities are integrated throughout the research and are transparently acknowledged and discussed. Without this reflexivity, research can serve to maintain the gender binary divide between men and women, sustaining gendered understandings of a social order which subordinates women to men, affirming organizational power to men and, therefore, denying power to women (Gherardi, 1994). Power is a key issue in gender research as a continual interacting process between people in organizations and is understood to be implicit as individuals make choices, shape, resist or accept gender expectations (Alvesson and Due Billing, 1997) against a backcloth of patriarchy. Thus the significance of gender research cannot be underestimated.

Gender can result in both harm and pleasure in the world. As Connell (2009: 143) points out, the 'harm of gender' is the system of inequality where women and girls are exploited, discredited and made vulnerable, and this harm is also found in specific patterns of gender order that have power to affect the world by the collective resources of society. The pleasure of gender comes from how it organizes sexual relationships, our relations with children and is integral to cultural richness. This harm and pleasure is potentially reflected in the political nature of gender research. We raise this as an issue because gender research is grounded in explorations of 'power structured relationships, arrangements whereby one group of persons is controlled by another' (Millett, 1972: 23) and where gender inequalities are generally expressed in terms of women's lack in relation to men, for example, power, income, wealth, social honour and cultural authority (Connell, 2009). However, while gender issues are not just about women – they are as much about men – we argue that to embark upon gender research is to commit to examining and exposing inequalities grounded in power. There will be those who resist this exposure as a threat to their own power, and those who do not see the inequalities, which has implications for the research and the researcher as well as those who share the motivation to expose. Participant responses to gender research have implications for the construction of knowledge within a political context for both the researcher and the researched.

PARTICIPANT–RESEARCHER RELATIONSHIPS AND THE RESEARCHER'S POSITION IN GENDER RESEARCH

Gender research can be highly sensitive as participants are often reluctant to discuss experiences of organizations on the basis of being a man or woman. Depending on participant motivations, individuals may want to be recognized for competence and position power, not for gender. An example of this comes from our current research project 'Senior Women at Work' (2011 to 2013) exploring women's relations with other women at work. In recruiting women to the project we were completely transparent about the topic; our motivations to explore women's relations with other women; how women can progress careers within organizations. Eighty-one women participants self-selected into the study. However, we did experience, in the minority, a number of women who did not support our motivations. During the interview they wondered why they had agreed to do the research and/or did not want to discuss their experiences of being a woman at the top of an organization. We also experienced, more generally, participants who did not think that being a woman had anything to do with their career success to date but were happy to talk in a gender neutral way about being in their current roles and how they got there. Here we were cognizant reflexively of how the researchers' and participants' conflicting positions on gender were influencing the way we constructed knowledge about gender, how the data was being produced and the impact on the subsequent analysis.

The debate of whether to declare your assumptions, values and principles as a gender researcher can be finely balanced. As women researchers and as feminists, we make sense of the world in a myriad of ways, bringing differing, even conflicting assumptions to our research, but 'feminism speaks with one voice in characterising the world it experiences as a patriarchal world and the culture it inherits as a masculine culture' (Crotty, 1998: 160). Our feminism is articulated in our research through a commitment to feminist standpoint research: the focus on women's experience as a basis for research, including the development of theoretical frameworks; the notion of the researcher as accountable to research participants and to a wider feminist constituency; acknowledging that the personal or private realm is also political; and a reflexive perspective on research as part of a knowledge evaluative framework which has tended to reflect the concerns of dominant groups (Griffin, 1995). Regardless of commitments to feminism, gender research is always political when exposing inequalities which can also lead to the risk of 'taint' for gender researchers located within business and management schools primarily focused upon gender neutral/blind education and research. In this context, as a woman, to lead on the gender research agenda opens up space for others (more powerful) to decide upon how the researcher and their performance are perceived and to attach value or not to the research itself. Such micro-political contexts can lead to constrained careers and limits on the resources open to gender researchers, thus reproducing gender inequalities.

TAKING OUR OWN MEDICINE!

To summarize our discussions so far, we have introduced the following key issues for consideration by gender researchers in HRD:

1. *Researcher reflexivity* is critical before a gender research project begins, for example, personal understandings of gender; individual researcher values and philosophical positions on gender; their motivations for research; and awareness of how gender research may construct researchers in their own professional settings and how research participants may respond to gender research.
2. Gender researchers need to be consistent and transparent in establishing/positioning their *understandings of gender* and the gender binary, in their *research methods, 'treatment' of gender, intersections with social categories* and relationships with *participants. Power* is a central concept in researching gender and cannot be ignored.
3. The researcher's *feminist ideals, gender philosophy and epistemological position* should be acknowledged, with consideration of the impact on participants and the research itself in producing knowledge, as *participants* may not share the researcher's commitment to exposing power relations and investigating gender and/or feminist ideologies.

4. Gender researchers need to consciously remain open to additional diverse discussions within HRD and multi-disciplinary perspectives concerning the advancing nature of the study of gender.

As white, middle-class, academic (elite) women, during our careers we have committed to gender, activism, development work and research, and as a result of our experiences in grappling with and confronting the issues outlined, we next outline a Multi-Stakeholder Framework developed to research gendered media constructions of UK women leaders. Through the Framework we make transparent how we have 'taken our own medicine' and are guided by our recommendations for gender researchers. In the discussion that follows we outline the literature drawn upon; the multiple methods within the Framework; how we operationalized the elements; and how we considered key issues for gender researchers in our research approaches.

A MULTI-STAKEHOLDER FRAMEWORK: GENDER–MEDIA–LEADERSHIP RESEARCH

Our current 'Gender–Media–Leadership' research concerns the marginalized position of women senior leaders in organizations, reflected by the lack of women on UK company boards, despite ongoing efforts to achieve more women in leadership positions (Davis, 2011). This is a gender issue where explanations can be explored through the experiences of women in organizations and reflect the growing body of contemporary research exploring how women leaders, and particularly women political leaders, are gendered through media representations and reporting (Mavin, 2009; Mavin et al., 2010; Skalli, 2011). We understand this gendering of women in the media as significant, as media reflect dominant social views (Tuchman, 1978), and are interested in understanding further *how women leaders are gendered in the UK media*, particularly in regional business media. Underpinning the research is our assumption that how women are constructed as leaders and how leaders are constructed in the media will have an impact on audiences, who, according to feminist media studies, construct meaning for their own lives from such sources (e.g. Ang, 1996; Ang and Hermes, 1996; Kelan, 2013), and, as such, will influence women's progress as leaders in organizations, that is, women's 'acceptance' as leaders.

As researchers with a feminist commitment to understand women's experiences and progress (or otherwise) in organizations, we drew upon the Global Media Monitoring Project (GMMP) (Macharia et al., 2010), which highlighted a dearth of women in business and economic media reporting and sensitized us to geographies of gender relations (Billing, 2011; Connell, 1987, 2009; Connell and Messerschmidt, 2005) – gender relations constructed globally, nationally and at local levels as well as within everyday interactions. We pursued this through a gender analysis of media constructions of women in a UK regional newspaper 'Annual Supplement' (Supplements) which presents the 'Top 500 Influential Leaders' in the geographical region. We therefore aimed to investigate the potential for multiplicity reflected through local variations in gender relations, while also being cognizant of the social context and that interactions and gender relations are influenced by background assumptions (regional, national or global) which reflect and maintain beliefs of the superiority of masculine hierarchical superiority (Knights and Kerfoot, 2004).

In developing our research methods we agreed to advance the limited research exploring how women's access to leadership positions is represented in the news media by using the methodological approach of Tienari et al. (2009) from organization gender studies and combining this with a method outside HRD which drew upon over thirty years of feminist analysis in media, gender and communication studies research (Carter and Steiner, 2004). Tienari et al. (2009) outline a discourse analysis process (see Box 23.1) to interrogate gendered constructions around quotas for more women on company boards in the Swedish and Finish news media, by focusing upon small sections of text while aiming to engage in 'mapping out more general social dynamics' (Tienari et al., 2009: 507).

We integrated this discourse analysis process into the first stage of a Multi-Stakeholder media analysis Framework adapted from Carter and Steiner (2004) (see Box 23.2) to reflect the media, gender and communication studies feminist literature which argues that media should be interrogated as articulated relationships between (1) texts, (2) institutions producing them and (3) audiences, to produce a multiple stakeholder and multiple methods approach.

This wider media, gender and communications literature addresses

---

BOX 23.1   THREE STAGES OF DISCOURSE ANALYSIS

1. Independent researcher discourse analysis of selected media texts.
2. Paired researcher reflexive comparisons of independent interpretations.
3. Research team identifying similarities and differences in interpretations of gendered discourses.

Source: Tienari et al. (2009)

BOX 23.2   CARTER AND STEINER'S FRAMEWORK –THREE LEVELS OF ANALYTIC FOCUS

1. Intertextual analysis to position the media text within its broader social context.
2. The technological/economic context of the publishers and their motivations in producing the media.
3. The audience practices.

Source: Carter and Steiner (2004)

---

a range of issues pertinent to our research, including women as (or in) entertainment; the news; the production of media; and audiences (Byerly and Ross, 2006). This critique supported our feminist ideals. It recognizes women's absence, reflects concern to raise women's voices and promotes women's participation in public and political life, by highlighting the extent of women's exclusion or misrepresentation in the media. Reviewing literature from beyond the boundaries of HRD, management and organization studies enabled us to establish that gender studies of media representations tell us something important about the messages media producers want to share with their audiences; something about perceptions of women's place and roles in social life which are socially acceptable, and contextual, therefore reflecting dominant social beliefs about public/private space (Norris, 1997), while also considering audience engagement (or rejection) of such messaging.

Management and organization studies media research has focused mainly on exploring researchers' interpretations of texts (Kelan, 2013). In developing the Framework and methods employed, we extend both gender media and communications, and management and organization studies literature which focuses upon discourse analysis of the discursive construction of media texts (Fairclough, 1995; Matheson, 2005; Sunderland, 2004; Tienari et al., 2009; Vaara et al., 2006), by including a media producer and an audience analysis. We therefore followed the shift in feminist media studies and the suggestion that the most influential feminist media analysis incorporates an appreciation of the media's contribution to the discursive negotiation of gender by exploring the interplay between text, production and the reception of media (van Zoonen, 1994; Carter and Steiner, 2004). We extend management media analysis by including the media producer and reflecting Carter and Steiner's (2004) media interplay between text, production and reception. We now move to explain the context and process of the Framework we utilized (shown in Table 23.1).

Table 23.1   A Multi-Stakeholder Framework for analysis of gendered media constructions of UK women leaders

Carter and Steiner's (2004) Three Levels of Analytic Focus	A Focus on Women's Experience as a Basis for Research		
	Our Focus	Research Method	Taking Our Own Medicine
Intertextual analysis Three Supplements of the Top 500 Influential Leaders in a UK Region (2008/2009 /2010). Sponsored by a recruitment/ HR solutions agency operating regionally and nationally. Produced by regional daily newspaper.	Identifying number of women in senior and professional positions (via SOCs in NOMIS) in the UK region. Exploring geographies of gender.	1) *Statistical analysis* of SOCs (senior manager and professional positions).	Identifying potential pool of leaders within region contributes to geographies of gender relations.
	Drawing on the extant literature to connect what is known of gender and management/ leadership against four researcher interpretations of three editorials, lead articles and media sponsor sections of the Supplements. Pieces chosen for analysis as they set the tone of the publication, communicate the understanding of 'influence' adopted: editorial, sponsor article and lead article (which focused on leadership and current issues/for the region).	2) *Discourse analysis:* a) Independently: four women researchers, followed by; b) Paired reflexive comparisons of interpretations; and c) Team identifying similarities and differences in gendered discourses constructing leadership in three Supplements (Tienari et al., 2009).	Through discourse analysis/ feminist standpoint utilizing doing gender well and differently theory, leadership as masculine and women as marginalized in analysis. Structured reflexivity through proforma, discussion and incorporating different gender and methodological interests in design/ analysis of the project. Reflexivity via individual, paired and team analysis of gendered discourses.

Institutional analysis Daily newspaper av. readership 88,000. Considers itself to be key part of regional business community.	Background and position of the news media within the region. To understand key issues in media producer's construction of Supplements: rationale for publication, technological constraints/opportunities, target advertisers, construction of leadership, stakeholders influencing inclusion of influential people, anticipated audience, response to NOMIS analysis.	3) One researcher conducted a *semi-structured interview* with lead journalist (man) from the editorial team of the Supplement.	Multi-disciplinary focus incorporating media and gender issues with media producer. Openness to challenge of research assumptions. Reflexivity post-comparison of assumptions regarding media producers' motivations vs findings of semi-structured interview. Influenced the overall project-data analysis.
Audience analysis	How do aspiring or current women leaders within the region respond to the Supplements and to initial NOMIS analysis?	4) One researcher conducted 3 *group interviews* comprising 17 women and 5 *semi-structured interviews* with women.	Commitment to women's voice. Transparency of research interests to group and individual interviews; inviting and exploring diverse participant perspectives. Reflexivity via responses to NOMIS analysis. No intersectional analysis due to low variation in participant backgrounds.

A team of four women researchers engaged in research to understand gendered media constructions of UK women leaders (women's experience as a focus for research), operationalizing a mixed method design (Saunders, 2012) involving: (1) statistical analysis of secondary data on women in senior positions in a UK region (geographies of gender); (2) analysis of three Supplements of the Top 500 Influential Leaders in the region via discourse analysis, independently, in pairs and as a group of four (gender intertextuality); (3) a semi-structured interview with a media producer (man) (gendered understandings); (4) group and individual interviews with a selected media audience (aspiring and current women leaders) (women's voice); and (5) various stages of ongoing researcher reflexivity (and accountability). All methods were employed before the overall analysis took place, and enough time was set aside for each stage of the methods. As researchers we were active in the interpretations and analysis and reflexive of our role in the process.

The statistical analysis of UK NOMIS[1] data, freely available to the public, of the top two Standard Occupational Classifications (SOCs) enabled a three year comparison of the percentage of women in the geographical region classified as holding senior manager and professional roles with the three Supplements. NOMIS results showed that the combined percentage of women in the top two SOCs in the region (40.9 per cent–38.4 per cent–40.6 per cent over three years) far exceeded the percentage of women profiled in the Supplements (16.8 per cent–17.2 per cent–18.2 per cent over three years). A UK regional comparison of the same SOCs highlighted that the geographical region was mid-table or above regarding percentages of women holding senior positions, although full statistical analysis of the figures was problematic due to the amount of estimation present in the percentages reported by NOMIS. However, the results challenged the assumption that the lack of women profiled in the Supplements was reflective of a geographical constraint and supported the researchers' assumptions that the media publication was not profiling sufficient women as influential leaders in the region.

For the discourse analysis, we followed Tienari et al.'s (2009) approach to critical discourse analysis of media texts, where individual texts are not subjected to linguistic in-depth analysis and the process is iterative. We combined Carter and Steiner's (2004) first level of intertextual analysis to position the media within its broader social context (connecting what we know of gender and management/leadership to the Supplement texts) with Tienari et al.'s (2009) approach, where all authors identify similarities and differences in original interpretations of media materials and note how to account for these apparent similarities and differences. We conducted discourse analysis of three lead articles (editorial, lead article, sponsor article) from the three annual media Supplements via individual, paired and group discourse identification. We were guided at each stage by a number of questions: what discourses contribute to framing the representations of gender and regional leaders in these texts? What factors have influenced the media producers? What technological or workplace issues have shaped the media texts? How is the text positioned or positioning? Whose interests are served by this positioning? Whose interests are negated? What are the consequences of this positioning in terms of gender and power? This process of staged discourse analysis produced a number of benefits. It identified diverse individual researcher perspectives/interests and, while individuals and pairs named discourses differently, there was resonance in the results and patterns identified, resulting in agreed final discourses through the group analytical stage. The development of the discourses was thorough, inclusive and comprehensive in that individuals, pairs and the four researchers returned to the Supplements and to their research notes (which were shared where appropriate) at each stage to check that all relevant extracts and interpretations for each discourse had been collated. The resulting discourses were checked against each other and back to the original data to ensure coherence, consistency and distinctiveness.

The audience analysis, comprising group and individual interviews conducted by one researcher, also raised gender consciousness (Martin, 2003; Mavin, 2006) to gendered media constructions and participant's responses to this media. Participants were given complete hard copies of the Supplements to read and discuss. Resulting data was analysed via template analysis (King, 2004; 2012), one of the most well-used forms of thematic analysis in the management field which can be applied to any kind of data (Cassell, 2012), to identify and compare key themes. We followed the conventions outlined by King (2004; 2012) and were guided by McGivern (2009), beginning with a *mechanical* exploration before moving on to the *intellectual analysis*. This consisted of one researcher conducting an initial exploration of the group interview data to get a 'feel' for it and to devise inductively the initial thematic categories. This was followed by the 'intellectual analysis' involving the other researchers in an iterative process of moving between the data and the literature, resulting in thematic resonance. This process of coding and interpretations enabled the researchers to discover links within and across categories/themes and enabled conceptual or theoretical links to be made (Cassell, 2012). The resulting themes provided resonance with the researchers' discourse analysis regarding audience responses to, and issues about, the Supplements. The audience analysis moved beyond the gendered constructions of women leaders and extended to the problematizing of 'leader' and 'leadership' constructed in the Supplements.

The semi-structured interview by one researcher with a lead journalist from the media producer was a key method to extend existing research in business media analysis. An existing relationship with the media producer facilitated access. The data was analysed again by template analysis (as above), and it challenged the research team's assumptions about how the Supplements were developed – who was involved; how leaders had been included or not; which images were included and of whom – and produced important insights into the production of the Supplements. The challenge to assumptions was recorded via researcher reflexivity, formalized via a proforma of individual reflexive data from experiences across the research methods, and subsequently discussed as a research team.

CONCLUSION

In summary, this chapter has outlined key issues for HRD gender researchers and how we reflected the issues within a Multi-Stakeholder (multi-method) Framework. We initially outlined how in gender research it is important to engage in researcher reflexivity regarding values, philosophical assumptions and understandings of gender, and how gender research (as political and grounded in power) may impact upon researchers and participants. We introduced debates concerning the gender–sex binary divide, geographies of gender, intersectionality and moving beyond HRD boundaries to advance gender research. We outlined how key issues for gender research impact on our choice of methods and our production of knowledge. The Framework enabled us to 'take our own medicine' in terms of operationalizing the key issues in a gender project; in our choice of multiple methods and stakeholder participants; and in extending research methods already in use. Producing data from various sources had the benefit of building resonance, credibility and confirmability of our findings and thus trustworthiness of the research (Lincoln and Guba, 1985) and facilitated development of the research team's knowledge, research skills and abilities. The constraints of the Framework – that it requires a research team, engagement in a time consuming process and access to producers of media, which can be problematic – are outweighed by the benefits it delivered for us as a research team and for the research question. From our experience, consideration of the key issues outlined can lead to the development of protocols which guide the research process and reflect the researchers' location within the issues raised, and we contend that this process produces transparent, credible, defendable contributions. Significantly for us, engaging with colleagues in gender research is incredibly rewarding and develops research teams to build credibility and trustworthiness in research.

ACKNOWLEDGEMENT

The authors would like to acknowledge 'Gender–Media–Leadership' research team members, Dr Patricia Bryans, Dr Nicola Patterson and Angela McGrane.

NOTE

1. http://www.nomisweb.co.uk/

REFERENCES

Acker, J. (1992). 'Gendering Organizational Theory'. In A. Mills and P. Tancred (eds) *Gendering Organizational Analysis*. Newbury Park, CA: Sage, 248–260.
Acker, J. (2000). 'Revisiting Class: Thinking for Gender, Race, and Organizations'. *Social Politics*, **7** (2), 192–214.
Alvesson, M. and Due Billing, Y. (1997). *Understanding Gender and Organizations*. London: Sage.
Ang, I. (1996). *Living Room Wars: Rethinking Media Audiences for a Postmodern World*. London: Routledge.
Ang, I. and Hermes, J. (1996). 'Gender and/in Media Consumption'. In I. Ang (ed.) *Living Room Wars: Rethinking Media Audiences for a Postmodern World*. London: Routledge, 109–129.
Billing, Y. D. (2011). 'Are Women in Management Victims of the Phantom of the Male Norm?' *Gender, Work and Organization*, **18** (3), 298–317.
Broadbridge, A. and Simpson, R. (2011). '25 Years On: Reflecting on the Past and Looking to the Future in Gender and Management Research'. *British Journal of Management*, **22** (3), 470–483.
Bryans, P. and Mavin, S. (2003). 'Women Learning to Become Managers: Learning to Fit in or to Play a Different Game?' *Management Learning*, **34** (1), 111–134.
Butler, J. (1990). *Gender Trouble: Feminism and the Subversion of Identity*. London: Routledge.
Butler, J. (2004). *Undoing Gender*. New York: Routledge.
Byerly, C. M. and Ross, K. (2006). *Women and Media: A Critical Introduction*. Malden, MA and Oxford: Blackwell.
Carter, C. and Steiner, L. (2004). *Critical Readings: Media and Gender*. Maidenhead, UK: Open University Press.
Cassell, C. (2012). 'Exploring Dignity at Work Using Three Types of Qualitative Data Analysis: Themes, Metaphors and Stories'. Paper presented to Research Methodology track, *The British Academy of Management Annual Conference, 11–13 September*, University of Cardiff.
Connell, R. W. (1987). *Gender and Power: Society, the Person and Sexual Politics*. Stanford, CA: Stanford University Press.
Connell, R. W. (2009). *Short Introductions. Gender*. Malden, MA: Polity.

Connell, R. W. and Messerschmidt, J. (2005). 'Hegemonic Masculinity: Rethinking the Concept'. *Gender and Society*, **19** (6), 829–859.
Crenshaw, K. W. (1991). 'Mapping the Margins: Intersectionality, Identity Politics, and Violence against Women of Color'. *Stanford Law Review*, **43** (6), 1241–1299.
Crotty, M. (1998). *The Foundations of Social Research: Meaning and Perspective in the Research Process.* London: Sage.
Davies, E. M. (2011). *Women on Boards.* Lord Davies Review.
Elliott, C. and Stead, V. (2008). 'Learning from Leading Women's Experience: Towards a Sociological Understanding'. *Leadership*, **4** (2), 159–180.
Fairclough, N. (1995). *Media Discourse.* London: Hodder Arnold.
Gherardi, S. (1994). 'The Gender We Think the Gender We Do in Our Everyday Organizational Lives'. *Human Relations*, **47** (6), 591–610.
Griffin, C. (1995). 'Feminism, Social Psychology and Qualitative Research'. *The Psychologist*, March, 446–448.
Hassard, J. and Holliday, R. (2001). 'Contested Bodies: An Introduction'. In J. Hassard and R. Holliday (eds) *Contested Bodies.* London: Routledge.
Holvino, E. (2010). 'Intersections: The Simultaneity of Race, Gender and Class in Organization Studies'. *Gender, Work and Organization*, **17** (3), 248–277.
Kelan, E. K. (2010). 'Gender Logic and Undoing Gender at Work'. *Gender, Work and Organization*, **17** (2), 174–194.
Kelan, E. K. (2013). 'The Becoming of Business Bodies: Gender, Appearance, and Leadership Development'. *Management Learning*, **44** (1), 45–61.
Kempster, S. and Stewart, J. (2010). 'Becoming a Leader: A Co-produced Autoethnographic Exploration of Situated Learning of Leadership Practice'. *Management Learning*, **41** (2), 205–219.
King, N. (2004). 'Using Templates in the Thematic Analysis of Texts'. In C. M. Cassell and G. Symon (eds) *Essential Guide to Qualitative Methods in Organizational Research.* London: Sage, 256–270.
King, N. (2012). 'Template Analysis'. In G. Symon and C. M. Cassell (eds) *Qualitative Organizational Research: Key Challenges and Core Methods.* London: Sage, 426–450.
Knights, D. and Kerfoot, D. (2004). 'Between Representations and Subjectivity: Gender Binaries and the Politics of Organizational Transformation'. *Gender, Work and Organization*, **11** (4), 430–454.
Lincoln, Y. S. and Guba, E. G. (1985). *Naturalistic Inquiry.* Newbury Park, CA: Sage.
Macharia, S., O'Connor, D. and Ndangam, L. (2010). 'Who Makes the News? Global Report'. *Global Media Monitoring Project.* Toronto: World Association for Christian Communication.
Martin, P. Y. (2003). '"Said and Done" versus "Saying and Doing": Gendering Practices, Practicing Gender at Work'. *Gender and Society*, **17** (3), 342–366.
Matheson, D. (2005). *Media Discourses: Analysing Media Texts.* Maidenhead, UK: Open University Press.
Mavin, S. (2006). 'Venus Envy: Problematizing Solidarity Behaviour and Queen Bees'. *Women in Management Review*, **21** (4), 264–276.
Mavin, S. (2009). 'Gender Stereotypes and Assumptions: Popular Culture Constructions of Women Leaders'. *10th International Conference Human Resource Development Research and Practice across Europe, HRD: Complexity and Imperfection in Practice*, Newcastle Business School, Northumbria University, UK, 10–12 June 2009.
Mavin, S. and Bryans, P. (1999). 'Gender on the Agenda in Management Education?' *Women in Management Review*, **14** (3), 99–104.
Mavin, S., Bryans, P. and Cunningham, R. (2010). 'Fed-Up with Blair's Babes, Gordon's Gals, Cameron's Cuties, Nick's Nymphets: Challenging Gendered Media Representations of Women Political Leaders'. *Gender in Management: An International Journal*, **25** (7), 550–569, an invited publication.
Mavin, S. and Grandy, G. (2012). 'Doing Gender Well and Differently in Management'. *Gender in Management: An International Journal*, **27** (4), 218–231.

Mavin, S. and Grandy, G. (2013). 'Doing Gender Well and Differently in Dirty Work: The Case of Exotic Dancing'. *Gender, Work and Organization*, **20** (3), 232–251.
McGivern, Y. (2009). *The Practice of Market Research*, 3rd edn. Essex, UK: Pearson Education.
Messerschmidt, J. (2009). 'Doing Gender: The Impact and Future of a Salient Sociological Concept'. *Gender and Society*, **23** (1), 85–88.
Millett, K. (1972). *Sexual Politics*. London: Abacus.
Norris, P. (1997). *Politics and the Press: The News Media and Their Influences*. Boulder, CO: Lynne Rienner Publishers.
Poggio, B. (2006). 'Outline of a Theory of Gender Practices'. *Gender, Work and Organization*, **13** (3), 225–233.
Saunders, M. N. K. (2012). 'Combined Card Sorts and In-depth Interviews'. In F. Lyon, M. N. K. Saunders and G. Möllering (eds) *Handbook of Research Methods on Trust*. Cheltenham, UK and Northampton, MA, USA: Edward Elgar Publishing.
Skalli, L. H. (2011). 'Constructing Arab Female Leadership Lessons from the Moroccan Media'. *Gender and Society*, **25** (4), 473–495.
Stead, V. (2013). 'Learning to Deploy (In)Visibility: An Examination of Women Leaders' Lived Experiences'. *Management Learning*, **44** (1), 63–79.
Sunderland, J. (2004). *Gendered Discourses*. London: Palgrave Macmillan.
Tienari, J., Holgersson, C., Meriläinen S. and Höök, P. (2009). 'Gender, Management and Market Discourse: The Case of Gender Quotas in the Swedish and Finnish Media'. *Gender, Work and Organization*, **16** (4), 501–521.
Tuchman, G. (1978). 'Introduction: The Symbolic Annihilation of Women by the Mass Media'. In G. Tuchman, A. K. Daniels and J. Benét, (eds) *Hearth and Home: Images of Women in the Mass Media*. New York: Oxford University Press, 3–38.
Vaara, E., Tienari, J. and Laurila, J. (2006). 'Pulp and Paper Fiction: On the Discursive Legitimation of Global Industrial Restructuring'. *Organization Studies*, **27** (6), 789–813.
Valentine, G. (2007). 'Theorizing and Researching Intersectionality: A Challenge for Feminist Geography'. *The Professional Geographer*, **59** (1), 10–21.
van Zoonen, L. (1994). *Feminist Media Studies*. London: Sage.
West, C. and Zimmerman, D. H. (1987). 'Doing Gender'. *Gender and Society*, **1** (2), 125–151.
West, C. and Zimmerman, D. H. (2009). 'Accounting for Doing Gender'. *Gender and Society*, **23** (1), 112–122.
Williams, J. and Mavin, S. (2012). 'Disability as Constructed Difference: A Literature Review and Research Agenda for Management and Organization Studies'. *International Journal of Management Reviews*, **14** (2), 159–179.

ANNOTATED FURTHER READING

Bryans, P. and Mavin, S. (2003). 'Women Learning to Become Managers: Learning to Fit in or to Play a Different Game?' *Management Learning*, **34** (1), 111–134. An introduction to key issues in the debate on gender, learning management and HRD.
Carter, C. and Steiner, L. (2004). *Critical Readings: Media and Gender*. Maidenhead, UK: Open University Press. We recommend chapters 1 and 2 which overview the importance of media representations of gender and the relevance of multi-levels of analytic focus when choosing research methods.
Wetherell, M., Taylor, S. and Yates, S. J. (eds) (2001). *Discourse Theory and Practice: A Reader*. London: Sage. A collection of classic articles on discourse research which provides an overview of key themes.
Wetherell, M., Taylor, S. and Yates, S. (eds) (2001). *Discourse as Data: A Guide to Analysis*. London: Sage. This book provides step-by-step guidance on how to do discourse analysis from a range of different perspectives.

24. Leadership development as a method of enquiry: insights from a post-structuralist perspective
Carole Elliott and Valerie Stead

SUMMARY

In this chapter we explore how adopting a post-structuralist sensitivity to leadership development practice opens opportunities for 'research in action' within the classroom. Within it we present examples of how leadership development methods can also act simultaneously as methods of enquiry, constituting a research–teaching cycle.

INTRODUCTION

The chapter will explore how adopting a post-structuralist sensitivity to leadership development practice opens opportunities for 'research in action' within the classroom. Extending the notion of 'classroom as real world' (Reynolds and Trehan, 2002) and previous work interrogating the significance of the 'social' in social learning theory (Swan et al., 2009), we present examples of how leadership development methods can act simultaneously as methods of enquiry, constituting a research–teaching cycle.

In broad terms, as a critical practice, post-structuralism employs deconstruction as an analytical tool and is concerned to challenge and question espoused foundational knowledge (Briggs and Coleman, 2007) and interrogates interrelations between individuals and society. In this regard, a post-structuralist perspective supports relational and socially situated understandings of the learning of leadership, so encouraging a view of learning as experiential, emergent from and responsive to participation in social practices, such as leadership, and within particular historical and social contexts, such as organisations (Gherardi et al., 1998; Hamilton, 2006; Kempster, 2006; Lave and Wenger, 1991). Working within this understanding of leadership learning as an experiential and social process, we focus on two examples of developmental activities that draw our attention to the performative nature of teaching materials – such as frameworks, templates and typologies – that seek to represent people's experiences of leadership learning. Post-structuralism recognises how discourse is performative (cf. Butler, 1993); the effects of teaching materials, for example, will bring particular understandings into being. We examine how, on the one hand, as management educators, we subscribe to an understanding of learning as an experiential and social process, but, on the other hand, we recognise how the classroom environment can have a sanitising effect when we seek to communicate others' experiences, thereby detracting from the messiness and situatedness of leadership learning.

Drawing on our experience of navigating the research–teaching cycle, we discuss how we have been made aware of the difficulties of bringing the immediacy of research into the classroom when discussing women's leadership learning. We present how we can introduce methods of enquiry, traditionally used to gather, analyse and conceptualise information, to leadership development/Human Resource Development (HRD) interventions. We illustrate this by reflecting on our experience of introducing a typology of women's leadership learning (Stead and Elliott, 2013) – the culmination of a qualitative research project whose aim was to understand the experiential nature of women's leadership learning – to two separate leadership development interventions. We then propose how conceiving the typology as an epistemic object, as an artefact that mediates learning, opens up the possibility of collective reflexive enquiry as a means to challenge and problematise understandings of leadership.

THE METHOD OF EXPERIENTIAL LEARNING

We begin our consideration of how leadership development interventions can simultaneously serve as a research space by reviewing the significance given to the role of experience in leadership learning and development. Experiential learning has been described as an approach that challenges the notion that learning involves the transmission of knowledge from an expert to a novice (Reynolds and Vince, 2007) and is a developing focus of empirical attention in the leadership development literature (DeRue and Wellman, 2009; Gherardi and Poggio, 2007; Kempster, 2009; Stead and Elliott, 2009). Learning is considered to be 'a collaborative process, one in which people critically examine the ideas they use to make sense of "experience"' (Reynolds and Vince, 2007: 7). Underpinning the experiential perspective is the notion that learning is inherently social. However, as several authors have highlighted, some of the most popular models of experiential learning, including Kolb's learning cycle, assume that events are separated from 'people as participants, creators and observers' (Ramsay, 2005: 221), so the significance of the social is not explicitly acknowledged (Miettenen, 2000: Ramsay, 2005; Swan et al., 2009; Stead and Elliott, 2013). In our research we have been specifically concerned to draw attention to how the social, and therefore experiential learning, is structured by gender, class and race. Taking an understanding of leadership learning as an inherently social process to the teaching of leadership, we suggest, encourages an approach that facilitates participants' ability to 'develop analytical frameworks within which to examine and interrogate experience' (Swan, 2007: 204) and to critically reflect on the everyday small occurrences, the micro-practices (Cunliffe and Eriksen, 2011), of leadership practices and interventions. In other words, conceiving leadership learning and development as a social activity draws attention to its empirical possibilities – its potential as a site for enquiry.

Thinking about experiential learning, and the social processes inherent to learning, has drawn attention to experiential learning theory's (ELT) lack of a 'theoretically critical foundation' (Reynolds, 2009: 390). Kayes (2002) proposes a post-structuralist approach to ELT, where he argues for the benefits of 'defining managerial practice grounded in concrete language' (p. 146) that makes use of methods such as storytelling, life story writing, critical incident interviews and 'conversational learning' (Baker et al., 2002) to help learners connect personal knowledge and social knowledge (Kayes, 2002). This post-structural perspective resonates with developments in understandings of leadership that perceive it as a relational, negotiated process (Fletcher, 2004; Ford, 2006; Cunliffe and Eriksen, 2011) that emerges from a particular context, developments that are now being reflected in the teaching of leadership (Reynolds, 2009). It also mobilises a more critical underpinning to the notion of 'classroom as real world', which has also been criticised for its lack of attention to issues of power relations within the classroom (Reynolds and Trehan, 2001). Not to address the power relations inherent to pedagogical processes is, Reynolds and Trehan (ibid: 368) suggest, 'to collude – unwittingly perhaps – with the processes through which inequity is generated and to lose an opportunity for learning about them as parallels of "the power and privilege of the secular world" (Johnson-Bailey and Cervero, 1996, p. 153)'.

In previous work (Stead and Elliott, 2013), we too have adopted a post-structuralist sensitivity to draw attention to the gendered nature of social practices, processes, activities and interactions that shape leadership activity (Acker, 1995; Wharton, 2005). Informed by our experience of leadership development practice and research into women's leadership learning (Elliott and Stead, 2008; Stead and Elliott, 2009), we have developed a greater appreciation and awareness of women's leadership learning as a social process that provides educators and students with access to a 'critical discourse' (Kelan and Jones, 2010: 39). Providing access to a critical discourse, we argue, challenges the prevalence of normative masculine leadership practices. In the following sections we go on to describe leadership development interventions where we have drawn on experiential learning approaches to critically interrogate objects of enquiry, such as typologies, to illustrate how leadership development can also act as a site for enquiry.

LEADERSHIP DEVELOPMENT INTERVENTIONS

Two leadership development interventions alerted us to how objects of enquiry, within instances of experiential learning, can themselves become the stimulus for additional cycles of enquiry. Both interventions, one a workshop with full-time master's students and the other a regional business development event for women leaders, employed a typology of women's leadership learning we had developed. The two-hour seminar for master's students was attended by 16 students (10 women and 6 men), and it was introduced as an opportunity to examine 'learning from difference' and aimed to encourage students to think about the impact of social conditions such as gender on leaders' learning. The event began with a presentation of the typology, including some in-depth discussion on examples of women's leadership learning strategies. Smaller group discussions then took place during which the students were asked to use the typology as a way of thinking about their own experiences. The keynote presentation at the regional business development week was attended by around 130 people, the majority of whom were women, and was promoted by the organisers as providing an insight into women's leadership skills. The presentation was followed by a 15-minute question and answers session and then by a 'networking' lunch.

The typology acted as a summary of key themes we had identified in the literature regarding women leaders' experiences, including the strategies that are reported as important to women's learning of leadership. However, when using the typology we experienced a sense of unease. In seeking to represent women leaders' learning through this format, we recognised that we risk homogenising women's experiences; intended as a helpful object to facilitate discussion, the typology worked to contradict our own position on women's leadership learning as well as denying the range, depth and diversity of women leaders' experiences. In mobilising the typology as a pedagogic tool we realised that we were in fact reinforcing an asymmetric view of the gender and leadership relationship.

LEADERSHIP DEVELOPMENT AS A SITE FOR ENQUIRY: ADOPTING A POST-STRUCTURALIST SENSITIVITY

In this section we discuss our use of the leadership development interventions as sites of enquiry. First we explain how we adopted a post-structuralist sensitivity to critically interrogate those interventions. Second we draw on this discussion to suggest a critical framework for reflexive enquiry that might be employed as a method for enquiry.

The particular dilemma that we faced was how can we represent women's leadership learning to participants, while simultaneously developing a critical appreciation of the subtleties of these experiences? Informed by post-structuralist understandings of the performative impact of discourse (Ford et al., 2008), we entered into a series of reflective cycles to deconstruct the construction (Stead and Elliott, 2013) of women's leadership learning.

We adopted what we call a post-structuralist sensitivity based on ideas from post-structural and feminist post-structural perspectives as a critical methodology to examine the interventions. With a concern for the 'social', and in recognition that post-structuralism is concerned with how people's lives are 'inextricably interwoven with the social world around them' (Collinson, 2003: 528), we first looked at how the experiences highlighted ways in which the intervention illuminated the social and cultural context of the participants' experiences. For example, in relation to both activities we identified how men and women reacted differently to the typology. When we presented specific examples from the typology that show how women leaders develop social capital, the women attending the business development event openly commented on how similar this was to their own experience. In the master's seminar too there was recognition, but also whispered conversations between some students. Once the seminar had ended, one female student approached Valerie to say how interesting she had found the session and how 'much of this has happened, and is happening to me' (Stead and Elliott, 2013: 384). Other women meanwhile expressed little empathy with the women leaders' experiences summarised in the typology, and stated clearly that gender was not 'an issue' (ibid.) for them. Male participants were less forthcoming in their comments; they found it interesting to engage with the typology but difficult to comment upon. In terms of looking at leadership they felt that the typology excluded, rather than invited, their participation.

Post-structuralist ideas draw attention to how ideas of the self as fixed are rejected, emphasising instead the dynamic nature of the self, the multiple and shifting nature of identities (Collinson, 2003, 2005). These ideas encouraged us to examine the performative effects of the interventions, that is, how the leadership interventions brought into being different representations of leadership identity. Ford et al. (2008), in their study of leadership identity, argue that 'reading, writing and talking are not innocent activities but are actively productive' (p. 10). Relating this to the typology, we can see how social representations of leadership in the typology can have a performative effect and bring particular leadership understandings into being. Taking this perspective we could then examine how the participants identified with, rejected or challenged particular representations of leadership articulated in the typology. For instance, in discussing examples of how women access social capital through networks, some participants highlighted how because of their gender they might struggle to be seen as leaders, while others found that because they were in the minority this brought more attention to their leadership identity.

Using these aspects of post-structuralist approaches to examine leadership development interventions has been helpful as a method of enquiry in a number of ways. It has enabled us to gain useful insights into how we theorise leadership; our experiences of using the typology have illuminated for us the disruptive nature of women's leadership, including how it counters and challenges traditional leadership discourses. Taking a post-structural sensitivity has also provided insights into how we teach leadership, including how we might use epistemic objects such as a typology or conceptual framework in the classroom. Our experiences and the reactions to our typology have highlighted the ways in which epistemic objects might be used, for instance, as a way to question and challenge leadership ideas, as a way to draw attention to power dynamics in the classroom, including how models or frameworks might enable some to express ideas while hindering others. The variety of responses to the typology therefore heightened our awareness of the knowledge creation possibilities within the classroom.

A CRITICAL FRAMEWORK FOR REFLEXIVE ENQUIRY

Our experiences suggest the opportunities created by a conscious deployment of a critical framework of reflexive enquiry in the classroom. Such a framework follows a process of three main reflective cycles of activity that begin prior to entering the classroom.

Reflective Cycle 1: This first reflective cycle involves preparing the classroom as a research site. If we explicitly use the 'classroom as real world' (Reynolds and Trehan, 2001), this requires us to recognise the social and relational dynamics inherent in any classroom activity. Models, frameworks, typologies, ideas or other epistemic objects might therefore be chosen as a basis from which researchers and management educators can directly access the everyday experience of a phenomenon such as leadership. They might be selected in the extent to which they enable deconstruction, disruption and critique. For instance, we have used typologies of women's experiences of learning as a way to stimulate critique and discussion on leadership development programmes. This preparatory stage invites initial reflection on the choice of object or ideas that will form the basis for the classroom research activity.

Reflective Cycle 2: This reflective cycle of activity involves the engagement of participants with the chosen epistemic object. In this reflective cycle participants, through their questioning and challenging, their participation or non-participation, alert us to consistencies, anomalies, spaces and dilemmas in the theory/practice divide. We have observed in our own teaching how explicit inclusion of participants in this critical exercise can be beneficial, for instance by introducing epistemic objects primarily as frameworks for critique and inviting participants to challenge and question. Data can be collected during this reflective cycle in a number of ways, including observation by facilitators and researchers of the response to epistemic objects as highlighted in Stead and Elliott's (2013) study. Other forms of data collection might include flip chart notes by participants documenting their discussions and critiques, video-taping of group or feedback sessions or through individual diaries.

Reflective Cycle 3: The classroom activity leads to a further reflective cycle where we can observe the performative effects of epistemic objects in the classroom, that is, the way in which the objects encourage particular ways of thinking or talking about the phenomenon under question, for example how we discuss and understand leadership (Ford et al., 2008). We can therefore reflect on both the participants' reactions and discussions at an immediate level as well as at a deeper level in consideration of how these reactions reflect broader social relations and discourse. This reflective activity might be captured through recording and documenting conversations between co-researchers and facilitators and participants during and after the classroom activity.

Employing this critical framework raises a number of issues for consideration. The level of interaction involved with participants presupposes a class number and setting that can work comfortably in groups and has sufficient time to discuss and feed back conversations. The timing of this kind of research–teaching intervention can also be important, for instance whether participants might feel comfortable enough with each other or confident in expressing their views and opinions. Furthermore, researchers may want to consider the benefits and limitations of including participants of different gender, race, ethnicity or class in the activity and the extent to which this mix might offer richness to the research experience.

A post-structuralist sensitivity, coupled with cycles of reflective activity, comprises a critical framework for reflexive enquiry that is both critical in exposing developmental activities to critique and reflexive in informing the development of theory and continuing educational practice.

REFERENCES

Acker, J. (1995) Feminist Goals and Organizing Processes. In: Ferree, M.M. and Martin, P.Y. (eds). *Feminist Organizations: Harvest of the New Women's Movement*. Philadelphia, PA: Temple University Press; pp. 137–144.

Baker, A.C., Jensen, P. and Kolb, D.A. (2002) *Conversational Learning: An Experiential Approach to Knowledge Creation*. Westport, CT: Quorum Books.

Briggs, A.R.J. and Coleman, M. (eds) (2007) *Research Methods in Educational Leadership and Management*. 2nd edition. London: Sage.

Butler, J. (1993) *Bodies That Matter: On the Discursive Limits of 'Sex'*. New York: Routledge.

Collinson, D.L. (2003) Identities and Insecurities: Selves at Work. *Organization* 10(3): 527–547.

Collinson, D. (2005) Dialectics of Leadership. *Human Relations* 58(11): 1419–1442.

Cunliffe, A.L. and Eriksen, M. (2011) Relational Leadership. *Human Relations* 64(11): 1425–1449.

DeRue, D.S. and Wellman, N. (2009) Developing Leaders via Experience: The Role of Developmental Challenge, Learning Orientation, and Feedback Availability. *Journal of Applied Psychology* 94(4): 859–875.

Elliott, C. and Stead, V. (2008) Learning from Leading Women's Experience: Towards a Sociological Understanding. *Leadership* 4(2): 159–180.

Fletcher, J.K. (2004) The Paradox of Postheroic Leadership: An Essay on Gender, Power, and Transformational Change. *Leadership Quarterly* 15(5): 647–661.

Ford, J. (2006) Discourses of Leadership: Gender, Identity and Contradiction in a UK Public Sector Organization. *Leadership* 2(1): 77–99.

Ford, J., Harding, N. and Learmonth, M. (2008) *Leadership as Identity: Constructions and Deconstructions*. Basingstoke, UK: Palgrave Macmillan.

Gherardi, S., Nicolini, D. and Odella, F. (1998) Toward a Social Understanding of How People Learn in Organizations: The Notion of Situated Curriculum. *Management Learning* 29(3): 273–297.

Gherardi, S. and Poggio, B. (2007) Tales of Ordinary Leadership: A Feminist Approach to Experiential Learning. In: Reynolds, M. and Vince, R. (eds). *Handbook of Experiential Learning in Management Education*. Oxford: Oxford University Press; pp. 155–168.

Hamilton, E. (2006) Entrepreneurial Learning in Family Business. *Working paper*. Lancaster University Management School.

Johnson, J. and Cervero, R.M. (1996) An Analysis of the Educational Narratives of Reentry Black Women. *Adult Education Quarterly* 46: 142–157.

Kayes, D.C. (2002) Experiential Learning and Its Critics: Preserving the Role of Experience in Management Learning and Education. *Academy of Management Learning and Education* 1(2): 137–149.

Kelan, E.K. and Jones, R.D. (2010) Gender and the MBA. *Academy of Management Learning and Education* 9(1): 26–43.

Kempster, S. (2006) Leadership Learning through Lived Experience: A Process of Apprenticeship. *Journal of Management and Organization* 12: 4–22.

Kempster, S. (2009) *How Managers Have Learnt to Lead: Exploring the Development of Leadership Practice*. Basingstoke, UK: Palgrave Macmillan.

Lave, J. and Wenger, E. (1991) *Situated Learning: Legitimate Peripheral Participation*. Cambridge: Cambridge University Press.

Miettenen, R. (2000) The Concept of Experiential Learning and John Dewey's Theory of Reflective Thought and Action. *International Journal of Lifelong Education* 19(1): 54–72.

Ramsay, C. (2005) Narrative. From Learning in Reflection to Learning in Performance. *Management Learning* 36(2): 219–235.

Reynolds, M. (2009) Wild Frontiers – Reflections on Experiential Learning. *Management Learning* 40(4): 387–392.

Reynolds, M. and Trehan, K. (2001) Classroom as Real World Propositions for a Pedagogy of Difference. *Gender and Education* 13(4): 357–372.

Reynolds, M. and Vince, R. (2007) Experiential Learning and Management Education: Key Themes and Future Directions. In: Reynolds, M. and Vince, R. (eds). *The Handbook of Experiential Learning and Management Education*. Oxford: Oxford University Press; pp. 1–18.

Stead, V. and Elliott, C. (2009) *Women's Leadership*. Basingstoke, UK: Palgrave Macmillan.

Stead, V. and Elliott, C.J. (2013) Women's Leadership Learning: A Reflexive Review of Representations and Leadership Teaching. *Management Learning* 44(4): 373–394.

Swan, E. (2007) Blue-Eyed Girl: Jane Elliott's Experiential Learning and Anti-Racism. In: Reynolds, M. and Vince, R. (eds). *The Handbook of Experiential Learning and Management Education*. Oxford: Oxford University Press; pp. 202–220.

Swan, E., Stead, V. and Elliott, C. (2009) Feminist Futures and Challenges: Women, Diversity and Management Learning. *Management Learning* 40(4): 431–437.

Wharton, A.S. (2005) *The Sociology of Gender: An Introduction to Theory and Research*. Malden, MA: Blackwell Publishing.

ANNOTATED FURTHER READING

Ford, J., Harding, N. and Learmonth, M. (2008) *Leadership as Identity: Constructions and Deconstructions*. London: Palgrave Macmillan. Informed by post-structuralist perspectives on identity, this text provides an overview of mainstream leadership theory and also introduces the authors' studies of leadership, which illuminate how these theories are adopted by organisations. The book includes a chapter on post-structuralist theory, drawing particularly on the work of Derrida.

Reynolds, M. and Trehan, K. (2001) Classroom as Real World Propositions for a Pedagogy of Difference. *Gender and Education* 13(4): 357–372. This paper seeks to illuminate how difference in the classroom can be recognised and valued as a stimulus for learning, while acknowledging the classroom as a microcosm of the broader social context. The paper draws on feminist critical pedagogy to reflect on the authors' experiences in working with participative learning designs and to highlight how even critical pedagogies are not necessarily adequate enough to address issues of difference in the classroom setting.

25. Navigating *extra* sensitive research topics utilising content analysis and Computer Assisted Qualitative Data Analysis Software (CAQDAS)

Thomas Garavan and Clíodhna MacKenzie

SUMMARY

This chapter explores the issues associated with researching organisational issues that are extra sensitive due to their potential for negative personal, organisational and institutional outcomes. It highlights innovative approaches to source primary and secondary data and the use of Computer Aided Qualitative Data Analysis Software in HRD research.

INTRODUCTION

Often, the most challenging and compelling topics for social science researchers involve sensitive organisational issues (Jehn and Jonsen, 2010; Sieber and Stanley, 1988). Sensitive research topics often emerge following extreme events that have significant financial, economic or social impact (Buchanan and Denyer, 2013; Vaughan, 1999). These extreme events invariably prompt governments to convene public inquiries into establishing how and why these extreme events occurred (e.g. FCIC Hearing, 2010a; Treasury Select Committee, 2010; US Senate Hearings, 2011) and these can be a very useful primary and secondary source of data for social science researchers. Public inquires serve two purposes: (a) to ensure mistakes are not repeated (Buchanan and Denyer, 2013; Gephart, 2004) and (b) to enable institutions to regain some degree of legitimacy following organisational failure predicated on a lack of institutional oversight (Brown, 2004). Public inquiries therefore provide unique opportunities for organisational and management scholars to gain access to sensitive organisational topics which would ordinarily prove impossible to investigate (Bahn and Weatherill, 2013; Buchanan and Denyer, 2013; Gephart, 1993).

Within the category of sensitive research topics lies a subcategory we refer to as *extra* sensitive organisational issues. Extra sensitive research topics such as *greed, corruption, unethical/illegal behaviour, organisational/leadership psychopathy* and *fraud* can play a central role in organisational crises and/or disasters (e.g. Ashforth and Anand, 2003; Ashforth et al., 2008; Campbell et al., 2011; Fligstein and Goldstein, 2010; Shrivastava et al., 1988; Sims and Brinkmann, 2003), making them vitally important to social science researchers from a crisis post mortem and theoretical development perspective. Extra sensitive research topics are differentiated from more benign organisational issues due to the potential for negative personal (loss of trust/power/authority), organisational (reputational damage/ethical flexibility), institutional (deligitimacy/illegitimacy) and societal (socioeconomic) outcomes.

While the sensitive nature of these organisational topics may have wide appeal to social science researchers, access issues, lack of organisational transparency, participant resistance and institutional interference can deter all but the most committed of researchers. In our research exploring Human Resource Development (HRD) failures in the context of the global financial and economic[1] crises in Ireland, the US and the UK we remained cognisant of these challenges yet resolute and undeterred. The potential benefit of advancing our understanding of *how* and *why* many areas of HRD responsibility failed far outweighed the many roadblocks, challenges and setbacks commonplace among research pursuing sensitive topics (Alison et al., 2001). Gaining access to participants is not a panacea as research on sensitive topics may result in either low response rates or social desirability bias (Gephart, 1997, p.585). Challenges for HRD and indeed any social science scholar pursuing sensitive and difficult-to-study topics includes not only *how* to gain access to participants who may or may not respond truthfully to questions on sensitive organisational issues but whether the methods used are appropriate for this type of inquiry. Indeed, the real challenge for research scholars is twofold: first, knowing *where* to look for the data that already exists but may be fragmented, obscured, contextually detached or presumed to be irrelevant and, second, knowing *what* replicable analysis methods can augment the unobtrusive measures of sourcing relevant, reliable and representative data. While we accept that no research method is without some bias, the utility to the researchers of adopting an innovative approach to data gathering and data anlaysis is cogently articulated by (Webb et al., 1966, p.1):

> Interviews and questionnaires intrude as a foreign element into the social setting they would describe, they create as well as measure attitudes, they elicit atypical roles and responses, they are limited to those who are accessible and

will cooperate, and the responses obtained are produced in part by dimensions of individual differences irrelevent to the topic at hand

Webb et al. highlight an important issue associated with researchers influencing the dynamic of the interview – merely by being present, the researcher can change the behaviour of the interviewee, memory recall and outcome. While unintentional, the researcher has the capacity to create an outcome that bears little or resemblance to the reality of the phenomenon under investigation. Banking crises, organisational failures and economic recessions reflect rare events that insiders[2] consider sensitive subject matters, but are made extra sensitive when evidence emerges that *greed, corruption* and *unethical behaviour* may have played central roles in these crises (Brown, 2005; Weick, 2010). Although public inquiries provide both a valuable source of empirical data that potentially circumvents the 'access' issues associated with investigating sensitive organisational topics, researchers still face other challenges, not least of which is the selection and application of appropriate methodologies to investigate the phenomeon. Banking failures are considered 'low-probability, high-impact' events that threaten 'the viability of the organization' and are 'characterized by ambiguity of cause, effect, and means of resolution' (Pearson and Clair, 1998, p.60). Accordingly, they are unique data sources for researchers exploring senstive organisational topics. Indeed, it was the availability of this rare and insightful data that prompted our own sensitive topics research.

In this chapter we discuss the challenges and opportunities for HRD scholars who engage in researching sensitive and difficult-to-study topics. We highlight innovative approaches that we have incorporated into our own research to source primary and secondary data, utilising content analysis (CA) as a research method that stresses 'systemacity and procedural transparency' (Lee, 2000, p.107) along with the sophistication of Computer Aided Qualitative Data Analysis Software (CAQDAS). We outline why sensitive research topics might be best approached from an unobtrusive perspective (Webb et al., 1999) rather than gaining trust from the participants and organisations central to the research topics under investigation. Finally, in our discussion we argue that the use of CA frameworks with the sophistication of CAQDAS provides a systematic analysis process that can augment the 'non-reactive unobtrusive' method of data collection that has the potential to facilitate the discovery of truths behind sensitive research topics that traditional research methods may be less capable of doing.

RESEARCHING SENSITIVE ORGANISATIONAL ISSUES

Sensitive research topics are emotive and can result in societal judgements from those looking in (outsiders – *context unaware*) and a reluctance to engage in dialogue and discussion from those looking out (insiders – *context aware*). Sensitive research predominantly involves people and their behaviour; therefore, given HRD's *raison d'être*, it can be a challenge to objectively investigate people and organisational failures, especially when HRD practitioners are considered part of the organisation's management team (MacKenzie et al., 2011). For HRD scholars, this is both a blessing and a curse. The close proximity of HRD practitioners to organisational leadership makes it virtually impossible for them to uncover sensitive truths and realities about organisational life in any value-free manner (Bierema, 2009; MacKenzie et al., 2012). Moreover, HRD scholars who rely on organisational insiders to provide access and/or accurate information about sensitive organisational issues are often left to infer causal determinants based on incomplete or inaccurate data. Indeed, 'veiled silences' (Mazzei, 2003, p.365), which refers to 'participants' providing answers to questions that are *not* asked, is an indication of the challenges HRD researchers face even when they have *no* access issues. These challenges are further complicated when dealing with participants who may be 'seduced' by the interview process to disclose 'something they may later regret' (Dickson-Swift et al., 2007, p.331) or may simply be so shocked and traumatised that their responses are likely to be emotionally charged (Buchanan and Denyer, 2013, p.216). These issues have serious ethical implications for *any* social science researcher. Consequently, the importance of utilising qualitative research methods that can uncover the richness and detailed descriptions of context-specific organisational actions and behaviours (or *mis-behaviours*) is often overshadowed by the difficulty in getting participants to disclose that which may be self-incriminating or organisationally damaging (Alison et al., 2001; Gephart, 2004; Webb and Weick, 1979). The *real* challenge then for HRD scholars engaged in sensitive research is *how* to get close to the data (and respondents) without having to traverse the ethics minefield, manage participant exposure and/or grapple with organisational or legal intervention. The challenge is how to achieve what we might call 'engaged disengagement'.

PRIMARY AND SECONDARY SOURCES

What constitute primary and secondary sources of data is somewhat contested in the literature, and this can lead to novice researchers dismissing a
particular source of data because the researcher is unsure as to what constitutes primary and secondary sources. Easterby-Smith et al. (2008, p.11)
define primary data as that which is collected 'directly by the researcher'.
Maylor and Blackmon (2005, p.172) provide a similar definition but
go further to delineate between primary and secondary sources stating:
'primary data are data you have collected yourself specifically for your
project and secondary data are data other people have collected for their
own research projects or commercial purposes.'

Within the academic research literature, Buchanan and Denyer
(2013, p.212) contend that although investigation and (public) inquiry
reports may be 'grey literature' they can be considered 'proxy research'
as they provide explanations about 'conditions contributing to particular
incidents' and have 'methodological significance as primary and secondary data'. Additionally, the use of internal organisational documentation
such as emails, presentations and memos serves to anchor reflections of
organisational behaviour as spatially and temporally bounded records –
free from witness recall bias. Researchers such as Brown (2005), Gephart
(1997, 1993, 2004) and Perrow (1999) have utilised public inquiries and
first-hand accounts of disasters as both primary and secondary sources.
Further complicating the issue of what constitutes primary and secondary sources is the definition proposed by Handlin, Schlesinger, Morison,
Merk, Schlesinger Jr and Buck (1970; cited in Goodman and Kruger,
1988, p.315):

> Primary sources are first hand testimony about an historical event; secondary
> sources are descriptions of the event derived from and based upon primary
> sources. The primary source represents the view of the eye witness, the second-
> ary source the view of the journalist or scholar who comes along later and tries
> to reconstruct the story.

While we consider public inquiry audio, video and transcripts to be
exceptionally valuable and rich sources of data that are often overlooked
by management or organisational behaviour scholars (Buchanan and
Denyer, 2013; Gephart, 1993) we consider Saunders et al. (2003) as
offering the best compromise in understanding the differences between
primary and secondary data. Saunders et al. (2003, pp.188–189) argue that
researchers rarely consider the 'possibility of reanalysing data that have
already been collected for some other purpose' – this data may be 'raw
data, where there has been little if any processing'. In the context of public

inquiries hearings, while the data reflects 'eye witness' accounts (Goodman and Kruger, 1988), it is still categorised as data collected for a 'potentially' different purpose by someone else and should, for the purposes of research in the business and management field, be considered a secondary source. Historically, HRD scholars have overlooked this type of data source, perhaps in part because it was collected for a different purpose by someone else as argued convincingly by Saunders et al. (2003) and in part because of an inability to see beyond the 'noise' – the 'amoratization' issue raised by Webb and Weick (1979, p.652). One could argue then that HRD scholars have a responsibility to utilise *any* empirical data source that can potentially illuminate failures of HRD policies, practices and procedures.[3] We characterise HRD failures as any intervention that forms a well-accepted function as defined by Swanson (2001, p.304): 'HRD is a process of developing and/or unleashing human expertise through organization development (OD) and personnel training and development (T&D) for the purpose of improving performance.'

These interventions have a major influence on 'shaping organizational culture, developing current and future leaders, building commitment among organization members and anticipating and managing responses to changed conditions' (Gold et al., 2009, pp.28–29). The valuable insight that is to be gained from analysing publicly available data that include, for example, public inquiry transcripts, audio and video interviews, and company reports (e.g. Chatterjee and Hambrick, 2007; Gephart, 1993; Brown, 2005) is succinctly illuminated by Poland and Pederson (cited in Morison and Macleod, 2014, p.695) who argued: 'what is not said may be as revealing as what is said, particularly since what is left out ordinarily far exceeds what is put in.' Ironically then, by distancing themselves from the actors at the heart of the sensitive research topics under investigation, HRD scholars can gain a unique perspective and are more likely to remain objective in their analysis of sensitive organisational issues.

Common reasons why social science researchers decide against exploring sensitive research topics were highlighted by Alison et al. (2001), who argued that the selection of appropriate methodologies that facilitate academic rigour is quite limited, especially when the data being analysed are not considered primary data, that is, the data were generated for a different purpose by another researcher. Webb and Weick (1979, p.652), however, argue that proponents of unobtrusive methods believe in amortisation in that no matter how and for what purpose the data was collected it has more than one use. Indeed, Lee (2000, p.9) argued convincingly that data obtained 'opportunistically should not be seen as inherently inferior to data designed for a particular purpose'. This is something that novice researchers who have limited research exposure and experience should consider when grappling with what constitutues acceptable primary and secondary sources of data. The availability of data sources that might be considered novel, unorthodox or outside of mainstream sources provides novice researchers with a multitude of perspectives with which they can address their research questions, aims and objectives. Armed with an expanding array of qualitative tools and methods, sensitive research topics no longer remain only within the reach of the most ardent and determined HRD research scholars. The use of CAQDAS, such as NVivo, used in conjunction with CA frameworks offers a level of sophistication that has the potential to uncover more than structured and semi-structured interviews might when dealing with sensitive and difficult-to-study organisational issues. We make the distinction between both CA and CAQDAS in that CA offers a framework intended to serve three purposes:

> Its *prescriptive* purpose is to guide the conceptualization and design of practical content analytic research; its *analytical* purpose is to facilitate the critical examination and comparison of the published content analyses; and its *methodological* purpose is to point to performance criteria and precautionary standards that researchers can apply in evaluating ongoing content analyses. (Krippendorff, 2004, p.29)

In contrast, CAQDAS offers 'tools to mechanize tasks of ordering and archiving texts, and represents software for data administration and archiving' rather than 'tools for data analysis' (Kelle, 2000, p.285). A distinction was also allueded to by Lee (2000, p.106), who argued that 'software tools' can aid in the 'analysis of textual' data. This distinction is important as it highlights the subtle difference between both CA and CAQDAS. HRD scholars who have obtained data in its natural state (i.e. public inquiries/publically available organisational documents) can objectively analyse audio and video archieval evidence knowing that they have not injected themselves into the interviewer/interviewee dynamic (Webb et al., 1966).

Although there may be 'nothing that forbids research on sensitive issues', there is the very real possibility that because the issues under investigation are considered sensitive or potentially damaging to individuals within the organisation, 'powerful forces' may be 'working against the conduct of such research' (Sieber and Stanley, 1988, p.49). As we found from our own experience, obtaining access to participants (bank officials/finance professionals/state agencies) willing to talk *on the record* proved somewhat fruitless. Indeed, in our endeavours to secure transcripts of interviews carried out by 'publically funded consultants' exploring the Irish banking crisis, we were informed by an Irish state agency that the [Irish banking crisis] report was externally-commissioned with the *Department* receiving only the final report, for that reason, we do not hold interview transcripts or other preparation material relating to this report . . . [the external consultants] were similarly not required to retain any such records following the publication of their report. (State Department)

This is a stark illustration of what Sieber and Stanley (1988) refer to as powerful forces working against the pursuit of sensitive research topics. It is something that we as researchers experienced first hand and were acutely aware of throughout the entire research project.

ADDRESSING ETHICAL CONCERNS

The use of CAQDAS such as NVivo has the capacity to uncover more than structured and semi-structured interviews might when dealing with sensitive and difficult-to-study organisational issues (Alison et al., 2001, p.242). Along with documents from the US and the UK financial crisis pubilc inquiries, our research utilised NVivo to analyse over 200 hours of public inquiry video evidence as well as approximately 150 hours of audio evidence, a job that would historically have required a team of researchers to analyse the data. The utilisation of CAQDAS also has the potential to aid in the development of new theories through reducing interviewer contact and contamination of the environment, allowing for the discovery of themes, meanings and patterns in the natural state. This allows for the interpretation of how concepts are operative in the data (Bazeley and Jackson, 2013) without influencing participant responses or exposing participants to undue pressures, thus bypassing potential ethical issues associated with asking the right question without compromising the respondent's sense of what is right or wrong. Buchanan and Denyer (2013) argue that researchers need to consider 'novel' approaches to getting truthful responses from respondents by utilising what is accessible rather than developing intricate strategies to gain trust and honesty. When dealing with sensitive organisational issues, developing a relationship based on trust in order to elicit key information from respondents is at best questionably ethical. Gaining trust while cognisant of the research objectives is perhaps one of the greatest challenges for sensitive topic researchers. By utilising public inquiries to provide 'native accounts' (Czarniawska, 1997) of witnesses central to organisational crises or disasters, researchers can minimise contact, reducing the ethical concerns other researchers face when 'in the field' (Dickson-Swift et al., 2007). NVivo allowed for the disassembly and reassembly of large text samples into more manageable and meaningful key passages which could then be expanded and linked through sophisticated analysis features into more conceptually meaningful reflections of the hidden narratives often missed when researchers are focused too much on the ethical issues associated with sensitive research. This is one of the many benefits of engaged disengagement.

Accessing the sworn testimony of public inquiry witnesses enabled us to minimise the ethical quagmire associated with conducting sensitive research and its potential consequences or implications as a direct result of the interview process. Consequently, the interviews conducted by various public inquiry committees and commissions that sought to uncover the 'truth and hard facts' about what caused the (financial) crisis (FCIC Hearing, 2010b, p.3) was considered a non-issue for the purposes of this research. Lee (2000, p.57) argued that people who do not know they are being studied 'do not change their behavior'; however, studying people 'without their consent' violates the ethical standards one expects from qualitative researchers. This is a critical concern that all qualitative research needs to be cognisant of. Notwithstanding Lee's cogent argument, when utilising public inquiry hearings that are being televised, the ethical concerns regarding personal autonomy are deemed neutral. Confidentiality and anonymity in the case of both the UK and the US public inquiries were deemed less important than uncovering root causes and any potential learning opportunities to minimise any recurrence (US Senate Report, 2010).

UTILISING CONTENT ANALYSIS FOR SENSITIVE RESEARCH TOPICS

CA provides an alternative means of conducting qualitative research in business and management research (Bryman and Bell, 2007). Although primarily a qualitative methodology, CA also includes quantitative features which potentially provide advantages over 'purely qualitative methods such as literary interpretation and hermeneutics' (Aguinis et al., 2009, p.76). Krippendorff (2004, p.18) defines CA as a 'research technique for making replicable and valid inferences from texts (or other meaningful matter) to the context of their use'. Although Krippendorff identifies texts as data sources, the content can include video, audio, signs, symbols, artefacts or even numerical data. CA offers a number of benefits to social science researchers exploring sensitive management or organisational issues. CA can provide a replicable methodology to access deep individual or organisational structures such as cultures, cognitions, values and attitudes and provide 'insights into managerial cognitions which surveys or interviews cannot provide' at the same level of detail (Pollach, 2012, p.263). Moreover, there are theoretical benefits to be derived as Sonpar and Golden-Biddle (2008, p.797) contend – CA has the potential to elaborate and develop 'adolescent theories' by linking disparate concepts and themes that allow for an underdeveloped theory to be progressed. While there are many benefits to utilising CA for sensitive research, researchers must remain cognisant that while there is an abundance of available data, this is no guarantee that data are reliable. To that end, Bryman and Bell (2007), citing Scott (1990), suggest the following should be considered when assessing the quality of documentary evidence as primary and secondary sources of data:

- Authenticity – are the data genuine and of unquestionable origin?
- Credibility – is the evidence free from error and distortion?
- Representativeness – is the evidence typical of its kind, and, if not, is the extent of its untypicality known?
- Meaning – is the evidence clear and comprehensible?

In our sensitive research, we utilised the replicability of CA to explore public inquiry data units such as audio, video, interview transcripts, internal organisational documentation (e.g. emails, presentations and memos) and publically available data such as financial reports, which allowed for a systematic evaluation and categorisation of the data (Chanchai, 2011; Krippendorff, 2004). The structured approach of CA allowed for the construction of text into categories (concepts/themes) based on explicitly defined coding rules (Miles and Huberman, 1994; Pollach, 2012) and did so by utilising non-reactive data that allowed for multiple interpretations considering alternative voices, diverse perspectives and oppositional readings (Krippendorff, 2004, p.88). This was particularly useful in our research as we needed to interpret the data from mulitple ideological perspectives. Accordingly, our choice of methodology was determined by the context of the phenomenon, availability of reliable data and sensitive nature of the research topic. While we experienced access issues in respect of Irish banking institutions and government agencies consistent with the literature on sensitive research topics, unrestricted access to public inquiry testimony from the US and the UK hearings proved an exceptionally rich data source. The difficulty in gaining access to organisations willing to participate and provide *truthful* answers to probing questions can limit the researcher's pursuit of objectives; as such, CA has become an accepted research methodology (Alison et al., 2001; Jehn and Jonsen, 2010) that can effectively and robustly explore sensitive research topics.

In his textual analysis of risk and blame in disaster sense-making, Gephart (1993, p.1466) cited the use of newspaper articles and government documents as a source of rich data 'describing organisational events at a level of detail not otherwise available'. Duriau et al. (2007, p.5) also noted that the growing acceptance of CA as a research methodology in business and management research derives from the need to 'explore many important but difficult-to-study issues of management research'.

The use of CA therefore provides for a 'replicable methodology in accessing, analysing and understanding individual or collective dimensions such as 'values, intentions, attitudes and cognitions' while also adhering to methodological rigour, reliability and validity requirements (Duriau et al., 2007, p.6; Krippendorff, 2004, p.109). Krippendorff provides a number of CA frameworks that may assist content analysts in ensuring their methods are replicable, empirically sound and systematic in their approach to data analysis. As the CA components illustrate, it is a very strucutred and systematic approach to analysing available data in pursuit of the research agenda.

Content Analysis Components

- Unitising – various types of 'content' which may inform the research (e.g. text, video, audio)
- Sampling – economising of data into manageable statistically/ conceptually representative data such as text paragraphs, soundbytes (audio) and video clips
- Recording/Coding – bridges the gap between the unitised data so that data can be coded/recoded over time
- Reducing – allows for the efficient representation of data, especially when dealing with very large volumes of data
- Abductively inferring – relates to deriving contextual phenomena from the data bridging the gap between descriptive accounts, what they mean, entail or provoke
- Narrating – makes comprehensible what the researcher has inferred from the research. This is perhaps the most important aspect of the CA in that the researcher may need to explain the practical significance of their contribution to the literature.

Although the above components illustrate a useable framework for novice content analysts, Krippendorff (see pp.81–96) provides a number of variants that offer a more simplified approach for those familiar with CA. As with any methodology, CA must take into consideration context, theories and literature central to the research area under investigation. We utilised the CA components identified by Krippendorff and derived our own process-based Qualitative Content Analytic Framework (QCAF) (see Figure 25.1). Our QCAF provided a systematic and iterative

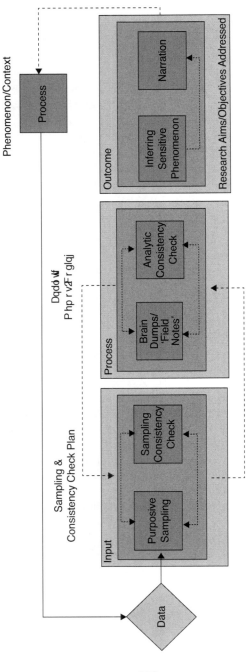

Source: Derived from: Bazeley & Jackson, 2013; Krippendorff, 2004; Saldana, 2012

Figure 25.1 Qualitative Content Analytic Framework

process-based method by which we could analyse the sophistication of CAQDAS to interpret and develop concepts unique to our own investigation. Indeed, we utilised this framework throughout the entire research project to ensure consistency and validity in the themes and concepts we derived from our data.

While no research method is without some fault, utilising CA with CAQDAS over other methods such as structured or semi-structured interviews or questionnaires does have a number of advantages. Researchers engaged in sensitive research face a number of obstacles that must be overcome; for example, the researcher(s) must ensure that (s)he builds a level of trust and rapport with the participant such that (s)he feels it is a safe environment in which to disclose/open up to the researcher (Dickson-Swift et al., 2007, p.338). Aside from the challenges researchers face in gaining the trust of the participants, they also run the risk of becoming 'desensitised' if they have been exposed to prolonged periods of sensitive research. This desensitising effect can paradoxically reduce objectivity wherein the researcher sees only similar patterns and concepts in the context of the research, which may reduce the researcher's ability to see connections due to insensitivity bias.

Another issue that qualitative researchers engaged in sensitive research face is that of participant resistance. This occurs when the participants actively engage in evasive behaviour when dealing with topics that are sensitive or uncomfortable. In this environment, the participants' limited responses may act as 'noise that veils or masks their inability or unwillingness' to engage with the researcher, leading to incomplete or inaccurate analysis and findings (Morison and Macleod, 2014, p.708). The limitations of questionnaires and interiews have best been articuated by Webb et al. (1999, p.174), whose criticism was not of the questionnaires or interviews per se but the tradition that allowed them to become a 'methodological sanctuary' to which the 'myopia of operational definitionalism permitted a retread'. That said, CA is not without its limitations. CA is only as good as the data on which the research is based. With public inquiries there is an abundance of sources and types (units) of data that provide multiple perspectives and narratives; however, if the researcher focuses too much on written reports or organisational documents, then there is a bias on the part of those who generated the reports (selection of what to include/not include) or, in the case of organisational documents, the potential for an idealised view of the organisation. Another issue is centred on coding, and specifically the interpretation of the data. Each researcher will have a different world view and may interpret the data in slightly different ways. This is less of an issue when the researcher is working alone; however, this can present problems for those working on team projects, especially if those teams are internationally based.

NAVIGATING THE MINE FIELD OF SENSITIVE ORGANISATIONAL ISSUES – EVIDENCE FROM OUR INQUIRY OF THE GLOBAL FINANCIAL CRISIS

Consistent with any approach to qualitive research, in our study we focused on design, data collection and analysis (Webb and Weick, 1979, p.650). However, given the sensitive nature of our inquiry we sought more innovative means of achieving this. For us, data collection preceded and drove the design and analysis, due in part to the many obstacles we encountered vis-à-vis organizational access and institutional resistance. Our approach was very much dictated by whether or not we could access reliable empirical data (Duriau et al., 2007; Krippendorff, 2004) and how innovative we were willing to be in order to analyse it (Buchanan and Denyer, 2013).

The appeal of getting close to the actors central to the financial crisis without having to face issues surrounding probing questions, and building rapport and establishing trust with the participants (Bahn and Weatherill, 2013; Jehn and Jonsen, 2010, p.314), meant we could spend significantly more time in the data analysis and interpretation phase of our research. While there are legitimate concerns that the data we planned to gather, analyse and interpret was collected for a different purpose (Alison et al., 2001, p.242), the potential benefits outweighed these issues. Concerns associated with our data being considered 'grey literature' (Buchanan and Denyer, 2013, p.212) or being perceived in some communities of practice as lacking 'closeness to the data' that could result in our alienation from the data also weighed heavily on our decision-making process. However, fears were minimised given that the public inquiry investigations were being conducted by seasoned investigators and addressed similar themes to the ones we were interested in, such as *why did people behave the way they did; why did organizations appear to engage in similar decision-making processes; in what way might emotions have impacted on decision-making*. Schütz 1973 (cited in Czarniawska, 1997, p.12) noted that one cannot understand human intention when one is removed from the setting in which that intention makes sense. To us, this observation reflected our desire to utilise *any* available and reliable data source that provided a native reflection of why excessive risk-taking and poor decision-making behaviours were commonly accepted in many banking institutions. Indeed, we pondered whether or not we would have elicited truthful and insightful responses from participants even if we had no access issues. Without the benefit of someone with legitimate authority to ensure a response from participants, sensitive research topics may be deemed too difficult to pursue. Ultimately, the public inquiry setting offered an excellent source of reliable empirical data.

When dealing with sensitive research topics, the truth often lies in what is *not* said rather than what *is* said. Given that extreme events such as the financial crisis are often sudden, unexpected and highly impactful, access can prove impossible, so alternative sources of data are vitally important to the success of the research project. In what they refer to as 'non-traditional data souces', Buchanan and Denyer (2013, p.216) cite the use of official government documents, archival records, interviews, commercially available video and news reports as important alternative data sources that provide not just 'colourful descriptive accounts' but are 'part of the causal fabric of the sequence of events under investigation'. These sources of data have a very real benefit for HRD and other social science researchers concerned about 'costs' and 'research completion times'.

The use of unobtrusive methods used in combination with these very rich data sources can uncloak sensitive organisational issues. An example of how researchers can adopt unobtrusive methods to explore highly sensitive issues is illustrated by Chatterjee and Hambrick (2007, p.363), who utilised unobtrusive measures such as 'prominence of CEO's photographs in the company's annual report, CEO's prominence in company's press releases and first-person singular pronouns in interviews' to explore the concept of CEO narcissism. In this example, the innovative approach to researching such a sensitive issue was dictated by the potential for low response rates, participant bias in self-report measures and available instruments such as the NPI-40/16 and CPI that were considered blunt tools that may not have provided accurate or truthful insights.[4] In their research, Chatterjee and Hambrick were undeterred by the limitations relating to access and non-responsiveness of participants and developed an innovative approach to gathering the publically available data as a proxy measure for CEO narcissism. More recently, Brennan and Conroy (2013) utilised discourse analysis to interpret the CEO (of a failed Irish bank) letters to shareholders to explore the concepts of narcissism and hubris and found evidence that the tenure of the CEO resulted in more pronounced narcissistic (hubris) behaviour. It is doubtful if this insight could have been elicited without the benefit of unobtrusive methods.

As researchers, we faced a similar dilemma. The global financial and economic crisis provided us with a unique opportunity to explore a very sensitive and difficult-to-study organisational event by utilising public inquiries. In order to fully understand the financial crisis, we as researchers needed to get to the story behind the intellectual and knowledge failures (UK Hearings, 2009) that manifested as the excessive risk-taking and poor decision-making behaviour of many banking institutions. While these behaviours may not have been considered sensitive organisational issues, the associated negative organisational, institutional and societal impact were. Public inquiries provided a very rich narrative from the perspectives of recipients of HRD interventions including learning and development, career development, management/leadership development and organisational development inter alia. As Bruner (1990; cited in Czarniawska, 1997, p.20) cogently remarked, 'the function of the story is to find an intentional state that mitigates or at least makes comprehensible a deviation from a canonical cultural pattern'. To explore why HRD interventions failed, we utilised documentary evidence such as public inquiry transcripts and audio/video testimony, government commissioned reports, academic literature, newspaper articles and periodicals as well as valuable empirical data sources from within the organisations and institutions under investigation. We utilised Swanson's definition of HRD, as well as areas of responsibility highlighted by Gold et al. (2009), Ardichvili (2013), Garavan et al. (2004) and Peterson (2008) that HRD can have a major influence on, when identifying what constituted HRD failures. Table 25.1 provides an example of our data's emergent structure and reflects the raw data, 1st Order Categories, 2nd Order Themes and HRD intervention failures of our analysis. The sensitive nature of organisational failure does not lend itself to social science research; however, when that failure is replicated in many institutions globally, it is highly unlikely that social science researchers would have the ability to obtain credible insight into organisational failures without the help of non-reactive methods *and* valuable data sources such as public inquiries. Accordingly, unfettered access to public inquiry transcripts, video and audio provided an unobtrusive measure of HRD failures that would have proven impossible for us explore and understand even if we did not experience access issues.

Our research explored behavioural issues associated with excessive risk-taking and poor decision-making in multiple banking institutions in Ireland, the UK and the US. For the reasons previously highlighted, we accepted that CA and CAQDAS offered the most appropriate analytical approaches to address our research aim and objectives. We utilised public inquiry testimonies, transcripts and other supporting documentary evidence (units), which provided a comprehensive account of how multiple institutional actors at the centre of the financial crisis engaged in similar risk-taking and decision-making strategies.

Table 25.1 Data structure representation

Raw Data	1st Order Category	2nd Order Theme	HRD intervention failure
Senior management would periodically distribute emails detailing their *departments' market share. These emails were limited to managing directors only. Even if the market share dropped by a few percentage points, managers would be expected to justify 'missing' the deals which were not rated. Colleagues have described enormous pressure when their market shares dipped.*	• Maintain market share at all costs • Applying pressure on management to achieve organisational goals • Pressure to meet or exceed Targets	• Performance Targets • Management & Leadership pressures • Organisational Performance Driven Culture	• Anticipating & maintaining responses to changed conditions • Developing current and future leaders • Shaping organisational culture • Failure of 'high road' HRM strategy (includes HRD strategies)
While, to my knowledge, senior management never explicitly forced the lowering of credit standards, it was one easy way for a managing director to regain market share. I do not believe that this was done in a deliberate manner. Instead, during the bubble years, it was quite easy to rationalize changes in methodology since the nominal performance of the collateral was often quite exceptional. Easier still was avoiding asking whether the collateral standards had declined or whether some of the parties had ulterior motives in closing the transaction.	• Implicit coercion of employee behaviour • Manipulation of processes & practices to maintain competitive advantage • Short-term supernormal profits impacting on cognitive processes • Social Silences maintained	• Coercion • Organisational Strategy • Cognitive Impairment • Power Distance	• Failure of Leadership Development (LD) • Misalignment of organisational goals/learning & development (L&D) interventions • Shaping organisational culture

Table 25.1 (continued)

Raw Data	1st Order Category	2nd Order Theme	HRD intervention failure
I would also say I was not involved in 2007, as this information went through with the folks who rated subprime directly. But *there was almost a feeling when dealing with them that there was a 'see no evil, hear no evil' sort of attitude, and partly I think it is because people who had done these deals, rated these deals, did not want to believe what was going on, partly profit motivated, partly because they were part of this market, and it just should not be happening.* Senator Levin. Part of that culture. Mr Kolchinsky. Part of that culture. Closed eyes.	• Cognitive awareness of questionable practices • Cognitive Dissonance and rationalisation of improper behaviour • Collective Cognitive Capture of market participants	• Irresponsible Behaviour • Emotional Impairment • Institutional Identity	• Shaping organisational culture • Failure of HR Strategic Partner role • Failure to facilitate the functional building of commitment among organisational members • Employee Advocacy failures (sustainability failures)

384

Primary and Secondary Data

Our US data consisted of video and audio testimony provided by witnesses to both the Financial Crisis Inquiry Commission (FCIC Hearing, 2010a) and the US Senate Permanent Subcommittee on Investigation (US Senate Hearings, 2010). Data sources from the UK consisted of the House of Commons Treasury Select Committee (UK Hearings, 2009) oral hearing transcripts and analysis of video testimony where possible. The systematicity of CA and sophisticated analysis features of CAQDAS allowed us to gather a comprehensive list of witnesses whose responses were recorded on video, audio and written format. This list consisted of 102 banking and finance professionals, 33 central bankers/Federal Reserve governors/regulators, 26 government officials, and 35 academics and quasi-regulatory (ratings agency) professionals. We also reviewed additional documents such as company memos, financial reports, emails and other communications that were sourced by the various committees as supporting evidential data. In total, approximately 420 hours of video and audio testimony directly related to the public inquiries were viewed and reviewed. The transcripts from the UK and US public inquiry witness testimonies totalled almost 7500 pages, with approximately 500 pages of follow-up documents provided by the witnesses. In addition, the US Senate made publically available over 2000 pages of 'evidence' which were also used as reliable data sources. To provide some idea of how much data was available, the FCIC noted that during its investigation it 'reviewed millions of pages of documents, interviewed more than 700 witnesses and held 19 days of public inquiry hearings' (FCIC Report, 2011, p.xi).

Research Phases

In the initial stages of our research, which we referred to as Phase 1 (P1), or the data gathering stage, we set about establishing which data we could reasonably access (see Figure 25.2 for a research phase flowchart). Our focus was on understanding the excessive risk-taking and poor decision-making behaviour of banking professionals and government agencies. To this end, we needed to obtain a representative selection central to our research aim and objectives. To do this, we utilised purposive or theoretical sampling (Miles and Huberman, 1994; Stake, 2005), which allowed us to identify a representative sample of individuals who would have had authority to engage in excessive risk-taking or poor decision-making behaviour and were 'theoretically meaningful groups, or cultures' (Gephart, 1993, p.1479) associated with the financial crisis inquiries. There was a total pool of 292 potential witnesses. Utilising purposive

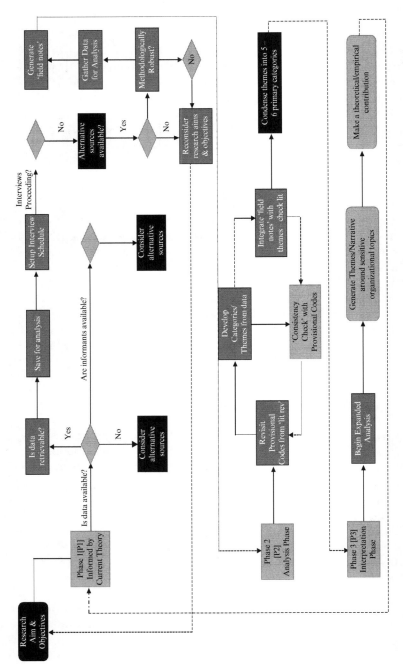

Figure 25.2   Research Phase Flowchart

sampling, we excluded anyone who was not working for a banking institution, government agency or regulator. Consultants, academics and other professionals not fitting this criterion were excluded, although we did analyse the interviews of some non-eye witnesses if additional insight was required. The final representative sample size was 196.

Given the initial impact the financial crisis had on economic stability in Europe and the US, it was assumed that individuals who worked in banking institutions in Ireland and played no part in the excessive risk-taking behaviour symptomatic of the crisis would be willing to discuss organisational dynamics to which they were privy. We were wrong. Employees who were approached and given assurances of anonymity (in line with ethical considerations) were either reluctant to discuss 'on or off the record' or were concerned that even being seen 'talking' to an 'outsider' they could lose their jobs. We had the same issues when approaching government institutions looking for 'redacted' or 'anonymised' interviews that formed part of the official (Irish) government reports. While the lack of engagement with individuals who had 'inside' financial institution knowledge was somewhat expected, we were surprised by the legalistic approach taken by government agencies in Ireland when we requested access to documents that formed the basis of these official reports. In one exchange, a Irish State Department cited the Commissions of Investigations Act, 2004, to curtail any further requests for data that might inform our research. Indeed, the State Department made it clear that further request for transcripts central to the investigation into the causes of the Irish banking crisis were not welcome. The State Department indicated that any record that may illuminate organisational/institutional dynamics were 'exempted from FOI legislation by virtue of section 40 of the Commissions of Investigations Act 2004'. Rather than a deterrent, this institutional resistance prompted us to become more novel and innovative in our approach. We considered the reluctance by government agencies reflective of its desire to reassert a dominant position and reclaim legitimacy by limiting what may have exposed the government (Buchanan and Denyer, 2013) and engaging a strategy to control the narrative played out in public discourse (Brown, 2005; Riaz et al., 2011).

The 'access issues' that emerged during P1 forced us to consider the use of proxy research to achieve our aims and objectives. The benefit of utilising a proxy as the method of choice are numerous. First, we were able to develop a considerable database utilising public inquiry data units from the Irish, UK and US financial crises without the expense of travel and time to develop relations with potential participants, organisational/legal gatekeepers, inter alia, as is associated with traditional methods of qualitative inquiry. Second, because witnesses appearing at the public inquiries were senior officials at many banking or government institutions, truthful responses were more likely due to (a) re-establishing credibility with 'stakeholders' and (b) all witnesses were 'sworn in' indicating the legal reach of the public inquiries in establishing the truth (Buchanan and Denyer, 2013, p.212).

In Phase 2 (P2) we remained within our 'data making' (Krippendorff, 2004, p.83) structure and utilised 'field notes' or 'brain dumps' developed from P1 when reviewing video evidence from the public inquiries. We also utilised our field notes from listening to the audio transcripts between federal investigators and financial crisis witnesses (e.g. Sabeth Siddique and Susan Bies). Field notes or analytic memos were a useful tool that allowed us to observe body language (video testimony) and tone (video and audio) as well as responsiveness of the witnesses under questioning, which transcripts alone do not provide. We considered this a 3-D representation of the data (audio, video and transcript). These analytic memos allowed for the documenting and reflection process providing anchors for the coding process and coding choices. Analytic memos facilitated the inquiry process and reflect on the patterns, associations, categories, subcategories and themes that would ultimately emerge as the data analysis moved from a loosely fitting bag to a tailored suit. As Saldana (2012, p.32) cogently observed: 'Analytic memos are somewhat comparable to researcher journal entries or blogs – a place to "dump your brain" about the participants, phenomenon, or process under investigation by thinking and thus writing and thus thinking even more about them: memos are sites of conversations with ourselves about our data.'

This proved particularly insightful on a number of occasions when witnesses either engaged in evasive answers or redirection, as in the case of Federal Regulators Sabeth Siddique and Susan Bies. Both Sabeth Siddique and Susan Bies had warned the Federal Reserve Board that the quality and underwriting standards of loans in many banking institution had deteriorated to the point that they were likely to go sour. These two expert witnesses provided insight into the institutional reluctance to call into question the excessive risk-taking behaviour of many banking intitutions because it would 'potentially stifle innovation' (FCIC Report, 2011, p.173). Analysis of the FCIC report highlighted the names of these two witnesses who had been interviewed by the commission investigators but for whom there were no interview transcripts. A decision was made to include the audio transcripts as they had the potential to uncover a narrative that illuminated the institutional pressures faced by regulators. Again, without a rich source of valuable, reliable data and innovative methods, it is highly improbable that *any* research would get this close to the eye witnesses while removed from the narrative.

In Phase 3 (P3) we could engage in the interpretation phase of our research, in understanding and addressing the aim and objectives of our research. The benefit of a replicable process-based method provided us with a degree of confidence that the subjective nature of our qualitative research was consistent with the requirements of academic rigour and validity. While we benefited hugely from both the CA frameworks identified by Krippendorff as well as the sophisticated analysis that CAQDAS provided, we must also recognise some of the limitations and issues we ourselves faced. The biggest issue for us in terms of the CA approach to sensitive research was time. While the public inquiries in both the UK and US were invaluable sources of data, it took over 18 months to gather, analyse and interpret even with the benefit of CAQDAS. This can present as a significant issue for reserachers who are constrained by time limitations arising from funding or research output demands. There is simply no shortcut. For example, the FCIC had over one million pages of evidence, had interviewed hundreds of witnesses and took nine months to complete the public inquiry. During this time, audio interviews took place in conjunction with the televised inquiries. Any researcher utilising this type of data unit has no choice but to watch (and rewatch) multiple times to determine what is useable and what is not (purposive sampling). This approach is replicated for any other public inquiries that may form part of the research project. In our case, we viewed both the FCIC and the US Senate hearings convened to investigate Wall Street and the financial crisis. Along with the video evidence of witnesses, we determined that listening to the audio evidence was an important dimension of our overall research strategy. This part of the reserch project was painstakingly slow.

Another issue we found with the CA approach to utilising public inquiries was the pressures it placed on other research we were conducting. When taking on a very large project such as the one we were involved in, other research projects and work commitments are sometimes neglected. The knock-on effect of this can be a reduced focus due to trying to balance the various other projects and work commitments. There is a high potential for burnout. The biggest issue, however, with researching sensitive research topics is funding. If the research has the potential to highlight significant organisational or institutional failures, difficulties may arise when trying to source funding that will pay for the research. This is exacerbated if the research is both sensitive and controversial as one might not even find an audience or journal willing to publish the findings once the research has been concluded.

The question then arises, why would anyone engage in researching sensitive organisational topics? If the benefit derived from deep immersion exploring sensitive research topics is minimal then how could the research be justified? The answer to that question can only be addressed by the researchers. For us, we were driven by Ghoshal's (2005, p.87) sage advice: 'social scientists carry a social and moral responsibility' because hiding ideology in the pretense of science can ultimately cause more harm than good. Sensitive research topics in the social sciences field serve as a warning sign that something may be fundamentally flawed or broken, either with the theory or our understanding of how that theory operates in practice. Utilising innovative non-mainstream research methods need not be a zero sum game. Every research method has its strengths and weaknesses, but perhaps a willingness to see beyond the tried and tested methods and a leap of faith in unobtrusive methods will see the myopia of operational definitionalism that permits a retread relegated to the annals of qualitative research history.

DISCUSSION

The unobtrusive approach and CA/CAQDAS should not be viewed as a 'silver bullet' for sensitive research topics; yet the same holds true for other methodologies widely used in the field. As with any methodological decision that has to be made by the researcher, CA provides many benefits that allow social science researchers to get inside the organisation without actually getting inside the organisation. For qualitative researchers, CA provides a reliable, transparent and relatively flexible research method. Used in conjunction with CAQDAS, researchers are able to analyse vast quantities of data and derive multiple conceptual/thematic interpretations. The availability of publically available documents enables the researcher to gain a detailed understanding of the organisation or institution even before (s)he progresses to analysing video/audio for tone, inflection and other body language signs. For quantitative researchers, CA allows for clearly defined and set out coding schemes and systematic sampling procedures so that the research can be replicated and augmented at a later stage by the original researchers or others interested in the topic. CA is also flexible when considering longitudinal analysis given the structured frameworks and CAQDAS's ability to analyse significant data sets.

The use of publically available reliable data units, while considered 'grey literature' (Buchanan and Denyer, 2013, p.212), is by its very nature unobtrusive from the perspective of the researchers. Utilising this type of data removes the researcher from the environment in which (s)he can influence the behaviour of the participants. This can also prove particularly useful when analysing secondary sources of data that are typically free from social desirability bias. For example, newspaper reports and television interviews carried out with CEOs of organisations during economic expansion may reflect a very confident (perhaps over confident) disposition. Researchers working on sensitive organisational issues can analyse and compare this secondary data if there is an organisational failure or instance of fraud or corruption in that organisation. Comparisons and inferences can be made between the 'before event' and the 'after event' to see how the individual's or organisation's dispostion or orientation has changed. Examination of internal organisational memos, emails and company documents prior to the event means that texts can be 'treated as traces of an author's [witnesses'] world view, preserved at a point in time and immune to retrospective construction' (FCIC Hearing, 2010b, p.3). This approach significantly decreases the potential for actor recall bias, potentially highlighting conflicts and organisation–institution dynamics that might not otherwise emerge.

CA offers a methodogically sound, empirically robust and academically rigorous systematic approach to the analysis of large data sets when exploring sensitive organisational topics because once the data has been collected, analysed and interpreted it can become a significant resource for future data mining and research on topics not considered 'core' to the original investigation. The development of a reuseable database cannot be underestimated and may not be understood until long after the intial research has been concluded. With CAQDAS, the ease with which a database can be data mined once collected is one of the most important reasons for considering CAQDAS as a qualitative approach that has the potential for significant research output well beyond the completion of the original sensitive research project.

NOTES

1. The global financial and economic crises will be referred to as the finanical crisis
2. Insiders refers to organisational/institutional actors with similar professional/ideological affiliations.
3. HRD policies, practices and procedures will be referred to as HRD interventions.
4. The NPI 40 is the Narcissistic Personality Inventory (Raskin and Terry, 1988) and the NPI 16 (Ames et al., 2006) are psychological inventories designed to measure narcissism as a personality trait in the social psychology field. The CPI or California Psychological Inventory (Gough 1957, 1987; Gough and Bradley 1996; McAllister 1996) is an instrument to assess social performance.

REFERENCES

Aguinis, H., Pierce, C. A., Bosco, F. A. and Muslin, I. S. 2009. First decade of organizational research methods. *Organizational Research Methods*, *12*, 69–112.

Alison, L. J., Snook, B. and Stein, K. L. 2001. Unobtrusive measurement: using police information for forensic research. *Qualitative Research*, *1*, 241–254.

Ames, D. R., Rose, P. and Anderson, C. P. 2006. The NPI-16 as a short measure of narcissism. *Journal of Research in Personality*, *40*, 440–450.

Ardichvili, A. 2013. The role of HRD in CSR, sustainability, and ethics: a relational model. *Human Resource Development Review*, *12*, 456–473.

Ashforth, B. E. and Anand, V. 2003. The normalization of corruption in organizations. *Research in Organizational Behavior*, *25*, 1–52.

Ashforth, B. E., Gioia, D. A., Robinson, S. L. and Trevino, L. K. 2008. Re-viewing organizational corruption. *Academy of Management Review*, *33*, 670–684.

Bahn, S. and Weatherill, P. 2013. Qualitative social research: a risky business when it comes to collecting 'sensitive' data. *Qualitative Research*, *13*, 19–35.

Bazeley, P. and Jackson, K. 2013. *Qualitative Data Analysis with NVIVO*, London, Sage.

Bierema, L. L. 2009. Critiquing Human Resource Development's dominant masculine rationality and evaluating its impact. *Human Resource Development Review*, *8*, 68–96.

Brennan, N. M. and Conroy, J. P. 2013. Executive hubris: the case of a bank CEO. *Accounting, Auditing and Accountability Journal*, *26*, 172–195.

Brown, A. D. 2004. Authoritative sensemaking in a public inquiry report. *Organization Studies*, *25*, 95–112.

Brown, A. D. 2005. Making sense of the collapse of Barings Bank. *Human Relations*, *58*, 1579–1604.

Bryman, A. and Bell, E. 2007. *Business Research Methods*, New York, Oxford University Press.

Buchanan, D. A. and Denyer, D. 2013. Researching tomorrow's crisis: methodological innovations and wider implications. *International Journal of Management Reviews*, *15*, 205–224.

Campbell, W. K., Hoffman, B. J., Campbell, S. M. and Marchisio, G. 2011. Narcissism in organizational contexts. *Human Resource Management Review*, *21*, 268–284.

Chanchai, T. 2011. Content analytic approach to measuring constructs in operations and supply chain management. *Journal of Operations Management*, *29*, 627–638.

Chatterjee, A. and Hambrick, D. C. 2007. It's all about me: narcissistic chief executive officers and their effects on company strategy and performance. *Administrative Science Quarterly*, *52*, 351–386.

Czarniawska, B. 1997. *Narrating the Organization: Dramas of Institutional Identity*, Chicago, The University of Chicago Press.

Dickson-Swift, V., James, E. L., Kippen, S. and Liamputtong, P. 2007. Doing sensitive research: what challenges do qualitative researchers face? *Qualitative Research*, *7*, 327–353.

Duriau, V. J., Reger, R. K. and Pfarrer, M. D. 2007. A content analysis of the content analysis literature in organization studies: research themes, data sources, and methodological refinements. *Organizational Research Methods*, *10*, 5–34.

Easterby-Smith, M., Thorpe, R. and Jackson, P. R. 2008. *Management Research*, London, Sage.

FCIC Hearing. 2010a. *First Public Hearing of the Financial Crisis Inquiry Commission: 1st Session*, Wednesday 13 January [Online], Washington, DC. http://fcic.law.stanford.edu/hearings/testimony/first-public-hearing [accessed 10 August 2011].

FCIC Hearing. 2010b. *First Public Hearing*, Wednesday 13 January [Online], Washington, DC: Financial Crisis Inquiry Commission. Available: http://fcic.law.stanford.edu/hearings/testimony/first-public-hearing [accessed September 2011].

FCIC Report. 2011. *The Finanical Crisis Inquiry Report: Final Report of the National Commission on the Causes of the Financial and Economic Crisis in the United States [full report]* [Online], New York. Available: http://fcic.law.stanford.edu/ [accessed October 2011].

Fligstein, N. and Goldstein, A. 2010. The anatomy of the mortgage securitization crisis. *In:* Lonsbury, M. and Hirsch, P. M. (eds.) *Markets on Trial: The Economic Sociology of the US Financial Crisis*, Bingley, UK: Emerald Publishing.

Garavan, T. N., Mcguire, D. and O'Donnell, D. 2004. Exploring Human Resource Development: a levels of analysis approach. *Human Resource Development Review*, *3*, 417–441.

Gephart, R. P. 1993. The textual approach: risk and blame in disaster sensemaking. *Academy of Management Journal*, *36*, 1465–1514.

Gephart, R. P. 1997. Hazardous measures: an interpretive textual analysis of quantitative sensemaking during crises. *Journal of Organizational Behavior*, *18*, 583–622.

Gephart, R. P. 2004. Normal risk: technology, sense making, and environmental disasters. *Organization and Environment*, *17*, 20–26.

Ghoshal, S. 2005. Bad management theories are destroying good management practices. *Academy of Management Learning and Education*, *4*, 75–91.

Gold, J., Holden, R., Iles, P., Stewart, J. and Beardwell, J. 2009. *Human Resource Development: Theory and Practice*, Basingstoke, UK, Palgrave-MacMillan.

Goodman, R. S. and Kruger, E. J. 1988. Data dredging or legitimate research method? Historiography and its potential for management research. *Academy of Management Review*, *13*, 315–325.

Gough, H. G. 1957. *Manual for the California Psychological Inventory™*, Mountain View, CA: CPP, Inc.

Gough, H. G. 1987. *The California Psychological Inventory™ Administrator's Guide*, Mountain View, CA: CPP, Inc.

Gough, H. G. and Bradley, P. 1996. *CPI™ Manual* (3rd edn), Mountain View, CA: CPP, Inc.

Jehn, K. A. and Jonsen, K. 2010. A multimethod approach to the study of sensitive organizational issues. *Journal of Mixed Methods Research*, *4*, 313–341.

Kelle, U. 2000. Computer-assisted analysis: coding and indexing. *In:* Bauer, M. W. and Gaskell, G. (eds.) *Qualitative Researching with Text, Image and Sound: A Practical Handbook*, London, Sage.

Krippendorff, K. 2004. *Content Analysis: An Introduction to Its Methodology*, London, Sage.

Lee, R. M. 2000. *Unobtrusive Methods in Social Research*, Buckingham, UK, Open University Press.

Mackenzie, C., Garavan, T. N. and Carbery, R. 2011. Understanding and preventing dysfunctional behavior in organizations. *Human Resource Development Review*, *10*, 346–380.

Mackenzie, C. A., Garavan, T. N. and Carbery, R. 2012. Through the looking glass: challenges for Human Resource Development (HRD) post the global financial crisis – business as usual? *Human Resource Development International*, *15*, 353–364.

Maylor, H. and Blackmon, K. 2005. *Researching Business and Management*, Basingstoke, UK, Palgrave Macmillan.

Mazzei, L. A. 2003. Inhabited silences: in pursuit of a muffled subtext. *Qualitative Inquiry*, *9*, 355–368.

McAllister, L. W. 1996. *A Practical Guide to CPI™ Interpretation* (3rd edn), Mountain View, CA: CPP, Inc.

Miles, M. B. and Huberman, M. A. 1994. *Qualitative Data Analysis: An Expanded Sourcebook*, Thousand Oaks, CA, Sage.

Morison, T. and Macleod, C. 2014. When veiled silences speak: reflexivity, trouble and repair as methodological tools for interpreting the unspoken in discourse-based data. *Qualitative Research*, *14*, 694–711.

Pearson, C. M. and Clair, J. A. 1998. Reframing crisis management. *Academy of Management Review*, *23*, 59–76.

Perrow, C. 1999. *Normal Accidents: Living with High Risk Technologies*, Princeton, NJ, Princeton Paperbacks.

Peterson, S. L. 2008. Creating and sustaining a strategic partnership: a model for Human Resource Development. *Journal of Leadership Studies*, *2*, 83–97.

Pollach, I. 2012. Taming textual data: the contribution of corpus linguistics to computer-aided text analysis. *Organizational Research Methods*, *15*, 263–287.

Raskin, R. and Terry, H. 1988. A principal-components analysis of the Narcissistic

Personality Inventory and further evidence of its construct validity. *Journal of Personality and Social Psychology*, *54*, 890–902.

Riaz, S., Buchanan, S. and Bapuji, H. 2011. Institutional work amidst the financial crisis: emerging positions of elite actors. *Organization*, *18*, 187–214.

Saldana, J. 2012. *The Coding Manual for Qualitative Researchers*, London, Sage.

Saunders, M., Lewis, P. and Thornhill, A. 2003. *Research Methods for Business Students*, Essex, UK, Prentice Hall.

Shrivastava, P., Mitroff, I. I., Miller, D. and Miglani, A. 1988. Understanding industrial crises. *Journal of Management Studies*, *25*, 285–303.

Sieber, J. E. and Stanley, B. 1988. Ethical and professional dimensions of socially sensitive research. *American Psychologist*, *43*, 49–55.

Sims, R. R. and Brinkmann, J. 2003. Enron ethics (or: culture matters more than codes). *Journal of Business Ethics*, *45*, 243–256.

Sonpar, K. and Golden-Biddle, K. 2008. Using content analysis to elaborate adolescent theories of organization. *Organizational Research Methods*, *11*, 795–814.

Stake, R. S. 2005. *Handbook of Qualitative Research*, Thousand Oaks, CA, Sage.

Swanson, R. A. 2001. Human Resource Development and its underlying theory. *Human Resource Development International*, *4*, 299–312.

Treasury Select Committee. 2010. *House of Commons Treasury Select Committee Banking Crisis: Oral Evidence Volume 1* [Online]. Available: http://www.publications.parliament.uk/pa/cm200809/cmselect/cmtreasy/144/144i.pdf [accessed March 2010].

UK Hearings. 2009. *House of Commons Treasury Committee: Banking Crisis Volume 1 Oral Evidence* [Online]. Available: http://www.publications.parliament.uk/pa/cm200809/cmselect/cmtreasy/144/144i.pdf [accessed March 2010].

US Senate Hearings. 2010. *Wall Street and the Financial Crisis: The Role of Investment Banks* [Online], Washington, DC. Available: http://www.hsgac.senate.gov//imo/media/doc/Financial_Crisis/042710Exhibits.pdf?attempt=2 [accessed June 2011].

US Senate Hearings. 2011. *Wall Street and the Financial Crisis: The Role of Regulators* [Online]. US Permenant Subcommittee on Investiagations. Available: http://www.hsgac.senate.gov/subcommittees/investigations/hearings/-wall-street-and-the-financial-crisis-the-role-of-bank-regulators [accessed June 2011].

US Senate Report 2010. *Wall Street and the Financial Crisis* [Online], Washington, DC: US Permanent Subcommittee on Investigations: Wall Street and the Financial Crisis – the role of Regulators, Investment Banks and Ratings Agencies. Available: http://www.hsgac.senate.gov/hearings?rid=4de12200-15ad-4ba8-9f48-d4cdb546ba68&type=sub [accessed 24 July 2011].

Vaughan, D. 1999. The dark side of organizations: mistake, misconduct and disaster. *Annual Review of Sociology*, *25*, 271.

Webb, E., Campbell, D., Schwartz, R. D. and Sechrest, L. 1966. *Unobtrusive Measures: Nonreactive Research in the Social Sciences*, Chicago, Rand McNally & Company.

Webb, E. J., Campbell, J. L., Schwartz, R. D. and Sechrest, L. 1999. *Unobtrusive Measures: Revised Edition*, Thousand Oaks, CA, Sage.

Webb, E. and Weick, K. E. 1979. Unobtrusive measures in organizational theory: a reminder. *Administrative Science Quarterly*, *24*, 650–659.

Weick, K. E. 2010. Reflections on enacted sensemaking in the Bhopal Disaster. *Journal of Management Studies*, *47*, 537–550.

ANNOTATED FURTHER READING

For any researcher considering how or why to approach sensitive research topics, below are a couple of papers and a book that may aid in the decision-making process.

Buchanan, D. A. and Denyer, D. 2013. Researching tomorrow's crisis: methodological innovations and wider implications. *International Journal of Management Reviews*, *15*,

205–224. This provides some exceptional insight into how researchers can utilise 'innovative' means to investigate organisational issues using proxy data. This paper is extremely insightful, but the real contribution this paper offers to prospective sensitive research scholars is that it can act as a 'springboard' into other seminal articles that utilised non-mainstream, innovative methods to pursue sensitive research topics.

Gephart, R. P. 1993. The textual approach: risk and blame in disaster sensemaking. *Academy of Management Journal*, *36*, 1465–1514. This seminal piece is the exemplar in respect of how he approaches a very sensitive organisational disaster utilising public inquiry data. The detail and richness of analysis in Gephart's paper makes it a 'must read' for researchers utilising public inquiries.

Perrow, C. 1999. *Normal Accidents: Living with High Risk Technologies*, Princeton, NJ, Princeton Paperbacks. This is perhaps *the* one example of a research that has made a career from delving into and utilising unobtrusive measures and innovative methods to address the 'hard questions' and seek answers from the data that is in plain sight. Sometimes the best research comes from what is freely available – you just have to look for it.

Index

Academy of Human Resource
    Development (AHRD) 48, 313
    findings of survey methods 231
action learning research (ALR)
    concept of 158
action research (AR) 151–2
    definitions of 142–4
    in HRD research 141–2, 144–5,
        151–2
        context 145, 149
        design 146, 150
        discussion/extrapolation 147–8,
            150–51
        methodology/methods 145–6,
            149–50
        narrative/outcomes 146–7, 150
        purpose and rationale 144–5,
            149
    use on OD 142
Actor Network Theory (ANT) 184,
    187
    enrolment 194
    network assemblages 187, 191, 194
        impact of non-human actors on
            194
    symmetry 187, 194
    translation 187, 194
    use in DA 187–9, 196
Adult Education Quarterly 301
Analysis of Variance (ANOVA) 315
    one-way 335
anthropology 79–80, 200, 292
applied management research 168
Aristotle 51, 55–6
Association of Internet Researchers
    (AoIR)
    *Ethical Decision-Making and
        Internet Research* (2012)
        187–8
autoethnography 5, 92–4, 102–4
    advantages of 97–8
    collaborative 101–2
    concept of 95–7

co-produced 102
disadvantages of 98–9
role in HRD research 99–100, 103
teaching of 100–101

Bayesian estimation 288
behavioural item questionnaire (BIQ)
    24

Chartered Institute of Personnel and
    Development (CIPD) 37, 94, 252,
    255
    HRD Conference 37
    professional development scheme 47
Chicago School 80
China 316
    Hong Kong 325, 332
    SMEs in 325, 330, 333, 336
Clean Language 6, 204–5, 210
    concept of 201
        development of 201–3
    influence in qualitative interviewing
        200
    potential influence on research
        interviewing 208–11
    questions 206
comparative fit index (CFI) 277
Computer Aided Qualitative Data
    Analysis Software (CAQDAS) 9,
    367, 369, 382, 385, 389, 391
    NVivo 121, 373–5
    use in visual data analysis 121–2
    use with CA frameworks 373, 379,
        389–90
consensual qualitative research
    (CQR)
    concept of 21
constructionism 20
constructivism 14, 23
    concept of 17
content analysis (CA) 369, 382, 385,
    390
    components of 377